BY FRANK FREIDEL

Franklin D. Roosevelt: *The Apprenticeship*

Franklin D. Roosevelt: *The Ordeal*

Franklin D. Roosevelt: *The Triumph*

Franklin D. Roosevelt
The Triumph

Franklin D. Roosevelt

The Triumph

by

FRANK FREIDEL

With Illustrations

Little, Brown and Company · *Boston* · *Toronto*

LIBRARY OF CONGRESS CATALOG CARD NO. 52-5521

FOURTH PRINTING

The author wishes to thank Harper & Brothers for permission to quote briefly from *Roosevelt in Retrospect* by John Gunther.

Published simultaneously in Canada
by Little, Brown & Company (Canada) Limited

PRINTED IN THE UNITED STATES OF AMERICA

To
Dorothy Edith

Contents

List of Illustrations

Franklin D. Roosevelt

The Triumph

CHAPTER I

Roosevelt Takes Command

> This day is notable not so much for the inauguration of a new Governor as that it marks the close of the term of a Governor who has been our Chief Executive for eight years.
>
> — FDR, INAUGURAL ADDRESS AS GOVERNOR, *January 1, 1929.*

TUESDAY, January 1, 1929, was a bleak, miserable day in Albany. The streets, slippery and slushy with snow followed by rain, were packed with crowds more intent upon crying farewells to the outgoing Governor than in hailing the new one. For just as Franklin D. Roosevelt had been outshone at his wedding by Theodore Roosevelt, he was overshadowed at his inauguration by Alfred E. Smith. The slight melancholy of many of the onlookers and the somewhat forced gaiety of Smith were signs of the general awareness that an era had come to an end in Albany. The crowds had no premonition, of course, that for the country as a whole, still basking in the Republican prosperity of the '20s, the end of an era was also fast approaching.[1]

Yet, for Roosevelt and for those few workers who owed their personal loyalty to him, it was a day of triumph. In part it was a comeback politically from the election of 1920, when as James Cox's running mate he had been buried in the Harding avalanche. In a larger degree it was a comeback physically from an attack of polio so serious that it would have permanently eliminated most men from public life. Stubbornly refusing to retire to invalidism, Roosevelt had continued active in business, had built for himself an influential behind-the-scenes role in politics, and had exercised ceaselessly to try to regain the use of his legs.

While Roosevelt's influence in Democratic councils grew, his physique also improved, especially after he began devoting much time to swimming and exercising in the pool at Warm Springs, Georgia. It was as a broken young man that he had first gone there (as old

Josephus Daniels always remembered), his physical condition in tragic contrast to what it had been when he had served under Daniels as Assistant Secretary of the Navy in the Wilson Administration. Speaking at Warm Springs in 1947, Daniels reminisced:

"How young and debonair, striding and strong he had been. I am glad I can remember not only that he was great but that he was beautiful as well. He came here as a cripple to recruit his strength. It is sad but instructive to remember that he came in the early 20s when the world also, which had been so strong, so beautiful in its purposes for democracy and for peace, was crippled with the paralysis of bitterness at home and abroad." [2]

The Roosevelt who returned to Warm Springs in November, 1928, was far from a cripple in appearance or attitude. Fresh from his startling election victory in New York State, where he had snatched the governorship from the ruins of the national Democratic collapse, he was self-confident, vigorous, and radiant with good health and high spirits. When he took the train from New York at Pennsylvania Station on November 9, he pointed out to newspapermen, "I couldn't stand on my legs about a year ago. But now I can stand without the aid of braces, although I can't walk without losing my balance. I still wear the braces for that reason and carry a cane." [3]

Even in boom times, the assuming of the governorship was not easy, and it was of foremost importance for Roosevelt to rest thoroughly in order to eliminate every trace of campaign fatigue. Certainly the environment was ideal for this at Warm Springs. The day he arrived, the sky was cloudless; a warm breeze lightly stirred the pines. Mornings he spent at the swimming pool, relaxing or playing water polo. On Thanksgiving, he celebrated the dedication of a new thirty-thousand-dollar glass-enclosed swimming pool given by Mr. and Mrs. Edsel Ford by participating vigorously in a game of water football. The "football" was a sponge wrapped in oilcloth. There were six players on a side; in order to make a "first down," they had to reach the center of the pool in four tries. Roosevelt facetiously boasted in advance, "We specialize in aerial attack and in fake and trick plays and we have a number to uncork." His threats were empty, for although he played valiantly at left tackle, the young women physiotherapists who made up the opposing team overpowered his side 12–0. Later he recouped some glory by winning a tin loving cup in a "crab race," in which he sat in a life preserver and with his hands outpaddled his competitors.[4]

Roosevelt's vigorous vacationing well illustrated that although he could not walk unaided, he had spectacularly recovered his strength physically as well as politically. He had time at Warm Springs to ponder on the tasks ahead, and he was fit for them even though they were to be compounded in difficulty by the economic paralysis which was to strike the country before he had been governor for a year. Whatever faith in himself he may heretofore have lacked, he had gained. A few days before he took office, he remarked to Frances Perkins, "You know, I didn't feel able to make this campaign for governor, but I made it. I didn't feel that I was sufficiently recovered to undertake the duties of Governor of New York, but here I am." [5]

From the outset, Roosevelt acted as though he personally had a rendezvous with destiny. He carried himself with the air and gusto of a big man, even if his actions sometimes fell short of his bearing. His lighthearted attitude toward adversity and his blithe refusal at times to face up to unpleasant matters caused many to misgauge him as a gubernatorial lightweight. At times he did indeed lack depth; but he demonstrated a remarkable willingness to improvise when doctrinaire approaches were inadequate, and he displayed a real brilliance in formulating and executing complex political programs of action. His course was usually eclectic, but behind it was the firm humanitarian tradition, Christian faith, and sense of *noblesse oblige* that he had inherited from his parents and learned from Endicott Peabody of Groton and Theodore Roosevelt. His were the background and attitudes, and the aspirations, to point him toward greatness.

Roosevelt made ready for his inauguration determined to be an outstanding governor. His confidence both in himself and in his political fortunes was on the rise at the very time that the world, crippled, as Daniels pointed out, teetered toward chaos and the American economy rushed toward a precipice. Because he did not have to meet the challenge of world crises, and was oblivious to the approaching domestic crisis, his task of preparation was relatively simple. In 1938, from the perspective of ten years, he wrote of his earlier attitude:

"Let me say with complete frankness that during the twenties, I in common with most liberals did not at the start visualize the effects of the period, or the drastic changes which were even then necessary for a lasting economy. We knew that many changes in monopolistic practices and in the concentration of the control of wealth in the hands of a few — changes fought for by Theodore Roosevelt and Woodrow Wilson — were long overdue. But we did not understand the real depths of the problem." [6]

This was just as well, perhaps, for even at the time Roosevelt's agenda for the governorship seemed long enough. He had time to grow in office before he had to grapple with the weightier problems. Afternoons at Warm Springs, sitting before a wood fire on a lounge in his cottage, he dictated correspondence, held conferences, and devised strategy to meet the problems of his new office. He had less than two months in which to answer large quantities of mail, write his inaugural and his annual message to the legislature, and tentatively prepare the state budget — in short, to decide upon policies and personnel upon which to base his administration, his reputation as governor, and hence his political future. More than that, he must find ways to take advantage of the unparalleled opportunity to sweep into the power vacuum inside the Democratic party created by the apparent abdication of Smith. Within New York, he must, if he could, devise means to top the resplendent record of Smith as governor. Nationally he must try to win the goodwill if not the active support of both the bitterly antagonistic pro-Smith and anti-Smith factions within the battered party.

All these difficult tasks he assumed so blithely and handled with such dispatch that even some of those closest to him saw only one or another segment of his planning, and failed to realize how each part fitted into an over-all scheme. Here was no bewildered political tyro elevated by events into a great office beyond his capacities, but one of the most skilled of political craftsmen, who without waste effort quietly erected in a few weeks the scaffolding for both the governorship of New York and the candidacy for President in 1932. The former he built in full view of everyone; the latter would serve its purpose only if it were unseen. Perhaps both structures were fully visible only to Roosevelt's gnarled, cynical secretary, Louis McHenry Howe, who had dreamed for so many years of putting Franklin into the White House. Certainly as sharp a young observer as Samuel I. Rosenman was not aware of it. Rosenman, an ardent Smith progressive, had worked loyally and capably during the campaign, preparing speeches for Roosevelt. When he came to Warm Springs to help Roosevelt construct his legislative program, he saw Roosevelt only as the governor-elect, not as a potential presidential nominee. Rosenman remembers that although the New York Democratic leaders who traveled together to Warm Springs spent much time speculating upon Roosevelt's future as governor, not one raised the question of the presidency. At a barbecue a few days later when a Georgian lauded Roosevelt as a future President, Rosenman discounted it as simply expansive Southern praise of an adopted favorite son, which no one took seriously.[7]

This was all to the good, since it was highly to Roosevelt's advantage during the next two years to function behind the scenes, as indeed he already had for so long. There was no need for him to point publicly to his strong national political position; events did that. Election as Governor of New York (in part because of the weight of New York's huge block of electoral votes) automatically made him a leading contender for the presidential nomination. In nine out of the sixteen campaigns since the Civil War, one of the major-party candidates had been a governor or former governor of New York.*

In Roosevelt's case there was in addition his remarkable feat of winning the election while Smith, who had always been a powerful vote-getter in New York, lost the state. Further, Smith with a tone of finality had abdicated as a contender for the presidential nomination. "I have had all I can stand of it," he proclaimed the day after the election. "As far as running for office again is concerned — that's finished." This seemed to leave Roosevelt as a particularly available heir apparent. Some of Smith's friends at once climbed aboard the Roosevelt wagon, and even predicted that if Smith had the naming of the 1932 nominee it was very likely he would favor Roosevelt. If Roosevelt could only win re-election as governor in 1930, they predicted, he would have a clear road to the nomination. The Olympian New York *Times* demonstrated the seriousness of this sort of speculation by devoting two of its editorials to Roosevelt's presidential prospects:[9]

"It is too early to select the new leader of the Democratic Party or to predict nominations for a date so remote as 1932. Steadily FRANKLIN D. ROOSEVELT has made this point when hailed by enthusiastic orators in New York and the South as the dominant national figure of his party. Yet by a most extraordinary combination of qualities, political fortunes and diversified associations, Governor-elect ROOSEVELT is within reach of the elements of party leadership." [10]

* Horatio Seymour, Samuel J. Tilden, Grover Cleveland (three times), Theodore Roosevelt (twice), Charles Evans Hughes, and Alfred E. Smith.[8]

The eclipse of Smith did more than facilitate the emergence of Roosevelt. Smith's rise had done both great service and disservice to the Democratic party. He had performed a service through winning to the enthusiastic support of the party hundreds of thousands of city voters of immigrant background. Samuel Lubell has pointed out that women of these groups went to the polls in numbers for the first time in 1928, and they went to vote Democratic. For the first time, the total vote of the twelve largest cities in the country went Democratic. As Roosevelt emphasized in the weeks and months after the election, Smith had led the way to a considerable resurgence of the Democratic party. He had polled fifteen million votes — more than any previous Democrat, and more than Coolidge four years earlier. The percentage of the Democratic vote had risen from 34.1 per cent in 1920 and 28.8 per cent in 1924 to 40.8 per cent in 1928.* In the cities, the Democratic party had never been in better shape; if it could hold its gains, in the future it would be a serious threat to the Republicans. Smith's disservice had been in the rural areas, where his Wet, Catholic, Irish background had repelled voters almost as strongly as it attracted the masses in the cities. In the South especially, the Democratic party seemed shattered.[12]

The challenge to Roosevelt was to repair this damage without losing the gains Smith had made in the cities. He told newspapermen upon his arrival in Georgia that he was optimistic about the future of the party. He thought that the quantities of Southern Democrats who had bolted to Hoover could be brought back into the party if the leaders used tact. Certainly Roosevelt himself was ready to do this, and the time was propitious. He was able to reach toward political power at the exact moment when, for the first time in the 1920's, the disastrous schism in the Democratic party was capable of being bridged. The fiasco of the 1924 convention had eliminated the leader of the Dry, anti-Catholic wing of the party, William Gibbs McAdoo; the Hoover landslide had buried the Wet, Catholic leader. The way was clear to unite under a moderate. Many leaders of both factions looked to Roosevelt as potentially this man.[13]

Thus it was of real significance (as the New York *Times* recog-

* In a form letter widely distributed, FDR declared, "The defeat of Governor Smith was of course a deep disappointment but I have no patience with those who deduce from it that the Democratic Party is in any danger of extinction. Of the additional votes cast in the election the Democratic nominees apparently received many more than half, and the casting of fifteen million votes for our ticket shows that our party has gained tremendous strength since 1920 and 1924."[11]

nized) that while Smith followers in the cities talked favorably about Roosevelt, nearly a thousand people assembled from a radius of six counties at the Methodist Church in Chipley, Georgia, to attend a barbecue in his honor. A distinguished Georgia editor, Julian Harris, son of Joel Chandler Harris, wrote, "It is difficult to convey in cold type the fervor of the devotion of Georgians to Governor-elect Roosevelt." Southern backers were even quicker than Northerners to take Smith at his word when he said, "Never again." One after another, they came to Warm Springs to confer with Roosevelt.[14]

As Roosevelt and Howe had long known, this sort of public attention was useful as long as it remained within limits. It habituated people to think of Roosevelt as presidential timber. But if he received too much notice, or if the publicity could be traced to sources close to him, it might backfire. Americans demand an almost doltish modesty of their heroes; aspiring politicians are quick to snap at the heels of one of their number who moves too soon toward the front of the pack. In consequence, Roosevelt said publicly again and again (as he had four years earlier) that it was much too soon to talk about presidential candidates, that this could only be disastrous to the cause. Instead, all good Democrats must concentrate upon rebuilding the party. When reporters queried him about Roosevelt-in-'32 predictions, he retorted, "I want to step on any talk of that kind with both feet. That is colloquial but clear."[15]

This in substance was Roosevelt's reply to the hundreds of people outside of New York State who wrote congratulating him upon his victory. On November 12, 1928, Howe wired him that six hundred letters had come in that morning, of which four hundred were out-of-state letters referring to national matters. He suggested a form reply to go both to these correspondents and to a select list of two thousand others. Roosevelt revised the reply to put the emphasis upon the vitality of the Democratic party and the necessity of creating a permanent organization to operate between campaigns. In this same tenor, he sent letters again, as after the 1924 election, to all those who had been delegates to the Democratic Convention, to all state and county Democratic chairmen, and to all successful and defeated Democratic congressmen, asking their opinion why the Democrats had lost, and inquiring whether a day-in-and-day-out Democratic organization should not be established. Thus cleverly Roosevelt called himself directly and flatteringly to the attention of the rank and file of the Democratic leadership in the entire United States. To those who charged that he was engaged in advancing himself as a presidential aspirant, he could point out that he had done the same thing four years earlier.[16]

Nor was Roosevelt solely interested in calling attention to himself. He himself examined closely the hundreds of replies he received from all over the United States. Howe employed a young Kentucky newspaperwoman, Lela Stiles, to compile a state-by-state analytical summary of them. The whole, a substantial bound volume entitled the *National Political Digest*, provided Roosevelt in this era before public-opinion polls with a remarkable over-all view of local Democratic opinion. The letters themselves gave him insight into the problems and prejudices of the Ku Kluxers and the Catholics, the mediocre mass, the stupid and the brilliant among the Democratic workers.

A defeated Kentucky congressman, Fred Vinson, who, although a Dry Protestant, went down amidst the reaction against Smith, warned Roosevelt that the national leaders of the party must concentrate upon issues which would be attractive everywhere in the country.[17] The significance of letters like this was not wasted on Roosevelt, who long since had felt that the Democratic party must avoid issues like Prohibition, concerning which large sectors of the party could not agree. He was sympathetic too with assertions like that of a fledgling Florida lawyer, Claude W. Pepper, who wrote, "For one, I want the Democratic party genuinely to become the liberal party of this Nation." [18]

And in the realm of concrete issues, Roosevelt was ready to accept the forecast of a leading Democratic congressman, Henry T. Rainey of Carrollton, Illinois. The approaching tariff revision, Rainey predicted, would be a stiff further revision upwards. It would provide Democrats with a fine issue in 1930 because the results would be disastrous to American interests abroad as well as at home. Farm relief would be inadequate and fail; the Hoover Administration would be sympathetic to the aggressions of the power trust. The result might be depression. He asserted:

"We will have plenty of issues two years from now about which [to] . . . unite. . . . The recent drop in the stock market is a warning as to what may come in the near future . . . under the policies which I am sure will be put into operation with the coming Hoover administration." [19]

Several other political leaders in the Middle West, West, and South wrote Roosevelt in a vein similar to Rainey's. Well before Roosevelt had received any of their letters, he embarked upon lines as governor-elect which demonstrated beyond question that he had independently come to the same conclusions. His problem was first to establish a course of action as governor which would raise him above the shadow of Smith, who had been one of the greatest governors in the history of New York. Secondly, through this course he must appeal beyond the boundaries of the state to all those voters anywhere in the country who might suffer from the policies of Hoover and the Republicans.

To top Smith's record as Governor of New York would be exceedingly difficult, for against the tide of the '20s he had kept the government of the State of New York progressive, and, even more remarkably, he had made it efficient. Smith had forced through a reluctant Republican legislature measures limiting rents and encouraging the construction of low-cost housing in crowded city areas. He had obtained bond issues for the elimination of grade crossings, improvement of state hospitals, and the building of state parks and parkways. Under his administration, state appropriations for teachers' salaries increased nearly tenfold. He obtained equal pay for women teachers, and a law which in theory at least limited the work week of women to forty-eight hours. At the same time, he was able to take credit for substantial tax cuts. Above all, after years of effort, Smith achieved the thoroughgoing reorganization of the state government from a hodgepodge of 187 agencies, many of them almost entirely independent, into 18 administrative departments, for the most part responsible to the governor. This reorganization, which had been in effect for only two years, gave Roosevelt a fine opportunity to run the state efficiently.[20]

Smith even left an impressive agenda of unfinished issues with Roosevelt — issues which Roosevelt, like Smith, could try to force through a hostile legislature, and upon which he could campaign for re-election two years hence. Prime among these was the public development of water power. But there were many others. When the legislature had adjourned in March, 1928, Smith had stingingly denounced it as the most fruitless he had seen in twenty-five years, "dominated entirely by partisan and petty politics," and disposed to sidetrack great questions of importance to the state and all of her people in favor of "the promotion of local politics and senseless, useless legislation." Aside from grade-crossing legislation, it had ignored every one of Smith's specific proposals, which included aid to women and children, especially the physically handicapped; improvement of education; protection of labor; and reorganization of town, county, and state governments.[21]

Much of this program would be of value to Roosevelt, and for that matter he had little choice but to endeavor to carry it out. It is difficult to determine how deep his admiration for Smith actually went at this time. When Henry Morgenthau, Sr., proposed to him that Smith receive the Woodrow Wilson Award, he admitted his distinct shock at first thought because "it seemed a bit incongruous," but he conceded that "Smith has accomplished more than anyone since Wilson to awaken interest in broad governmental questions during the past few years." He took much the same line with reporters. "Needless to say, the wonderful reforms effected by Governor Smith have put the government of this state on a more businesslike footing," he commented to one of them, adding that since Smith had not been able to finish the job, it was up to the new administration to carry on. On another occasion, after Roosevelt had conferred at length with Smith, a reporter asked him if he would continue the Smith policies. "Generally," he replied, "for that is what we said all through the campaign."[22]

This was somewhat less than dynamic, and with reason, for while Roosevelt had no intention of deviating from the direction in which Smith had been heading, he was determined to go up the road alone.* Consequently, while he publicly paid as much obeisance to Smith as courtesy and obligation demanded, he made the Smith program the foundation but not the structure of his enterprise.

This became almost immediately clear as Roosevelt day after day in talking to reporters threw emphasis upon first one, then another aspect of the program he expected to present to the legislature. Superficially it was Smith's with the emphasis shifted somewhat from urban to rural matters. To the state Democratic leaders, all ardent Smith

* In an interview just before he took office, FDR made emphatic the progressive nature of his thinking:

"I believe that in the future the State — and when I say the State I do not mean New York alone — will assume a much larger role in the lives of its citizens. Public health, I believe, is a responsibility of the State, and I think there will be a general widening of its activities to promote general welfare. The State educates its children. Why not also keep them well?

"Now some people are going to say this is socialistic. My answer to them is that it is 'social,' not 'socialistic.' "

But then he stated his faith that "after all the best government is the least government."[23]

men, who conferred at Warm Springs with Roosevelt, this seemed eminently sound.* He was not abandoning any of the legislative demands that would appeal to city voters; he simply was putting more stress upon those that might win upstate Republicans to the Democratic party. The best possible strategy within New York was to try to hold what Smith had gained, and build farm support in addition.

In retrospect, Rosenman saw the value of the planning sessions. They dealt with two matters, the plotting of a feasible, forward-looking program of legislation, and the strengthening of the Democratic party organization. "In later years," Rosenman has written, "Roosevelt taught me how closely these two subjects were intertwined, how important both were to success at the polls — a good affirmative liberal program and a good party organization." [25]

The conferees were so preoccupied with New York politics that they may not have noticed how intertwined Roosevelt's state program was with the national demands of disaffected farmers and former progressives. He ignored for the time being the question of Prohibition repeal, which had brought so much national antagonism as well as support in Smith's direction, but he did take over Smith's water-power issue. It had won Smith considerable progressive endorsement throughout the country — most notably that of Senator George Norris of Nebraska. Immediately after the election, Roosevelt congratulated the voters of New York upon having saved themselves (by defeating his opponent) water sites capable of developing two and a half million horsepower. Several times in ensuing days he came back to the power-development question. Although he advocated piece by piece almost every other item on the Smith agenda, power was the only one he underscored.[26]

Rather, where Smith emphasized aid to the poorer classes in cities, Roosevelt concentrated upon farm relief. Smith had been too much a New York City figure to win much farm support upstate, let alone in the nation. He had gained only limited backing during the campaign, even though he accepted the schemes of Midwestern agricultural leaders. A young Republican, Henry A. Wallace, made several speeches on his behalf in Iowa, and more Northern farmers voted Democratic than in 1924 or 1920. But most farmers voted reluctantly

* These were Democratic State Chairman William Bray, Lieutenant Governor-elect Herbert H. Lehman, the Democratic leaders in the assembly and senate, Maurice Bloch and Bernard Downing, and the Democratic Legislative Bill Drafting Commissioner, Rosenman.[24]

for Herbert Hoover, whom they had never regarded as their friend, and lamented that Frank Lowden of Illinois had not received the nomination. Smith had been incapable of tapping the mainspring of agricultural discontent. Roosevelt already in 1928 demonstrated keen interest in it. Despite his lack of awareness that a depression was in the offing, he had, as he wrote ten years later, "grasped the fact that the progressive decline in agriculture was a thing of danger."[27]

The problems of New York farmers differed from those in the Middle West; they did not produce the great staples which were in surplus. Neither, for that matter, could Roosevelt in a single Eastern state work out useful solutions to agricultural problems national in scope. But he could do some things to relieve the poverty of many of the farmers within the state, and he could do so in a way that would attract wide attention. In devising a program he could count upon the active aid and encouragement of the agricultural experts at Cornell University, and of his friend and Dutchess County neighbor, Henry Morgenthau, Jr., editor of the *American Agriculturalist.* Above all, he could depend upon his own considerable knowledge of upstate rural conditions and his political experience of fifteen years earlier when as state senator he had become known as a friend of the farmer.

Immediately after the election Roosevelt conferred with several farm leaders, including the heads of the State Grange. Within a week he wrote agricultural specialists asking suggestions. These he followed by creating a commission, which met and reported a concrete program that he accepted. All this took place before the end of December. If Smith's welfare bills were to be the foundation of Roosevelt's administration, certainly farm-relief measures would be the capstone.[28]

Almost every day Roosevelt had something to give to the reporters as he gradually unfolded his program; thus day by day one or another aspect of it appeared to advantage in the headlines, attracting more attention than it would as part of the single complicated parcel in his message to the legislature. In addition, he made several speeches after his return from Warm Springs in which he outlined his plans and fascinated at least some of his listeners into accepting them. When he spoke late in December before the Merchants' Association of New York City, he described himself as being both a city businessman and an upstate farmer. He promised to run the state on a sound business basis without regard to party lines, pledged a survey of taxes, demonstrated Smith's knack for making figures come alive, and strongly defended the New York milk-shed system as being a protection to both dairy farmers and consumers. It was a typical Roosevelt display of virtuosity of the sort that forced Republican leaders to recognize well before he arrived in Albany that here was a formidable successor to Smith.[29]

A large part of what Roosevelt was demanding was similar to what Republican voters too had wanted. Consequently, upon Roosevelt's return to New York, the Republican legislative leaders tried to undermine his appeal upstate by accepting the olive branch which he was repeatedly offering to them. They announced that while they would oppose Roosevelt on administrative reforms (these would cut into Republican strength) and on state development of water power, they would cooperate on tax and farm-relief measures. Of course Roosevelt, who in actuality had nothing to lose by appearing above party considerations too, said he was "perfectly delighted," since "about 90 per cent of the legislation ought not to be taken up from a partisan point of view." [30]

With men as well as measures, Roosevelt cautiously asserted his independence without destroying Smith's valuable foundation. He kept on almost all of Smith's department heads, whether popular or unpopular. Most notably these included Colonel Frederick Stuart Greene, State Superintendent of Public Works, one of the most capable of the "Smith Republicans," an urbane gentleman who in his leisure time wrote short stories. Colonel Greene was the target of several upstate Democratic leaders because he resisted their demands for petty patronage; much more important to Roosevelt, he had the reputation for being an honest and efficient road builder with a knack for getting one hundred cents out of every dollar. Similarly Roosevelt announced he would keep on the Commissioners of Mental Hygiene and of Correction because he was impressed with their work.[31]

On the other hand, the Industrial Commissioner under Smith, Dr. James A. Hamilton, a Bronx Democrat, had been seriously criticized for his handling of the State Insurance Fund. Smith had been dissatisfied with Hamilton and had repeatedly bypassed him to place much of what normally would have been Hamilton's responsibilities on the Chairman of the Industrial Board, Miss Frances Perkins. When Smith informed Roosevelt that Hamilton would have to be replaced, Roosevelt inquired if Miss Perkins would make a good commissioner. Smith praised her as being fair and possessed of common sense, but warned Roosevelt that the men who worked as factory inspectors and on compensation boards might be reluctant to take orders from a woman. Later Roosevelt asked Miss Perkins to be commissioner. He told her what Smith had said, chuckled, and added, "You see, Al's a good progressive fellow but I am willing to take more chances. I've got more nerve about women and their status in the world than Al has."

"I laughed too," Miss Perkins recalls, "but I could not resist the temptation to say, 'But it was more of a victory for Al to bring himself to appoint a woman, never appointed before, when I was unknown, than it is for you when I have made a record as a responsible public servant for almost ten years.' "[32]

What made Roosevelt even less daring was the additional factor which Mrs. Roosevelt frequently pointed out to her husband: it was politically valuable to recognize women in making appointments. This had only recently become true, and Miss Perkins was only the third woman to head an important state department. One of the previous two had failed abysmally.[33]

Miss Perkins had not been overanxious to accept the appointment; she had enjoyed her work as Chairman of the Industrial Board, and knew she would run into inefficiency and perhaps even corruption in the Labor Department. She told Roosevelt these things as he talked to her about industrial problems while driving her around Hyde Park, showing her his new trees and other improvements to his farms. He gave her his firm assurance that she might go ahead, investigate, and fire whomever necessary, whatever the political repercussions from labor leaders and insurance companies. On this basis she accepted.[34]

Two other shifts were not as pleasant for Smith. He recommended to Roosevelt that Robert Moses be kept as Secretary of State. Moses, a man of ability and integrity, nominally a Republican, had been a useful adviser to Smith. The duties of Secretary of State were not onerous, and Moses had busied himself with many other things — most notably the development of a park and parkway system on Long Island. In the process he had clashed with various persons, frequently in a sharp and exciting manner. Unfortunately, one of them had been Roosevelt, who as chairman of the Taconic Park Commission had been trying to build a similar system from New York City north into Dutchess County.* Consequently, Roosevelt turned instead to Bronx boss Edward J. Flynn, who had been energetic on behalf of Roosevelt during the campaign and vigorous in his protection of

* For details of this dispute, see Frank Freidel, *Roosevelt: The Ordeal*, 219–220.

Roosevelt's interests during the critical days when the ballots were being counted. He could serve as an adroit adviser to Roosevelt on the many touchy problems involving the city machines.[35]

An infinitely deeper disappointment to Smith was Roosevelt's decision to dispense with Belle Moskowitz. She was a powerful, domineering woman, able brilliantly to plan and execute schemes, and completely loyal to Smith. Probably like Smith she felt Roosevelt incapable of being governor in his own right; she and Smith apparently conceived it to be her task to keep things straight in Albany. Undoubtedly she could have done so admirably, but it would have been a continuation of the Smith administration, not an inauguration of Roosevelt's. Certainly from the start Roosevelt had planned differently, but he keenly disliked to stir up unpleasantness. When Smith recommended to Roosevelt that he make her the Governor's Secretary, and extolled her ability and reliability, Roosevelt nodded his assent (to her valuable qualities, not her appointment) and did not commit himself. It had rankled him during the previous campaign summer, when he had expected to be one of Smith's closest advisers, that she and Raskob had kept Roosevelt isolated from Smith and treated him at headquarters "as though I was one of those pieces of window-dressing that had to be borne with because of a certain political value in non-New York City areas." Nor had Howe failed to report to Roosevelt that it took Mrs. Moskowitz only a few seconds to veto the purchase of Roosevelt's *Happy Warrior* as campaign literature.[36]

Not wanting to affront Smith, Roosevelt postponed coming to a definite decision as long as possible. Frances Perkins, who was quite close to all the principals in the matter, thinks that he might well have drifted into accepting Mrs. Moskowitz except for Eleanor Roosevelt. Mrs. Roosevelt, who had worked under Mrs. Moskowitz during the 1928 campaign, was highly impressed with her ability, but pointed out firmly to her husband that he must make up his mind whether or not he wanted Mrs. Moskowitz shaping his program. Obviously he did not, and when Miss Perkins came as an emissary from Smith to raise the question a second time, he told her so.[37] Years later she recalled:

"Roosevelt said, 'You know, I've thought about that a great deal. I admire Mrs. Moskowitz. I think she is very, very able. I think she did a great deal for Al. I am sure she could do a great deal for any man who is Governor, but — ' Here he looked off out the window, and for the first time I realized how much he had gained in self-analysis and self-knowledge. '—I've *got* to be Governor of the State of New York and I have got to be it MYSELF. If I weren't, if I didn't do it myself, something would be wrong here.' He tapped his chest. '. . . I am awfully sorry if it hurts anybody, particularly Al.' "[38]

Just before the inauguration, Roosevelt announced to the press that he had not had a single conference with Mrs. Moskowitz. He told Smith that he was appointing as his secretary Guernsey Cross, whose only notable qualification was that he was a big, strong man who could aid Roosevelt in walking at public appearances.[39]

Yet in areas where Smith's knowledge and judgment could be of value, Roosevelt called upon him for advice. He asked Smith to suggest strong appointees to the Transit Commission. On December 14, he conferred with Smith for four hours concerning taxes, water power, and especially the budget. On December 22, Smith planned to come to Hyde Park, but because of the cold weather stayed in Albany and spent ten or fifteen minutes going over the budget figures with Roosevelt by telephone. He assured Roosevelt that the surplus would be twenty-five million dollars, twice as large as the year before. Had Smith been willing subsequently to be of service to Roosevelt without trying to dominate him, cordial relations between the two men still might have continued. Roosevelt may have hoped Smith would cooperate this way, for he wrote privately on January 7, "I am very certain that he can be tremendously helpful to the cause of liberalism, and it is the duty of all of us to keep him active. I begged him to let me put him back on the Port Authority in New York, but he wants nothing definite for the next six months."[40]

Understandably, Smith was no more disposed than Roosevelt to take a back seat. Bewildered already by his smashing defeat nationally, he was sharply hurt by Roosevelt's assertion of independence. Most of all, he was upset over Roosevelt's unwillingness to take Mrs. Moskowitz, and referred to it again and again in conversations with Miss Perkins. Mrs. Moskowitz herself kept prodding the sore with Smith, while Howe did the same with Roosevelt. However, Mrs. Moskowitz was only the key point of conflict; the basic issue was whether Roosevelt should be his own governor, or should preside under the paternalistic guidance of Smith and his staff. Upon this, Roosevelt, ordinarily a master of compromise, would not give ground in the slightest. Tension began to develop between the two men—tension which gradually curdled into rancor. It wounded both men,

Roosevelt so much so that a decade later he dictated an account of what had happened in a letter to a former political associate, decided not to send it, and instead did something almost unique for him: sent it to the files marked WRITTEN FOR THE RECORD. His long-smoldering resentment betrayed him into a statement less than fair to Smith:

> I think [Smith] was sincere when he told me over the telephone at Warm Springs that if I were elected Governor, I could be sworn in and then go South for January and February, leaving the Governorship to Herbert Lehman in the meantime, and returning a few days before the close of the Legislative Session.
>
> In line with this he planned, as you know, to stay in Albany at the De Witt Clinton Hotel for several weeks after January 1, 1929, to help me, and then Herbert Lehman, to carry on the work.
>
> You know, of course, that I kept sixteen of his eighteen Department heads, but he was furious because I put in Miss Perkins in place of old man Hamilton, who had been a complete stuffed shirt as head of the Labor Department, and because I put in Eddie Flynn as Secretary of State in place of Bob Moses, whom I left, however, as Chairman of the State Council of Parks and as President of the Long Island Park Commission.
>
> Furthermore, about a week before Christmas, 1928, Al came to see me and told me that Mrs. Moskowitz was preparing my Inaugural Address and Message to the Legislature. Honestly I think he did this in complete good faith, wanting to help, but at the same time with the rather definite thought that he himself would continue to run the Governorship. His first bad shock came when I told him that I had already prepared my Inaugural Address and that my Message to the Legislature was nearly finished. As I remember it, I told him that I would show both of them to Mrs. Moskowitz before I went to Albany on January first, but it is my recollection that I did not find an opportunity to do so, though I really meant to at the time. It would not have made much difference one way or the other because I knew just what I wanted to say and had it all down on paper.[41]

Thus it was that when Roosevelt arrived in Albany for the inauguration he had already fully set the stage for both the new administration and the ultimate break with Smith. "Both Mrs. Roosevelt and I were in every way cordial and considerate of the Smiths on Inauguration Day," Roosevelt later asserted. Nevertheless, for Smith and his adherents, the proceedings had some of the atmosphere of a wake.[42] On the afternoon of December 31, the Roosevelts arrived at the Executive Mansion in Albany. Already it was undergoing alterations to fit Roosevelt's personal needs. Within the mansion, an elevator was being installed; in the back yard, Smith's private zoo was being dispersed, the greenhouses dismantled, and a swimming pool was about to be constructed. A crowd of almost a thousand people stood outside the gates of the mansion as the Roosevelts drove up. For them, the Governor and Governor-elect put on an effective display of cordiality. "A thousand welcomes," Smith greeted Roosevelt. "We've got the home fires burning and you'll find this is a fine place to live." Roosevelt with equal warmth turned to several friends and said, "I only wish Al were going to be right here for the next two years. We certainly will miss him." It seemed to a reporter who watched Smith depart, waving his brown derby while the crowd sang "Auld Lang Syne," that Roosevelt, inside the mansion, was wearing "a smile that had a trace of wistfulness." [43]

Much the same sort of sentimental public display of mutual devotion took place at the inauguration on January 1. Because of the bad weather it was held in the Assembly Chamber in the Capitol. The crowd was the largest to attend a Democratic inaugural since 1911. Roosevelt had invited every member of the Democratic state committee, and every county chairman and vice-chairman. By scheduling important party conferences to follow the inauguration, he had guaranteed their attendance. In addition he had invited almost every Democrat of the slightest prominence outside the state; several from nearby states had accepted. Altogether Roosevelt had six hundred guests. As a result, the Assembly Chamber was so jammed with Democratic dignitaries that when the members of "the Honorable the Senate of the State of New York," almost all of whom were Republicans, were announced by the sergeant-at-arms and entered, they found their seats pre-empted. They filed up the steps onto the platform, and, thoroughly angry, were escorted through a rear door out of the chamber.[44]

At noon, Smith and Roosevelt, entering from the rear, walked down a runway together to the front of the platform. Smith outwardly dominated the occasion. From time to time someone in the jammed rear of the chamber would yell, "Where's Al?" The customary inaugural proceedings were altered to permit him to deliver a valedictory, and he made the best of it. Within a minute his audience was with him as he launched into a description of his achievements as governor. Toward the end, he gripped the hand of the new governor and said to Roosevelt, "A personal word. Frank, I congratulate you. I hope you will be able to devote that intelligent mind of yours to the problems of this State." There was great applause. Smith shifted his attention to Sara Delano Roosevelt, sitting proudly in a front seat on the platform. "I congratulate the mother," he remarked. "It is a great day for her. I remember my mother. My mother was on the platform with me for two inaugurations. I know how she enjoyed it and how she felt about it." Smith's wife cried, and Sara Roosevelt brushed away tears.[45]

Next Roosevelt walked to the rostrum with the aid of a cane, grasping the arm of his eldest son, James. Solemnly, his left hand placed on the family's two-hundred-year-old Dutch Bible, he took the formal oath of office.* Smiling cordially, he departed from his prepared speech to address himself first to Governor Smith — Al: "To Alfred E. Smith, a public servant of true greatness, I extend on behalf of our citizens our affectionate greetings, our wishes for his good health and happiness and our prayer that God will watch over him and his in the years to come." [46]

With the demands of sentimentalism met, Roosevelt in his "rather higher, more cultured voice" launched into a brief, clear exposition of the progressive principles upon which he was ready to base his actions as governor. It was an eloquent address which formed an admirable preface to the concrete proposals to come in his message to the legislature. The old regime was gone; the new regime had begun.[47]

Smith was well aware by this time that he was to have little part in it. "I guess . . ." Roosevelt reminisced in 1938, "it had become pretty evident that I was not going South and that I was going to be my own Governor and not [somebody else's]. You know, too, the politics in any Capitol. My Inaugural Address and the Message to the Legislature were both pretty strong documents and the crowd sensing the implication began to flock around their new Governor. Thus without any premeditation or action on my part, Al, I think, got the

* The outgoing Secretary of State, Moses, administered the oath. The night previously FDR and Lieutenant Governor Lehman had privately been sworn in by Lehman's brother, Judge Irving Lehman of the Court of Appeals, so that they could legally deal with any emergency that might arise after midnight, when their terms began.

impression that to hang around Albany would be a grave mistake on his part."[48]

Smith stayed only long enough to review the inaugural parade with Roosevelt, then slipped into the Executive Mansion ahead of the new Governor to say a few final farewells. Less than two hours after the inauguration he left Albany. Roosevelt was in command.[49]

CHAPTER II

A New Regime in Albany

> Most of our problems are not political: they can be solved by the same kind of cooperation on your part which I as the Executive of the State hereby offer you.
>
> — FDR TO THE NEW YORK STATE LEGISLATURE, *January 2, 1929.*

THE day after his inauguration as governor, Roosevelt returned to the rostrum in the Assembly Chamber to deliver his first annual message to the legislature. This time the fifty-one men just sworn in as senators who filed in to join the hundred and fifty assemblymen had no trouble finding seats. On the platform, flanked by the presiding officers of the two houses, Roosevelt, radiating graciousness and conciliation, by word and gesture tried to impress a nonpolitical air upon the proceedings.

In a manner reminiscent of the way Jefferson in his first inaugural had assured his Federalist adversaries that all Americans were really of one party, Roosevelt greeted his preponderantly Republican legislature with "the hope and belief that neither you nor I are entering upon our offices with partisan purpose." Assuring them that most questions facing them were not political, he proceeded to outline a legislative agenda which duplicated large parts of what the Republicans had enumerated in their platform of the previous fall or in their legislative manifesto of December 31.

As for a few questions upon which there might be an honest difference of opinion, Roosevelt said he hoped they could "find a practical solution by frank discussion and honest effort to obtain results." What he meant became clear as he detailed his proposals. For weeks he had been feeding them to the press a crumb at a time; now he set them forth as a unified whole.

Both on the farm problem, where Republicans were in substantial agreement with Democrats, and on issues which Republicans were not likely to touch, Roosevelt made strong specific recommendations. On some matters where he could not possibly hope for legislation he took a firm Democratic position to satisfy pressures within his own party. His labor proposals were a good example. These he copied intact from the A. F. of L. manifestoes, Smith's earlier annual messages, the state Democratic platform, and his own campaign speeches. Year after year Democrats had demanded them; Republican legislators had ignored them. For lost causes like these obviously he would find no point in fighting very hard.

Between these two kinds of areas — sure legislation and the impossible — stretched a wide no man's land of controversial matters where Roosevelt hoped he might tactfully maneuver the recalcitrant Republicans into ultimate compliance with his wishes. Here, rather than making concrete proposals, he discreetly asked Socratic questions. On the most important of these issues, that of power, he carefully dropped queries both to stimulate the legislature, in his annual message, and to stir the public, in his inaugural address.

In the inaugural he fished for support from upstate middle-class voters (the mainstay of the Republicans) with the bait of cheap electricity in a measurably short time. Dramatizing the losses resulting from Republican inaction, he pointed out, "In the brief time that I have been speaking to you, there has run to waste on their paths toward the sea, enough power from our rivers to have turned the wheels of a thousand factories, to have lit a million farmers' homes. . . . It is intolerable that the utilization of this stupendous heritage should be longer delayed by petty squabbles and partisan dispute." He raised three technical questions concerning how far the state should go to guarantee that consumers receive power at the least expense: Should it construct the dams and power plants? Should it erect the transmission lines? Should it make final distribution to homes and factories?[1] In addressing the legislators, Roosevelt, less rigid than Smith, declared the development should begin that year, and with public control over the power. Turning with a smile to the Republican speaker, Joseph A. McGinnies, he added, "This is one of those questions on which I hope we can reach an agreement." McGinnies smiled back rather hesitantly, and the legislators snickered.

Like the inaugural, the message was brief. Roosevelt kept it to about twenty minutes' length, the briefest in the memory of any of the legislators. It was clear in outline, but its generalities invited compromise of the sort observers considered indispensable if a Democratic governor and Republican legislature were to join in enacting a constructive program. It was above all a dramatic answer to those critics of Governor Smith who claimed that his greatest hold upon the voters had been an idealistic but unfulfilled program which year by year he requested, and which annually the legislature failed to enact. Roosevelt, having so genially proferred an olive branch, challenged the legislators to pass good bills. "Let us all at this session rid ourselves forever of that blighting dread of following in the rear guard of another's triumphal procession along the road to better government," he declared. "It is of small moment who first points out that road." [2]

There was not much the Republican leaders could do except to reiterate their pledge of the previous month that they would go along with Roosevelt on a reasonable program. And certainly most of what he had outlined in his message seemed reasonable: a balanced budget, aid to agriculture, improvement of parks, elimination of grade crossings, judicial reform, and the like. Consequently, they granted that it was a satisfactory message. "I like its spirit of cooperation," declared the majority leader of the senate, John Knight. They could carp only that most of the proposals were about the same as Smith's. One Republican senator grumbled in satirical comment upon the contrast between Roosevelt's smoothness and Smith's gruffness, "The voice is Jacob's but the hands are the hands of Esau." [3]

The only serious sounds of displeasure came not from Republicans but from devotees of the firm Smith position on public development of power sites; some of these feared that Roosevelt's bland words meant that he would retreat to a system of short-term leases to private companies under state supervision. Roosevelt repeatedly refused to tell reporters whether or not this was what he had in mind. He would say only that he expected shortly to discuss the power problem with Republican leaders. This was a minor jarring note which Democratic leaders in the legislature of necessity overlooked. They vied with each other in making flattering statements about the message.[4]

Thus, in the most cordial atmosphere that had greeted any new governor in Albany in many years, Roosevelt began his term. Later in the afternoon, after delivering his message, he arranged to receive the congratulations of visitors in the executive chamber, a large anteroom to his private office, ornately decorated in red velvet plush, the walls covered with portraits of former governors, including Theodore Roosevelt. He felt fully at ease in his new surroundings, he declared. There had been so few changes since he had left the state senate in 1913 that it was "just like renewing acquaintance with old friends." [5]

To a singular extent Roosevelt was able to communicate to others the feeling that all was well. On one occasion in January or February Miss Perkins attended an informal hearing in the executive chamber. About a hundred people, many of them strangers to Roosevelt, were present. The door to the Governor's office opened and he entered, one hand on his cane, the other clenching the sturdy arm of his secretary, Cross. It was a considerable distance to the desk, and he did not walk as skillfully as later. Miss Perkins observed:

"It was but natural common courtesy for those in the room to rise and wait until the Governor reached his desk. It took him a long, long time. . . . The tenseness in the audience grew as it waited in dread, wondering if he would make it. . . . Painfully, slowly, and awkwardly he walked along with Guernsey Cross. About halfway to the desk he realized the tension of the audience. He began to smile and nod, tossing his head up gaily. He waved the cane, saying cheerfully, 'That's all right. I'll make it.' "[6]

Certainly, from January 2, 1929, on, Roosevelt functioned as confidently as though he had been governor for years. It would take the legislature weeks to process bills, but he began at once to gather to himself power both as Governor of New York and as leader of its Democratic party. Theodore Roosevelt and Woodrow Wilson had long been his idols as strong Presidents; he was quick to profit from their examples as governors.

While the honeymoon with the legislature lasted, much of his task as chief executive was unspectacular but nonetheless essential if he was to build his strength as governor. During January, while he readied the budget for the legislature, he became familiar with the ordinary tasks of his new position. This was not difficult, for he had behind him the experience of seven years of administrative routine in Washington. In this, he had never allowed himself to be overwhelmed by petty details, nor had he failed to retain command.

Roosevelt found it simple to organize his cabinet; like the President, he had the power to determine its membership and procedure. He invited nineteen department heads, or commissioners and assistants, including Lieutenant Governor Lehman, but not Attorney General Hamilton Ward. The attorney general, who was an elected officer, was a Republican and, unlike several Republicans in the cabinet, was an active politician. At the first meeting in the executive chamber on January 10, 1929, Roosevelt decided that the atmosphere must be kept informal. To insure that it would be, he ordered that no stenographer should be present to take down what was said and thus inhibit the free flow of comments and suggestions. Then, as the business of the first meeting, he discussed with the cabinet officers devices to obtain more prompt and accurate reports from state agencies.[7]

In handling these reports and most of the other detailed work, Roosevelt found he had to function as jack-of-all-trades. Fortunately, since his interests were catholic, the role appealed to him. He pointed out to Robert L. Duffus that as governor he had to supervise the care of prisoners and of the insane, the promotion of child welfare, the schools, and the highways. Each day he had to see four or five of his department heads, each of whom would bring him quite a different sort of problem.

In a single field, construction, he was in effect as governor the largest individual contractor in the state. The annual construction bill for a multitude of public works, ranging from roads, hospitals, and prisons down to barns, silos, and pigsties, was more than eighty million dollars. Earlier he had acquired some basic knowledge about construction, first in the Navy Department, later as president of the American Construction Council, so the task appealed to him. He kept track of the progress of about one hundred and fifty projects currently under way, marking on a chart each week the degree to which each was up to schedule and approaching completion. In addition, Roosevelt as governor considered himself the superintendent of normal schools, state parks, and military camps. If anything went wrong, he told Duffus, he had to be the trouble man, or, as he called himself, the "glorified janitor." He was custodian, responsible for the maintenance, repair, and improvement of about a billion dollars' worth of state property, which in 1929 seemed a staggering amount.

There were numerous speeches for Roosevelt to prepare, and although he had the aid of Samuel I. Rosenman, Louis Howe, and others in gathering the material and drafting them, the final responsibility fell upon Roosevelt himself. He expended much time and imagination upon them, and they almost invariably in the end bore his unmistakable touch. Then came the public appearances which he had to make when he delivered them, except over the radio, with all the handshaking, hurried conferring, and imperative cordiality that they required.

In the office itself, day in and day out, there were streams of visitors, some on state business, some from other parts of the country on political missions to a possible presidential nominee, some who simply wished to see a governor and prominent political leader. Cross turned away most of those whose business was not definite, and could not guarantee that the many who came without appointments could get in. Usually when Roosevelt went home there were still ten or fifteen disappointed ones left in the anteroom, but these were few compared with the large numbers whom he saw and conversed with receptively, often at length.

Correspondence was relatively light at first. Roosevelt received not much more than two hundred and fifty letters a day, about fifty of which he answered personally. In addition, he signed his name to many kinds of minor documents – requisitions and the like – which could have been as easily handled by a clerk, but which the antiquated New York laws specified must bear the governor's signature. Each day there were a hundred or more of these. More serious, there were questions of pardons and extraditions constantly passing over his desk; at times these thrust upon him the terrible final decision of whether or not the state should take a man's life.[8]

Even in quiet times the constant flow of paper and people flooded Roosevelt with a substantial work load. If he were to keep afloat it would be impossible for him to follow the sort of regimen that Dr. Leroy Hubbard of the Warm Springs Foundation prescribed for him. Dr. Hubbard, who was in charge of Roosevelt's treatment, greeted the Governor at the inauguration, then turned to newspapermen to say:

"Mr. Roosevelt is in fine general health and there is no question that if he keeps to the proper routine he will continue to improve. He should go to bed not later than ten or ten-thirty o'clock and should rise about nine-thirty o'clock. He ought to have an hour's rest lying down after lunch and he should have his regular exercises. And, above all, he ought to try to keep away from the frills as much as possible, the handshaking and all that sort of thing." [9]

Perhaps Dr. Hubbard hoped that by publicly announcing his instructions to Roosevelt he could intimidate his vigorous patient into following them. His attempt was a complete failure. Roosevelt's only concession to Dr. Hubbard was not to arrive at the Capitol until about ten-thirty in the morning, but his round of work then belied any implication that he might be a semi-invalid. He would handle his mail quickly and begin a round of appointments that extended into the late afternoon. During the noon hour he remained at his desk and at about one o'clock ate a lunch brought him from the Capitol restaurant. Officially he was through at five-thirty, but usually he did not leave until six-fifteen, and some days had his dinner brought in also, so that he could remain in the office until ten o'clock. Almost always when he went home he had to take with him quantities of papers to read and study.[10]

In addition to the long hours he devoted to the business of the State of New York, Roosevelt had to give much time and thought to being a political leader. Thus on January 2, the very day when he delivered a nonpartisan message to the legislature in the afternoon, he gave a rousing political talk to the state Democrats at their victory dinner in the evening. He told them that he had already pledged himself to "act upon all public business with a single view as to what is good for the state." He urged those Democrats who were in the legislature to do likewise – to support all wise and good bills regardless of which party originated them. This nonpartisanship should not hamper any Democratic worker from laboring constantly to inform every voter in the state where the Democratic party stood on fundamental principles: "It is a moral duty for us to spread the Democratic gospel."

The task in many of the rural areas, as Roosevelt well realized but did not state in his speech, was that the Democratic party had to be built from the bottom up. It had no grass roots. Almost no Democrats existed, and the rural prejudices against Democrats, as against many another city heresy, had never been more powerful than in the previous election.* To spread the Democratic gospel among these farm and small-town people would require far more "educational publicity" than Democrats had used in the past. To get this to the voters posed an acute problem, since radios were still far from universal in the country, and the upstate daily and weekly newspapers were mostly Republican, either openly or in the disguise of being independent. The only reason for the existence of many so-called Democratic papers was to publish legal advertising that had to appear in both a Republican and a Democratic paper.

As a practical step which could start immediately to bring results, Roosevelt proposed the creation of an efficient publicity service in Albany. "We must not expect the rural editor to be able to keep in close touch with the progress of our party at Albany or Washing-

* As an illustration of rural prejudices, FDR commented, looking at the Democratic state vice-chairman, "There are still three or four counties up-State where you, Mrs. O'Day, or my wife would not dare to be seen smoking a cigarette." Amidst the laughter, he explained that he was reliably informed that neither of the women smoked.[11]

ton, or to be able by some kind of intuition to understand fully what important Democratic achievements and policies have been deliberately misrepresented or suppressed by a partisan Republican press," he explained. "You, as the State organization, must immediately set about to provide . . . fair and accurate information." [12]

With a will, the Democratic delegates voted immediately after the speech to put Roosevelt's recommendations into action. They unanimously passed resolutions to establish a permanent information service in Albany, and to appoint a finance committee to raise the $100,000 a year that it would cost.[13]

At once Roosevelt put his mandate into operation. Before the end of the month, he opened a publicity bureau staffed with trained writers, several of whom were from western New York. It began turning out detailed news free of cost for the upstate newspapers. In previous years, Mrs. Moskowitz had run a press bureau for Smith, but it had concentrated upon obtaining national publicity for his presidential candidacy. For the time being, Roosevelt preferred to have Howe promote his candidacy undercover from New York City. The Albany press bureau concentrated upon the country weeklies which could not afford the regular news services. It sent them releases they were likely to print because they were straight news rather than merely Democratic publicity, news about the votes and the remarks of their local legislators. It was newsworthy in even the most heavily Republican areas if the assemblyman from one of these districts failed to appear in his seat for a week, failed to vote, or voted wrong on an important bill. Republican papers upstate began to carry these innocent-appearing press releases. Though not outwardly Democratic propaganda, they served two important functions: they helped keep wayward legislators in line, especially in their voting on the farm program, and they almost invariably reported on specific benefits rural people were receiving from the administration of Governor Roosevelt. A sure proof of their immediate effect was the hasty Republican reassembling of their own press bureau, which they had thought they could safely dismantle after the campaign.[14]

Among those people, whether in the city or in the country, who had radios, Roosevelt hoped further to circumvent the virtual Republican monopoly of the press through monthly addresses in which either he, the Lieutenant Governor, or the Democratic legislative leaders would discuss developments in Albany. In these talks he could, if need be, speak more openly as a Democrat. Or if he were faced with a legislative impasse, he could use the microphone, as Governor Charles Evans Hughes had once used the newspapers, to make an appeal to the people. The Democratic party contracted for an hour of radio time a month on a state-wide hookup.[15]

Long since, Roosevelt had grasped the significance of radio as an invaluable political medium for the Democrats which would enable them to break through the paper curtain of the publishers and appeal directly to the voters. In an address to the Tammany Speakers' Bureau in mid-January he explained the shift he felt was taking place.* Originally in American elections, he declared, the "silver tongues" had swayed many voters. Then as newspapers had become giants, they had taken over, and the influence of orators had declined. Radio was changing this:

"The pendulum is rapidly swinging back to the old condition of things. One can only guess at the figure, but I think it is a conservative estimate to say that whereas five years ago ninety-nine out of one hundred people took their arguments from the editorials and the news columns of the daily press, today at least half of the voters sitting at their own firesides listen to the actual words of the political leaders on both sides and make their decision on what they hear rather than what they read." [16]

Roosevelt's promise to use these new techniques to the utmost, and his energetic assumption of immediate leadership, enheartened Democrats throughout the state. With considerable aplomb he managed to retain favor among both the city and the country factions. The unfriendly New York *Post* claimed that he was passing out too many political favors to Tammany men for the upstaters to feel much enthusiasm for his party building. On the contrary, the upstaters were highly pleased with Roosevelt's political program, since it gave them the first slight hope in years that they might win power in their districts. They had repeatedly presented similar plans to Governor Smith, but he had doused them as a needless waste, since he considered the territory above New York City hopelessly lost. Roosevelt in his initial enthusiasm was talking about fighting for assembly seats in the 1929 fall elections. This encouraged the building of new Democratic organizations in many heretofore solidly Republican counties.

None of this displeased the New York City wing of the party, for it held strong promise of a continued Democratic administration for

* FDR planned to deliver this speech on radio by telephone from Albany, but ironically the connection failed and someone else had to read it.

the state — an administration which Roosevelt demonstrated from the outset was ready to cooperate with the city machines. Both before and after his inauguration he conferred privately over appointments with Tammany Boss Olvany and Brooklyn Boss McCooey. Bronx Boss Flynn was his secretary of state.

Also Roosevelt kept on superficially good terms with Smith, who, while he did not dominate the machines, was the idol of their voters. Once he called Smith to Albany to secure further advice on putting finishing touches on the executive budget; Smith was gratified. Several other times he saw Smith more casually, and, in March, Smith engaged in mild horseplay by helping the reporters interview Roosevelt at a press conference. These encounters gave the impression that all was well between the two leaders, and forestalled any suspicion among city Democrats that Roosevelt might slip back into his old antiorganization ways.[17]

Not surprisingly, one Westerner complained: "Out here, you seem to have the brand of Tammany Hall and its 'clique.' I feel that if you do not help to eliminate the unworthy men in your party, the Democratic standard will be very much lowered and will doubtless go down again in defeat in '32." [18]

Roosevelt put the letter in a pile to go to Howe, who ghosted this reply:

> I suppose it is rather useless for me to attempt to convince you that your ideas of Tammany Hall and its relation to the Democratic National Party are founded on untruth and vicious propaganda. If you ever come East I think you will revise your views very much. . . .
>
> It is very hard for the Democrats, with a press so hopelessly Republican, and in the face of such enormous sums of money spent for the dissemination of the most atrocious libel, to get the truth before the people. If I had never heard anything except the propaganda disseminated against the Democratic Party and its candidates last year and had no means of hearing the other side, I dare say I would have found it difficult to remain loyal to my Party.[19]

The words were Howe's, but the ideas were clearly Roosevelt's. He worried less about being identified with Tammany than he did about the emotional tirades against it and Smith which Republican propagandists had whipped up during the 1928 campaign. He was so bent upon exposing them that he probably was not at all conscious that he himself was making use of what he decried, a thoroughly emotional appeal to the rabidly pro-Smith Democratic leaders and voters. In effect he was using the "bloody shirt" technique. Just as Republican leaders held the support of their following for decades after the Civil War by reminding them periodically of old wartime grievances and hatreds, so Roosevelt prodded at the still-bleeding wounds the campaign had inflicted upon Smith supporters.

The device was to release a long statement about the three thousand replies Roosevelt had purportedly received in his Democratic survey after the election.* Since Howe sent it to the papers in time for the Monday-morning editions, when news was at an ebb point, it received much space in a prominent position. The statement was no dispassionate statistical analysis of the letters, since that was not yet ready. Nor was the opening part startling, for it carried, as the consensus of the letter writers, Roosevelt's long-standing protest against laying away the Democratic National Committee "in cotton wool after each election, to be taken out and dusted off just before the next." Rather, what made the headlines was Roosevelt's implied comparison of the defeat of Smith with "the theft of the Presidency in the case of Mr. Tilden" in 1876:

"Bigotry, ignorance of Democratic principles, the spread of unspeakable and un-American methods of the most atrocious falsehoods, unfair and improper pressure brought to bear upon workers in specially favored Republican industries, false claims for the prosperity of the country and kindred propaganda cheated, so my correspondents feel, our party out of the Presidency." [20]

These strong words undoubtedly did Roosevelt and his cause more damage than good. Whatever enthusiasm they may have inspired among the die-hards who had fought in Smith's lost cause, they disturbed those who considered themselves independent voters. Nicholas Roosevelt, a distant cousin on the Oyster Bay side of the family, who was an editorial writer for the New York *Times*, challenged the Governor to produce evidence. The Governor replied that he was merely quoting his correspondents. He went on seriously to argue that propaganda, the cost of which ran into the millions – in Georgia, "vile handbills with pictures of Governor Smith dancing with an almost naked Negro woman," in New York State, anti-Catholic papers sent to multitudes of voters – swayed an ignorant twenty or twenty-five per cent

* The actual number of replies was about a thousand.

of the voters, and thus defeated Smith. Whatever the merits of this argument, many people felt it did not offset the harm Roosevelt was doing. The Democratic National Chairman, John Raskob, who came to Albany the next day to confer with Roosevelt on other matters, told reporters he had not read the statement, but let word leak out indirectly that he did not approve of it. The New York *World*, which had rather mildly supported Smith during the campaign, announced editorially that it must dissociate itself from such a baseless accusation.[21]

Roosevelt chafed under the criticism, the first he had received as governor. When Representative Joseph W. Byrns strongly commended those sections of the statement recommending that the party organization remain active, Roosevelt immediately took it as an endorsement of his bigotry statement. He complained to Byrns:

"Personally I feel that a campaign of slander was tried experimentally in a few states against Wilson and that our failure to ever mention it afterwards emboldened the Republicans to conduct wholesale propaganda of scandalous libel very thinly disguised during the last campaign. If they find that we are intending to keep forever silent about the kind of campaign they waged last year, it is almost certain that we will see the most outrageous lies openly circulated four years from now and I could not let the occasion pass without saying something about it." [22]

The lesson seemed to be almost as much for Roosevelt as for the Republicans. Roosevelt may have gone far to ingratiate himself among Smith followers, but he did not again try to appeal so directly to the emotions. In chiding him, the New York *World* had stated the truism that what the Democrats needed were "convictions, a program, and a leadership which the country will recognize as a genuine alternative to that which the Republicans supply." Roosevelt returned to the less spectacular but considerably safer task of trying to provide them.[23]

CHAPTER III

A "Sanely Radical" Program

> You are right that the business community is not much interested in good government and it wants the present Republican control to continue just so long as the stock market soars and the new combinations of capital are left undisturbed. The trouble before Republican leaders is that prevailing conditions are bound to come to an end some time. When that time comes, I want to see the Democratic party sanely radical enough to have most of the disgruntled ones turn to it to put us in power again.
>
> — FDR TO HERBERT C. PELL, *January 28, 1929.*

ISSUES are the fuel that provides motivating force for modern political machines; without them they can seldom run very far. No one was more aware of this than Roosevelt. Consequently, he lost no time in compounding potent ones for his new engine for Democracy. He devised them carefully to entrench the party within the state and attract favorable attention from without.

In the early months of 1929, agricultural measures could best serve this purpose. National interest focused upon the forthcoming special session of Congress which President-elect Hoover had promised he would call to enact farm-relief legislation. "I am inclined to think that you are going to have a most interesting session," Roosevelt prophesied to Congresswoman-elect Ruth Bryan Owen, "and that the Republican majority is headed for real trouble both on farm relief and on prohibition. For eight long years they have managed to carry water on both shoulders, but there is a limit to the success of that form of juggling." [1]

On Prohibition, Governor Roosevelt himself was wise enough to continue his own water carrying. On farm relief he was fortunate enough, because of the specialized agricultural problems of New York State, to be able to present vigorous recommendations for local farm relief without in any way committing himself on any of the controversial proposals for dealing with the high surpluses and low prices of wheat and the other great staples. It was to his advantage that he could promote aid to agriculture in New York in ways for the most part inapplicable to the nationwide problems. This aid would suffice to label him as a friend of the farmer without bringing down upon him the attacks of partisans or opponents of any of the major farm proposals, such as the McNary-Haugen plan. Even though any farm program for the State of New York would be minor compared with a national one, there would be some measure of profit for the Democrats if Roosevelt in Albany could achieve success while Hoover in Washington floundered.

With the plight of agriculture drawing so much national attention, what Roosevelt proposed could not help receiving some notice. By the time he took office he had already so firmly announced himself a friend of farmers that Frank O. Lowden, the darling of the Corn Belt, wired Roosevelt congratulations upon his inauguration. Roosevelt replied at once, inviting Lowden to come to Albany to talk about farm matters. At a farm conference at Cornell University a few weeks later, Roosevelt boasted that his administration was going to do so much to solve the agricultural problems, not only of New York but of other states as well, that "people will turn again and will say, 'See what New York has done.' "[2]

New York was a leading farm state. It had 190,000 farms – 25,000 fewer than Iowa, but 25,000 more than Kansas. Yet the total value of New York farm acreage was only two thirds that of Kansas and a third that of Iowa. The value of crops raised in New York similarly lagged. The overproduction and marketing problems in New York revolved around truck crops, apples, and milk rather than corn, hogs, and wheat. The soil, far from being overbounteous, was much of it so poor that farms were being abandoned at an alarming rate – four million acres in the previous forty years. There was little excepting politics to link the farm problems of New York with those of the Middle West.[3]

Roosevelt, writing later, frankly granted the restricted potential of agricultural legislation confined to New York:

"In most respects a farm relief program for an individual State must perforce be a limited one, for an adequate farm program must disregard State boundaries and deal in national terms. Not only is there the factor of competition from the farms of other States, but the whole agricultural problem is so tied in with the activities of every group of the nation's population and of every section of the country, and is so closely bound up with such Federal matters as the tariff, the currency, and foreign trade, that treatment by any one State alone must necessarily be inadequate." [4]

In 1929, Roosevelt as governor chose a somewhat different line of approach: There was no single nationwide solution to farm problems because they varied so greatly from one area to another, he pointed out. Creation of an equalization fee on wheat, the McNary-Haugen proposal, would give little relief to New York farmers. What New York farmers needed was a New York program. In his message to the legislature he suggested what he had promised in the campaign: specific solutions to specialized New York problems — the forthcoming recommendations of his commission on farm abandonment, rural taxation, and distribution of farm products.[5]

"The ultimate goal," he asserted, "is that the farmer and his family shall be put on the same level of earning capacity as his fellow American who lives in the city." In the months that followed, he never failed to call attention to the basic principle that the economic life of the city and country were so strongly interrelated that the nation could not long go on half prosperous and half depressed: "If the farming population does not have sufficient producing power to buy new shoes, new clothes, new automobiles, the manufacturing centers must suffer." And again, to justify lifting some of the farmer's tax burden: "We are all in the same boat and if we put too large a burden on the rural sections, the cities must and will inevitably feel the reaction just as too heavy a burden on the cities will in the long run retard the progress and prosperity of the farms." [6]

No one would gainsay this principle. The Republicans, as Roosevelt had expected, rushed to endorse it with fervor, trying to forestall the loss of farm votes. For all his bland assurances of nonpartisanship, Roosevelt had acted early in expectation of these countermeasures. This was why as governor-elect he had unofficially appointed an agricultural committee whose members met at their own expense and used the offices of Morgenthau's *American Agriculturalist*. Roosevelt thus hoped to keep the Republican legislature from taking over. He claimed that eighteen of the twenty-one members of his committee were Republicans. This may well have been, but they were not Republican politicians.[7]

Within his first week as governor, Roosevelt appointed the same people to a second unofficial Agricultural Advisory Commission, asked Morgenthau to serve as chairman, and requested recommendations for a farm program. It was not much more than a formality, since the previous month the members of the commission had already made proposals which were acceptable to all major farm organizations in the state. But the success of the Governor's commission forced the Republicans into a ludicrous scramble for the credit. The Republican leaders of the legislature promptly announced that they would hold a conference of farm leaders on the opening day of the annual meeting of the state Agricultural Society — the same day that Roosevelt's commission was scheduled to meet. This, they pointed out, would make the commission unnecessary.[8]

"There is no crossing of wires," Roosevelt assured newspapermen. He claimed Speaker McGinnies did not in the slightest object to what he was doing, or he to the speaker's plan. Nevertheless, there was a decided chill between the two groups when the Agricultural Society convened. Morgenthau's commission duly met, deliberated for six hours the day before the legislators' conference, met again the next morning, and succeeded in issuing a report only an hour or so before the rival conference began. In it they recommended equalizing the tax burden on farmers, a two-cents-a-gallon tax on gasoline to lift from them much of the expense of highway construction and maintenance, rapid extension of rural electrification, continued work to eliminate tuberculosis among dairy herds, and increased support for agricultural research.[9]

There was nothing drastic or radical about this program — especially the central point in it, the readjustment of farmers' taxes. Undoubtedly the farmers were suffering an injustice under the existing system, but rural tax relief was little more than a peripheral attack on the farm problem. It had an enormous advantage from Roosevelt's standpoint in that it was a concrete program that he could put into effect speedily because it was unassailable. Every farm pressure group was behind it; Republicans could only scurry to advance it as their own proposal. Even on the key means of bringing tax relief to farmers without unbalancing the budget, a gasoline tax, they could fight no more than with a minor delaying action. New York was the only state in the nation without a gasoline tax.[10]

Smith was at least in part to blame for this; perhaps his earlier association with the trucking industry made him overappreciative of its point of view. In December, 1926, Roosevelt had urged Smith to recommend the tax to the 1927 legislature. Smith had assured Roosevelt he favored it in principle, but did not want to ask for any further taxes that year in order to forestall Republican charges of extravagance. At that time, Roosevelt already had heartily favored a gasoline tax because he had "seen its excellent results in the south." As governor, he slowly and methodically marshaled support for it. Even before he took office, he had the state Tax Commissioner, Mark Graves, advocate it at a meeting of the strong New York State Farm Bureau Federation. Naturally, the federation went on record in favor of the shift. The Agriculture Commissioner, Berne A. Pyrke, who was a Republican and responsible to the legislature rather than to Roosevelt, went to New York City in November to discuss tax readjustment with the Governor-elect.[11]

Roosevelt in writing to state farm leaders a few days later made use of Pyrke's arguments. He proposed altering the farm real-estate tax to make it correspond to the taxes on businessmen: "The businessman [primarily] pays a tax on his profits and on his income. . . . The farmer pays a real-estate tax, but he pays it whether he is making any money or not." [12]

The Republicans tried to make these arguments their own by advancing them through their nonpartisan legislative conference. To appear above party considerations, they invited Governor Roosevelt to address them, but slipped when they failed to ask the Morgenthau commission to attend the conference. Morgenthau directed attention to this and added, "I would be glad to go if I had an invitation." Legislators replied that there must have been an oversight.

The serious oversight was in allowing Roosevelt to appear, for he could so skillfully outplay them at their own game. They might better have dropped the pretext of being nonpolitical. When the conference convened in the Assembly Chamber, he came before them in his guise as a private citizen – one who had grown up in a rural community – to tell them about the work of his Agricultural Advisory Commission. He said that he agreed with the Republican leader, Senator Knight, that there were some long-range questions which would require continued study, but pointed out that there were some things that could be done immediately. Then came the cleverest stroke of all: he suggested to them that they do what they were already planning to do, appoint a committee of agricultural experts to cooperate with the legislature. For his own part, he pledged, "After I go downstairs to my desk, you will find an Executive who wishes to go along with you the whole way." Even the Republican legislators were forced to applaud. Obviously they would have a difficult time stealing the spotlight back from Roosevelt.[13]

While Roosevelt took his stand above party, the Democratic leader of the assembly, Maurice Bloch, issued a statement declaring, "Blame for the do-nothing policy that has prevailed rests squarely upon Republican shoulders, for the Legislature has been in their control, year in and year out." [14]

Whatever the actions of the two parties might have been in the past, in 1929 both were ready to work in the same direction. On January 28, both the rival committees met at the same time and later came out with almost identical recommendations. The Republicans still could not entirely stomach the gasoline-tax proposal, and for a while the chairman of their Agricultural Advisory Commission toyed with the idea of substituting a ten-million-dollar revolving fund for farmers. But this would have involved a constitutional amendment and hence delay at a time when the farmers were clamoring for immediate action, and Roosevelt was promising action to them. Consequently, the Republicans soon capitulated entirely.[15]

On February 1, 1929, when Roosevelt went to Syracuse in the heart of the Genesee Valley to explain his program to a hundred country publishers, he shifted his emphasis from tax relief to the need for improved efficiency in town and county governments.* Upon the editors, Roosevelt declared, must fall the task of improving the efficiency of county and town governments. If local burdens were to be eased, these must operate more economically at the same time that the state government contributed more tax money.[17]

Roosevelt talked individually with a large number of the newspapermen. He found eighty-five per cent of them Republicans, willing to accept his pledge of nonpartisanship and to write editorials promoting his program of tax relief and reorganization of town and county governments.[18]

Two weeks later Roosevelt returned to the tax-relief issue when he addressed three thousand rural New Yorkers at the Farm and Home Week Conference at Cornell University. Once more identifying him-

* Democratic Assembly Leader Bloch had already pointed to the extreme contrast between the per capita cost of government in the counties of New York City and some of the sparsely populated ones upstate:

Bronx	$1.48	Madison	$9.48
Manhattan	3.31	Delaware	8.91
		Allegany	8.39 [16]

self as a farmer, he declared, "All we farmers are asking is a square deal and we propose to get it." [19]

Again the response was gratifyingly warm. "The trip to Ithaca was a grand success," Roosevelt reported to his son James. In order to reach an even wider audience, he took his arguments directly to the people of the state in a radio talk early in March. It too was a grand success. The dismayed Republicans could only counter feebly by killing Roosevelt's bills and rushing through the legislature almost identical Republican substitutes recommended by their own commission.[20] Obviously they would have a fairly hard task persuading people upstate that the Republican party, not the ingratiating farmer from Hyde Park who sat in the governor's office downstairs, was the best friend of the rural voters.[21]

In courting Republican farmers, Roosevelt did not entirely neglect the Democratic faithful in the cities. One of their most urgent needs, to which social-welfare agencies were continually calling attention, was for a program of old-age assistance. In 1929 this was still a relatively new idea in the United States, but Roosevelt had backed it during the campaign and in January took the first steps to redeem his pledge. He called for a commission to investigate and to draw up legislation for old-age security. Both he and the legislature should appoint members to the commission; it should operate under the leadership of Dr. Charles H. Johnson, Director of the State Board of Charities.

Two types of old-age security were necessary, Roosevelt declared. First, a contributory system for wage earners which would insure them against want when they grew old. Second, in the rural districts and among those who were not wage earners, something to eliminate or cut to a minimum the use of the "badly coordinated and probably wasteful systems of county poor farms, [and] almshouses." There was considerable popular support for old-age security; Roosevelt received quite a few favorable letters after he first mentioned it, yet he felt he must defend it from the stigma of radicalism: "I want to emphasize that there is nothing socialistic in a program of this kind. No greater tragedy exists in our civilization than the plight of citizens who find themselves, after a long life of activity and usefulness, unable to maintain themselves decently." [22]

In his budget, Roosevelt included a figure of $25,000 for the establishment of a commission. Republicans felt under no pressure from their constituents to further this proposal as they had farm relief; on the contrary, many of the conservative Republican contributors of campaign funds firmly opposed it. Rather than create headlines for Roosevelt, the Republican legislators preferred to bury it quietly in committee. Roosevelt was not in the least disposed to let it remain there. He sent a special message again strongly recommending a commission. New York City liberals were quick to rally to his support, since the problem was already becoming a serious one. There were over half a million people in New York State over sixty-five years of age; and, in New York City alone, between forty thousand and forty-five thousand of these were dependent upon relatives or outside assistance for their livelihood.[23]

Finally, on March 5, 1929, the legislature held hearings. More than two hundred representatives of welfare, civic, and lobbying organizations attended. Spokesmen for the National Civic Federation and the manufacturers' and real-estate associations denounced Roosevelt's proposal; it would ultimately result, the real-estate representative warned, in high taxes on property.

"I suppose," Rabbi Stephen S. Wise retorted, "within the next few days legislation will be introduced to subsidize poor and downtrodden industry. Real estate owners are not the goats; they are getting the goats' milk at present." He went on to suggest a commission to which the legislature might appoint a few members, but which the Governor would staff chiefly with experts. Rabbi Wise's testimony was along lines he had developed in conversation beforehand with the Governor, for Roosevelt had succeeded in enlisting the wholehearted support of the great liberal religious leader. "I think you did a splendid piece of work before that hard boiled committee," Roosevelt later thanked Wise. "I wish you could come up here once a week regularly to give me courage and enthusiasm."[24]

As a compromise, Wise suggested to Roosevelt the possibility of establishing the commission so that the trustworthy experts plus the Democrats would form a majority. Roosevelt tried to negotiate some such arrangement with the Republicans, but they were willing only to agree to a commission upon which their appointees would outnumber his six to three. Promptly Roosevelt announced this at a welfare workers' luncheon. He went on to declare that the legislature could set up its own commission, and that as soon as the lawmakers went home he would, as he was constitutionally entitled to do, establish a "real commission of experts." Unfortunately, he could not provide it with sufficient funds. There the matter rested for the time being. Even in a period of relatively full employment like the first half of 1929, the problem was a significant one, but Roosevelt did not yet consider it urgent.[25]

Water power was urgent — or at least liberals considered it so. Week after week they read with alarm in magazines like the *New Republic* that the giant public-utilities companies were growing larger, and fattening upon outrageously high power rates. Large numbers of middle-class New Yorkers who had never heard of the *New Republic* agreed. Smith had done much to help make them power conscious, and Roosevelt had concentrated effectively upon power during the campaign. Like farm relief it was a national as well as a state problem and of even greater significance in the West than in New York. The attitude that many powerful Western leaders might assume toward Roosevelt would depend in part upon his stand on power. Within the state, too, it would have bearing upon his political future. Already his vague remarks when he took office were leading to speculation. They were of the sort which would be helpful for a short while but demanded relatively early clarification.

New York led all the states east of the Rockies in power potential and in the entire United States was exceeded only by the three Pacific Coast states. In developed water power it stood first in the nation until 1925. Its share of the tremendous undeveloped resources of the Saint Lawrence River would provide energy equivalent to that produced by twenty-four to forty million tons of coal per year. Yet for nearly twenty-five years, since the progressive Charles Evans Hughes administration, the legislature and administration had been deadlocked over whether the power should be developed by public or private interests. Some years earlier, progressives had prevented a combination of the Du Pont, Mellon, and General Electric interests from obtaining the sites. On the other hand, those who wished public development had never been strong enough to get a bill through the legislature, although measures had come before it at least a dozen times in as many sessions.

Even the Republican position was equivocal. Although H. Edmund Machold, the state chairman, was one of the most powerful utilities magnates in New York,* the Republican party did not dare go further than to advocate the long-term leasing of the power sites rather than their sale. The precarious position of the Republicans was apparent in

* Machold had resigned as Speaker of the Assembly in order to become the banking partner of Floyd L. Carlisle, who in 1929 became Chairman of the Board of Niagara-Hudson Power Corporation.

their platform of the previous autumn, in which they asserted their "unalterable opposition to any sale of the State's interest in the water power resources" at the same time that they advocated prompt development of them under existing laws.[26]

Roosevelt also had promised prompt development, although of a different sort. There was no more than a slight possibility that he could get it, partly because of the Republicans, but also because of serious questions. Owing to the efficiency of modern steam plants, would the power actually be a superlative bargain? More important still, since private companies owned the riverbank and the Federal Government and Canada claimed jurisdiction over the water, could the state clear away legal obstacles to the building of dams and plants? Yet Roosevelt risked a serious political setback if he failed to do anything or achieved action only through substantial compromise. At a time when liberal alarm within the state was being heightened by rumors that a great Morgan-Mellon power combination was about to move into New York to annex its utilities companies into their great holding-company structure, Roosevelt would have been most foolhardy to make concessions. The hope of the New York *Times* that Roosevelt would favor improved public regulation, rather than a Power Authority such as Smith had proposed, was in vain. The nature of political support that Roosevelt was trying to gain both within the state and without pushed him toward an advanced stand on power development and regulation.[27]

Keeping his own counsel among the legislative leaders, but conferring earnestly with a number of power experts, Roosevelt quietly devised a plan. It was no compromise with the Republicans, for indeed Roosevelt did not even try to arrive at an arrangement with them. Knight, the president pro tem. of the state senate, complained later that although Roosevelt had promised all through the legislative session that he would confer with the Republican leaders on the power problem, he did no more than call them in at the last moment to tell them that his plan had already been formulated.

On March 12, 1929, Roosevelt again went upstairs in the Capitol to deliver his power message in person to a joint session of the legislature. There were few auditors, since not many people knew Roosevelt was to appear. He spoke quite briefly, only about twenty minutes, but what he had to say made national news. It heralded to every progressive in the country that Roosevelt was "correct" on the power issue — that he would not compromise with the Republicans.

What Roosevelt had to propose was much like Smith's earlier suggestions, as the irritated Republican legislators pointed out. He urged them to establish a five-man body to be known as the Trustees of the Water Power Resources on the Saint Lawrence River, to be composed of great public figures like Smith and Hughes. They should have the right to plan and negotiate, subject to approval by the legislature, for the construction of a dam and generating facilities on the Saint Lawrence. Private companies should have the opportunity to build power lines and handle distribution, but under firm regulation. They must accept rates set by the trustees on the basis of the actual cash outlay, in keeping with the rules of the Federal Power Commission, rather than under the more lenient surveillance of the state Public Service Commission. Under the state commission, Roosevelt claimed, some utilities companies were allowed as much as fifty or even one hundred per cent annual return on the original investment. These proposals of his, said Roosevelt, were neither Republican nor Democratic.[28] He threw down a challenge to the legislature:

"I want to see something done. I want it done in accordance with sound public policy. I want hydro-electric power developed on the St. Lawrence, but I want the consumers to get the benefit of it when it is developed. They must not be left for their sole protection to existing methods of rate-making by Public Service Commissions. Are the business men of this State willing to transmit and distribute this latent water power on a fair return on their investment? If they are satisfied, here is their opportunity. If not, then the State may have to go into the transmission business itself. It can not on the one hand let this power go to waste, nor on the other be required to yield to anyone who would aim to exploit the State's resources for inordinate profit." [29]

Behind this fair promise was Roosevelt's threat, more than half implied. This was that to protect the public the alternative would be state ownership and operation not only of the production facilities but of the distribution system as well. In Washington, Senator Norris granted that Roosevelt had taken "a very brave step in the right direction," but lamented that he had "stopped to change horses in the middle of the stream" by not making an outright demand also for public distribution of power. Norris believed that the criterion south of the Saint Lawrence in New York should be the same as north of it in Canada: the government should provide power to the public at cost.[30]

South of the Saint Lawrence, the halfway step that Roosevelt had proposed seemed to Albany newspapermen to be twice as far as he was likely to go. Several days after Roosevelt's power message, they held their annual dinner. As the Governor had announced his intention of touring state waters during the coming summer, they built it around the theme "Captain Frank's Show-Off Boat." Lustily they sang, "Old Man Power, he's Frank's right bower," but then showed Captain Frank (at this point Admiral Roosevelt) on his junket encountering the Pirate of the Saint Lawrence, Republican Chairman Machold. Despite the fierce cannonading of a huge weapon labeled "Democratic Publicity Bureau," the pirates took over, and the Admiral was forced to surrender his sword.

"Whoever would have thought Machold had so much power?" Admiral Roosevelt exclaimed.

"It wasn't Machold's power that sank you," was the reply. "It was water power."

"Same thing," sighed the Admiral.[31]

In reality, in March, 1929, Admiral Roosevelt was not as yet engaged in battle with the Republican pirates over his basic program on farm relief, old-age security, or water power. Rather, he was engaged in a fierce hand-to-hand struggle with them over what at a superficial glance seemed a rather technical matter, the executive budget.

CHAPTER IV

The Battle of the Budget

> I am getting into a grand little fight with the Legislature and from now on, for five weeks, it will be a general row.
> — FDR TO JAMES ROOSEVELT, *February 20, 1929.*

POLITICAL honeymoons are seldom long lasting. In New York in the 1920's they were of no more than wartime duration, since the assembly was elected every year and the governor and state senate every two years. Hence they were the briefest of interludes following the shotgun marriages which a public sense of propriety demanded between two necessarily incompatible political forces. Of the two partners, the Republican legislatures were the more reluctant, and with reason.

Smith's bombastic rows had been disastrous to them. Roosevelt's genial waving of the olive branch was potentially as great a threat since if they passed a comprehensive and constructive series of bills, he would profit at the polls. Not much more than a month after Roosevelt first took office, he was embroiled in a battle which would have a bearing upon a second term. Consequently, the Republicans could not afford sweet cooperation with a Democratic governor for more than a few days. Roosevelt, like many an adroit politician before him, stood so firm in a position of eminent reasonableness that his opponents were forced into firing the first shot.

It came not over power but the new budget. The Republicans opened up their volley in an effort to keep Roosevelt from entrenching himself as an effective executive. This his budget would have made possible. The New York State budget was the third largest governmental budget in the United States. Only those of the Federal Government and New York City exceeded it in size. One of Smith's hardest-won reforms was to put it on a scientific basis — to take away from the legislature the opportunity to harvest from it a rich crop of patronage plums and political loot. Governmental experts and indeed most educated people hailed the change with approval. The Federal Government had adopted a budget system a few years before; consequently, most newspapers and magazines for some time had carried articles explaining and praising the concept of a scientific budget. Well-read people, believing in it, could not very well take the position that what was worthwhile for a Republican administration in Washington was not equally good for a Democratic one in Albany. This is why so many fair-minded people thought Roosevelt was in the right when he challenged the attempts of the legislature to tamper with the new scientific budget. They felt that he was defending sound principles of public administration.

Consequently, it was with at least fair public support that Roosevelt stood firm against legislative encroachment upon what he considered to be executive prerogative. At the first point where he had either to give way or prove himself a dominant governor, he put up a powerful, effective fight in keeping with all of his past experience and thinking.

An amendment to the New York State constitution had destroyed the old inefficient agency of budget making. This was the Board of Estimate, through which the legislature had negotiated budgets with the executive, and within the privacy of committees had increased allotments for pet projects and raised the salaries of political favorites. The purpose of the change was in part to strip the cloak of secrecy from the legislature. The legislature could strike out or reduce items; its power to embarrass the governor in these respects was unaltered. But it could add items only by stating them separately and distinctly in individual bills, each of which must refer to a single object or purpose. Since the governor could veto these, the new budget seriously limited its opportunities for political aggrandizement.[1]

On the other hand, while the governor could make lump-sum requests for appropriations, he must clearly, specifically, and in detail list the manner in which they were to be spent. The Republican legislators claimed that the use of this lump-sum proviso would have the unjustifiable end of enabling the Democratic Roosevelt to distribute funds for purposes of party building and patronage.* Hence they tried, as had so many of their predecessors since early colonial times, to establish legislative control over the expenditure of funds. This was no more than a new ramification of the age-old struggle for the power of the purse. Around this issue the battle began; it soon spread to encompass the entire legislative program.

Roosevelt joined the issue by sending the budget message to the legis-

* The Republican Attorney General Ward requested and received such an item in the budget for his department.

lature on January 28. He had meticulously followed the legal specifications by collecting data on financial needs from the chiefs of departments and reviewing their proposals at hearings in the presence of the chairmen of the assembly and senate finance committees. The final 411-page document contained, as the law specified, "a complete plan of proposed expenditures and estimated revenues." In it, Roosevelt and his assistants had explained in terms readily understandable to any intelligent reader every item of proposed appropriations. Moreover, the increases for which he asked were not large for a boom year – out of a total of $256,418,000, less than twenty-four million dollars. Very little could go into patronage under any circumstances. Only about three millions were for personal services, and over a million of that would provide additional personnel to staff the growing hospitals, charitable and penal institutions, and to police state parks. A small amount was to enable Miss Perkins to overhaul her labor department. More than half of the over-all increase was for the construction of new hospitals, highways, and bridges; most of the rest was for schools.[2]

In transmitting his "scientific budget" to the legislature, the Governor called upon the Republican leaders to decide upon it in open sessions rather than in committees. He declared that the overwhelming vote of the people of the state in favor of the amendment creating the new constitutional budget indicated public distaste for the traditional trading of favors which surely would continue in the privacy of committee deliberations. All budget deliberations should receive pitiless publicity, he proclaimed, adding in Wilsonian terms that the result must be "open covenants openly arrived at."

This put the Republican legislators in a difficult spot. Their only hope of obtaining political gain through the budget was to pare it as drastically as they dared, not, as Roosevelt implied, to ladle out pork to themselves. Yet if they did this cutting openly on the floor of the legislature the Democratic publicity bureau would quickly carry the names of the ax wielders to the special-interest groups they were hurting. Even the New York *Times*, favorable as it was to the "scientific budget," conceded that open deliberations were scarcely practicable. Consequently, the Republicans took the unpopular course of voting down proposals for open consideration and sending the budget to committee as always.[3]

Roosevelt, continuing to play a role of forbearance, did not protest unduly. Later the Republicans claimed that he agreed upon their formula for handling the budget. If he did so, he agreed privately and orally, for he took a different position publicly and in writing. When the legislature passed a bill providing that he and the department heads should have the right to appear before committees to testify on the budget, he signed the measure on the grounds that it was an additional prerogative which did not take away from him the right to appear before the two houses in session.[4]

Among intimates, his pose was one of amused annoyance. To his wife's Aunt Corinne (Theodore Roosevelt's sister) he apologized for sending a typed note since he found longhand letters impossible "until the silly, old Republican Legislature takes it into its head to go home and leave me in peace to run the affairs of the State." He added, perhaps not in entire sincerity, "It must be grand to belong to a legislature which has a Governor of its own faith! Up here in Albany I do not know which suffers the most – the Legislature or myself." [5]

The answer was simple: the legislature. Roosevelt could afford to continue the harmony indefinitely; they could not. For him the best politics was to assume the pose of being above politics. While they were pleased with the easy time they were having in contrast to the rows with Smith, they worried about the growing popularity of Roosevelt upstate. "They are a little afraid," Ernest K. Lindley of the *World* reported, "that even if the 'era of good feeling,' already impaired so far as Gov. Roosevelt and the Republican leaders personally are concerned, is patently disrupted by open conflict in the closing weeks of the Legislature, they will not be able to separate the Governor entirely from some claim to the rural New Yorker's gratitude." [6]

Nevertheless, they took that risk. They misgauged their man as so many others had misgauged him earlier; his bland smile and continuing good humor lulled them into underestimating him. They forgot how he had initially made his name in that same capitol building eighteen years earlier by leading a knock-down, drag-out legislative revolt against Tammany. The novice had committed some crudities in that first fight; in the years since he had lost none of his toughness but had grown greatly in smoothness and political skill. He was quite ready to appear an ingratiating easy mark compared with the rough-and-tough Smith if that would help throw the opposition off balance. Certainly he was anything but the pushover they thought him to be.

In mid-February the legislators hurled the first dead cat. Professing astonishment over the budgeted twenty-five millions of lump-sum appropriations which only Roosevelt could allocate, the Republicans anonymously aired their indignation to newspapermen. One asserted that it was not conducive to economy. They tried to give the impression that it was full of Democratic boodle, but specific claims were relatively modest. One item of $112,000 would provide for new state police in Long Island parks; another, $5250, for jobs in the State Athletic Commission, headed by James A. Farley, Secretary of the Democratic State Committee. These, the Republicans charged, were blinds to aid the Democrats in building the party, and they virtuously slashed them from the budget.[7]

At the same time they took a far more serious step. They introduced a bill providing that the Republican chairmen of the fiscal committees should have a direct voice in allocating lump-sum appropriations. This was intolerable to Roosevelt since it would force him to relinquish some of his power to the legislative leaders.

For the moment he made no retort but sent the legislature his supplemental message on farm relief in which he recommended a gasoline tax and a twenty-per-cent cut in the state income tax. At once the Republicans challenged this too by introducing their own measure. This time they varied the pattern they had set earlier in the session by making in addition a significant change in Roosevelt's recommendations. By now they were willing to accept a gasoline tax, but they threw out the income-tax cut and instead, as they had pledged in their platform, eliminated the direct tax on real estate. It was as bold a bid for rural support as any Roosevelt had made earlier, but it involved the risk of displeasing many of their well-to-do supporters, mostly in cities, who would benefit more from an income-tax cut.[8]

Roosevelt had indeed held fire until he could see the whites of his opponents' eyes. He opened up at point-blank range. "I will stand back of the income-tax reduction," he told reporters on February 26, "because it is the reduction which will mean the greatest good for the greatest number." He bluntly warned Speaker McGinnies that either the legislature must pass his income-tax reduction and plan for tax equalization, or he would veto the gasoline tax and accompanying farm-relief measures. McGinnies stood firm and retorted that the Republicans would stand firm on that – if Roosevelt vetoed the bills, he would be leaving things as they had previously been. To this Roosevelt replied with the threat that the legislature might have to remain in Albany all summer or come back for a special session in order to balance the budget. This, said McGinnies, would be satisfactory; the Republicans were willing to take the fight to the electorate in the November assembly election.[9]

With more strong words, the Republicans immediately brought out from committee their own "perfected budget." Roosevelt was ready for them. The same day, February 27, he sent them a strong, dignified message charging them with grave breaches of constitutionality and principles of good government. He declared that their bills failed by fifty per cent to follow the simple, clear legal procedure which would show the press and the public how they had altered the budget. Most important of all, these bills gave the legislature a voice in spending lump-sum appropriations. Roosevelt brought this long-simmering issue to a boil. The time had come, he stated, "to give heed to a grave question directly related to our American form of representative government":

> I have serious doubts on many grounds as to the constitutionality of requiring the approval of two members of the Legislature before appropriations made in the spring by the Legislature can be spent during the following fiscal year.
>
> Among these reasons, I raise the broad question affecting the division of governmental duties between the executive, the legislative and the judicial branches of the government. To the same degree that the Governor should never be given legislative functions so the members of the Legislature should never be given executive functions.[10]

In addition to this primary objection, Roosevelt denounced the legislative policy as being bad administrative practice, since it could hamstring the executive branch of the government if the committee chairmen were unavailable to countersign the governor's allocations of money. They might be on vacation. Worse still, for a period each year, actually no such officers of the legislature existed. During this time, the governor would not be able legally to spend any lump-sum moneys. Finally, Roosevelt pointed out that the entire matter was greatly exaggerated since the lump-sum appropriations constituted only a small amount of the total budget.[11]

To all this, Republican orators replied with heat rather than careful argument. A Syracuse assemblyman, referring to the Governor as "that man downstairs," declaimed, "The very foundation of the state is in danger with this message of avarice, usurpation and presumption." After this bombast, the Republicans pushed through both houses of the legislature the "perfected budget" bill, giving them a veto over lump-sum expenditures.[12]

Roosevelt, taking advantage of the statutory time allowed him to study the budget bill, for the time being held his peace about it. Instead he broadened his attack upon the legislature to encompass a number of issues probably more understandable and interesting to most voters. Gradually these differences developed into a battle royal of the sort that both Roosevelt and the public found exciting. It began fairly quietly, overshadowed for days early in March by the events surrounding the inauguration of Herbert Hoover. By the middle of the month, as Washington news settled down, that from Albany became a bit more spectacular. Rollin Kirby, cartoonist for the rather friendly New York *World*, portrayed a fit and serious Governor, wearing glasses, boxing cautiously with a bloated, evil-appearing "G.O.P. Legislature." One of Roosevelt's banker friends protested that it was unfair to portray him wearing glasses, but the Governor himself disagreed: "I decided that the eyeglasses were a compliment as there is a neat implication that 'the big bozo' is about to receive a wallop in the tummy which will result in at least acute appendicitis! Anyway I have not had to take off my glasses so far." [13]

Indeed, Roosevelt figuratively had no need to take off his glasses. He was boxing so rapidly and swiftly that he landed repeated stinging blows which kept the unwieldy legislature so off balance that most of its heavy counterpunches whistled harmlessly through the air. During the month that followed the initial blows over the budget, he peppered the legislature with messages recommending constructive legislation, much of it noncontroversial, all of it widely supported among voters:

February 28, he asked for a commission to study the need for an old-age pension system.

March 4, he proposed a program to readjust the tax burden on rural school districts, provide for the better support of country schools, and enable a minimum wage of $1200 per teacher.

March 12, he delivered his significant (and debatable) message calling for a Saint Lawrence power commission.

March 16, he asked for $168,000 for three agricultural research studies.

March 20, he recommended a referendum on a four-year term for governor.

March 21, he requested a commission to study the business of courts and the administration of justice.

March 21, he also recommended a law requiring the prompt filing of election returns.

March 22, he sent a message supporting a number of pieces of social legislation and labor bills.

March 22, he recommended a study of the further development of Saratoga Springs.

March 25, he recommended the creation of a public-utility survey commission.

March 26, he called the attention of the legislature to the critical needs of hospitals and other state institutions and recommended a fifty-million-dollar bond issue for the construction of new buildings.

March 26, he again requested establishment of a Saint Lawrence power commission.[14]

Of all this, and what Roosevelt had earlier proposed, the legislature passed only the farm-relief measures and those creating commissions to investigate old-age security, the public-service law, judicial reform, and the development of Saratoga. Even these were not administration bills but Republican substitutes.[15]

Roosevelt in part compensated for this technique of substitution by seeing to it that it received wide publicity. The dean of legislative correspondents, Axel "Baron" Warn, reported in the New York *Times* that whenever Roosevelt let it be known that he intended to recommend certain legislation, the Republican leaders would introduce a bill along the same lines. Their bill would embody some feature not foreshadowed by the Governor's statement, in order to lure away from him some additional group of voters.[16]

Thanks to his friendly manner with reporters, Roosevelt was able to get several such accounts into Republican as well as Democratic newspapers. In part, the Republican papers counteracted this with hostile editorials. Consequently, Roosevelt could be much more effective by taking his complaints against the legislature directly to the public. Even there he tried at first to be conciliatory toward the legislature. He drafted a strong radio address on his rural program and income-tax cut for delivery on the evening of March 7. That afternoon he held it as a club over the Republican legislative leaders when he conferred with them. Although he gave them a few mild raps in the conference, he abandoned his belligerent attitude of the previous week. They too gave way, so it was a pleasant hour and a half, and compromise again seemed possible. Immediately he toned down his address before delivering it that evening.[17]

As soon as Roosevelt had given his radio talk, the Republicans spurned compromise and returned to their attack. Certainly they were in a formidable position in favoring abolition of the direct real-estate tax as the change that would most help poor upstate landowners. It would benefit far more people than a lowering of the income tax. While, as Roosevelt said, 530,000 people paid an income tax, the Republicans pointed out that only four thousand of these taxpayers, or three fourths of one per cent, would receive fifty-three per cent of the benefit from the proposed twenty-per-cent cut. The bottom 335,000 would benefit an average of only $1.28 each. Speaker McGinnies further undermined Roosevelt by promising to take under advisement a twenty-five-per-cent cut on the tax on earned incomes up to ten thousand dollars. This would give greater relief to the smaller taxpayers.[18]

Luckily for Roosevelt, his opposition was not so clever and sound in other moves against him. The legislature, by its wholesale slaughter of almost all other progressive bills, gave him the opportunity to denounce it sternly. On March 9 he told New York social-welfare experts precisely how the legislature was blocking their bills:

> Measures which are in no sense political are being murdered in committee rooms without full and fair consideration and without a record vote. When your senators and assemblymen come up for reelection you will have great difficulty in finding out how they stood on any of these measures. . . .
>
> I am not opposed to the legislative committee as an institution, but I hold that bills of this character . . . should be given a fair, open discussion on the floor of each house and record votes taken on each measure. Then, if we are beaten we cannot say we did not at least have a chance. . . . I have done all that I could, but I can't pass legislation.[19]

Roosevelt proclaimed two main grievances against the legislature. The first was that they passed and sent up to him such a large number of "fool measures" that he had to spend time studying them that he should be giving to vital public questions. Of the nine hundred to a thousand bills he could expect from the legislature, he considered two thirds unnecessary. Yet each took time to consider. They came to the Governor in a gray wrapper accompanied by memoranda, letters, and telegrams relating to them. One bill had 1500 telegrams with it. Yet many of these bills were absurdly trivial: one was to change the number of a law passed at a previous session with the wrong number attached; another would legalize five hooks on a line rather than three for a certain kind of fishing.[20]

At the same time that the legislature ground out these trivia, it unhesitatingly slaughtered significant bills in committee. This was the major grievance Roosevelt aired again and again. "Take the holocaust . . . last week," he pointed out, referring to the work of the Assembly Judiciary Committee on March 7. "These gentlemen got together and in an hour and forty minutes, just 100 minutes, they killed 250 measures which had been referred to their committees." Some of these had the widespread backing of civic groups, and were under the sponsorship of Republicans as well as Democrats. The most notorious was their destruction of a bill to outlaw the "ambulance chasing" tactics of unscrupulous lawyers. "Aw, the hell with it," a member of the committee exclaimed, and they killed it.*

Irresponsibility of this sort, Roosevelt told R. L. Duffus, illustrated why the next major reform in the state government (now that Smith had overhauled the executive branch) should be the scientific reorganization of the legislature. "For years we have put up with legislative machinery which would not be tolerated in any private business," he said. Yet he profited from its very incompetence. Because of the way in which the Republicans were mismanaging it, Roosevelt was able to proclaim with some point that by a curious development at Albany, the majority party had become the party of opposition.[22]

From the general, Roosevelt returned to the specific, the executive budget. He consulted his counsel and other lawyers, and conferred with Smith and the former Secretary of State, Robert Moses. All of them agreed with him that the legislature was violating the state constitution in insisting upon control over lump-sum appropriations. But they persuaded him that he should not, as he had planned, accept the bill and undertake the difficult maneuver of taking it to the courts for a ruling. Instead, he should exercise his prerogative to veto the offensive items. Consequently, on March 13 he sent back to the legislature the appropriation bill with all the lump-sum items vetoed — some fourteen pages of them totaling fifty-four million dollars.† [23] In language so firm that it could not be misunderstood he reiterated his belief that

* Chairman Edmund B. Jenks concluded this remarkable performance by asserting, "I am a Republican, but I am not in the least inclined to play politics with the legislation." [21]

† The legislature, to gain additional control over the budget (and perhaps to conceal certain increases), had more than doubled the lump-sum items.

joint legislative and executive supervision of the expenditures was "contrary to the spirit and letter of the constitution of this State:

"It is wholly contrary to the whole plan of the American form of representative constitutional government to give two-thirds of a purely executive duty to the legislative branch of the government. The Executive Budget was not approved by the people of this State with any such thought in mind. I will not assent to a precedent depriving the present Governor or future Governors of a large part of the constitutional duties which are inherent in the office of Chief Executive." [24]

The Republican leaders retorted angrily; Speaker McGinnies questioned the constitutionality of the Governor's vetoes. Yet along with his vetoes, Roosevelt proposed a compromise. He announced he would resubmit the vetoed items to the legislature in two forms of bills: as lump sums to be spent with the authorization of the governor, which would be more efficient; or itemized in detail, which should eliminate the objection of the legislature to giving him discretion over expenditure. Either of these he would sign because either was constitutional. Finally, he announced that if he were given authority over lump-sum expenditures, he would keep the finance-committee chairmen informed of all steps he made in handling them.[25]

For the moment, the Republican leaders seemed to succumb to Roosevelt's attitude of reasonableness. At first they agreed to accept the itemized bill he would submit, then thought better of it. On March 18, when the assembly received Roosevelt's new budget message and the bills, at first it voted, 82 to 59, against permitting them to be introduced. Two days later it shifted strategy and allowed them to be filed, only for the purpose of amending them back to the identical form that Roosevelt had vetoed. Even though the Republicans might seem to be unreasonable in the face of Roosevelt's conciliatory attitude, they did not wish to pass up the opportunity to place him in a predicament. They assumed Roosevelt considered resort to the courts for a test impossible. "The court test is out of the window," he had declared to reporters at the time of his vetoes.[26] Consequently, the Republican leaders thought they could force him either to accept lump sums with legislative control, or call them back into a special session in which they could be as balky as he. Fortified with a ruling by the Republican Attorney General upholding the constitutionality of their actions, they went ahead, impervious to the Governor's protests.[27]

When the Republicans brought the amended budget bill back onto the floor of the senate, two of the Democratic leaders, flushed with anger, yelled their protests. Senator Knight shouted in reply that the Republicans were struggling once again in the historic American battle against taxation without representation. "All great fights in history," he thundered, "have arisen . . . between the people and an oligarchy or a despot." The Democrats tried to apply this same logic against Knight. They charged him with trying to steal power from the governor, and challenged him to accept Roosevelt's itemized budget, which would automatically eliminate the lump-sum controversy. "We graciously took it and this is our reward," Knight hypocritically explained. "We restored the lump sum for the Departments of Labor and Law, because the department heads want to be free to reorganize their departments. The Governor's segregation for these departments was hasty and unscientific." [28]

Quickly the Republicans shifted attention away from this weak argument to a far more effective one. They brought forth a shocking illustration of the alleged misuse of funds which could take place if they did not retain control over lump allocations: the Taconic State Park Commission at a time when Roosevelt was a member had received $100,000 for land, but had spent only $304.53 for land and over $68,000 of the amount for personal services.* With this as justification for their position, they passed their budget, rushed through a great mass of legislation, and adjourned, leaving Roosevelt in what they considered to be a hopeless impasse.[30]

Republican newspapers hailed their victory and hooted at the apparent impotence of the Governor. Roosevelt was politically weaker than three months previously, contended the New York *Post:* "From the Republican standpoint the session was a howling success, but from

* Francis R. Masters, chairman of the commission, replied immediately that the Republican charge was grossly misleading:

> "Like other regional State park commissions, this commission was never given sufficient funds by the Legislature for planning and overhead expense. The law in connection with the $100,000 appropriation referred to specifically states: 'Where money is appropriated by this act for the acquisition of lands, so much as may be necessary may be used for the purpose of making surveys, examinations of title and other expenses incidental to the acquisition of such lands.'
>
> "These facts were never hidden from any one. Obviously it would have been senseless to expend money for land without adequate studies as to what land should be acquired. No apologies are due to any one for the use of bond money for plans and surveys. Personal service had to be employed for this purpose as well as for title surveys and other incidental expense.
>
> "In the past two years the commission has acquired 4,350 acres of land for park and parkway purposes at an average cost of $46 an acre." [29]

the Democratic viewpoint it was almost a complete 'flop.'" The Republican triumph had "brought the Legislature back into its own." The New York *Herald Tribune* agreed in more solemn tones, chiding Roosevelt for his failure: he should not have attempted Smith's tactics when he lacked Smith's political skill and dramatic gifts.[31]

What these papers overlooked was the Pyrrhic nature of the Republican victory. The legislature had won only at the cost of much of the progressive program which a majority of the voters had favored time and again at the polls. Governor Roosevelt was not so much the loser as were all the people of the state. He pointed this out to the people immediately.

"Possible partisan advantage, instead of being forgotten," he declared, was "the supreme test as applied to any legislation. . . . Having, apparently, practically no constructive ideas of their own, the legislative majority has deliberately assumed the role of the party of the opposition. Such suggestions of my own as have apparently survived the unintelligent riot of these closing days are so altered for political reasons as to require a somewhat careful examination . . . before I can be sure whether they are mine . . . or merely changelings dressed up to look like meritorious legislation."[32]

The legislators returned home from the battlefield in Albany to celebrate their victory. They returned too soon and celebrated mistakenly. Roosevelt had only just begun to fight.

CHAPTER V

Appeal to the People — and the Courts

The Legislature is ending in a burst of profane glory against practically every one of my recommendations. They have come out in the open and shown their hand, which makes the record very clear and will give a splendid opportunity for carrying matters straight to the people.

— FDR TO GEORGE FOSTER PEABODY, *March 27, 1929.*

THE very day that the recalcitrant legislators took their triumphant departure for home, Governor Roosevelt began his task of undermining their victory. First he began to appraise their handiwork — the nine-hundred-odd bills they had passed in the last frenzied rush — and to determine how much of it he would let stand. He had thirty days after their adjournment in which to study these and decide which to sign and which to veto. His most difficult decision would be whether he should again veto the critical budget bill, which the Republicans had repassed in identical form. Should he capitulate or fight in the courts?

Studying bills was the lesser part of Roosevelt's task. He must concentrate even more upon making dramatically clear to the voters of the state, and those keeping a watchful eye from beyond New York's borders, how badly the legislature had behaved and how well their Governor was performing. While the unruly ending of the session was still in the headlines, Roosevelt began his onslaught. He easily assumed a role congenial to him, but highly irritating to the Republican leaders, that of the benign schoolmaster whose task is to lecture his charges on the principles of government. He wrote Morgenthau, "I am inclined to think that some day we will not stop compulsory education at the age of fourteen, but will compel every citizen throughout life to attend a school of information once a week."[1]

Of course, Schoolmaster Roosevelt could run his class only on a voluntary basis: the willingness of New Yorkers to turn on their radios. On April 3, 1929, and again a week later, speaking over WGY and other stations in the state, he fought for the first time with one of the most effective political weapons in his armory. This was what later in the White House he called the "fireside chat." In an intimate, quiet way rather than in an oratorical manner, he projected his personality through the microphone into the sitting rooms of New Yorkers. This was the reverse of Smith's political brimstone, and with good reason, for Roosevelt's purpose was not to devastate but to persuade. Smith spoke as an indignant East Sider, his inflections and vocabulary flavored with the tones and phrases of the New York sidewalks. Roosevelt with his cultivated accent spoke as a friend of the common people, but not as one of them. His talks were clear, logical, simple, and carried a note of authority. Roosevelt talked much as he must have when he discussed next year's crops with his tenant farmer, Moses Smith. In one respect he had not developed his full power. He spoke a good bit more rapidly than in later years; his delivery was to grow in mellowness and strength, but already it fascinated radio listeners.

Newspapers gave little advance notice to these first two radio addresses, and people were not yet in the habit of tuning in on Roosevelt. Probably his audience was not wide, but it was enthusiastic. The talks were effective. Proof of this was the angry Republican retort that they would not stand by idly while Roosevelt attacked them unjustly – that he was not a benign patriarch but a political governor.[2]

In his first half-hour radio address on April 3, Roosevelt charged that the Republican party had failed to live up to its platform. It had charged the Smith administration with waste and extravagance, yet the Republican majority in the legislature had passed appropriations totaling thirty-three million dollars more than those of the year before. It had ignored platform promises to reform the patchwork tax system, promote social-welfare legislation, and improve state hospitals. It had promised to develop sound policies to utilize water power, but it had made "not a single move . . . to put forward any program, sound or unsound."

The fault, Roosevelt asserted, lay with despotic Republican chairmen of committees, who buried almost all sound legislation, Republican as well as Democratic. He argued that the chairmen, themselves in most cases acting under orders from others, had run the legislators. A majority of the Republicans had been mere rubber stamps. The Republican strategy had been that of "preventing all discussion, of waiting until the last minute before even reporting such measures as the Republican leaders conclude to allow to go through, so that they are hurried through with hundreds of other bills by a mumbled roll call, without any attempt at honest debate." The remedy must lie with the voters, who should make sure their candidates were "more than dummies voting 'Aye' or 'No' dutifully when so told to do." [3]

Newspapers throughout the state interpreted Roosevelt's strictures as the prelude to a hopeless fight for a Democratic legislature. Obviously, because of the disproportionate number of districts in solidly Republican upstate areas, the Democrats could not win the legislature. Even in the later depression years of Democratic landslides, the assembly went Democratic only once. In the boom spring of 1929, it would have been the height of folly for Roosevelt to attempt the fight, since the inevitable failure would cost him prestige. In interviews, Roosevelt denied he had any dreams of trying to win the assembly; he granted only that the Democratic party would make an extraordinarily energetic attempt to win more seats in the fall. In his second radio address, a week after the first, he emphasized that he was not trying to "play politics on behalf of a Democratic Legislature," that what was important was not the election of Democrats or Republicans but of good legislators.

Yet his implication was obvious when he went on to describe the progressive planks of the Democratic platform – unenacted because the Democratic minority in the legislature did not have the votes to push them through. A measurement of the platform against achievements made "a rather long list of persistent efforts to secure the passage of legislation which we had promised and a rather discouraging unwillingness on the part of the majority to go along with us and forget politics."

The one outstanding exception was the Democratic promises and the solid achievements on behalf of agriculture. Roosevelt refused to grant to strong Republican claims the credit for this. Rather, he cleverly ascribed it to the Governor's Agricultural Advisory Commission, which he himself had appointed the previous November. He reminded his listeners that nineteen of the twenty-three members of the commission were Republicans, but behind them was not the party but the Dairymen's League, the Farm Bureau, the Grange, and other leading agricultural organizations. The program which the Republican legislature had passed was basically that of the Advisory Commission. Roosevelt tried to clinch this point by emphasizing that while the Republicans had been in control of the legislature for years, they had not even suggested anything substantial for the benefit of the farmer until the Advisory Commission pointed the way. As a result, the farmers had gained considerable relief through the shifting of much of the tax burden for roads and rural schools from counties and towns to the state.

Roosevelt enumerated a number of pieces of minor legislation which had passed, but the total was not very impressive. The reason for this small total, he implied, was Republican fear of giving him political credit.* This was immaterial, he concluded. "I can only say that I rejoice in what the majority members of the Legislature have given me of my program and regret their failure to adopt the rest."[5]

Undoubtedly these radio speeches, together with the steady flow of favorable press releases from the Democratic publicity bureau, made a start toward recouping whatever prestige Roosevelt had lost to the legislature. His vigorous veto policy during the month after it adjourned brought him still more prestige. He worked rapidly through the mountain of measures the legislature had passed heedlessly in its final days. Within a week after adjournment, he had already signed 268 of them; he took six hundred more with him to Hyde Park for study, joking to newspapermen that he wondered if he should not get a trailer to carry them.[6]

Many of these, like a measure to pay twenty dollars a day to members of the Nassau County mosquito extermination commission, were of a petty pork-barrel nature. Roosevelt vetoed them as useless increases in the cost of county government. Others were small special bills to provide compensation to individuals, which he vetoed because there was general legislation to accomplish the same purpose. And there were many other sorts of minor bills. Toward the end of his task, Roosevelt disposed of seventy-nine of these in a single omnibus veto.

A few vetoes were more significant. He refused to sign a measure to weaken the Workmen's Compensation Law. Also, he vetoed a bill to establish a commission on the administration of justice. The commission, as the Republicans wished to create it, would have been composed solely of lawyers and legislators; Roosevelt strongly advocated a commission which would contain lay as well as legal experts. Other-

* One piece of Republican legislation that FDR grudgingly signed was a bill increasing state income-tax exemptions for single persons from $1500 to $2500, and for heads of families of married persons from $3500 to $4000. He denounced it as an unscientific addition to a "jerry-built tax system." Yet it gave income-tax relief at the bottom while he would have given it at the top of the income brackets.[4]

wise, he felt it would be incompetent to study the broad questions involved.[7]

One veto towered above all the others in importance. On April 12, he killed three segregated lump-sum items in the executive budget in order to force a court test. Before doing so, he had again consulted various legal experts. He sent his law partner, Basil O'Connor, to discuss the constitutionality of his stand with one of the most eminent of Republican lawyers, George Wickersham, who had been one of the sponsors of the executive budget amendment to the New York constitution. Wickersham granted that he had some doubt whether the legislature had power to go as far as it had, although he leaned in its direction. But he stated what Roosevelt was eager to hear: "I do think that the question of the budget legislation might well be submitted to judicial determination." [8]

Previously Roosevelt had not seen how it would be possible to test his stand in the courts, even though his counsel, Griffin, and others had assured him that he was constitutionally correct. Now the Republicans were ready to cooperate with him; they announced that if he again vetoed the lump-sum items they would take the budget to court. On this basis, Roosevelt exercised his veto, strongly stating his conviction that an important constitutional principle was at stake.[9] He appointed William D. Guthrie, former President of the New York City Bar Association, to represent him in the case, and expressed his hope that the courts would deliver a decision before the beginning of the new fiscal year.[10]

Although the Republican leaders assented to the court test, they publicly accused Roosevelt of bad faith. Even before the veto, Senator Knight and Speaker McGinnies jointly declared that they were not going to sit by quietly while Roosevelt "bombards the Legislature through the press and over the air with ridiculous and groundless charges." Following the veto, Knight told a Republican meeting that Roosevelt was seeking for political purposes to smear the legislature on the budget issue. Knight asserted, "Having once openly agreed upon the procedure relating to the budget, the Governor suddenly and without warning to the Legislature reversed his attitude and charged, in substance, that the Legislature was trying to force secret, rather than public, consideration of budget bills." Crying "Unfair, unfair," he claimed that Roosevelt had promoted strife rather than harmony, and had spurned the legislature when it was ready at any time to go more than halfway.[11]

This was on the face of it a stretching of the facts that could not have been very convincing to Roosevelt's independent supporters. Because as an individual he personified the state government, it was easier for New Yorkers to credit him rather than the legislature for advances in government. Similarly, the fact that he had vetoed more trivial bills than any of his predecessors in years, even including Smith, made him look like a sound administrator.

There had been no sure way out for the Republicans, who controlled the legislature. Had they passed a more extensive program, he would have benefited politically more than they; besides they were considerably more conservative than many of their constituents, and did not want to pass liberal measures. It was they who had balked and engaged in subterfuge. But in so doing, they slipped back into the villain role they had so long played during the Smith era. It was easy for liberal voters to blame the legislature for its failure to obtain one law or another; Roosevelt, who had pushed hard for these measures, to a considerable degree remained their champion.

Consequently, despite the gibes of the Republican politicos and press, Roosevelt was able to view his first bout with the legislature with equanimity. Certainly it had added rather than detracted from his exhilaration over being governor. Indeed, it probably helped distract him from the normal vicissitudes falling upon the head of a large family. A few days before the legislature went home, he wrote an old friend:

"This family is going through the usual tribulations. James is getting over pneumonia; Elliott is about to have an operation; Franklin, Jr. has a doubly broken nose and John has just had a cartilage taken out of his knee! Anna and her husband, Curtis Dall, are taking a short holiday in Europe and their baby is parked with us at the Executive Mansion. Eleanor is teaching school two and a half days a week in New York, and I am in one continuous glorious fight with the Republican legislative leaders. So you see that it is a somewhat hectic life."[12]

It was also financially a rather difficult existence for Roosevelt. His governor's salary of $25,000 per year was no more than he had received as vice-president of Fidelity and Deposit, and in becoming governor he had had to give up various minor positions which brought in a certain amount of income. He received five hundred dollars per month for the maintenance of the Governor's Mansion, but this could not possibly have covered his additional expense there.[13]

However pinched Roosevelt may have been, he enjoyed living in the mansion. Occasionally on warm nights the noise from festivals in the nearby Italian district kept him awake, but that was a minor annoyance. Like his mother's old-fashioned house at Hyde Park, the mansion had many comfortable ties with the past of a sort that he savored. "It is still the same old house, with much of the rather dreadful original furniture in it," he wrote Grover Cleveland's widow, "but it has many memories." He was much more interested in adding to these than in modernizing. From former governors, their relatives and descendants, he begged without much success for pieces of furniture associated with their regimes in the Albany mansion.[14]

With aplomb that bordered on zest, he accepted the liabilities too that went with being a prominent public figure. He seemed to regard a threat on his life with more fun than fear. Early in April, a porter in the sorting room of the New York City post office stepped on a package addressed to the Governor. Smoke began to come out; the porter managed to put out the flames and prevent the explosion of a crude, homemade bomb. When news reached Roosevelt, late at night upon his return from Hyde Park, he showed nonchalance. "I am very sleepy," he told reporters, "I am going to bed and I expect to sleep well." And it gave him the opportunity to add in typical fashion that such things were nothing new to him; when he had been Assistant Secretary of the Navy a bomb had been sent to him, but was discovered before it reached his office. (This was an incident no one had ever heard of before.) Mrs. Roosevelt took the affair a little more seriously; she was sufficiently alarmed to request that special state troopers be placed on guard at the mansion and the Roosevelt homes.* The Governor continued to take it lightly. "I am very certain that the bomb was not sent by a radical," he pointed out to a correspondent, "but, as I stand fairly well with labor and the more liberal element in the population . . . by somebody with a fancied grievance."[16]

A few days later, Roosevelt's lighthearted attitude proved correct. The porter who had discovered the bomb admitted that he himself had made it and planted it, in the hopes that by apparently saving Roosevelt's life he might win promotion; he was having difficulty in supporting a widowed mother on a low salary. Roosevelt, far from

* Mrs. Roosevelt told a women's gathering, "I suppose it was the work of some crank. I think that if someone is kept on watch for a short time in Albany to guard against anything of the kind, that will be sufficient precaution. . . . I am not particularly frightened."[15]

being angry, felt "awfully sorry for the poor fellow," and sent the District Attorney a check for one hundred dollars to help him out. A year later when the man appealed to Roosevelt for a job, the Governor asked Labor Commissioner Perkins to help find him one. "It is very like you to be concerned about him," Miss Perkins replied, "and since I am the same kind of a fool myself, I will help you turn the other cheek." [17]

Roosevelt's warmth and gaiety spilled over into many another area, and in the process gave reporters numerous human-interest stories. In the spring of 1929, there was the "company" he formed with Henry Morgenthau, Jr., to grow a few acres of squashes. They had heard that there was a good market for them. He burlesqued the enterprise into what he called "Squashco." It was a business venture actually not much different from many a one into which he had entered more seriously.* Following a letter describing the planting instructions he had given his farmer, Roosevelt wrote Morgenthau:

"Please write me any further directions as to how the common stock should be planted, whether it should be watered, whether the distribution should be wide or closely harrowed, whether it carries any bonus (besides bugs), other stock in the same rows, etc. I am writing Moses Smith to visit your Squashco vaults at the Fishkill Farms Security Company to inspect the Squashco safe deposit cellar accommodations." [19]

And, of course, this made a news story at a time when things were dull in Albany.[20]

Things were dull there most of the spring, for in late April and during the entire month of May, Roosevelt left the governorship almost entirely behind him in order to resume his old routine of swimming and exercising at Warm Springs. Like a tired businessman on a holiday, he wrote Morgenthau, "It is heavenly weather and the pool is perfect, especially since all of the new work is completed." He continued his serious interest in the physical therapy that the staff was giving to polio sufferers. "Things are booming," he exulted, "and for the third successive month we are full up, with a long waiting list." Roosevelt announced that he was at Warm Springs for a rest, and he broke it only for the most urgent New York State business, a few

* In the fall of 1929, FDR resumed the burlesque, by proposing that "Squashco" absorb the "Pine Mountain Water Melon Corporation," "which ought to afford our holding company a glorious opportunity for hydrating the stock. Another offer will shortly be made for the sale of the 'Shiloh Valley Beef Cattle Co.' This also looks attractive, as we can afford to sell a little more 'bull.'" [18]

visits with political leaders, and a speech or two to the people of Georgia. These talks were probably more recreation than serious work. In them he exhorted Georgians to build good roads, expressed his repugnance for war, and extolled the scenic glories of New York State.[21]

Inevitably, newspapers carried stories after Roosevelt went to Warm Springs, such as the one in the Elmira *Advertiser* that "he was an exceedingly tired man when he went South," and that "the office proves a severe tax upon his strength, for he is by no means well." There may have been some measure of truth in this during Roosevelt's first months as governor; certainly he was having to labor far longer hours than he had at any time since the campaign of 1920. Morgenthau told Henry Wallace in 1932 that Roosevelt's first months as governor had put a strain on him. But at this time Roosevelt, reacting energetically, sent strong rebuttals from Warm Springs.

"I not only am but have been throughout this year and for several years past extremely well," he wrote the Elmira editor. "As a matter of fact, all through the legislative session and until I came South, I was in the pink of condition, except for a slight cold which lasted for, I think, four days early in February." But with considerable concern, Roosevelt asked the editor not only to correct the misimpression among his readers, but to let Roosevelt know the source of the bad news. "Several editorials in mid-western papers of late . . . have insinuated that I was on my deathbed!" Roosevelt explained. "Like T. R., I like to run down reports of this kind before they are made more general." [22]

To a Kansas editor, Roosevelt wrote in even more emphatic fashion:

> Outside of my absence at this time for five weeks and my absence next autumn for three weeks, I am spending the whole of my time in the duties of Chief Executive.
>
> I did not bring a doctor here, have no doctor, and while I am here merely take the regular exercises in the pool, which I find are of great benefit in improving the leg muscles.[23]

These answers indicated the vigor with which Roosevelt acted to quash politically damaging reports. The candor of his reply to the Kansas editor was so completely disarming that the editor replied expressing both his apologies and increased admiration.[24]

In the meanwhile, Acting Governor Lehman, in an unspectacular but efficient fashion, dealt with several complicated problems in Albany. For the moment the most important of these seemed to be the budget. He negotiated satisfactory arrangements with the Attorney General to enable the state to continue to spend funds while the suit was brought before the Court of Appeals.

When the court delivered its decision June 21, some weeks after Roosevelt's return, it dealt him a serious blow. It sided with the Republicans, ruling that the governor must consult with the legislative finance chairman in allocating lump sums, but granting that this was a hairline question which might well be decided the other way. Roosevelt at once had the case appealed to the state Supreme Court. During the summer, while it was pending, he quietly and without difficulty shared his allocation power with the Republican finance chairman.[25]

By this time, popular interest in the budget question had simmered down to insignificance. Few people paid much attention to Roosevelt's temporary setback in the courts. For his part, he was quite ready upon his return from Warm Springs to draw public attention to other matters. For a short while during parts of June and July he abated his appeal to the people and courts of New York. He seemed to be addressing himself primarily to the rest of the nation.

CHAPTER VI

A Quiet Summer Campaign

> It is probably because of the warm weather and the lack of real news that my young gentlemen friends of the Press are inventing Arabian night tales about the Presidential possibilities and candidacies for the somewhat far distant date of 1932.
>
> — FDR, DRAFT STATEMENT, *July 20, 1929.*

DURING the politically languid summer of 1929, Roosevelt worked diligently but quietly at touring, speaking, and being ingratiating to people. To friends and enemies alike it was clear, regardless of his protestations to the contrary, that he was conducting a campaign in low key. What was not so clear was whether he was campaigning for re-election as Governor of New York or for the Presidency of the United States. Of course, he was cautiously building toward both.

His firm statement of the previous January that he was in no sense a presidential aspirant had done nothing to stop sporadic mention of him. It increased when on his way to Warm Springs in April he stopped in Washington to attend the newspapermen's annual Gridiron Dinner. There he, rather than Al Smith, filled the niche as leading Democrat. He was one of three speakers; the other two were President Hoover and Chief Justice William Howard Taft. As he arose to speak, the audience sang:

Oh, Franklin, Franklin Roosevelt,
  Is there something in a name?
When you tire of being Governor,
  Will you look for bigger game?
Will you wish for something higher
  When at Albany you're through?
When you weary of the State House
  Will the White House beckon you? [1]

Roosevelt's talk to the Gridiron members was off the record, but his speeches in the early summer seemed to lend some credence to their ditty. He began to talk and act like a person receptive to the Democratic nomination. In quick succession he delivered addresses on three campuses in which he dealt with broad principles appealing to the latent progressive sentiments of the American middle class. Of course, his rationale, as he declared later in the summer, was that these principles related to his work as governor:

"As almost every State problem has its national aspect it is, of course, necessary for me, from time to time, to study and refer to national matters. It seems a pity not to be able to do this without untrue insinuations about thoughts which, as a matter of simple fact, are not in my head." [2]

Basically, the theme that ran through these and other talks of the summer was a re-examination of Federal-state relationships. To this extent he was candid in declaring that what he said grew out of his thinking as governor. Even more, though, it was an examination of what Roosevelt regarded with alarm as an undemocratic, unholy alliance between big business and big government. This he referred to privately as the "tendency away from democracy and towards the new form of state socialism under dictatorship or oligarchy." [3]

At Hobart College on June 10, 1929, Roosevelt, in words cut out of the old fabric of Woodrow Wilson's thought, warned against this sort of concentration of economic and political power:

"Every day that passes . . . a hundred small storekeepers go out of business or are absorbed by the new business device known as the chain store. That means that a hundred independent owners of their own businesses either transfer to some other business or become employees of a great impersonal machine. We see the same trend in every form of manufacture, in transportation, in public utilities, and in banking."

Similarly, in the world of government, Roosevelt declared the nation was drifting into federal centralization, not through deliberate choice, but through the default of local government. Arthur Schlesinger, Jr., has suggested that Roosevelt, like any strong administrator, wished power on his level. Certainly in 1929 he was critical of the drift of power toward Republican Washington:

"If there is failure on the part of a State to provide adequate educational facilities for its boys and girls, an immediate cry goes up that a department of education should be established in Washington. If a State fails to keep abreast with modern [health] provisions, immediately the enthusiasts turn to the creation of a department of health in Washington. If a State fails adequately to regulate its public service corporations, the easiest course is to ask the Interstate Commerce Commission or the Federal Trade Commission to take jurisdiction." [4]

At Fordham University in New York City two days later, Roosevelt cut his address to the trim of an urban audience and praised those innumerable young men and women who were turning their backs on careers which might lead to fortunes in order to devote themselves altruistically to social service. They would dedicate their lives "to the purpose to which their minds, rather than their pockets, call."

The president of Fordham, in citing Roosevelt for an honorary degree, commented that his future might yet include the Presidency of the United States. The audience of ten thousand applauded.[5]

Later that week, Roosevelt again developed the same theme as Phi Beta Kappa speaker at Harvard: the present era was the "age of social consciousness." He received a great ovation when he entered the auditorium (where as an undergraduate he had gone to hear Theodore Roosevelt) on the arm of his son James, who was a Harvard junior. Robert Hillyer, '17, who delivered the Phi Beta Kappa ode, presented Roosevelt with a copy inscribed, "With homage, admiration, and a vote in 1932 (albeit from Connecticut)." [6]

The occasion meant far more to Roosevelt than the slight political prestige it might have carried. It was one of the high points of his life, for just twenty-five years after he had graduated, not quite the top leader of his class that he would have liked to have been, he became the center of attention and received all of the highest honors. He had failed to earn a Phi Beta Kappa key as an undergraduate; now Harvard gave him an honorary one. A few days earlier, Hobart also had elected him an honorary Phi Beta Kappa – and to the confusion of the jewelry firm which supplied keys, he insisted he wanted one from each institution.[7] More than this, Harvard granted him an honorary doctor-of-laws degree.* When President A. Lawrence Lowell informed him in advance of the honor, he replied, like an undergraduate winning an almost unattainable prize:

"I have been, and still am, quite overcome by your news, and it has taken me 'all of a heap.' If I ever had thought of the possibility of a Harvard honorary degree, it would have been with the feeling that perhaps I might deserve it at the age of 70 – certainly not at this time." [8]

Above all this, there was what Roosevelt had always regarded as

* FDR also received degrees in June, 1929, from Hobart, Fordham, and Dartmouth.

the supreme honor, to be chosen from among all the members of Harvard '04 to be Chief Marshal of the commencement. "It certainly is grand," he bubbled to his old crony, Livingston Davis. "I assure you that being Governor is nothing in comparison." And he worked at it with a corresponding degree of intensity and enthusiasm. During commencement week, he and Mrs. Roosevelt stayed in one of the old freshman dormitories, where he had never been willing to live as an undergraduate, and participated in a multitude of class activities. "The five days in Cambridge were a tremendous success — " he wrote triumphantly upon his return to Albany, "over eight hundred men, women and children from 1904." [9]

On the Fourth of July, Roosevelt was in entirely different surroundings, but ones which, like Harvard, had had much to do with his early education. For the first time since 1917, he addressed Tammany Hall at its big annual festivities. Almost everything had changed except the aged Sachem John R. Voorhis, who was about to celebrate his hundredth birthday. The formidable Boss Murphy had long since departed, and Roosevelt, who had once come as a young supplicant, appeared as a powerful governor. Even as in 1917, he was ambitious. Here was a sounding board superior to the commencements for the proclamation of his basic theme, and he stated it most emphatically.

Widespread alarm over the impending Morgan-sponsored power merger in New York State gave Roosevelt the opportunity to propose a new Declaration of Independence against the growing mammoth aggregations of capital and the partnership of business and government. Out of their combination in Washington, he charged, would come such products as the new exceedingly high Hawley tariff bill which would hurt every consumer. Out of it came excess charges for electric power. The solution, Roosevelt boldly told his auditors, was for them to don liberty caps like their Revolutionary forebears to fight against this new economic feudalism. Unless they resisted, all property ultimately would be concentrated in the hands of a few, and the overwhelming majority would become serfs.* Fortunately,

* Nearly a year later, when a congressman quoted from this speech, FDR amplified what he had meant: "There is no question . . . . that there will be a gain throughout our country of communistic thought unless we can keep Democracy up to its old ideals and its original purposes.

"I know that you will agree with me in believing that we face in this country not only the danger of communism but the equal danger of the concentration of all power, economic and political, in the hands of what the ancient Greeks would have called an Oligarchy." [10]

he added, they could battle for their rights with ballots rather than muskets.[11]

The fifteen hundred assembled Tammany braves cheered Roosevelt as the "next President of the United States." Far to the westward of their new brick wigwam, many a man who had learned such slogans from his Populist parents was ready to take up the cry, for Roosevelt's sentiments were of a sort likelier to appeal to poverty-stricken Republican farmers than to employed Democratic workingmen. Roosevelt received quantities of letters asking for copies of the speech, but apparently did not wish to be quoted too closely, for he replied that it was extemporaneous and that no stenographer had taken it down. From Los Angeles, Will Rogers asserted that the speech "just about threw [Roosevelt] in the ring as the next Democratic candidate."[12]

On July 16, Roosevelt pounded spectacularly on a different aspect of his theme: the inability of a large government to cope successfully with the organized crime of the Prohibition era. The occasion was one where he might have expected difficulty in shining – the Governors' Conference at New London. It was the first he had attended, and there was little reason to think that he could succeed in stealing the spotlight from the twenty-three other governors assembled there. Many of them were powerful, and most of them more experienced. Many were curious to see Roosevelt because he was a potential candidate, but after all there were many potential candidates. At the conference he was not likely to be more than just one additional governor. Yet at the opening session he delivered a spectacular address which almost completely dominated the three days' proceedings.

There was a dangerous tendency, Roosevelt warned the governors, for the national government to encroach upon state supremacy in police powers and administration of justice. States must overcome this by cleaning out antiquated laws and substituting scientific crime prevention. A first step would be the collection of satisfactory statistics on crime; the next, the enactment of state codes embodying fundamental principles of uniformity. Also states should establish crime commissions like that in New York, create competent identification bureaus, and adopt scientific police methods.

All this was carefully stated and was sound. It bore the unmistakable imprint of Howe, who for some years had worked for the National Crime Commission. But the speech as it stood was not spectacular, despite the great popular interest in crime and its prevention. What made it sensational was the conclusion: a lengthy letter from George

W. Wickersham. A few weeks earlier, President Hoover had, amidst great fanfare, appointed Wickersham chairman of a commission to study crime and law enforcement. This meant, above all, he must analyze the breakdown of Prohibition and the accompanying rise of gangsterism. Wickersham, despite much pressure upon him from newspapers, had made no public statement. Hence his letter to Roosevelt made banner headlines: states should take over from the Federal Government part of the burden of enforcing the Prohibition Amendment.[13]

Wickersham's letter on Prohibition enforcement caused nationwide excitement. After reading it, Roosevelt proposed that the governors bar reporters and go into executive session in order that they might discuss all phases of the problem with complete freedom. The governors declined to do so, instead entering into hot debate, in which they aligned themselves into Wet and Dry factions. Roosevelt, who could not fail to make enemies by choosing one side or the other, wisely remained silent. In the end, the governors voted to shelve Wickersham's suggestion. Almost the only gain had been in added publicity for Roosevelt. There were those who suggested that he had published Wickersham's spectacular letter without permission.* Roosevelt feebly answered these criticisms by pointing out that he had written Wickersham for suggestions two weeks earlier, and that the reply had mentioned no limitation upon its publication.[15]

On the whole, Roosevelt had made a favorable impression upon the governors. Afterwards he sent them a follow-up letter, inviting them to visit him if they passed through Albany. As a result he was able to launch into a correspondence on politics with several of them, like Governor Cary A. Hardee of Florida, and build additionally toward 1932.[16]

Thus by midsummer 1929, Roosevelt had once again done a good bit to attract national attention as a potential presidential candidate — enough so that politicians would not forget about him. Had he done more, they might have been tempted to nip his budding candidacy. The time had come to bury it once more in the root cellar. Roosevelt did not have to be reminded by one of his oldest newspaper-editor

* The beginning of Wickersham's letter (which FDR edited out in making it public) intensifies suspicions that Wickersham had not intended publication: "I have run away from Washington for a fortnight of change of air, and your letter of 3rd was forwarded to me here. I should have been very glad to have talked with Mr. Howe about your opening address, but at this distance it is hardly feasible."[14]

friends that a premature bloom would invite frostbite. He prepared a lengthy statement, which in itself called further attention to his possible candidacy, and sent it to Howe for later release. Howe obviously worried even more than Roosevelt that the bloomlet might get out of control. He shortened the statement into a terse insistence on Roosevelt's part that he was not a candidate for President and was concentrating entirely upon the man-sized job of administering the government of New York State. Roosevelt had planned to hold the statement until the end of August; Howe released it immediately in mid-July. And for the moment the speculation died down.[17]

What had taken place would be of ultimate value to Roosevelt in 1932, but only if he won the 1930 election in New York State. If he lost, his chances for the presidential nomination would be blighted. The key to the statehouse continued to be upstate votes, and it was to the winning of them that Roosevelt devoted the bulk of his time and effort during the summer of 1929. He spent weeks in a grand tour back and forth across the rural counties engaged in what politicians refer to as fence mending. In Roosevelt's case it was almost literally road, bridge, and institution building.

The first of the tours began on July 7, when he headed toward Buffalo on the New York State Barge Canal (which had replaced the old Erie Canal) aboard the glass-roofed yacht *Inspector*. The thought of the journey had made him "laugh whenever I compare it with the old Navy days," when he had dashed about the Atlantic aboard a destroyer, and he had sarcastically predicted, "It will certainly be a rough and exciting voyage." [18]

Whatever it lacked in thrills it compensated for in tangible political satisfactions. He made three sweeps, partly by boat and partly by automobile, across the Genesee Valley, up the Saint Lawrence, and back down through the northern counties, and a second time across the tier of counties just above Pennsylvania. Like almost everything else he did, he found it delightful:

"For mile after mile the canal as it is today is a very beautiful and charming river, a place for recreation and a place to spend a real vacation. . . . As far as seeing the natural beauties of the State is concerned, I would much rather see them while being seated in a comfortable chair on the deck of a boat going along at a speed of six or seven miles an hour, than I would from the most luxurious automobile ever made travelling along at forty or fifty miles an hour. You really see the country and, incidentally, on this trip, I saw many people, too, and that was mighty interesting." [19]

Seeing the people was what was most important to Roosevelt. He talked earnestly with all sorts of citizens, both leading and unimportant. Most of them were Republicans, and he saw to it that local Democratic dignitaries did not push them out of the way. When that nearly happened at Olean, he firmly remarked that he was governor of all New Yorkers, and could not have been elected without Republican votes. He demonstrated his feeling by bringing the sidetracked Republican mayor to the platform to speak with him. Of course he left Olean more popular than when he had arrived. On another occasion, he took a Republican assemblyman from Syracuse in tow for two days; at the end of that time, the assemblyman was an enthusiast for Roosevelt's power ideas.[20]

Melvil Dewey, ardent Republican and champion of simpler spelling, wrote Roosevelt from the Lake Placid Club:

"It was a myti short visit yu paid us but it was astounding to see how meni warm frends wer made in thoz fu minits. The Lord gave yu a fase & vois & maner that makes yu veri danjerus in a republican stronghold." [21]

The Republican state chairman ponderously tried to inoculate party members against Roosevelt's disarming ways by announcing, "He is now engaged in a tour of the State ostensibly to inspect State institutions, but in reality, I am sure to make votes for himself and his party." The inoculation did not take. Republican leaders had to concede that wherever he went, Roosevelt gained political strength. He listened to the requests of dignitaries for local public works and, as often as possible, promised to fight for them. He listened too to the complaints and comments of lesser persons; through them he helped to take the public pulse.

There was, for instance, the fine-looking woman in her eighties at the town of Montezuma who came down to the *Inspector* to see him. Her story was not very exceptional, and it was partly for that reason that Roosevelt related it in a speech.[22] She had lived since she was a baby on a large and formerly prosperous farm; on it she had raised a large family in comfort, but by 1929 she had to struggle to make ends meet. The example, Roosevelt concluded, was "typical of thousands of acres which two generations ago provided a prosperous livelihood for an intelligent and progressive population." [23]

On his trip, Roosevelt seemed concerned most with talking to farmers and appealing to them. In his speeches, he proposed further to improve their economic position through the establishment of "vegetable sheds" like the milk shed as a means of stabilizing the market. This involved regional planning for the production and consumption of agricultural products. It also involved, although Roosevelt did not say so that summer, limitation of crops, and limitation of the area from which farm products could enter the New York markets. He went no further than to point out that New York apple growers could not hope to compete with those in the Pacific Northwest until they learned to produce fine-appearing, well-packed apples. He boldly predicted, "I look for the day when, throughout the length and breadth of the United States, zones will be established for the production and consumption of whatever the soil within that zone is best fitted to raise and whatever the demands of consumption require. As a step in this direction, New York should lead the way with a great farm survey." [24]

For the most part, Roosevelt concentrated upon explaining to farmers how much he, or rather his Agricultural Advisory Commission, had already achieved for them. On August 23, 1929, he sent open letters to the taxpayers of each of the fifty-seven counties beyond the Bronx, addressed to editors of local papers, calling attention to the savings in their individual counties due to farm-relief legislation. In his letter to the voters of Sullivan County he pointed out that various bits of relief, which he enumerated, would save $198,108 plus sizable amounts for rural schools and an uncertain sum for grade-crossing elimination. The total for the entire state, Morgenthau estimated, was $21,000,000 – but the smaller sums that Roosevelt listed were more effective in winning votes because taxpayers could readily understand them. Roosevelt gave as his reason for sending the letters his vital interest in seeing the savings passed along to the citizens. The Republicans, of course, once more shouted "Politics," and printed editorials in rural papers claiming all credit for the farm legislation. Roosevelt countered not only with statements of his own, but by directing his press bureau to "get local people to write letters to the Republican papers which are getting out the deliberately false statements." [25]

In this fashion, Roosevelt was trying to counteract the Republican viewpoint which Morgenthau had discovered upon sampling farm opinion after the legislature had adjourned. "What hits me most is the very high percentage of ignorance," Roosevelt commented. "I am not concerned about prejudice, personal stupidity or wrong thinking so much as by the sheer, utter and complete ignorance displayed by such a large number of farmers." On his tours and through his press bureau and radio appeals, he tried to charm them into knowledge.[26]

On his crisscrossing of the state, Roosevelt likewise tried to win middle-class urban support for various of his ideas. The canal itself fascinated him, as anything having to do with water always did. He proposed that various parts of the waterway be developed into state recreation areas, and lamented that enterprising citizens did not organize a company to run pleasure excursions through the scenic parts. What concerned him more about the canal system was that it was a heavy drain on the state, little used compared with the Canadian canal system paralleling the Saint Lawrence. Because of its shallowness and fixed bridges, it was suitable only for barges. Despite all these disabilities, he could not recommend abandoning it because of the howl that would have gone up from interested shippers and from cities along its route. Rather, he cleverly proposed that it be turned over to the Federal Government for development into an Atlantic-to-Great Lakes ship canal, as an alternative to the Saint Lawrence waterway. It was by no means a feasible scheme, but it made western New Yorkers happy without arousing much wrath among Saint Lawrence waterway proponents in other parts of the nation.[27]

This web of political gossamer served the negative use of deflecting pressure upon the state to fritter away additional sums on inadequate improvements on the barge canal system. In other directions, Roosevelt's interest in public works took a constructive turn which would appeal strongly to Republican liberals.

In the early summer of 1929, after his return from Warm Springs, where he had spent much of his time at the pool encouraging fellow paraplegics, the crying necessity for improved hospital care was in the forefront of his thinking. While he was South, Acting Governor Lehman had been visiting crowded, understaffed hospitals, keeping alive the hospital bond issue upon which the legislature had failed to act. Republicans, planning to make economy a major item in the fall election, played into his hands by taking the view that a bond issue was unnecessary.[28]

Roosevelt, at a conference with Democratic leaders at his New York City home on June 3, decided to put pressure on the Republicans.

For a while he considered calling the legislature into special session, and indeed discussed the possibility with the Republican leaders on July 2, 1929. He told them that the state was lacking 10,625 beds with which to care properly for patients, and that the shortage would increase acutely in the next few years. The surplus in the state treasury would not be large enough to cover the increase in hospitals. The only answer, Roosevelt told the Republicans, was a fifty-million-dollar bond issue. This they refused to countenance. Since they produced no plan of their own, they were forced into a compromise with the Governor. He agreed to abandon his demand for a bond issue in return for their promise that at the next session of the legislature they would pass an appropriation to provide for five thousand (or, if need be, six thousand) new beds. Further, they would find the money for these.[29]

During his tour of the state, Roosevelt inspected numerous state institutions. When his party arrived at each, the superintendent would come out to join the Governor in his car. Together they would drive around the grounds and look at the outside of the new buildings. Walking was too difficult for Roosevelt to go through them himself, but he was not satisfied merely to listen to the reports of the head. He had had too many years of experience with inspections when he was Assistant Secretary of the Navy. Consequently, he would remark to the officials that Mrs. Roosevelt would be delighted to go through the institution. And so she would, serving as his eyes and ears.

At first when she came back and reported to her husband, he would laugh heartily at her amateurishness. He asked her if there was overcrowding; she replied that she did not think so. "Idiot," he joked, "didn't you look to see if there were beds put away in closets or behind doors?" He taught her also to ask how great the distance was between beds, so she could determine whether there was adequate air space for each person. Next, he asked her what the inmates were having to eat. She reported what she had seen on the menus; it was not mealtime so she had not seen the food. "Look into the pots on the stove," he instructed her. From this time on, she did, even though the officials dreaded having her go into the kitchens. As a result she soon got to know prisons and hospitals so well that by the time she came to Washington she had a fine background of experience and a basis for comparison when her husband sent her on inspections throughout the nation.

When they drove up to one mental hospital, Roosevelt always

liked to recount, he was much impressed because one man on the lawn stopped cutting grass, and stood cap in hand bowing to them as they passed. Then someone glanced behind. The man was still standing there – thumbing his nose.[30]

This may have been at the Utica State Hospital for the insane. When Roosevelt visited it in the summer of 1929, he conferred with the acting superintendent, and found that although the capacity was only 1279, it had 1700 patients. Immediately he expressed his horror over the "shocking and disgraceful conditions." The next week he proposed two new hospitals, and promised to renew his fight for adequate appropriations. There was not much the Republicans could do but capitulate. Speaker McGinnies pledged that the next legislature would support the Governor's program; Roosevelt promptly enlarged it. He demanded six thousand more beds, and ordered plans drawn for $18,975,000 worth of new buildings. The state would get its hospitals, and the Republicans rather completely lost their economy issue for the forthcoming campaign.[31]

In the course of the summer, the outbreak of destructive riots at Dannemora and Auburn drew Roosevelt's attention even more sharply to frightful conditions in prisons. They were so badly congested that 1500 prisoners were without cells; the food was deplorable, and discipline was breaking down. On July 22, 1929, at Dannemora 1300 prisoners rioted for five hours, setting buildings on fire and storming the walls. Three prisoners were killed and twenty wounded. Less than a week later at Auburn, prisoners burned $250,000 worth of buildings.[32]

Immediately Roosevelt assigned R. F. C. Kieb, Commissioner of Corrections, to investigate the outbursts and announced that he was taking steps to prevent their recurrence. He visited the Great Meadows Prison, the newest in the state, and pointed to it as a model along the lines of which he wanted every prison in New York modernized.[33]

The acute overcrowding in state institutions was a serious dilemma. Roosevelt could not hope to solve it, but he did demonstrate an earnest interest in ameliorating it at once.

Development and control of public power in the state posed an equally difficult problem. The Fourth of July speech to Tammany had indicated not only the seriousness with which Roosevelt regarded it, but his willingness to relate it to the national political and economic order. During the remainder of the summer he talked more specifically about the problem in New York State. He had dramatically told

Massachusetts Democrats in June* that only two heartbeats – his and that of Lieutenant Governor Lehman – separated the great power monopoly from the public resources of the State of New York.[35]

Within the state, he spelled out his meaning in detail during his summer travels. He was slowly preparing the way for whatever power program he might propose to the next session of the legislature. His first step, late in June, after capitalists announced they planned to merge several power corporations into a huge holding company, Niagara-Hudson, was to call upon the Republican Attorney General to investigate whether or not the holding company would be a monopoly in violation of the state laws. He pointed out to the Attorney General, and thus the public, that the merger might affect not only the commercial and manufacturing interests of the state, but also the monthly electric-light bills of millions of people.[36]

For the moment, Roosevelt's purpose was less to prosecute than to embarrass the Republicans. He did so at the precise time when the dominant position of the power corporations in the Republican party in New York was becoming a marked liability. The state Republican chairman, Machold, was one of the prime organizers of the merger. Whether because the negotiations occupied too much of his time, or because they made him too great a political liability, he resigned his party chairmanship in June. Unfortunately for New York Republicans, the same faction continued to control the leadership. W. Kingsland Macy, a dynamic and imaginative young man who could have made things lively for Roosevelt,† failed in his bid. Instead, the Republican committee elected Machold's choice, W. J. Maier, and Roosevelt was able to continue his efforts to make the Republican party and the power trust seem almost synonymous to New Yorkers.[38]

Attorney General Ward unwillingly helped Roosevelt along. He

* FDR did not think too well of this effort afterwards. He wrote, "I felt conscious personally of making a very rambling speech, but I was so tired after the various activities of the week that my thinking apparatus was not working as well as it should." [34]

† Macy, Chairman of the Suffolk County Committee, was almost the only Republican in the state who could land blows squarely on FDR's jaw. When FDR, by implication at least, took credit for all the tax cuts the farmer received, Macy retorted, "He fails to record that he was opposed to the elimination of the direct State tax on real estate brought about by the Republicans for the benefit primarily of the up State. Neither does he recall that he advocated a method of income tax reduction that would have benefited the wealthy taxpayer greatly without bringing relief to the little fellow. He does not say that the Republicans insisted on giving greater relief to the small rural schools than he was willing to grant." [37]

spent two weeks preparing an elaborate report for the Governor, covering, as Roosevelt wryly pointed out in a public reply, "23 printed pages, followed by 44 printed pages of exhibits and charts," but not stating whether or not the merger would be legal. Roosevelt pressed the question upon Ward a second time. The Attorney General could no longer delay his reply – that the formation of Niagara-Hudson would not constitute violation of any existing statute.[39]

The creation of a power monopoly, Roosevelt began to proclaim throughout the state, would lead to grossly unfair utility rates. Indeed, he pointed out to farmers at the state fair, rural rates were already far too high. The Public Service Commission was failing to regulate the power corporations, which were making enormous profits through being allowed a fair percentage of return upon unfairly overcapitalized valuation of their plants. To obtain the graphic sort of evidence he always liked to use, and to enlist local Republican support, he sent letters to the mayors of towns and villages, most of whom were Republicans, inquiring about their local power rates. Many of them sent him indignant replies, backing up his contention. Next Roosevelt outlined the solution: state development of power plus firm public control of the power corporations in order to bring rates down to a fair level.[40]

In the middle of September, 1929, Roosevelt, back in Albany, was able to look with considerable satisfaction upon his summer's activities. On September 17, he made a radio report to the people of the state, his first since April, in which he described his travels and his inspection of state institutions and public works. His purpose, he told them, was also "to learn at first hand, from the citizens, of the needs and thoughts of the various localities." [41]

To a considerable degree he had succeeded not only in learning their thoughts but also in convincing them that these were his also. The Republicans, who the legislative correspondents had predicted would sink Admiral Roosevelt on his summer voyage, seemed far closer to foundering than their intended victim at the end of his quiet warm-weather campaign.

CHAPTER VII

Crash and Ascent

> Because [large corporations] have seemed, at least, to bring prosperity and to bring us comforts and luxuries, it has become unfashionable to speak even a whisper of warning against the danger of letting them eventually assume the mastery of us all.
>
> — FDR, *December 10, 1929.*

BY the early autumn of 1929, Roosevelt could congratulate himself upon having won a reputation as governor that would carry him as far as any Democrat could go during those years of Republican prosperity. Although he could count on no more than a narrow margin of success, everything indicated he would win re-election as governor in 1930. With reasonable luck he might have the honor of running against President Hoover in 1932, if he wished to do so. But Hoover and the Republican party were so popular that Roosevelt could not expect to make much of a showing; at best he could win a few more electoral votes than James Cox, John Davis, and Al Smith. In this case, he would be written off as one more defeated Democratic nominee, and this was not his goal. Friends, no doubt inspired by Louis Howe, whispered that while, true enough, he would be first-quality presidential timber in 1932, he would be a real threat by 1936.[1]

As a result Roosevelt concentrated that fall upon long-range plans for building his power and prestige as governor. The most important of these was his extended private study of a public-utilities program which would require years to execute. Secondarily, but only secondarily, he tried as always to attract favorable attention throughout the country. His eyes indeed seemed to be on 1936, not 1932; yet in a few weeks unforeseen economic circumstances took a big tuck in his timetable. In the fall of 1929 came the big stock crash.

Roosevelt had no more idea than anyone else that the boom economy was about to crack up. He made no wildly optimistic predictions like

FDR and Raymond Moley. Library, Hyde Park,
the Governor's chair

By permission of the Director of the Franklin D. Roosevelt Library, Hyde Park, N. Y.

Fishing while on a picnic party at Warm Springs, in 1930

By permission of the Director of the Franklin D. Roosevelt Library

In his "Governor's Chair," at Albany

By permission of the Director of the Franklin D. Roosevelt Library

Speaking at the Capitol in Albany. c. 1930?

Democratic National Chairman Raskob.* Neither did he issue official warnings against the runaway speculation on Wall Street, nor did he call for a tightening of state regulation of the New York Stock Exchange, although it was within the power of the state to curb the market. In private correspondence, it is true, he predicted that the follies of the Republican policies would lead to disaster, but he had routinely uttered such jeremiads all through the '20s. Those of 1929 were more of the same and indicated less a foreboding of immediate trouble than a belief that a debacle was inevitable sometime in the indefinite future.

When Roosevelt toured upstate New York through the summer of 1929, he should have noted new ominous signposts as significant as the perennial distress of the farmers: construction was in the doldrums, automobiles were piling up in dealers' garages, freight-car loadings were down, and wise operators were beginning to sidle quietly out of the stock market. In spite of these portents, the bull market roared on its way, pushing stock prices farther and farther into the sky, stretching further and further the tenuous tie between market prices and the economic realities of production and profits. Few people noticed that the tie was stretched close to the breaking point. Small speculators continued to buy on margin, counting on rising stock prices, not dividends, to win them a large quick return.

On September 3, the market reached its peak when United States Steel soared to 261¾ and General Electric to 396¼. The Dow Jones industrial average was 381.17. Then the market turned soft and nervous. In little more than a month, the value of securities on the New York exchange dropped two and a half billion dollars. Nevertheless, in mid-October, Charles E. Mitchell, head of the National City Bank, asserted that he saw no sign of the slump that pessimists were always predicting; Roosevelt's acquaintance, Professor Irving Fisher of Yale, proclaimed that the high level of the market was permanent.

Confident statements were a fine thing, but they proved no more effective than pebbles wedged behind the wheels of a truck slipping backwards downhill. The week after these "all is well" statements, the cataclysm struck. On Monday, October 21, the market began to drop badly. The following day, it gained sharply, but slid again near the

* Raskob had been quoted in the *Ladies' Home Journal* in August, 1929, as saying, "I am firm in my belief that anyone not only can be rich, but ought to be rich." Anyone who put fifteen dollars a month into good common stocks, Raskob predicted, would have at the end of twenty years an investment of eighty thousand dollars yielding four hundred dollars per month income.[2]

close of trading. At two o'clock on the afternoon of October 23, the crash began. Everyone rushed to unload, and by the close of trading, stockholders had suffered a paper loss of four billion dollars. The next day, "Black Thursday," panic-stricken speculators began selling with the opening gong; by the end of the day, 12,894,000 shares of stock had changed hands. Temporarily, J. P. Morgan and Company and a group of big bankers staved off total disaster, but the following Tuesday, October 29, Morgan's transfusions proved ineffectual and the market collapsed worse than ever. The end of that day saw sixteen million shares sold, and the total losses for the month reached nearly sixteen billion dollars.[3]

This was more than a catastrophe among financiers. It marked the point when the easy money, the faith in permanent prosperity, the facile optimism of the '20s vanished into oblivion. Growing pessimism and a mammoth deflationary spiral had taken their place. The crash had not caused the depression, but did precipitate it. President Hoover, instantly grasping the extreme seriousness of the crash, grasped also the fact that it had caused a reversal of the economic mood of the country. He seized upon this: the optimistic nation had been a prosperous one, but now optimism was gone; therefore a necessary step was to get that optimism back. He conceived it his task to issue sanguine statements designed to bolster public confidence. Further panic would lead only to further deflation; the greater the dislocations in the intricate credit structure of the country, the worse the depression that would follow. Consequently, the anxious President declared, "The fundamental business of the country, that is production and distribution of commodities, is on a sound and prosperous basis."[4]

This was like trying to reinflate a punctured balloon with a bicycle pump. Later Governor Roosevelt's hindsight made this fact very clear to him and he was sharply critical of the nervous optimism President Hoover pumped into the collapsing economy in order to try to ward off the depression. Despite Roosevelt's perennial pessimism about the way the Republicans ran the country, there is no shred of evidence in his public and private statements at the time that he had any real grasp of what was happening. On the morning after Black Thursday, he wired a New York newspaper from Warm Springs, "Do not know detailed conditions but firmly believe fundamental industrial and trade conditions are sound." This seems to have been his view for some weeks after the first rumblings of the landslide became perceptible. Apparently he regarded it as no more than a just punishment which immoral speculators had brought upon themselves. If he was aware of its implications for the national economy, he kept them to himself.

On the very day that Hoover proclaimed his confidence in continued prosperity, October 26, 1929, Roosevelt admonished a churchmen's organization in Poughkeepsie, "It is not good for anyone to go too far on the theory of getting something for nothing." He explained to his audience that while much of the stock-market transactions were legitimate and proper, "in some cases improper schemes and questionable methods have been used in stock promotion and many investors have lost sight of the real purpose of the Exchange in a fever of old-fashioned speculation." [5]

On the evening of the worst day of the panic, Roosevelt spoke at a political dinner in Massachusetts. Some wag sent a bogus telegram signed "Al Smith" which the hoaxed chairman read to the gathering: Would the crash be blamed on the Democrats? Everyone laughed. For the moment, even Roosevelt, who was to become the greatest political beneficiary of the crash, did not try to blame it on the Republicans.[6]

A month later, when President Hoover was trying to rally the country into a voluntary program to stave off the looming depression, Governor Roosevelt still did not take it very seriously. The President sent telegrams to all the governors calling upon each of them to engage in the "energetic yet prudent pursuit of public works." Roosevelt replied that he intended to recommend to the legislature a much needed construction program for hospitals and prisons. But he had been planning this for a long time anyway. He added with a conservatism that exceeded even the prudence Hoover recommended, "The program will be limited only by the estimated receipts from revenues without increasing taxes." [7]

Nor could it be argued that Governor Roosevelt, like Hoover, feared the worst but did not wish to make public statements which might further depress public confidence. Perhaps the only comment in a private letter that Roosevelt made at the time was when in requesting Howe to attend an auction at the Anderson Galleries he wisecracked, "It is just possible that the recent little Flurry down town will make the prices comparatively low." [8]

Except for the exceedingly small percentage of Americans who had been playing the market, the pattern of the slump unfolded only slowly with gradual cancellation of orders and a slackening of employment. The prosperous United States of the '20s seemed, even as President Hoover declared it to be, relatively intact with only the paper profits torn away. Governor Roosevelt felt free to concentrate upon winning Democratic gains in the fall elections to the state assembly, and upon perfecting a reform program to present to the legislature in January.

The election came in the first numbing days after the crash, too soon to be affected by it. Roosevelt, as was proper in an off year, kept the campaign on a relatively low key and high plane. There were four great issues, he told the voters over the radio on October 30, 1929: state control over public utilities, improvement of hospitals and prisons, reform of the administration of justice, and modernization of county and town governments.[9]

In his campaigning, Roosevelt abided by his wise decision of the previous spring. He did not openly call for a Democratic majority in the assembly; rather, he demanded first-rate assemblymen. These he defined as men financially and mentally honest, "unwilling to stoop to petty deceits," farsighted enough to see beyond their own districts to view the state as a whole in the future as well as the present. There was no point in sending a robot representative to Albany. If he had no function but to count as one vote on a roll call, Roosevelt declared, it would be cheaper for the voters to vote for the party label; the leaders could then cast proxies in the legislature. If legislators behaved in this fashion, Roosevelt argued, the voter was to blame, since no man could be gagged against his will, and, "as it is the fault of the man we elect, it follows that the first fault lies with us in electing such a man."[10]

No one could quarrel with these noble generalities, which Roosevelt uttered from his position above and aloof from the sometimes noisome local campaigns. "I think it will be for the best interests of all concerned if I keep out of all local election matters," Roosevelt explained to an old associate. "If I were to do anything in New York City I should have to do it in Albany and Syracuse and Rochester and Buffalo and many other places."[11]

From his Olympian watchtower, Roosevelt directed the coaching of Democratic assembly candidates in the large policies which he was trying to establish as campaign issues. Louis Howe, operating from Roosevelt's New York City home, acted as unofficial majordomo of the campaign. Checking each move with Roosevelt, who spent part of the campaign period at Warm Springs, he worked out strategy with

James A. Farley, secretary of the state committee, and Maurice Bloch, Democratic leader in the assembly. They arranged several conferences for Democratic candidates for the assembly to brief them on the issues, and provide them with copies of Roosevelt's water-power message. In Albany, the Democratic press bureau cooperated. It was the kind of concentrated, coordinated strategy which Roosevelt and Howe had developed successfully the previous fall. The organization was clearly Roosevelt's; Howe, Farley, and Bloch operated smoothly and loyally within its framework.[12]

Not so with William Bray, chairman of the Democratic state committee. Bray, a Utica politician, owed his position to Al Smith rather than Roosevelt, and from the outset of Roosevelt's term as governor showed little disposition to become part of Roosevelt's organization. In the spring, when Roosevelt established the Democratic press bureau, which was peculiarly Howe's baby, Bray was disappointed over the choice of Howe's rather than his candidate to be its director. During the summer he was somewhat less than cooperative. Partly because of this, Roosevelt turned for political counsel to Farley, who was loyal, ambitious, and energetic. At the end of September, someone leaked the quarrel to the newspapers, together with the prediction that Farley would be made chairman. Howe, deeply upset, gave several editors his personal assurance that the story was untrue, and managed to get them to kill it. From Warm Springs, Roosevelt wired a denial which Howe edited and gave to the newspapers. "Of course the originator of this yarn must have known its utter untruthfulness and disseminated it in a deliberate attempt to sow discord," Roosevelt declared.[13]

The flurry did not end Bray's recalcitrance. On the ground that he was too deeply involved in a hot election fight in Utica, he planned to attend only the conferences at Albany, Schenectady, and Buffalo. Farley tipped off Howe, who wired Roosevelt in distress that by dodging the conferences, Bray might well wreck them. Much planning had gone into the conferences; all but three of the assembly candidates were planning to attend; and Farley and Bloch agreed to go to all of them, although it meant neglecting important matters elsewhere. At Howe's suggestion, Roosevelt sent word to Bray that he hoped Bray would take in all of the conferences. Bray did not budge; he went to only two conferences. Farley and Bloch attended all of them, and returned enthusiastic over the results. Howe was delighted; he felt that the only harm had been to Bray. To insure that it would be serious, he arranged for Farley and Bloch to see Roosevelt immediately upon his return from Warm Springs, to tell the Governor their story. The path was clear for Farley to become state chairman.[14]

The fight was of deep significance for the future of Roosevelt and Farley. Since Howe identified himself completely with Roosevelt, he was struggling less to increase his own power than to build an effective political organization of unquestioned loyalty to the Governor. Farley would fit into this; Bray would not. The other most valued adviser, Bloch, who had demonstrated a willingness and ability to work brilliantly, died suddenly a few weeks later. "You knew him and can appreciate what a sad thing this is," Roosevelt wrote to his son James, "and what a great loss to our leadership." Farley's lone star rose even more rapidly.[15]

While the factional struggle upstate may well have prevented Roosevelt from collecting as many farm votes as he had anticipated, the 1929 contest focused upon New York City. Roosevelt's strategy, perhaps dictated in part by national aims, was to concentrate upon upstate voters and issues, and to remain as far as possible aloof from Tammany. Republicans, on the contrary, were well aware that the source of Roosevelt's power was the enormous Democratic plurality in New York City, which comprised two thirds of the state's Democratic vote. New York City, Republicans reasoned, was the place to stop him from becoming a national threat, and the time to begin applying the pressure was 1929.

New York City was electing a mayor that fall. This, as it turned out, was the most important political contest in the United States. Jimmy Walker, the debonair darling of the jazz age, was running for re-election. At best, he had been a thoroughly incompetent mayor, devoting most of his time to processions and night life, as a kind of official drum major for the big parade. His Democratic organization – partly through neglect – was crawling with corruption. The previous spring, Tammany had put in a new leader, John F. Curry, who had administered splendidly on the district level, but Curry had not been able to regain the power that had been dissipated in the five years since Boss Murphy's death. In the two years since Howe had first reported to his chief that wine, women, and song were playing the very devil with Walker, the Mayor had not reformed, but fortunately for Roosevelt the public had not yet caught on to this fact. Although reformers raised an outcry about the dissoluteness of Tammany, so far they had not been able to make enough of their accusations stick.[16]

In New York City, Walker ran on a platform of his own personal popularity and that of the man whom the public linked with him, Al Smith. Against him the Republicans ran a candidate who should have had broad appeal. This was Major Fiorello H. La Guardia. He was part Italian and part Jewish, had fought bravely in the World War, and had attracted strong approbation as a progressive Republican in the House of Representatives. He was volatile, peppery, and dynamic, with as clever a knack as Walker for headline-hogging. But in 1929, La Guardia was weighed down by a foolish and incompetent Republican organization existing on what crumbs it could pick up from Prohibition and corruption. He suffered still more from the national stand of the Republican party on big issues. "Republicanism," as such, was something the great majority of New York voters firmly opposed.[17]

To the left of the Democrats stood a third candidate, Norman Thomas, a powerful Socialist crusader who pulled behind him most of the reformers in New York City. Within the city, Thomas hurt La Guardia by drawing away from him those anticorruptionists who could not stomach the Republican program. Within the state, in effect, he joined with the Republicans in putting pressure upon Governor Roosevelt.

The Republican grand strategy was to claim that there was widespread corruption in the city government, and to demand that Roosevelt, as governor, step in and clean up the mess. This put Roosevelt in an exceedingly delicate position. If he succumbed to Republican pressure, and launched an extensive cleanup of New York City, he would destroy the very organization which seemed essential to his continued political success. If he refused to budge, he would appear to be in league with criminals. This was the dilemma which the Republicans thrust upon Roosevelt with increasing pressure from 1929 through 1932. The harder they pressed him, the more adroitly he slipped around to keep from being forced into either of the two politically impossible positions. The Republicans found themselves trying to pin down a drop of mercury with a blunt instrument. But for a man who had originally catapulted himself into prominence by crusading against Tammany, this slippery performance was the height of inconsistency.

Governor Roosevelt had no reason to be dissatisfied with the New York City organizations. Their members in the legislature had followed his lead on all the issues and had supported him loyally. He in turn had thrown state patronage their way; he had consulted local leaders concerning appointments directly affecting their districts. He seemed in every way pleased with the election of Curry as Tammany leader, since Curry had been Walker's candidate. Curry's election seemed to mark the end of Smith's influence in Tammany.

As a result, Roosevelt was vulnerable to any attacks upon Tammany. That fall, La Guardia launched a fiery but inconclusive assault. He chose an issue over which tabloid editors had already whipped up the public appetite: the unsolved murder of New York's most notorious Prohibition-era gambler and racketeer, Arnold Rothstein. The police and district attorney had fumbled the case so badly that newspapers had long hinted they were covering up political scandal. La Guardia applied his verbal bellows to the issue and blew it up to a white heat. But he smelted out only one tangible bit of scandal. A Bronx magistrate, Albert H. Vitale, had borrowed twenty thousand dollars from Rothstein. Thomas broadened the attack to take in all the magistrates' courts. Together with La Guardia he directed several sizzling blasts Roosevelt's way. They demanded that the Governor make use of his powers of investigation to clean up New York City.[18]

Roosevelt cooled off these blasts by pointing out that his powers of investigation were narrowly limited. He could investigate only when definite facts were alleged.[19] If La Guardia and Thomas would appear before him or before a grand jury in New York City and present these facts, then he would act. He even toyed with the idea of summoning La Guardia and a vociferous former police commissioner before him. He would then insist "in the presence of a stenographer that they back up their demands for an investigation with definite facts. If they have the facts I will start an investigation; if not they will look silly." [20]

Since the candidates failed to make any new exposures, Roosevelt did not have to resort to this sort of showdown. For the moment he was in a safe position in refusing to go beyond his legal powers as governor. At the one point where New York City corruption had touched his state administration, he had demonstrated a willingness to investigate. This was the City Trust Company case. When the flamboyant Italian promoter who was president of the bank died suddenly at the end of January, 1929, the state Superintendent of Banks, Frank Warder, feared a run on the bank. Within a few days it became apparent that the superintendent had other reasons besides the death of the president for this particular fear. Auditors for A. P. Giannini, who was planning to buy the bank, uncovered forgeries, juggling of the account books, and fictitious foreign-credit items. In mid-February, Warder closed the bank, and quietly made his plans for a sudden trip to Europe.[21]

Fortunately for Roosevelt, Warder was not his appointee. The Governor had already chosen Joseph A. Broderick, a man highly endorsed by reputable bankers, but his term was not due to start until July 1. On April 22, Warder resigned, and Broderick became Superintendent of Banks. Several days later, while Roosevelt was at Warm Springs, Acting Governor Lehman, himself a banker, was shocked by banner headlines announcing that Warder had applied for a passport. After careful thought, Lehman, under the power vested in the governor by the Moreland Act, appointed a commissioner to investigate the relationship between the State Banking Department and the City Trust Company. His choice was a man Roosevelt would never have selected, Roosevelt's political antagonist, Robert Moses. Lehman explained to the Governor, "I knew that you felt that he was courageous and of great ability." It was significant that Lehman had made this politically touchy appointment without consulting Roosevelt by telephone.[22]

Lehman had guarded Roosevelt's interests well. Moses began so competent and thorough an investigation that Roosevelt was able to ignore the demands of the Republican gadfly, Kingsland Macy, that he immediately widen the investigation to include the entire State Banking Department. Subsequently Roosevelt announced that he would make a general inquiry into the department as soon as the City Trust case was closed. When Moses uncovered criminal evidence against Warder, Roosevelt appointed a state Supreme Court justice to hear the charges, and ordered a special term of the Supreme Court of New York County to be convened to investigate the mess.[23]

Although Moses had been one of Smith's most loyal lieutenants, in his report he lambasted not only Smith's appointee, Warder, but also a nephew of Smith's. This nephew had left a $3750 job with the Banking Department to become a $5000 part-time counsel for City Trust to represent it before the Banking Department. Further, Moses censured Francis X. Mancuso, judge of the Court of General Sessions, who had been chairman of the board of City Trust. As for the Banking Department, Moses found no further evidence of corruption, but much demoralization. The new superintendent, Broderick, was doing much to restore morale; salary increases would help even more.[24]

What all this meant politically at the moment was that Governor

Roosevelt had demonstrated a willingness to appoint a thorough and competent investigator where scandal touched the state government. This was so amply clear by the fall of 1929, and the reformers' charges against Tammany were so relatively unsubstantiated, that Roosevelt suffered no demonstrable political damage.

On the very day of the election, Warder was found guilty of having accepted a ten-thousand-dollar bribe. Serious charges were likewise being made against Judges Mancuso and Vitale. But Mayor Jimmy Walker waltzed through to re-election by a margin of nearly a half million votes over La Guardia. Although the Socialist protest vote was a startling 175,000, this was all but ignored in the excitement over the Democratic victory. Mainly as a result of the city vote, Democrats picked up three additional seats in the assembly. The total state-wide Democratic vote for the assembly exceeded the Republicans by about thirty thousand. Upstate Democratic organizations did better than usual; eleven cities, including Ithaca and Bray's Utica, elected new Democratic mayors. This looked impressive to distant Democratic workers, who read only the bare report in the newspapers. Roosevelt must be working political magic in New York State.[25]

The magic was the usual Roosevelt brand, a talent for collecting credit for greater political achievements than were his due. The shift toward the Democratic party in the assembly elections was only about sixty thousand compared with the last off-year election in 1927. That sixty thousand had been picked up almost entirely in New York City as a result of the mayoralty election. The upstate shift toward the Democrats was microscopic, a negligible three thousand votes. The Walker smile, not the Roosevelt grin, made 1929 a good year for New York Democrats. But it was Roosevelt who began at once to capitalize upon the victory.[26]

Before the end of November, another piece of political good fortune fell in Roosevelt's lap. The state's highest court, the Court of Appeals, handed down a unanimous decision upholding Roosevelt in the all-but-forgotten executive-budget case. A Republican, Judge Cuthbert W. Pound, wrote the decision reversing the Appellate Division. He declared that the two legislative finance-committee chairmen were violating the state constitution by participating with the Governor in the segregation of lump-sum items. The constitution forbade members of the legislature from holding any other position of profit, trust, or honor. Judge Pound further held that the heads of departments should segregate budget items without the approval of the governor or legislative chairmen. Some Republican newspapers, most notably the New York *Post*, made much of this restriction on Roosevelt. The Governor immediately denied that he had ever contended that he alone should supervise the expenditures, and jubilantly asserted that the decision was a "very great victory, all along the line, for constitutional government." Roosevelt was clever enough not to add that since department heads were responsible to the governor, the court's restriction was meaningless.[27]

Roosevelt had won a thumping victory over the legislature. "From now on I trust that instead of constant bickering and efforts to throw monkey-wrenches into the machinery, we shall have better cooperation and a clearer understanding of the governmental powers in Albany," he declared on November 23.[29] The Republican legislators did indeed look upon him with new respect. He had proved himself a strong governor by successfully holding fast against their drive to cut into his power.* It was an experience which would stand him in good stead later, if he were to become a strong President.

That December, with his own position strengthened in New York State and the Republican position weakening in the nervous weeks after the stock crash, Roosevelt once again began to act like a man with his eye on the White House. He made a spectacular appearance in Chicago on December 10. It was there, less than ten years before, that he had first thrust himself upon the national political stage by firmly proclaiming the Democratic party to be the party of progressivism. He made the same sort of speech on this second occasion. Addressing himself to distressed farmers, and to all those Midwestern and Western middle-class people who feared Wall Street and monopolies, he appealed to the tradition of populism and progressivism. The inflection was that of Groton and Harvard, but the words were those of Bryan and La Follette.

With Populist fervor he whacked at Joseph Grundy, the powerful Pennsylvania collector of Republican campaign funds and leader of the high-tariff lobby in Washington. Grundy was expressing the at-

* FDR was obviously thinking of congressional domination of President Andrew Johnson when in October he sent a statement for the lawyer arguing the case to present to the court: "No one of us can tell what the future will bring forth. We may again in our history pass through times of confusion, of bitterness and of attempt at highhanded usurpation. This controversy deals far more with the future than with the present. To overthrow even partially the separation of the functions of the executive and the legislative . . . would . . . create a definitely dangerous power in the legislative leaders to administer the affairs of every department of the State Government, including the Executive Department itself."[28]

titude of those who sat in power when, according to Roosevelt, he asserted in effect, "What right has the West to attempt to curb tariff rates demanded by our great protected industries of the East? Pay no attention to the demand of the 'Backward States.'" These states were not backward, Roosevelt countered; indeed they were the backbone of the nation. If in part they were poor and impoverished, who was responsible but Grundy and his Republican friends?

To insure that none of his auditors would fail to identify him with progressivism, he thumped Senator George Moses of New Hampshire for calling recalcitrant Western progressive Republican senators, like William E. Borah, "sons of the wild jackass." "Let me remind the distinguished senator from New Hampshire," Roosevelt pointed out with his silky air, "that it was to Balaam's ass that God granted the miraculous gift of sudden speech to warn his master from proceeding further on a path that led to irretrievable destruction."*

At the heart of the speech, Roosevelt made an attack upon the oppressors of the farmer, significant as an indication of his views at the onset of the depression:

> Because we have discovered that vast numbers of manufacturers and combinations of manufacturers employing hundreds of thousands of men can produce things which make for our own ease at prices within our incomes, and in so doing can produce millionaires at the top and better paid workmen at the bottom, we have, without much thought, given our tacit approval to such combinations, and have, indeed, become so obsessed with this apparent magic power that during the recent wild speculation and senseless inflation, any half-dozen of decrepit and moribund industries, by merely pooling their individual debts and inefficiencies, could attract the public's money to any stock issue they chose to float because they were a "combination," a "merger," or a "holding company."
>
> But the farmer was subject to no such mass possibilities of production. He was and always must be an individual. His labor and his profits are his. He cannot be exploited or bonded or united into stock companies, or be made the object of this new craze for consolidation and combination; and it has only been the recent realization that if the farmer starves today we will all starve

* From Washington, Charles Michelson, the Democratic press agent, sent out this attack to newspapers in the disgruntled areas. It made lively reading in Sioux City, Iowa, and other cities to the west.[30]

tomorrow that has brought him prominently before the attention of the public at all.

What solutions did Roosevelt propose? For the problems arising out of business combinations, he hinted at regulation, especially of public utilities. They must be good servants — "well paid as all good servants should be" — not bad masters. At all times they should be "under such control of government as will prevent them from becoming Frankensteins of our own creation."

He was more vague concerning answers to the farm problem. In effect, he said that lending money to distressed farmers would not be sufficient. For workable solutions, the farmers must look to the Democratic party, which was fundamentally progressive, rather than to the Republican party, which was basically conservative.[31]

Roosevelt was carefully evasive later that same day when he addressed the American Farm Bureau Federation. It was the most powerful farm organization in America, with its strength concentrated among the relatively successful corn-hog farmers of the Middle West. Its primary objective was not social reform but the raising of farm prices. Roosevelt was in fine form the day he spoke. At the outset he described himself as one who, having been born and brought up on a New York farm, had been in close touch with the farm bureaus for many years. In addition he labeled himself a Georgia-cracker farmer. Thereupon, thoroughly identified, he launched into a detailed exposition of what he was doing for the farmers in New York, and a plea for reorganizing and cutting the cost of local government. He was heartily cheered by the farmers. At the end of his talk they sang "The Sidewalks of New York" in his honor — which was about as relevant to Roosevelt as the things he told them were to their condition.[32]

At a dinner gathering that evening, the versatile Roosevelt addressed the Chicago Commercial Club on the necessity for bringing social-welfare agencies into a closer relationship with government.

It was a full day, a highly successful one, and its dominant note had been politics. Newspapers gave the headlines to Roosevelt's prediction that in 1930 the Democrats would carry the House of Representatives and slice seriously into the Republican majority in the Senate. Roosevelt himself was the beneficiary of the attention, for he appeared as a dynamic, positive leader. He was "frankly quite flabbergasted" when even the Republican Chicago *Tribune* editorially joined in the acclaim.[33]

The venture was an open move on Roosevelt's part to seize a larger share of party leadership. He sent copies of his main speech to every Democrat in Congress, except for the bombastic, racist Senator "Tom Tom" Heflin of Alabama, with whom he did not wish to communicate in any way. The warmth of the replies from prominent Democrats was a measure of his success. John Nance Garner, Democratic leader in the House, wrote that he had talked with a number who had heard the address, and they were loud in their praise of it. "As we would say down in Texas 'it is all right.' " Garner added: "It was expected, however, that it would be 'all right' coming from you." Senator C. C. Dill of Washington expressed his delight that Roosevelt was assuming leadership over the progressive Democrats.[34]

The only quibble came from a group of congressmen who, like Clarence F. Lea, thought the speech "somewhat deficient in concrete information in support of its theme."* In spite of this, Lea thought Roosevelt the most available Democrat for 1932. Wright Patman and Marvin Jones of Texas and John E. Rankin of Mississippi tried to commit Roosevelt to McNary-Haugenism: a controversial plan to raise domestic farm prices by subsidizing farmers to export their surpluses. Roosevelt would not commit himself.[36]

Patman wrote him with fervor that there was no overproduction in American factories; if farmers of the South and laborers of the nation were paid a living wage, there would be a shortage of automobiles, radios, and the other comforts and necessities of life. On the bottom of the letter, Roosevelt wrote Howe, "Prepare reply! Please!" And replies to letters like this had to be at once evasive and conciliatory.

Naturally Roosevelt conceived of his Chicago junket as being no more than another opportunity to exhort Democrats of differing political ideas in different regions to unite under a progressive program. With an almost proprietary interest in the Governor, the New York *Times* editorially decided that whether or not Roosevelt had intentionally tossed his hat, so far as the politicians were concerned, it was

* FDR made the clever but scarcely frank contention at the time he was preparing the Chicago speeches that "I should avoid in so far as possible a discussion of the national issues except in the most general terms for the very good reason that a whole lot of my well-meaning but silly friends will talk about my throwing my hat in the ring."[35]

sitting in the 1932 ring.[37] The *Times* felt called upon to give him some advice:

"Governor ROOSEVELT will gain attention from his party by what he said. But he and his advisers, after noting the pleasant post-mortems of the Chicago luncheon, might well call a conference to decide whether the method of proving faith by works will not be better tactics for a year or two." [38]

This was precisely what Roosevelt planned to do.

CHAPTER VIII

Victory over the Power Magnates

> The time has come for a complete restudy of the relationship between public utility companies and the State itself. Nobody wants to prevent public utility companies from earning a reasonable return on their actual investment, but we and they must always remember that they are operating under a State grant and must differentiate very sharply between a private corporation and a public utility.
>
> — FDR, *February 3, 1930.*

THE Governor Roosevelt who came before the legislature on January 1, 1930, to deliver his annual message was a far stronger public figure than the freshman governor who had appeared there for the first such occasion one year before. He had successfully beaten off the efforts of the Republican legislative leaders to encroach upon his executive authority, and had successfully established the issues upon which the session must concentrate. Confident of a strongly favorable public behind him, he proposed a program of enlightened reform, attractive to Republicans and Democrats alike.

There was a crying need for wise and immediate legislative action on several important matters, he declared. Through indifference and false economy, and the failure to apply scientific methods to the treatment of convicts, prisons had become incubators of new crimes. The meshes of the banking laws had "been woven so loosely as to permit the escape of those meanest of all criminals who squander the funds of hundreds of small depositors in reckless speculation for private gain." Selfish and indifferent people should not be allowed to escape the burden now being carried by the charitable: care and support for the poverty-stricken aged. All taxpayers must bear alike this common duty.[1]

In addition, Roosevelt called for reform of the administration of justice and of antiquated units of local government, and for the rehabilitation of hospitals. All these were issues upon which he had been hammering away since the legislature had adjourned. He suggested further aid to agriculture, but had already obtained his basic farm program. As yet the effects of the stock crash were only dimly felt; he saw no need to call for unemployment relief. Indeed, he was able to report the state treasury in excellent condition from an unexpectedly heavy increase in tax receipts.[2]

Rather, Roosevelt made power control the keynote of his second legislative program. By no accident he was following the lead of George Norris and many another progressive Republican leader. It was an issue which would appeal less to the urban masses, where Roosevelt could count upon overwhelming majorities anyway, than to the upstate middle classes, which were habitually Republican, but which also were chronically irritated by their high electric bills. "After all," Roosevelt explained to one of his experts, "our principal fight on the question of electrical power is in behalf of the household and farm consumer . . . for the rates to the very large consumers of industrial power are about as low as they well can be." [3]

This did not mean that Roosevelt was doing nothing more than fish for votes. He had always been deeply interested in the power question. From the day he was elected governor he had begun an even more intense task of self-education on the problem. It was an assignment in which numerous experts and liberal leaders substantially aided him in person, through letters and through quantities of books and articles. There was no other area, even that of agriculture, in which Roosevelt undertook such intensive study. In the course of it, he became acquainted with a number of authorities on the subject, some of them professors, who were to be important to him for many years. Here, as in other fields too, he developed the habit of depending upon specialists and academic men for technical advice.

Roosevelt's education on New York power questions had begun in November, 1928, when Morris Ernst, an energetic liberal lawyer, wrote him on behalf of the Public Committee on Power in New York State, which had long fought the utility interests. Ernst warned Roosevelt that Smith, by concentrating upon Saint Lawrence power development, had diverted public attention from unjustifiably high power rates. Ernst was so eager to present his committee's plans to Roosevelt that he volunteered to come to Warm Springs with Stephen Raushenbush, who had been pressing the power fight in the *New Republic*. Roosevelt begged off, but arranged to see Ernst when he returned to New York, and later read Raushenbush's writings.[4]

A few weeks later, Roosevelt shrewdly requested Senator Norris to send him power data, which of course Norris did by return mail. At about the same time he had a brief conversation about power with Senator Thomas J. Walsh of Montana, and borrowed a manuscript Walsh had unsuccessfully submitted to the *Atlantic Monthly*. From a third influential senator, Cordell Hull, he received a copy of a bill to clarify the responsibilities and rights of states and the Federal Government so that they could both proceed more vigorously with power development.[5]

Roosevelt received much counsel from the opposite side as well. Owen D. Young, an influential Democrat as well as head of General Electric, sent him thirty pages of memoranda on power development in New York in which, of course, he took the General Electric point of view. This was that water power in the United States should be developed, owned, and managed by the private light and power companies under government regulation. Others wrote Roosevelt in similar vein.[6]

To this side of the issue, Roosevelt paid little attention. He had committed himself long since to the Norris position. Liberals firmly supported him in it when he prominently announced it in his inaugural. A brilliant and ambitious Harvard law professor, Felix Frankfurter, who had known Roosevelt since early in the Wilson Administration, immediately sent his congratulations. "Hydroelectric power raises without a doubt," Frankfurter declared, "the most far-reaching social and economic issues before the American people, certainly for the next decade." From this point on, in this area as in others, Frankfurter bombarded Roosevelt with suggestions, many of which Roosevelt accepted. Soon Frankfurter was one of Roosevelt's most influential advisers * outside of the small coterie in Albany and New York.[8]

Roosevelt's first short step toward power reform had been to wrest from the reluctant legislature authority to create the Public Service Survey Commission, dominated by Republican legislators. Roosevelt was able to appoint a minority of its members. Frankfurter enthusiastically evaluated these appointees. He regarded Professor James C. Bonbright of Columbia as combining high competence with disinterestedness; Frank P. Walsh, long closely associated with Norris, was

* Concerning power, FDR asked one of his appointees to obtain full information on Massachusetts conditions from Frankfurter. In July, 1929, he inquired of Frankfurter, "Where are you going to be this summer? I wish much we might have a talk some day." [7]

"a fearless fellow of great experience in large-scale investigation," and David C. Adie, Executive Secretary of the Buffalo Council of Social Agencies, who had been on Frankfurter's staff of the War Labor Policies Board, "a man of character and thoroughness." [9]

Roosevelt lamented to Frankfurter that his three appointees could do no more than to make the scope of the investigation as broad and as fundamental as possible in order to see to it that the progressive side of the case obtained adequate publicity. The six Republican legislative members, he asserted, were "all of them not merely conservative but definitely reactionary." [10]

During the ensuing months, Roosevelt leaned heavily upon Bonbright and Walsh, and upon Professor William E. Mosher, Director of the School of Citizenship and Public Affairs at Syracuse University. In April, Mosher volunteered his services and those of his staff to carry on parts of the investigation, because for over a year they had been engaged in a study of the control of electrical utilities in the United States. In this they had used the services of a political scientist, an economist, an engineer, and an accountant. They had examined not only the public-service commissions, but also the role of the courts and holding companies. All this they had incorporated into a study entitled *The Electric Utilities: A Crisis in Public Control.* This kind of broad approach and the arguments of Mosher and his staff for scientific rate control appealed to Roosevelt. He made use of Mosher's services, read his book, and sent copies of it to several friends. "The whole question, in my mind," Roosevelt declared after reading the book, "is as to whether a public utility has the right to make any old profit that it can, or not, in other words, as to whether there is any real distinction between a public utility and a purely private business." Drawing upon Mosher's statistics, he cited the way in which the capitalization of utility companies had risen rapidly, to the disadvantage of both consumers and bondholders. The heavy profits had gone to stockholders.

Julius Henry Cohen, Counsel of the Port of New York Authority, who was a zealous advocate of utility regulation, called Roosevelt's attention to a particularly flagrant example of this in the summer of 1929. The advance in value of common stocks in the Insull Utility Investments Company had amounted to sixty-three million dollars in the previous six months; altogether the paper profit of Samuel Insull and his associates was about ninety-four million dollars.[11]

For Roosevelt, after reading Mosher's book, the answer seemed to be to get back to the basic principles that Charles Evans Hughes had advanced twenty-five years earlier. People who invested in public-utility common stock should do so with the assurance that through public regulation cutthroat competition would be eliminated and their investments protected up to about an eight-per-cent dividend. In return for protection they must not expect a return larger than this. Additional earnings or savings in operating costs should revert to the consumers in the form of reduced rates. Roosevelt concluded, "We have got a long way from [Hughes's] theory in the past 25 years." [12]

During 1929, Mosher carried on several lines of investigation for Roosevelt. He suggested to the Governor that the plan to develop transmission lines under state authority made imperative a study of the probable use of electricity under that system, both in urban and rural areas within the state. Roosevelt immediately authorized Mosher to prepare a report that could be the basis for part of his annual message to the legislature.[13]

Roosevelt was particularly interested in rural electrification as part of his farm reforms, and had already worked out tentative plans with Henry Morgenthau, Jr., for a Rural Power Authority. Morgenthau in turn had commissioned Professor George F. Warren of Cornell to prepare a report on rural electricity rates, and apparently wanted to keep this firmly part of the agricultural program. Roosevelt had a different master plan, so he requested Frank Walsh to discuss the idea with others of his minority on the Public Survey Commission so that they would put a strong statement on behalf of rural electrification into their report.[14]

Roosevelt further asserted his generalship when Bonbright inquired whether the investigation should encompass Saint Lawrence power development. This involved, Bonbright pointed out, the issue of state versus private ownership and operation. Roosevelt, after some delay, replied that he found it difficult to say either yes or no. "My own assumption is that the commission must primarily examine into the problem of proper regulation of existing private utilities," he declared, "but at the same time there is always the possibility in the future of public competition with private utilities, at least as a 'yardstick.' " [15]

The reason for this tack was that in his private negotiations, Roosevelt had reason to feel that he was already on the way toward a separate solution of the Saint Lawrence issue. At the end of November, he informed Cohen in confidence, "The Niagara Hudson people have asked me whether if they would take up the St. Lawrence solution

I on my part would take up the River Regulating Districts in the Adirondacks and I said I would be glad to consider the two matters simultaneously." In other words, a negotiated peace seemed within sight: in exchange for concessions in the Adirondacks, Niagara-Hudson might be willing to give way on the Saint Lawrence.[16]

The fact that the power trust would move toward compromise was a clear indication of how effectively Roosevelt had been carrying on his power campaign among the voters of New York State. Late in the year he carried it beyond the borders of the state in *Forum Magazine*, an influential liberal journal. In his article he redeveloped many of his earlier ideas, then advanced another step to take up the prudent-investment theory. The previous spring the Supreme Court in the O'Fallon decision had seemingly rejected the view long held by Justice Louis D. Brandeis that the valuation of companies upon which to calculate rates which would bring a fair return to stockholders should not be the cost of reproduction but a sum which would represent a prudent investment.* Since prices were high, railroads and utilities were determined to make reproduction cost the criterion.

The Supreme Court, Roosevelt asserted in his *Forum* article, had not held that reproduction cost was the true ultimate basis for valuation, and had not closed the door on the prudent-investment theory. As for Roosevelt, his main argument seemed to be that in an age of inflated costs of reproduction and spreading utility holding-company empires, any other basis than prudent investment would be grossly unfair.

"The real 'milk in the electric cocoanut,' " he declared in horrid metaphor, was whether the American people were "willing to accept the obvious hope of the electric utility companies to earn an adequate return on all of the pyramiding of stocks," or go back to "the principles which have stood for three hundred years." This meant, Roosevelt insisted, "differentiating sharply between a public utility and a private business, insisting that the rate of return shall be based on the prudent investment theory and on the right of the consuming public to get the lion's share resulting from improvements made in management and in modern science."

As for public development of power, here also Roosevelt advanced publicly to a new position. The Saint Lawrence, Muscle Shoals, and Boulder Dam projects, he declared, were the only great natural power

* Cohen, who wrote an article for the *Yale Law Journal* on prudent investment, had sent FDR a copy of Brandeis's dissenting opinion, and two draft statements which Cohen thought should appeal to investors as well as consumers.[17]

resources still owned by the people. "One of the most important arguments for their development by Federal or state authorities," he expounded, "is that, if so developed, they will remain forever as a yardstick with which to measure the cost of producing and transmitting electricity."

Because these three power sites were publicly owned, they were in the realm of politics, Roosevelt pointed out. "Very powerful financial groups want to have the use of the power for their own companies. They have strong political backing. On the other side are the unorganized citizens who want the disposal and physical possession kept in the constant control of the Federal or state governments."

Those who wished to see government power development and control of utilities, he concluded, "ought not to be howled at as Bolsheviks and dangerous radicals; for after all, they are seeking only a return to the ancient principles and the protection of the average man and woman in the reasonable enjoyment of social needs." [18]

Martin J. Insull, President of the Middle West Utilities Company, whose own gargantuan power empire was shortly to collapse, produced a weak and nerveless rebuttal to Roosevelt in a later issue of the *Forum.** The power of the Insull-type magnates was declining. The decade of denunciation by Norris and other advocates of power control was bringing results measurable upon the meters of public opinion. The reason why the J. P. Morgan-Niagara-Hudson interests were willing to make concessions was less Roosevelt's onslaught than the long indoctrination of the public with antipower views. Clearly the Republicans were on the unpopular side. The only possible solution for them was to follow the lead of Niagara-Hudson, and edge towards compromise. If they could clear away the power question, they might be able to concentrate upon politically more lucrative issues in the fall of 1930.

Roosevelt was well aware of the Republican strategy and demonstrated a canniness in negotiation. Just before Christmas the opposition came to the Executive Mansion to drink a friendly cup of tea with him. The visitors demonstrated by their presence the alliance that voters disliked between the Republican party and power. Among them were Carlisle of Niagara-Hudson, H. Edmund Machold, formerly state

* Insull accepted the principle of government regulation, but claimed that the real power problem was to provide consumers with the lowest possible rate in keeping with a fair return to investors. This private companies could best do if they did not suffer from too much interference.[19]

Republican chairman, also of Niagara-Hudson, and John Knight, Republican leader of the state senate. They proposed to Roosevelt that the legislature authorize a commission which the Governor could name in entirety. It should have complete freedom of action to investigate plans for the development of Saint Lawrence power, and for rigid state supervision of the rates, finances, and operation of the utility corporations to which the power would be sold.[20]

Roosevelt listened so sympathetically that his visitors left the mansion convinced he meant to accept their compromise. But after all, the unimpressive Republican showing in the 1929 upstate elections made it obvious that Roosevelt would have a sure-fire issue when he talked about power in the 1930 campaign. He had nothing to gain by accepting an investigating commission whose reports could be pigeonholed by the legislature. He went ahead, therefore, and wrote a section on power into his annual message. On January 1, 1930, when he appeared before the legislature, which was no more than formally polite, he stiffened his demand of a year earlier for state development of Saint Lawrence power by emphasizing that the state should finance and retain title to the transmission lines. If for no other reason, he argued, it would be worthwhile because the state could borrow the money for these so much more cheaply than private utilities that the saving in financing would amount to millions of dollars per year to pass on to consumers.[21]

Upon this point, toward which he had gradually shifted during his year in office, Roosevelt was thoroughly earnest. "Like you," he wrote in reply to the congratulations of Samuel Untermeyer, "the more I study the electric utility problem, the more convinced I am that in the long run the transmission lines will prove to be the key to reasonable consumer rates." [22]

The Republican legislators were furious. While Senator Knight had the good sense to hold his tongue, the assembly floor leader castigated the Governor for the sneering and superior tone and the holier-than-thou attitude he had assumed in delivering the message, "a marvel of skillfull obfuscation." On the following day, Republicans delivered such a violent series of attacks upon him from the floors of both houses that the veteran New York *Times* correspondent, Axel Warn, had to hark back to the pre-World War era to find a parallel. They charged that Roosevelt was responsible for the breakdown of his banking, public works, and prisons departments, and that a good bit of the time he was using his office as "an advertising bureau for future political campaigns, state or national." But they said little or nothing about power. In response to all this bombast, Roosevelt sadly expressed to newspapermen his disappointment over the sheer selfish partisanship of the Republican attitude.[23]

Roosevelt continued to negotiate with the Republicans but saw no reason for accepting an empty compromise that might end their discomfort. To add to it, the Republican maverick, Kingsland Macy, gathered his cohorts to launch an open attack upon the state leadership of the party. He called publicly upon the bumbling, pro-utility state chairman to resign. Then Macy came to Albany to confer with Knight and the Republican legislators. Macy insisted that the public had the impression that the chairman was on the wrong side of the power question, and was opposed to any compromise. "How can we elect a Republican Governor when the Republican State Chairman is viewed in this light by the voters?" Macy inquired. His solution was simple: "What the Republican party ought to do at this session of the Legislature is to dump the water-power problem right in Roosevelt's lap and say to the Governor, 'Go ahead and solve it.' " This, Macy thought, would dispose of Roosevelt and his visionary schemes.[24]

Roosevelt kept silent concerning power, although with regard to another Republican dumping proposal he remarked, unperturbed, that his lap was pretty broad. There seemed little reason to believe that he would accept meaningless compromise proposals, or that the Republicans would offer anything more solid. Even Eleanor Roosevelt was pessimistic about the likelihood of a solution. Carlisle of Niagara-Hudson addressed a public letter to Roosevelt calling upon him to hold in the executive chamber a nonpolitical discussion of the problems and possible solutions. He was slow to answer. When he did he commented that so many people would be interested in such a meeting that it would have to be held in the Capitol park.[25]

As a final gesture to put Roosevelt on the defensive, Senator Knight and Speaker McGinnies decided publicly to offer him a commission of much the sort they had suggested to him in private. They did so, confident that he would not consent to having the power problem foisted upon him. There was some question anyway whether it was not too late by a full year to eliminate power from the 1930 campaign. Nevertheless, they made what they considered a perfunctory challenge. They went as far as they had in private, and one small step further: the proposed commission must investigate Roosevelt's own power proposals before taking up any others. Since superficially the Republicans seemed to offer a generous-sized olive branch, they dreamed of reaping vast political capital from Roosevelt's certain refusal. They would authorize the Governor to appoint a five-man commission of his own choosing which would not need to be confirmed by the senate, and appropriate $200,000 for the commission to carry out its tasks. Roosevelt would slip away from the responsibility and they would harpoon him for insincerity.[26]

But this did not happen. When the supposedly spurious bill made its appearance at a Monday-evening session of the legislature, Governor Roosevelt at once obtained a copy. He took it home with him to the Executive Mansion, and there, seated in his study, went over it line by line with his counsel, Rosenman, his legislative leaders, and several experts. There was a story current later in Albany that Roosevelt even made a long-distance call to that wily veteran of the power fight, Al Smith, who was vacationing at Coral Gables, Florida. He came to a decision thoroughly startling to the Republicans. He accepted the bill. Not a person of halfway measures, he did not accept it mildly, but with volleys of skyrockets.

"This is one of the happiest days of my life and one of the most important for the people of the State of New York," Roosevelt told reporters when he announced acceptance at his news conference the next morning. Republican leader Senator Knight heard the news with mild incredulity. "Are you sure," Knight inquired, "that your information is right?" [27]

Roosevelt did more than accept gladly. He proclaimed that in passing this bill the Republicans had surrendered and admitted the error of their ways, and that he had won a correspondingly mighty triumph. He went beyond what the Republicans clearly had offered him (a commission which would investigate state development of power) to claim that they had accepted the concept of state development *per se*. He wired Smith that the Republican legislators had presented a bill "which seems to accept the great basic principles for which you and I have fought so long. There is no doubt it is a great victory." [28]

This was, Roosevelt publicly announced, a red-letter day in the history of the state. Everyone who used electricity had cause to rejoice. It ended a long controversy over a great principle, and removed it from the field of temporary politics. It was a definite recognition that the state should "retain constant control of its great electric power resources, develop it, and sell the electricity by contract, in such a way that the consuming public will be assured of cheap lighting and power." * Fortunately for Roosevelt, he was not alone in this interpretation, little as it may have been anticipated by Republicans. Walter Lippmann of the New York *World* assured Roosevelt that the *World* was interpreting the outcome as a complete triumph. Frankfurter elaborately remarked, "All too often public men compromise essentials on a vital issue, accept stone for bread and then comfort themselves with the metaphor that half a loaf is better than none. By holding out on your water power policy for New York you have vindicated courage in government." [30]

True enough, Governor Roosevelt had not accepted stone for bread. Rather he had snatched the insincerely proffered half loaf and was now trying by clever application of the old mirror trick to present it to his public as the whole loaf he had promised. There was nothing the resentful Republican politicians could do but accept the image of whole loaf for which he was thanking them. They did not even enjoy the satisfaction of having taken the issue out of politics, for Roosevelt was able to capitalize upon it. He reminded his listeners again and again during the election year that he had forced the Republicans to capitulate on power, and that only at his urging had they seen the light. Nevertheless, Roosevelt was aware – and reminded his public of the fact – that capitulation was not necessarily unconditional surrender.

His strategy, he explained privately to Frankfurter, was to take the position that the bill set up a policy, even though it might be only a temporary policy. It directed Roosevelt to appoint commissioners and directed them to bring in a plan based on this policy. Consequently, Roosevelt thought it right to appoint commissioners sympathetic with his viewpoint. The Republican press, he complained, was howling for the appointment of nonpartisan commissioners without preconceived notions. Roosevelt thought it inconceivable that anyone of real intelligence could still lack preconceptions, and besides thought it right to appoint men who would work day and night on his side.[31]

* FDR contended that the bill provided that the commissioners bring in a plan for development of the Saint Lawrence by a state agency, and the sale of electricity for consumers' use by the contract method. The bill provided that they should "study and report plans for the development and form of contract for the sale of hydro-electric power to be generated at power sites . . . owned or controlled by the people of the state." In addressing the New York State Bar Association January 18, FDR granted that under the third section of the bill, if the commissioners did not think state development feasible, they could bring in an alternate proposal. He asserted there had been nothing in his bill of a year earlier to prevent this.[29]

The Governor warned the public that the battle was not yet over. Not only must the commission bring in a favorable report, but the Republican legislature must vote funds before development could begin. The bill establishing the commission was a milestone, he declared when he signed it. "But like all milestones on the road of progress," he cautioned, "it is a milestone only and not a terminal. Even greater vigilance will be required on the part of the public to make sure that this progress is not halted by those who have so long successfully blocked all attempts to give back to the people the water power which is theirs." [32]

The Republicans, even though they were still in a position to win the final battle years later, had not gained much by their 1930 maneuver. It had helped catapult Roosevelt into such a position of national leadership in power questions that Senator Dill of Washington wrote to him for endorsement of a State of Washington referendum measure to authorize publicly owned power plants for country districts. Roosevelt obligingly replied firmly in the affirmative. "What rouses my ire," he declared, "is the loose talk that municipal or county or district supplying of electricity is socialistic! If that is the case, it is also socialistic for a city to own and operate its own sewage disposal plant. Some day the utility companies may cry 'wolf' just once too often." [33]

Within New York, Roosevelt put his Power Commission promptly to work. In January, 1931, it brought in a report substantiating all of his basic contentions. It declared that Saint Lawrence water power could generate electricity at forty per cent of the cost of steam power, and was therefore feasible and desirable. It recommended that the legislature should create a Power Authority to negotiate with the Federal Government over Saint Lawrence rights, and with the Niagara-Hudson Company over distribution of the cheap power. If the power monopoly would not contract to sell electricity at low rates, the authority should take whatever steps might be necessary to deliver cheap power to consumers.

Confident as always of his own skill in political maneuvering, Roosevelt intended that he, not the Power Commission, should deal with Niagara-Hudson and the legislature. "I told them to let me do the political fencing for them," he wrote Frankfurter, "and, without taking undue credit to myself, I think I am a better trader in this kind of work than they are! As a matter of fact, I find the best kind of trading is to go after the objective in the simplest and clearest way." [34]

And so Roosevelt did. When the Republicans in the 1931 legislature resorted to their usual tactics to try to wreck the Power Authority bill, Roosevelt engineered a great tide of protest from civic associations. The Republican leaders, almost inundated by this, surrendered when Roosevelt in addition threatened to denounce them over the radio.

In May, 1931, Roosevelt appointed a most eminent group of public-power experts to his new Power Authority. Frank P. Walsh was chairman, Leland Olds, executive secretary, and James C. Bonbright, Morris L. Cooke, and Fred J. Freestone, trustees. They undertook to study low-cost power development, and began discussions with the State Department over New York rights in the pending Saint Lawrence Treaty between the United States and Canada. They could do nothing to initiate actual power development until President Hoover acted, and he, unlike the state legislature, could not be hurried by any tide of New York protest. The State Department did not conclude a treaty with Canada until the summer of 1932. By that time, Roosevelt was ready to inject the issue into national politics.[35]

The initial Republican concession in 1930 did not even end the power issue in that session of the legislature, for Governor Roosevelt quickly shifted attention to the twin problem of even more immediate importance to New Yorkers, regulation of utility rates. The New York Telephone Company precipitated the shift on January 20 by announcing a general increase in telephone rates. This came at a time when other prices and consumer incomes were starting to plummet. It came in a provocative way, since the telephone company announced that it was basing its new higher rates on a Federal court decision of the previous December.[36]

The increases were not very spectacular; in New York City they would raise home telephone rates $3.42 per year, and upstate, $2.06. But they touched off a vigorous protest. Governor Roosevelt conferred with the members of the Public Service Commission; it announced that it would investigate the rates. At the same time, he ordered his counsel, Rosenman, to make a close study of the case in the Federal courts to determine if it could not have been appealed to the United States Supreme Court. He followed this with a message to the legislature requesting it to memorialize Congress to pass Senator Wagner's bill to remove original jurisdiction over intrastate utility cases from the United States district courts.* The legislature acted, although Speaker

* FDR declared, "Time and again we have seen utility companies rush into the

McGinnies scoffed that this was no more than a political move. Democratic Congressmen from New York and Republican Representative La Guardia spoke up loudly in Washington. Roosevelt urged his friend Senator Walsh of Montana to back the measure because it was vital to all states. All this attracted much attention, but, as McGinnies had prophesied, led to nothing except further affirmations of strong states'-rights principles on the part of Roosevelt.[37]

Roosevelt struck closer to the consumers' pocketbooks when he put pressure upon the Public Service Commission to intervene vigorously in establishing fair rates. He did so even though there was not much that the commission legally could do. The New York Telephone Company had recently obtained a Federal court decision after a lengthy suit. This set a relatively modest valuation of the company's property as the basis for setting rates that would bring an eight-per-cent return on the investment. But the telephone company tacked on another $133,000,000 in new capital expenditures, and, contending it was carrying out the Federal court ruling, announced raises in its rates. Roosevelt protested against this vigorously, and called for the greatest possible amount of state home rule in the setting of utility rates.[38]

Whether or not the Public Service Commission had much authority, on the day before its hearings on the telephone controversy Governor Roosevelt called upon it to resist the new rates. "Even though the Federal court has set up certain standards of values, the Public Service Commission is still the only rate making body of the State," he pointed out. "I am sure that the power of the State has not been so emasculated that this particular utility company can force upon us arbitrary rates, the basis of which has not yet even been considered by your body." [39]

Hastily the commission tried to devise means to forestall the increase. On the day before the new rates were scheduled to go into effect, it ordered the increase to be reduced temporarily by twenty per cent. This, it estimated, would still enable the New York Telephone Company to receive a return somewhat above seven per cent, although it cut the total increase from about fourteen million dollars to eleven million dollars.

Even though the Public Service Commission had forced a limited

---

Federal courts to obtain injunctions against state commissions. Although state courts are open to them, they have refused to accept state tribunals, but instead have sought the aid of Federal judges. I consider such action to be contrary to sound theories of government and an improper encroachment upon state home rule."

reduction upon the telephone company, Roosevelt let it be known around Albany that he was wondering if the commission had not outlived its usefulness. He felt that there ought to be an entirely new study of the relation of the state to public utilities. Perhaps, he was arguing in private, the solution would be for the state to make contracts with the utilities setting the rates.[40]

In these remarks, Roosevelt was echoing the spreading dissatisfaction with the commission which had led to the establishment of the committee to investigate it. During the fall and winter months, Professor Bonbright and Frank Walsh had labored hard for Roosevelt as a firm minority representing him in the investigation. Roosevelt's third appointee, Adie, was seriously ill. They were not able, as Roosevelt had hoped, to force out a report to the legislature earlier than the March 1 deadline, but they did keep Roosevelt informed of their progress.

Even the Republican legislators on the investigating committee gradually came to realize that the commission needed thoroughgoing changes, Bonbright wrote Roosevelt late in December. He felt that the investigation was clearly showing the utility-mindedness of the dominant members of the commission. This was notably true both of the Republican chairman, William A. Prendergast, and the leading Democratic member, George R. Van Namee. Van Namee had been Smith's preconvention manager in 1928 and, in name at least, Roosevelt's campaign manager, but since the campaign no warmth had developed between Van Namee and the Governor. As for Commissioner George R. Lunn, who had been associated with Roosevelt years earlier, his heart was in the right place, according to Bonbright, but he was hopelessly ignorant of the complicated techniques of public-service regulation. The counsel was defeatist, reluctant to initiate litigation, and quick to accept unfavorable decisions in the lower courts. Obviously what the commission needed were members with both the will and technical skill to regulate.[41]

During January, Chairman Prendergast came under public attack for his pro-utility bias in cases involving the telephone company, the Brooklyn Union and Borough Gas Company, and the Long Island Railroad. He was even criticized because his two sons were associated with utilities. To add to his anguish, he thoroughly disapproved of Roosevelt's determination that the commission should serve as a bulwark for consumers rather than as a quasi-judicial body holding a balance between utilities and citizens. He resented the Governor's orders to the commission to resist the telephone-rate raises and to take firm and aggressive action.[42]

On February 4, Prendergast conferred with Roosevelt for two hours over telephone rates. In the course of the conversation, he told the Governor he had a more personal matter to take up, and handed him a brief letter of resignation. Prendergast left the office smiling broadly, refusing to comment to reporters. Roosevelt restrained the jubilation he must have felt. "I was completely surprised," he remarked. "You could have knocked me over with a feather." [43]

After his resignation, Prendergast began publicly denouncing the Governor for tampering with the Public Service Commission. The New York *Times*, which had been friendly to Roosevelt, agreed that the Governor was exceeding his authority. This did not deter Roosevelt in the slightest. Repeatedly in speeches both before and after Prendergast's resignation he asserted that the utilities operated only on franchises from the people of the state: the purpose of the commission was to protect the rights of the citizens under these franchises. "Historically, practically, legally and in every other way," he declared, "Mr. Prendergast was dead wrong." Roosevelt's theory was so popular that even Senator Knight, who was heading the committee investigating the commission, did not openly refute it. Rather, he tried to capitalize upon the feeling of the man in the street by warning the utilities in an address that they must watch their step.[44]

The Public Service Commission announced immediately after Prendergast's resignation that it would heed the Governor's demand for aggressive action. Roosevelt pondered carefully the selection of a new chairman, and on March 1 announced a brilliant choice. This was Milo R. Maltbie, known as "the people's champion." When Governor Hughes had succeeded in obtaining a commission in 1907, he had appointed Maltbie to it, and Maltbie had served as a progressive member from 1907 to 1915. He had an unassailable reputation as a utilities expert. Professor Mosher wrote Roosevelt he was the best qualified person in the country to be chairman, and with his authority could be expected to revolutionize the administration of public-utility regulation. Senator Knight was not pleased, but did not dare oppose the confirmation.[45]

Roosevelt could be certain that Maltbie would lead the commission in vigorous action against the telephone company, since he had been the expert for New York City in the case. And so Maltbie did. The temporary reduction in the new rates applied only until May 1. At that time, the commission handed down a sweeping rejection of the company demands for rate increases, reduced the valuation of the company, and reduced the temporary schedules. It refused the eight-million-dollar increase the company requested, and instead cut rates a million dollars. In a sixty-six-page opinion, it castigated the company for allowing its operating expenses to rise, and sought to refute critics who claimed that regulation had broken down. "I think the Commission went about as far as it could," Maltbie informed Roosevelt, "and I am sure that recent events, particularly your attitude upon regulatory matters, has had an effect." Roosevelt expressed his gratification, and at once he put Maltbie to work checking on the overcapitalization of power holding companies.[46]

Roosevelt did not fare as well in his effort to dominate the investigation of the Public Service Commission. As had been foreshadowed by Senator Knight's speech, the Republican leaders tried to undermine the appeal of Roosevelt's militancy by themselves taking a mildly critical attitude. They made sure too that the report would be a Republican document for which the Governor could not take credit; at only one vital point did they refuse to accept the views of Bonbright and Walsh, but they made no effort to reconcile this difference in order to bring out a single unanimous report. Rather they rushed a preliminary majority (Republican) report to the newspapers; the Democratic minority followed suit. At a final meeting, when Bonbright and Walsh demanded an open session under threat of otherwise publicizing the transactions, the Republicans threw out the two Roosevelt appointees.[47]

This time Roosevelt's opponent was a worthy antagonist, the counsel for the investigating committee, William J. ("Wild Bill") Donovan, who also knew how to make exciting statements. Rate making was sheer guesswork, he declared in the preliminary majority report. That made the headlines. The majority granted that the commission was bogging down, and proposed as a solution the idea with which Roosevelt had been toying, the substitution of a contract system of regulation. The minority was somewhat harsher in its strictures upon the utilities; it recommended the prudent-investment base of evaluation.[48]

The Republican report did not disturb Roosevelt in the least. "It is certainly a very 'wishy washy' document," he commented to the Socialist Harry Laidler, who had been attacking Roosevelt's own views as wishy-washy. As for the minority report, he publicly proclaimed it a model of clarity which would for many years be a textbook throughout the country.[49]

Frankfurter, sharing the views of most experts on utility regulation, pointed out to Roosevelt that the Republican report "shrinks from the conclusions of its own analysis and suffers from the timidity of excessive conservatism and partisan alignment." As for the Bonbright-Walsh report, Frankfurter felt that it would serve as the basis for Roosevelt's recommendations, and as a means of educating the public mind toward legislation. It was "the most important contribution that has been made to modern problems of utility regulation." [50]

Frankfurter's attitude was important. He had been in intimate consultation with Bonbright and Walsh while they prepared the report, and it was he who labored diligently to hold Roosevelt to the prudent-investment line. Roosevelt had in a general way endorsed the scheme in his *Forum* article the previous December. Bonbright had emphasized to him at that time that the fatal weakness in the existing scheme of utility regulation was the vicious doctrine of the Federal courts in allowing the return to be determined by the present value of property. The danger, Bonbright granted, was that the courts would throw out a prudent-investment scheme on constitutional grounds. Nevertheless, he went ahead and wrote such a proposal into his report. Frankfurter was delighted. "As Professor Whitehead says generally about modern political issues," he commented to Roosevelt, "without considerable daring we get nowhere." [51]

Fear of constitutionality was giving Roosevelt considerable misgivings. Julius Henry Cohen played upon these to such an extent that in the spring of 1930, Roosevelt considered proposing a bill (in line with the Republican recommendation) to regulate utilities through contract. Frankfurter, despite the *O'Fallon* decision, demurred. He pointed out to Roosevelt:

"It is perfectly idle to find such tyrannous authority in the dicta of the Supreme Court in regard to valuation, or at least to have such fear of these dicta as is manifested by the Donovan report. One may be considerably confident that we have reached the peak of the Supreme Court's reactionary attitude and that the next ten years will find the Court going over gradually into a more liberal attitude. Moreover, with the drop in commodity prices, the utilities themselves will want to slide over to the 'prudent investment' basis. I have not a little basis for so thinking." [52]

When Frankfurter visited Roosevelt at the Executive Mansion a few days later, he argued strongly that it would be futile for the Governor to sponsor a voluntary-contract bill, that he would be throwing away the great political issue of adequate utility regulation. Moreover, the Supreme Court had not ruled on this precise policy. "In your speeches," Frankfurter wrote after his conference, "there need not be the slightest attack on, or a criticism of, the Court. You can take the offensive by saying that your policy is grounded in justice and in good economics, and let the other side prove that that which is good economics and socially just is unconstitutional." [53]

This in practice was exactly what Roosevelt did. In a state-wide radio broadcast on April 23, he insisted that New York should "return to the original theory of granting a reasonable return and only a reasonable return to the owners of utility companies." He did not mention the term "prudent investment"; instead he said rates should be based on "the actual cash put into the utilities by investors." He also suggested establishing more municipally owned companies as yardsticks to measure rates. As for the Supreme Court, he remarked only, "Under the lack of a plainly-stated policy by the State Government as to what the rate base shall be, the Supreme Court has gradually allowed large additional amounts to the rate base, based on what it would cost to reproduce the plant anew after many years have elapsed." [54]

The Republican legislature would have none of this. It defeated four bills based on the Bonbright-Walsh report, and after considerable modification passed twenty-six bills based on the Donovan report. Roosevelt denounced them as feeble and makeshift. He vetoed the valuation bill as doing no more than perpetuating the existing muddle. Concerning a batch of twenty which he did sign, he mused, "As I review them I wonder whether meticulous attention to the correction of typographical and verbal inaccuracies in the law did not distract the attention of those who wrote them from the crisis in the State's control of its huge utilities." [55]

On the day that Roosevelt finished a long hearing on the various public-utility bills, he wrote an acquaintance, "The mountain labored and brought forth a mouse! Out of the whole lot there is only one bill with any teeth in it — the one to control holding companies. The fight has only just begun." [56]

Far from being dead as an issue, the entire power question had become one of Roosevelt's strongest political weapons. In his radio address of April 23, he brought home what he meant by contrasting the widely varying and generally high power rates in New York with those in neighboring Ontario. A family with a four-room house using various appliances would have to pay $17.50 in Manhattan, but $13.50 in Brooklyn across the East River, $19.50 in Albany, only $7.80 in Buffalo, $6.93 in Dunkirk with a municipal power plant – but less than $3.00 anywhere in Ontario.[57]

One listener in Albany was so unkind as to add up his check stubs and report to Roosevelt that his total expenditures for gas and electricity during the previous year had been $74.07 – not the $234 Roosevelt's talk implied. Roosevelt retorted that the question was not whether the consumer could afford to pay what he was charged but whether the prices in and of themselves were reasonable.[58]

Outside New York, Roosevelt cautiously took a national position on power development. "As you know," he confided to a friend, "Senator Norris and I think very much alike on this whole subject." He obtained detailed information on Norris's fight in the Senate for public operation of Muscle Shoals, later the heart of T.V.A. Although he would not openly endorse Norris's stand, on the principle that he must keep out of Federal legislative questions, he authorized the newspaper *Labor* to report, "It is well known that Governor Roosevelt heartily approves of the government development of the big plant at Muscle Shoals."[59]

A measure of Roosevelt's success were the attacks upon his program. The Chicago *Journal of Commerce* called it "subsidized socialism." The Philadelphia *Public Ledger* sneered at him as "one of those prophets of the bright millennium who want to pave the way to better times by a relentless war on property." A report reached him that the leader of the Republican party in Connecticut, who was also head of the Connecticut Light and Power Company, planned to send money into New York State to fight Roosevelt's re-election as Governor.[60]

But Roosevelt was braced for the charge of the "light" brigade with that firmest of all supports a politician can have: knowledge that the little men who filled the ballot boxes favored the cause that he championed.

CHAPTER IX

Taming the Legislature

> I must certainly give credit to the Legislature for acting on a very large percentage of measures during the final two weeks, even though it was the same old story of sitting here in Albany month after month without action, while a small group of leaders were trying to make up their minds what to do.
>
> — FDR, *April 16, 1930.*

THE bitter and sarcastic onslaughts against Governor Roosevelt that marked the opening of the 1930 legislative session were the final fusilades of a retreating foe. After the Republicans' flare-up over the Governor's annual message and one further feeble attempt to control the executive budget, they shifted strategy. During the legislative session, their main offensive effort was to try to entangle the Governor in the growing investigation of crime and corruption in New York City. This obviously was to be the Republican campaign issue against him. Defensively, they sought compromise on almost every point of Roosevelt's constructive program in order to try to nullify its campaign value for the Democrats. On January 22, Roosevelt reported to the editor of the New York *Times* that "there seems to be a real, even though it may prove to be a temporary change of heart on the part of the Republican leaders. They now say they want to go along with practically the whole of the welfare program." [1]

They followed up their effort to take Saint Lawrence power development out of the campaign with similar strategic retreats in other areas. The result was the passage of a considerable array of constructive legislation. Whether the Republican legislators or Governor Roosevelt should receive credit for this would be for the voters to decide in the fall.

Certainly Governor Roosevelt demonstrated himself to be master of the legislature. Also, he looked upon its program as providing him with accomplishments with which to face the electorate.

Roosevelt's success in obtaining so much from the Republicans was in part due to the methodical way in which he went about it. With other issues besides public utilities, he drew upon the advice of experts as well as politicians in developing his own stand. He continued to make effective use of the press bureau and the radio to sway the public toward his position.

Beginning in the winter of 1930, he worked an improvement in the legislature by assuming direct, detailed leadership over the Democratic minority. He had clung, as Ernest K. Lindley has pointed out, to the old-fashioned notion that legislative bodies should hold debates. Certainly he himself as a young state senator had exploited his minority position against the party machines to the spectacular limit. Now he began coaching ambitious young Democratic legislators in ways and means to sabotage the Republican machine. Repeatedly he had deprecated the habit of the Republican leaders of eliminating debate and rushing their measures through at the last minute in rubber-stamp fashion. Even in the 1930 session, he was not able entirely to eliminate this. The Republicans refused to act upon any important measure for three months, then passed nearly a thousand bills in two weeks. "This way of handling business means, of course, that no proper consideration or debate can be given during the last few days, especially when bills are actually passing the Assembly or the Senate at the rate of two or three a minute," he pointed out. This might be usual procedure, "but it does not get away from the fact that the rank and file of Senators and Assemblymen have no opportunity to know anything about or study the great majority of bills that actually pass or are defeated." [2]

As a means of breaking this system, Roosevelt began assembling a group of Democratic legislators for lunch at the Executive Mansion on Mondays, the day the legislature met. There he usually fed them cold turkey, hence the participants came to be known as the "Turkey Cabinet." But the Republicans with more accuracy, and probably more to Roosevelt's liking, labeled the gatherings "The Governor's School for Legislators." After food came the instruction, as Roosevelt himself or an expert or department head guided the enthusiastic pupils through the intricacies of pending bills, and primed them for the forthcoming session.[3] The effect, according to Lindley, was painfully evident to the Republicans:

"The lawmaking machinery no longer sped swiftly on its course, and Republican attacks were no longer allowed to pass without more than a perfunctory reply. With the opening of the debate, a dozen Democratic legislators would spring to their feet, and the chambers soon would resound with familiar phrases – sometimes slightly awry, but still recognizable as Roosevelt doctrine." [4]

Roosevelt's class for the Democratic minority most irritated the Republicans at the session over his budget. When the Governor learned that the Republicans were planning to prune it, he assembled the Democratic floor leaders, Senator Downing and Assemblyman Irwin Steingut, together with a half dozen of the Democrats' best debaters from each house. They appeared for the "Turkey Cabinet" meeting with the copies of the budget under their arms. After lunch, Roosevelt's budget expert, Joseph H. Wilson, began his instruction. It lasted until late in the afternoon. Wilson assigned each legislator certain items in the budget and explained to each the reason why the Governor had put them into the appropriation bill, and the damage the Republicans could do by deleting them. To make sure they would not stumble over intricate details, he gave each of them a typewritten sheet explaining a point and suggesting how to ask a question about it.

The result that evening was an unprecedentedly hot discussion of the budget which lasted until nearly two in the morning. The Republican leaders, expecting only the traditional perfunctory protest from the minority, were irritated. The Republican Chairman of the Assembly Ways and Means Committee, Eberly Hutchinson, a slight, owlish engineer from the north country, reacted as though the Democrats were being unethical. He indignantly pointed to Budget Director Wilson, sitting in a front-row seat in the balcony, and accused him of having coached the legislators.

The stir delighted Roosevelt. The next day he remarked, "It is the first time in a decade that the budget has been debated thoroughly. I hope that next year the members on the Republican side of the House will have some idea of what the budget is all about." [5]

Nor was this Roosevelt's only technique for bedeviling the Republicans. Unexpected little things cropped up now and then which demonstrated as much as anything the persistence of his Fly Club sense of humor. In February, 1930, the Republican legislators solemnly caucused to decide upon three nominees for the state Board of Regents, which directed the New York educational system. In order to keep the regents out of politics, their appointment had been left with the legislature when the administration was reorganized. As a result, eleven of the twelve were Republicans, though, as Lindley points out, with no noticeable effect upon the school system of the state. In a routine fashion the Republicans prepared to add three more of their number. When they nominated these choices in the legislature, the Democratic leaders put into nomination one man – Owen D. Young. The Republicans in agitation arose and expressed their great respect and admiration for this eminent Democratic financial and industrial leader, then nevertheless voted in their own candidates. Roosevelt had made them look foolish in their claim to be above partisanship.[6]

Ten days later Roosevelt worked a variation on the same device. The woman members of the Republican state committee were about to arrive in Albany to listen to their legislative leaders discussing the main issues of the session. Roosevelt wrote them expressing his appreciation for their interest in public affairs, and invited them to tea at the Executive Mansion. The invitation, he explained, would be a token of his "heavy debt of gratitude to many of the Republican women of the State for the fine and powerful support they have given to those important issues endorsed in the platforms of both parties and on which there can and should be no division of opinion on partisan lines." The Republican ladies accepted and attended the tea. This was an unprecedented event.[7]

Roosevelt's clever and aggressive leadership, which brought him widespread public support, carried him through successfully in tilt after tilt with the 1930 legislature. Many of these battles were over vital matters.

Prison reform was one of these. When the legislature assembled at the beginning of January, the leaders vehemently blamed Roosevelt for the riots at Auburn and Dannemora, anticipating that these would serve as dangerous ammunition in the fall campaign. Their onslaught was bombastic and determined, but Roosevelt was ready for them. In the weeks before the legislature met, he had several times dramatically attacked the medieval conditions existing in the prisons, and he had held two widely publicized conferences with penologists and heads of prisons to formulate an over-all plan of reform. As usual he demonstrated a faculty for picking the brains of the experts and making their knowledge his own. "I was amazed to see the grasp which you displayed of the prison building program, on what must have been comparatively brief acquaintance," a consultant for the Russell Sage Foundation wrote after one of the meetings, "and I admired equally the skill with which you handled the different types of men who came together." [8]

When the legislature session began, the Governor was far better prepared than the Republicans to propose concrete and sound plans for reform. On January 2, he sent the legislature a message calling for emergency remedies, to be followed by reforms that would go to the root of the trouble. He proposed an immediate appropriation to construct outdoor camps to relieve the overcrowding, an increase in the food ration from twenty-one cents to twenty-five cents per day, and an increase in the number and pay of prison guards.[9]

Amid vehement accusations of mismanagement against Roosevelt, the legislators passed his bill. At the same time they established a commission to investigate the administration of the prisons, especially new construction. Here they hoped to uncover campaign material to hurt Roosevelt, and to establish themselves as proponents of scientific penology.[10]

Roosevelt both as a politician and a humanitarian suspected their motives. He not only welcomed the opportunity to undercut the Republicans in prison reform, but also was genuinely concerned with establishing a workable program. He demonstrated his systematic, scientific thinking when he wrote a correspondent that reform would involve three phases. These were: "the physical, which includes the buildings to eliminate overcrowding; secondly, the whole subject of industrial and agricultural work for the prisoners; and thirdly, a reorganization of the parole system and sentencing systems."

His first practical step to relieve overcrowding was to start five outdoor camps for one hundred men each. Even these, he realized, could create trouble. "Probably some poor idiots with only a short time left to serve will try to skip out from these camps," he commented, "but the fundamental idea is sound and most of the prisoners in them will be happy and contented, and at the same time perform some useful service." [11]

In the area of prison construction, Roosevelt had moved even before the legislature met. One of the sorest points was the expensive new prison in preliminary stages of construction at Attica in western New York. Many stories were circulating about its anticipated extravagance. It would cost twelve million dollars, or, critics claimed, about six thousand dollars for each of the two thousand prisoners. Fencing would cost more than a million and a half dollars, and the warden's house, seventy-five thousand dollars — more than the Governor's Mansion. Because there was quicksand on the site, the foundations might run the bill up to two million dollars above the original estimates.[12]

All this cast discredit on the administration. Roosevelt was very much dissatisfied with everything he heard about the site, and in November, 1929, in time to forestall the legislature, he ordered Lieutenant Governor Lehman to investigate some of the dubious points: who had been responsible for choosing the location, whether test borings had been taken, and whether the Departments of Public Works and Correction had passed on the suitability of the property for prison buildings and the requisite prison wall. Meanwhile, he was ready to hold up the contracts for preliminary construction until Lehman's findings were in.[13]

Lehman reported to Roosevelt in mid-December after consulting with both administrative officials and with Senator Knight and Speaker McGinnies. Estimates were up, he said, but the original estimates had not included many items. No borings had been made on the site before it was purchased, but it was not customary for the state to make borings. The silt deposits would increase the cost of the prison by three hundred and fifty to four hundred thousand dollars, but Lehman felt that any other site in western New York would have posed equal or greater difficulties. Consequently, he recommended that work proceed. Lehman demonstrated a high degree of responsibility in his report, for he might well have made political capital out of the records of the State Office Site and Building Commission, which indicated that Senator Knight had been responsible for the choice of the site in his district. At a meeting in May, 1929, he and the Prison Commissioner had been appointed a committee to purchase a site, and at a later meeting in September, 1929, he had been authorized to enter into an agreement to purchase the land. The agreement of purchase was concluded July 30, 1929.[14]

Nevertheless, after the legislature convened, the Prison Association of New York announced that the costs at Attica were much too high. Senator Knight, on the principle that the best defense was an offense, attacked Roosevelt for wastefulness and sluggishness at Attica, and at the end of January instigated a Republican legislative investigation. Roosevelt's Commissioner of Public Works, Colonel Greene, defended his revised estimates before the investigation commission as being reduced to less than the original, to eleven million dollars. As for Roosevelt, he replied crisply and with an air of finality to Republican statements that it was ridiculous for them to suggest building a fortress-like escape-proof prison with steel cell blocks: [15]

"Only last autumn I told the legislative leaders that the prison experts in two important conferences had gravely doubted the wisdom of going ahead with plans to build cell blocks for 2,000 prisoners at that place. The legislative leaders would not listen to any change or to any suggestion that accommodations other than steel cell blocks were feasible or safe. It is a comfort to know that these gentlemen have at least taken enough interest in our prisons to gain knowledge of some of the fundamentals. They at last see that the steel cell block is not a necessity for every prisoner of the State." [16]

Again, in the area of paroling and pardoning prisoners, Roosevelt moved rapidly. Out of the many investigations of the prison riots had come the indisputable fact that the Baumes law forcing life terms upon fourth offenders was defeating itself. Prisoners, many of them quite youthful, who could not hope to get time off for good behavior, and who faced only many dismal years in prison, could lose little if they made desperate attempts to escape. The New York system of paroling prisoners was out of date and needed thorough revision to be brought up to the standards of Illinois and other advanced states. Senator Caleb H. Baumes (author of the Baumes law) was proposing some revisions, but Roosevelt thought them silly. Instead, he decided to try to get the legislature to establish a full-time parole court. He turned to Sam A. Lewisohn, an eminent New York philanthropist and expert on prison problems who had formerly been a member of the Board of Parole of the New York State Reformatory.* On January 6, he asked Lewisohn to prepare for him a two- or three-page memorandum outlining the functions of the new court — "complete authority over parole and the parole and probation officers, and also the right to receive from the Governor pardon applications and [to] make recommendations on them to the Governor after careful examination and study of each individual case." [18]

Two weeks later, Roosevelt appointed an informal committee with Lewisohn as chairman to make a quick survey of parole problems and recommend the new system. It was an excellent committee: two of the members had engaged in probationary work, another member was an energetic Barnard College professor, Raymond Moley, who had been a member of the Cleveland Crime Survey and for several years Research Director of the New York State Crime Commission.

* When Lewisohn sent him a book on criminals, FDR replied that they should both take it as a warning, that there was no telling where they would wind up. "May I express the fervent wish that our [cells] will adjoin — also that they may be in the new prison and not Auburn or Dannemora." [17]

Louis Howe, who had gained considerable knowledge of these problems and those best suited to cope with them during his work for the National Crime Commission in the 1920's, had brought Moley to Roosevelt during the campaign of 1928.* Moley had helped draft a a speech for Roosevelt calling for reform of the administration of justice. His work on the parole commission was his first assignment for the Roosevelt administration at Albany; it led to bigger things.[19]

Within twelve days the commission reported back to Governor Roosevelt with a plan which incorporated the thinking of leading penologists. It recommended establishing a full-time parole board in the executive department, separate from the Department of Correction. It should be staffed with specialists and psychiatrists who could investigate pardon as well as parole cases. In transmitting the report to Baumes, Roosevelt commented that the saving of men and women from lives of crime was a matter of such great importance he trusted it would not be allowed to sink in the maelstrom of politics.[20]

Next Roosevelt planned a committee to report in a third area, to study the segregation of prisoners into different groups according to the seriousness of their offenses, and to plan employment for them which would not conflict with free labor and industry. He tried to get on his committees "men so big and so recognized not only by this state but by the whole country as being in constant daily touch with the details of manufacturing and distribution, as to make any decisions that they arrive at carry the greatest possible weight throughout the country." This, he hoped, would persuade other backward states to accept their conclusions. In addition to labor representatives, he hoped to persuade Marshall Field, the Chicago department-store owner, and Gerard Swope of General Electric to serve as industrial representatives on the committee. Roosevelt failed.[21]

Roosevelt's negotiations to obtain distinguished committee members were still dragging on when the legislative finance committee handed out to newspapermen advance copies of its report attacking Al Smith and Roosevelt for not having developed a prison policy, and proposing

* Moley first met FDR in the fall of 1928 when Howe, "with elaborate offhandedness, took me into Democratic headquarters 'just to have you meet "The Boss."' Roosevelt . . . was sitting at his desk sorting out letters. He looked up, smiled, and then explained, to my surprise and to Louis' dismay, that my visit wasn't at all unexpected. He wanted to simplify the administration of justice in the state. He wanted to say something about it in his campaign. Louis had suggested that I might 'shape out' some ideas he could use."

ideas very similar to those which Roosevelt himself was privately advocating. This was on a Thursday, and the release date was Friday, March 14. On Thursday evening Roosevelt beat out the legislators by a hairline: he announced he was appointing two committees, and outlined the very plans which the Republicans were attacking him for not proposing. His program appeared in the newspapers one day before the complaints of the legislators.[22]

The Republicans were furious. Assemblyman Hutchinson, whose ace had been trumped, arose in the chamber on Friday, and asserted that Roosevelt was guilty of an impudent attempt at plagiarism: "The Governor, apparently through some subterranean channel or through some particular aptitude of his own for petty larceny when it comes to the ideas of his opponents . . . has taken the recommendations of the committee and put them out as his own." Roosevelt, he concluded, had conducted himself "in a manner altogether disreputable and unworthy of the Chief Executive." [23]

When newspapermen carried word of Hutchinson's accusations downstairs to the Governor, he laughed heartily, and explained that any similarity between the two statements on prisons was coincidental, since he had prepared his ten days earlier. This was true. The incident did Roosevelt no political damage, for the public was interested in little beyond the practical results. Between the Governor and the legislature, New York obtained vital improvements in its prison system, a new parole board,* and a commission to make an intensive study and investigation of prison administration. Roosevelt appointed Lewisohn chairman of the commission, which introduced a powerful and cogent report the following year. In the spring of 1931, the National Committee on Prisons and Prison Labor awarded Roosevelt its medal for outstanding service in the cause of prison improvement. Roosevelt replied in a flurry of modesty that he was quite overwhelmed. "I am certainly not the one to receive an award . . ." he disclaimed, "for I have merely tied things together and made it possible for the real workers to carry on the battle." This was precisely what he had done.[25]

If the legislators could not make good campaign provender out of Roosevelt's policies for the rehabilitation of criminals, they felt perhaps they could do so over his failure to ferret criminals out in the

* At first the new parole board did not function too smoothly, but by January, 1932, Winthrop D. Lane, a noted penologist and director of parole in New Jersey, declared that the New York system held top rank in its field.[24]

government of New York City. The scandals that had been simmering there since the murder of Rothstein were coming to a boil. New disclosures encouraged Republicans to think that what had failed to prevent Jimmy Walker from piling up a huge plurality the previous November could ruin Roosevelt upstate in the coming November. They ignored the strategy of Kingsland Macy, who wisely proposed that they vote a legislative investigation of the city government. This might have led to the exposure of some Democratic villains and the building of Republican heroes. Instead, the Republican party was destined not to return to power in New York State until it produced a really crusading district attorney. The legislators did not wish to take on the task of investigation, rather they preferred to grant the power to Roosevelt in order to embarrass him. Senator Knight, smiling with glee – newspapermen claimed he never laughed – introduced an enabling bill to this purpose.

The Republican tactics were all too obvious. One of the most vigorous of the state senators, George R. Fearon of Syracuse, who combined the features and build of an Abraham Lincoln with the rough-and-tumble oratorical style of Al Smith, led the attack. In direct proportion to his ambition to gain the Republican nomination for governor, his invective against Roosevelt rose in volume and intensity, and by spring of 1930 he had blown himself into a red-hot candidate. He explained to the senate that Roosevelt was professing to lack power to probe Tammany; the Republicans wanted to help him out by delegating him that power. Democrats were well aware that his tongue was in his cheek, and were ready when it slipped. "All we want to do," he declared, "is to put the Governor in a position – "

Fearon got no further, one newspaperman reported:

"The Senate went into an uproar, the laughter of the members on the Republican side mixing with the guffaws of the minority.

"Bernard Downing, the Democratic floor leader, fairly leaped out of his chair. Above the tumult he shouted, 'Yes, you want to put him in a hole.' " [26]

The Republicans did their best to put him in a hole with their enabling bill, but he popped out of that hole with an instant and indignant veto. It was a pity for the sake of orderly government that the bill had been passed, he declared, for it would foist upon the governor the new and unheard-of responsibility for investigating the government of one particular city! Already the governor had the right to act when specific charges were filed; to act otherwise would be a violation of the principle of home rule. He pointed to the obvious lack of good faith and wholly political motivation of the bill, and added wryly that it was "within the right of the Legislature to go wholly outside of specific charges of specific facts about specific individuals and to go on any general fishing expedition it wishes." [27]

The legislature still did not wish to do so; during the months that followed, Knight and McGinnies continued to press upon Roosevelt demands for an investigation of New York City. He resisted stoutly with as yet no appreciable signs of political damage.

When the legislature adjourned in mid-April, Roosevelt was able to look back at the session with a feeling of triumph. Despite the heavy burden that adjournment placed upon him, he was in high spirits. He wrote a gay letter to Lehman, who was recuperating from appendicitis:

"There is little news here except an avalanche of bills, bills, bills, hearings, hearings, hearings, and telephone calls at the rate of three a minute from 9 A.M. to 11 P.M. I have acted on about 550 bills and there are less than 200 left, so I begin to see blue sky."

Toward the end of the session, the Republican legislative leaders had rushed through bills bearing the names of Republican senators and assemblymen in an effort to take credit for a progressive program. Of course, Roosevelt crowed to the people of the state that the legislature had given him a large part of what he had demanded. In the stampede for credit, he pointed out, they had dealt with more important subjects than in any average year.[28]

The legislature had given way at least to a limited extent on power development and public-utility regulation, on the building of hospitals, and on reform of prisons. It had also provided Roosevelt with the type of judicial reform commission he had demanded, had taken a few steps toward tightening the banking laws, had made elementary provision for old-age security, and had made what Roosevelt called rather grudging concessions toward his liberal labor policy. It had passed a number of minor pieces of legislation to aid agriculture. Finally, at the close of the session, it had made a large appropriation for Bernard Baruch's pet project, the development of Saratoga Springs as a great health center.[29]

As soon as the legislature went home, Roosevelt once again went to the people. In two radio chats, he discussed with them the achievements of the legislature. Again, in a fashion highly irritating to Republicans, he left the impression that all the achievements were his and the failures theirs. There was not much they could do about this.

The previous year they had failed conspicuously through being intransigent; this year they had failed through being cooperative. In 1929, Republican newspapers had hailed the end of the session as a crushing defeat for Roosevelt; in 1930 they could make no such claim. With the election only six months off, Republican prospects were dark. The main question seemed to be how large a majority Roosevelt could roll up.

CHAPTER X

Bread and Booze

> We are headed towards a saner course on the Prohibition question, which will bring the kind of action which, in a few years will promote a really sounder and greater temperance.
>
> — FDR TO HUGH C. LAUGHLIN, *September 25, 1930.*

IF anyone had characterized the Roosevelt of early 1930 as a political Houdini, escaping again and again from the traps hidden in the key issues of unemployment and Prohibition, the Governor would not have been offended. Both he and Louis Howe occasionally in lighter moments saw the public's Franklin D. Roosevelt as a political magician.

One of these occasions was his birthday party on January 30, 1930, which, following long custom, was rather like a private Gridiron dinner, crowded with stunts satirizing the past and predicting the future. Howe always indulged his dramatic talent by sketching elaborate skits for these events. On this January 30, his imagination teeming with bright ideas for the fall campaign, Howe presented Roosevelt with a "Politician's Magic Set" for use on the hustings. Its contents were wonderful indeed. There was a vanishing half dollar which Roosevelt could use to explain to rural audiences the increase in the budget: he could make two or three hundred million dollars disappear in just the same fashion. There was also a money-making machine for demonstrating to the chairman of the assembly finance committee where he could obtain the money for Roosevelt's budget. Finally, Howe gave the Governor a disappearing-pea trick and a set of magic disks with which to baffle Senators Knight and Machold: Roosevelt could thus instill in them inferiority complexes.[1]

Roosevelt could afford to laugh at Howe's pleasant nonsense. He knew perfectly well that his magic was built in and required no gadgets or gimmicks. No box of tricks he might take along on the campaign could help him outsmart and baffle the opposition more thoroughly than the sleight of hand of his basic political acumen. He had seldom lost in the game of wits which had begun with his inauguration, and he was not losing in 1930. As the pace of the game slowly increased in the weeks and months after the legislature adjourned, time after time the Republican leaders presented the Governor with the same old magic disks. Time after time he chose the right one.

Or perhaps it would be more accurate to say that he refused to choose the wrong one. Having failed to make headway by challenging Roosevelt on the positive issues, like power, farms, and prisons, the Republicans fell back upon crime in New York City. They continued to hope that by luring him into a trap on corruption, they could destroy him. He cleverly continued to outmaneuver them. Quite correctly he acted on the assumption that the economic issues growing out of the deepening depression would far overshadow any questions of corruption in one city, over which as governor he had no direct control.

As the effects of the stock crash of the previous autumn began to be felt, Roosevelt focused on the growing unemployment figures. He telephoned his Industrial Commissioner, Frances Perkins, asking for new figures more frequently than she had them to give, although she was sending him statistics once a week. She had to depend primarily upon monthly reports from industries on dwindling payrolls and employment, but prepared for the Governor weekly tables which she believed were far more reliable than those of the United States Employment Service. These Federal statistics were not a composite of industrial reports, but only of placement figures and job applications during the previous week.

When President Hoover at the end of January, 1930, announced on the basis of these U.S.E.S. figures that employment had risen, Miss Perkins was incensed. Her own New York figures indicated quite the reverse, and she feared that Hoover's unjustifiably optimistic statement would make the people being laid off in large numbers think that there was something wrong with themselves personally because they were losing their jobs. Impetuously, she issued a press statement contradicting President Hoover.

When it appeared in the newspapers the following day, she was overwhelmed with telegrams and telephone calls. In the middle of the morning, the call she was fearing came in to her office. Governor Roosevelt wished to speak to her. She answered with apologies and explanations, but quite needlessly, for Roosevelt had phoned to congratulate her. When she told him she was sorry she had not informed him in advance, he replied that he was glad she had not done so because he would have found it necessary to ask her not to issue the statement. Since she had done it without permission, Roosevelt did not have to take responsibility. He assured Miss Perkins that he thought it much more wholesome to have bad news out in the open.[2] There was a much more important reason for Roosevelt's good humor. Already he was beginning to match his actions in the state realm against what Hoover was undertaking on a national level. Within the State of New York, he wished to attack unemployment as he had the farm problem as a means of demonstrating what could be done throughout the United States. He might not be able to find national answers, and, as Miss Perkins has pointed out, he had not made up his own mind what ought to be done. At least he was beginning to realize the threatening implications of the problem, and he was ready to study and learn.[3]

"The situation is serious," he admitted at the end of March, 1930, "and the time has come for us to face this unpleasant fact dispassionately and constructively as a scientist faces a test tube of deadly germs intending first to understand the nature, the cause and the effect, and finally the method of overcoming and the technique of preventing its ravages."[4]

Though Roosevelt may not yet have known it, this was a disease which could spell political death to the doctor who failed to find a cure. He began to search for a remedy. The state Department of Labor index indicated a drop in factory employment of nine per cent since the previous October, 1929. A survey Roosevelt had made among labor organizations and chambers of commerce showed a decline in various communities averaging between ten and fifteen per cent. Reading this economic fever chart, he urged community officials to act immediately to collect unemployment figures, supervise public and private relief, undertake small job campaigns, create free employment clearing houses, and establish local public-works projects.

In effect, Roosevelt for the moment was doing no more than noting symptoms and prescribing aspirin. He also sought to analyze causes. The reasons for unemployment, he decided, were seasonal fluctuations chronic in some industries, technological unemployment growing out of the displacement of men by new types of machines, and the depression due to the business cycle — "an economic phenomenon recurring with some regularity throughout the nation as well as this State."[5] This, while correct as far as it went, resembled the doctors' diagnosing his polio as a severe chill caused by exhaustion and exposure to the elements.

In his search for a solution of one of the contributing factors, Roosevelt established a commission to study methods of ironing out seasonal fluctuations in employment. It was the first state commission of its kind in the United States. The problem had concerned Roosevelt in his business years, when he had sought means to even out employment in the building trades. One of the men he appointed to the commission was an expert who had done much in his own business. This was Ernest Draper, vice-president of the Hills Brothers Company, importers of dates. Hills Brothers had reduced seasonal unemployment in its Brooklyn plant through building cold-storage warehouses so that employees could pack dates more months a year, and, in otherwise slack periods, keep at work packing figs, shredded coconut, and other produce. Since Roosevelt always liked to think in concrete examples, Miss Perkins brought Draper to Albany to tell the Governor about these innovations.[6]

The commission's report a few weeks later enumerated a number of specific examples illustrating its recommendation that businessmen must adopt a new slogan, "Steady work the year around." It also amplified the Governor's recommendations to communities. As for the state, the commission was more cautious. It primarily advised that New York expand its employment service. It added in a minor and vague way that the state should sponsor public works, but this was something of a halfhearted footnote. Obviously at this time neither Governor Roosevelt nor his administrators nor his advisers had much more realization of the formidable nature of the nation's disease or the drastic nature of the required therapy than did President Hoover himself.[7]

This limitation did not prevent Roosevelt from deliberately planning to challenge Hoover on the issue of unemployment. Within several months after Miss Perkins's attack, Roosevelt readied himself for an offensive in his own name. In April, 1930, Frankfurter nudged him with the suggestion that he check up on the President's prophecy early in March that the unemployment problem would evaporate in sixty days. When Hoover's sixty days were up, Frankfurter advised, Roosevelt should "make clear [to the public] how all these statements from the White House about prosperity and unemployment are in truth efforts to 'dope' the public." Concurring, Roosevelt enthusiastically asked Frances Perkins to step up the supply of statistical ammunition. As it arrived from her office, he stockpiled it, awaiting the psychological moment to open fire upon the President. Yet, like Hoover, Roosevelt still regarded the situation as merely a worse-than-usual dip of the business cycle and still intended to rely almost entirely upon voluntary relief measures.[8]

During that same April, Roosevelt moved a step further toward an open role as national challenger of President Hoover. The occasion was the Jefferson Day dinner of the National Democratic Club at the Hotel Commodore in New York City. This was not just another Tammany rally; rather it was the national Democratic opening of the campaign of 1930. Governor Roosevelt was one of two featured speakers. The other was Senator Burton K. Wheeler of Montana, who six years before had run for vice-president on Robert M. La Follette's protest ticket against the conservative Republican Coolidge and the conservative Democratic Davis. He was back in the Democratic party, but remained a powerful spokesman for the same groups he had championed in 1924, groups that were rapidly becoming larger, hungrier, and more clamorous as economic distress spread. What Roosevelt and Wheeler had to say was carried by the NBC blue network to all sections of the country except the Pacific Coast. Both men addressed themselves not to New York City but to the depression-ridden Great Plains and Rockies.

Governor Roosevelt, speaking first, made a stirring attack upon the concentration of wealth in the United States. Having aligned himself with the foes of plutocracy in a fashion certain to please Westerners, he added that in the past week he had signed or vetoed some seven hundred and fifty bills, which had kept him at work until nearly three o'clock in the morning each day. Therefore, pleading exhaustion, he slipped away from the meeting.

As soon as Senator Wheeler began to speak, keen observers realized that Roosevelt had a reason more compelling than fatigue for absenting himself from the Democrats' kickoff rally. Montana's Wheeler confronted a Tammany audience which he disliked and distrusted and remembered as an unruly group more interested in the bottles under the table than in what he had to say. Over their heads, he appealed to the Westerners, whose grievances he so ardently shared. He launched into an attack upon greedy power magnates and manufacturers, pointing to the necessity of electing a President who could lead and win the fight for public-utility regulation and lower tariffs. He proclaimed:

"As I look over the field for a General to lead the people to victory under the banner of a reunited, militant progressive party, I cannot help but fasten my attention upon your Governor. The West is looking to Roosevelt to lead the fight and with him I feel sure we can win." [9]

Wheeler came out for Roosevelt, he recalled many years later, as a means of trying to head off a new Smith boom. He was fearful that Smith might be renominated, the Ku Klux Klan fight renewed, and the chances for a Democratic victory thus thrown away. In 1928, when Wheeler had carried Montana, Smith had lost the state. Wheeler did not want to take any chances in 1932; he wanted none of Tammany. Indeed, he had been so suspicious of the New York City Democrats that when they had invited him to speak at the dinner, he at first refused, and he changed his mind only at the urging of Jouett Shouse and Senator Robert Wagner. He gave no previous warning what he intended to say in his speech; it was only afterwards that he gave reporters his formal statement endorsing Roosevelt.

Nevertheless, the Roosevelt forces caught the scent in advance. During the dinner, one of Roosevelt's supporters, former Ambassador James Gerard, approached Wheeler to inquire if he planned to come out for Roosevelt. Wheeler replied affirmatively; Gerard told him to go to it. This was Roosevelt's cue to leave before Wheeler spoke. Thus, while the statement was not Roosevelt-inspired, it was certainly not quashed, for it fitted neatly into his grand stategy.[10]

Wheeler's bugle call created a sensation, for he was the first important Democrat to come out openly for Roosevelt. Amid the excitement of the next few days, Roosevelt turned sphinx. His sudden and uncharacteristic silence made Wheeler wonder for some weeks if he might have offended him. It was not until the beginning of June that Roosevelt sent Wheeler a friendly letter, and that communication, though amiable, was noncommittal.

A few of Roosevelt's friends and most of his rivals deplored the statement as premature. Shouse, who hoped for a more conservative candidate, such as Owen D. Young, greeted Wheeler ruefully upon his return to Washington. But Roosevelt's inner circle was obviously delighted with Wheeler's trial balloon, since they needed to take no responsibility for it. They were able to cover up easily by quoting Roosevelt's familiar refrain that he had plenty in his present job to occupy him, and that he undoubtedly would not want to run until 1936, when he would still be only fifty-four. They made it clear that Roosevelt would do nothing to advance the boom. He was leaving for three weeks at Warm Springs. After that, late in June, he was going to Salt Lake City to the Governors' Conference, and pointedly he was declining invitations to speak at cities on the way.[11]

Roosevelt, in a confidential note to his distant cousin Nicholas Roosevelt of the New York *Times,* wrote with a reticence which would have been more touching had it been genuine:

"Don't give a thought to 1932. That date has become a positive nightmare to me and the whole family. Why can't reporters, editorial writers and the politicians let a poor devil alone to do the best he can with a very current job? As a matter of fact, I am trying to put even November, 1930, out of my thoughts until at least September first. Whether the correspondents believe it or not, my trips through the state this summer will be wholly devoid of politics." [12]

Despite all these fine protestations, Roosevelt journeyed to Salt Lake City looking more like a potential presidential candidate than a reluctant governor who would not even make a move toward a second term until autumn. He had been endorsed for the presidency by a Western senator on behalf of the West; his immediate trip into that area was entirely coincidental, but the coincidence did not dim the significance. The New York *Times* sent its seasoned Albany expert, W. A. "Baron" Warn, to cover the conference. At Albany in 1911, Warn had queried state senators on their impressions of the newcomer to their group; at Salt Lake City in 1930, Warn asked Roosevelt's fellow governors what they thought of him. Did they consider him a presidential possibility? A surprising number answered affirmatively. Republican governors, hoping that an early bloom would blight Roosevelt's candidacy, assured Warn that Roosevelt was maneuvering at the conference to secure support for the nomination.

Whether or not this was so, certainly Roosevelt was the center of attention. When the Republican mayor of Salt Lake City, John F. Bowman, delivered an address of greeting to the governors, he startled them by speculating that one of them might become a presidential nominee. "I have in mind one," Mayor Bowman declared, "who, I think, if elected, would make one of the great Presidents of the United States." A few minutes later, Governor George Dern of Utah introduced Roosevelt as the first speaker, but even without this pointed sequence of events, everyone knew to whom Bowman was referring. To make sure no one would be in doubt, Bowman later told reporters, "Of course it was Mr. Roosevelt I had in mind." [13]

When he rose to speak, Roosevelt received such a lengthy and warm ovation that later he smilingly told the governors and their wives that they had made him feel like crawling under his desk. Nor did his remarks disappoint them, for he addressed himself to the ever-deepening unemployment problem. He chose this conspicuous appearance under the national spotlight as the occasion for which he had been waiting to hurl Frankfurter's harpoon into Hoover. While he did not mention the President by name, he berated the officials in Washington for juggling figures and distorting facts to hide the seriousness of the unemployment problem. Next he criticized their techniques for dealing with economic problems, indicating in his remarks how slightly he had as yet traveled from his economic training at Harvard a quarter century before. He lambasted the Hoover Administration for having departed from the economic orthodoxy of laissez-faire and the Manchester School. They had succumbed, Roosevelt charged, to a "wholly new economic theory that high wages and high pressure selling could guarantee prosperity at all times regardless of supply and demand." Roosevelt pointed to what he regarded as the fallacy of this: "Unfortunately for some of our Washington friends this new theory that although a man cannot pull himself up by the bootstraps a nation can, came a terrible cropper when it bumped squarely into the old law of supply and demand."

Roosevelt followed his denunciation of Republican radicalism by further aligning himself with conservatives. He was guarded in his commendation of public-works spending, upon which President Hoover was placing much reliance. He pointed out that New York State had cooperated with the President to the extent of increasing its expenditures a full twenty million dollars for the fiscal year, but warned that states must not depend too heavily upon public works to ease unemployment because over any period of time they would be too big a drain on the treasuries.

Then with his habitual blithe eclecticism, Roosevelt aired his liberal proposals for unemployment insurance and old-age benefits which would not be a mere dole or government handout but rather the product of joint contributions from employees, employers, and the government. Finally, he reaffirmed his states'-rights leanings by attacking the constitutionality of the Hawes-Cooper bill to limit interstate shipment of prison-made goods.[14]

This sleight of hand, flipping before each spectator the vision he wanted most to see, impressed gubernatorial listeners, both Republican and Democratic, but impressed them less with Roosevelt's economic thinking than with his presidential aspirations. Republicans told "Baron" Warn it was a blatant bid for the presidency; the six Democrats, confining themselves to praise for the speech, admitted they were sizing up Roosevelt as a potential candidate.

One of the Democrats, Governor L. G. Hardman of Georgia (a state where Roosevelt was even more of a favorite son than in New York), announced upon his return to Atlanta that he favored a Roosevelt-Harry Byrd ticket. Hardman declared that Roosevelt was easily the outstanding personality at the Governors' Conference, and would probably be able to carry the West. This pronouncement so excited Hollins N. Randolph that he wanted to come to Albany to explain in person to Roosevelt how he could sew up the delegates of the South. To this frenzied approval, Roosevelt replied with gracious words that sounded the way his cryptic smile looked: "It was very good of Governor Hardman to say what he did." [15]

The political maestro gestured the trumpets to crescendo with the right hand but hushed the kettledrums with the left; much as he wanted the nation's attention, he did not want a serious fight for convention delegates as yet. The Democratic governors assured Warn rightly that they were not aware of any organized Roosevelt-for-President movement, for there was none. Nor did Roosevelt overlook for an instant his immediate problem, to win re-election as Governor of New York. If he lost the Governor's Mansion, the mirage of the White House would instantly dissolve. The Republicans were equally well aware of this, and combined their public jeremiads against his greedy ambition with quiet plotting to oust him from Albany in the 1930 election.[16]

Aware of the Republican planning, Roosevelt at no point ignored even the minute workings of Democratic politics in New York State. Farley continued his tireless rebuilding of an upstate organization; Roosevelt went on personally watching upstate newspapers, trying to cajole or coerce them into printing favorable news and editorials. While he was in Warm Springs in the spring of 1930, he scanned the clippings and wrote Rosenman:

"I am enclosing an editorial from the Binghamton Press in regard to the Lord-Bentley grouse bill. Will you have a talk with [Conservation Commissioner] Alec Macdonald in regard to it and suggest to Alec that he write me a letter for me to send to the Binghamton Press to show them that there is no intention of creating an open season for grouse this year, and that their editorial is based wholly on misinformation.* Further, that he, the Conservation Commissioner, will keep the season closed, as he has a right to do, by a department order. He ought to be a little indignant at the thought that the Conservation Department will encourage the extinction of ruffed grouse." [17]

It was Roosevelt's slavish attention to even such picayune homework as the Binghamton *Press's* attitude toward grouse that made him such a difficult opponent for local Republicans to discredit. For a while they toyed with the idea of running a great name against him, and tried to enlist the Secretary of State, Henry L. Stimson. But Stimson had no interest in leaving his dignified office for the hurly-burly of the hustings in New York State. His try for the governorship there years earlier had ended in debacle. Obviously the Republicans would have to fall back upon some less impressive candidate and try to make up the difference by hard work on the issues. They continued to fertilize their hardy perennial, Tammany corruption; in the summer of 1930 they also nurtured into renewed bloom that sturdy old issue of the Smith regime, Prohibition.[18]

From one point of view they were wise to do this. In recent years Prohibition had wrecked many a candidate both locally and nationally. It was as difficult to straddle the distance between the boroughs and upstate opinion as between the East and West. Morality itself could no longer stretch far enough to keep a foot in both camps without splitting up the middle, for many of those who had advocated the Great Experiment found themselves forced by growing disgust with speakeasies and crime and racketeering into a gradual switching of sides. By 1930, the moralists who believed coercion could not dry up America combined with the more thirsty opponents of Prohibition into a force strong enough to push many a candidate off the fence onto the Wet side, even though it was still a political quagmire.

On the other hand, Prohibition could be a risky issue for the Republicans to use against Roosevelt. The last victim to sink from sight in the quicksands of the Wet side (if one excepts Al Smith) had been a Republican Senator, James Wadsworth, in 1926. The fact that the Republicans must choose these dangerous grounds in 1930 indicated their desperation, and perhaps their advance nervousness over Roosevelt as a potential national candidate.

Roosevelt had no intention of wading prematurely onto the Wet

* By the time FDR left office, he had a considerable dossier on grouse in his files, as on countless other rather trivial official subjects. Nothing seemed too small for his attention.

side. For many years he had sat on the fence, his feet dangling on the Dry side, righteously demanding that his split party forget Prohibition and unite on other really vital questions. Even his home life was a straddle. Mrs. Roosevelt was a devoted Dry who kept her leanings rather quiet; Roosevelt was personally Wet, but in a decidedly moderate way – a one- or two-cocktail man.* His great concern over Prohibition was that it must not wreck the Democratic party again. From the day he assumed office as governor, he handled Prohibition in a gingerly fashion.

The State of New York had had no Prohibition enforcement law concurrent with the Federal Volstead Act since Governor Smith had signed the repeal of the Mullan-Gage Act in the early 1920's. At the very outset of his term, on January 3, 1929, Governor Roosevelt obtained from his law firm a memorandum clarifying the role of the state in Prohibition enforcement: state law-enforcement officers should arrest those violating the Federal law, but must turn them over to Federal courts, since state criminal courts could not prosecute in the absence of a state law.† Roosevelt studied this jurisdictional problem, as he explained a month after taking office, "so as to be fore-armed in case something turns up, though at the present moment there does not seem to be even a rumble of trouble at Albany." Nor did trouble develop. When an occasional Dry complained because the state was not more vigorous in preventing the collapse of Prohibition, Roosevelt was able to respond in a conciliatory fashion, "The only difference between this state and states having a state enforcement act is that offenders are tried only in the Federal Courts and not in both State and Federal Courts." [19]

At the Governors' Conference in 1929, where Roosevelt had stolen headlines by quoting Wickersham on Prohibition, he had fostered a states'-rights solution of Prohibition enforcement. There had been some logic in his approach, since Federal enforcement was pathetically weak. When New York City police were attacked for not eliminating speakeasies, Police Commissioner Grover Whalen made a telling countercharge that the Federal agents were almost totally ineffective. Of

* In the campaign summer of 1932, when he could not get a cocktail at home, he frequently drove in the late afternoon to Wappinger's Falls to drink one in the Rosenmans' back yard.

† New York equity courts did exercise concurrent jurisdiction with the Federal courts in enjoining violations (padlock cases) under the Volstead Act, and all state courts recognized the illegality of selling or possessing liquor without a permit.

the prosecutions before Federal courts in New York City, Whalen pointed out, ninety-eight per cent were being initiated by the city police. He sent a copy of his reply to the Governor.[20]

While Roosevelt and his administration were ready to counter charges of laxness from the Drys, they were equally unwilling to take any step that might offend the Wets. At no time did Roosevelt recommend restoration of a state Prohibition law. His attitude toward both sides was summed up in an ambiguous reply he had his secretary send to the Genesee Annual Conference of the Methodist Church, which called upon him to enforce Prohibition as a state obligation. Cross wrote: "Governor Roosevelt . . . is heartily in accord with enforcement of the laws of the State."[21]

Until the summer of 1930, Roosevelt continued to straddle without much difficulty. By this time the tide against Prohibition was beginning to run strong. In June and July inspired rumors crept into the newspapers that Roosevelt would write a plank which would call for home rule for the Democratic state platform. This had been his basic position as early as 1911. Contradictory reports followed. Some declared that he would continue to straddle for fear a clear-cut stand would deprive him of the 1932 nomination; others asserted that he was, on the contrary, limiting his horizons strictly to 1930, and would soon speak out clearly to prove that he was not being cautious because of Washington fever. In any event, when the Democratic state committee met on June 17, he was still noncommittal. He announced that for the duration of the summer he would be silent on all campaign issues — a wise policy since Republican orators were rapidly running out of new ammunition with which to assail him.* If he gave them no fresh target they might be reduced to comparative silence.[23]

When after the committee meeting reporters queried Roosevelt about Prohibition, he parried, "Only the press seems to think the Democratic platform will be dry." The New York *Post* editorially needled him for being cryptic instead of clear, perhaps hoping that it could force him to take a stand. If so, it made no headway, for Roosevelt promptly wrote the publisher, "Mere question marks will not cause me to go outside my duties as Governor."[24]

During the summer months, Roosevelt said little but listened a great

* Before FDR returned from Warm Springs, Rosenman reported to him that the Republican big guns were making a series of speeches against him, each receiving smaller headlines than the one before. Rosenman advised Roosevelt to make no reply upon his return because it would merely revive the publicity for these men.[22]

deal. Early in August he conferred with Smith on utility rates, and also the Wet issue. As he had done during the previous summer, he intensively toured upstate waterways on his boat, the *Inspector*, insisting as always that he was not campaigning. Wherever he went, he talked earnestly with local leaders about state issues, and in the forefront of most discussions was unemployment and Prohibition. Clearly public opinion was shifting overwhelmingly in favor of some changes. Roosevelt bided his time, absorbing more information than he dispensed.[25]

Roosevelt privately revealed his hand to Frank Gannett, powerful upstate publisher, who complained of open saloons in Buffalo. Gannett demanded that Roosevelt explain why he permitted such conditions and opposed a state enforcement act when in contrast he had vigorously cleaned up Saratoga Springs.[26]

"Unfortunately, it is not such an easy task," Roosevelt replied. "The best comparison I can make is that of a simple, isolated boil on a human anatomy which suffers in every pore and joint and vein from a chronic disease — a disease which incidentally has not been cured or even arrested, in those states which have every known form of state and local enforcement law. I think we need a new doctor." [27]

Whatever he wrote in private, Roosevelt continued throughout the summer months to make no public statement, insisting that he was Governor of New York not a candidate for any public office, and so under no obligation to discuss future campaign issues. Then suddenly, on September 9, he broke his official silence by addressing a letter to Senator Wagner, congratulating him upon his selection as temporary chairman of the Democratic state convention, which was to meet later that month. This was the vehicle for his dramatic announcement: [28]

"It is my belief that in the State of New York an overwhelming public opinion is opposed to the Eighteenth Amendment. The crux of the matter is that the Eighteenth Amendment has not furthered the cause of a greater temperance in our population. . . . I personally share this opinion."

The solution, Roosevelt declared, must be to repeal the Prohibition amendment and replace it with a new amendment which would restore to the states real control over intoxicants. In states where the people desired it, the sale of liquor through state agencies should be lawful; in states where the people felt otherwise, they should have the right to bar the sale of liquor. Furthermore, this principle of home rule should extend down to the level of cities, villages, and towns.

In some states, and Roosevelt felt New York was definitely in this category, "a reasonable sale of intoxicants through State agencies would in the opinion of the great majority of citizens of these States do much to bring about less intoxication, less corruption and bribery, and more regard and respect for law and order." For those who feared a return to pre-Prohibition conditions of disorder, he advanced the proposition that moderate Wetness would serve as a powerful barrier against the return of wringing Wetness, such as Smith supposedly advocated. Roosevelt insisted that control over the sale of liquor must rest wholly in the states or state agencies as an effective guarantee that the saloon could never come back.[29]

The crucial political question was whether this exquisitely balanced statement could appease the Wets sufficiently without alienating the Drys irreparably. Would it jeopardize the hope of the White House? Of course Roosevelt and Howe did not launch the statement until they had cautiously weighed all possible reactions both in New York State and throughout the nation. Western politicos had given Roosevelt a useful cue to his action by expressing the hope at the Governors' Conference that he would block a Tammany "dripping Wet" plank with a damp one of his own. An even more significant indication that a damp position would not kill Dry support was the observation of the chairman of the Democratic committee in the Dry state of Utah that whether Roosevelt was Wet or Dry would make little difference. Knowing all this and more, Roosevelt had acted.[30]

Reaction from all over the country immediately confirmed Roosevelt in his belief that he had taken a wise rather than a reckless risk. There were a few protests from Dixie. The Governor of South Carolina asserted that Roosevelt had removed himself as a presidential candidate, and the Chairman of the Methodist Church South wrote Roosevelt that his statement would be perfectly acceptable to every brewer, distiller, ex-saloonkeeper, and immigrant in Eastern cities. There were far fewer denunciations of this sort than Roosevelt may have expected. He commissioned Rosenman to draft a form letter to send to those who wrote letters of protest, but there was little need for it.[31]

At the same time, Roosevelt's position was Wet enough to bring him hearty congratulations from Raskob, and somewhat watered-down approval from Governor Albert C. Ritchie of Maryland, who himself hoped to float into the White House on a Wet plank. Of twenty-nine members of the Democratic National Committee who answered a New

York *Times* query, only five bluntly opposed Roosevelt's stand, and of these five, two expressed personal esteem for him in spite of this.[32]

Within the state, Roosevelt's mildly Wet position, with its emphasis upon local option, could hurt him only slightly in rural areas. To critics like the Methodist leader, he could plead that many areas would remain Dry under his plan. Since present methods were a failure anyway, to give control over liquor to local governments might even increase temperance.* This threw the problem back into the laps of the local ministers. At the same time, Roosevelt's proposal was moist enough to stir enthusiasm among Wet urban Democrats. They were in no doubt what local option would bring about in their own neighborhoods.[34]

There was yet another factor. By taking a mild but firmly damp position, Roosevelt was undercutting somewhat the appeal of candidates like Ritchie among the Wets. This was true especially among those who were ready to blame Prohibition for bad public morals and gangsterism, yet feared the return of the saloon. To Drys also, Roosevelt's program was less alarming and more potable than Ritchie's. His timing was perfect. Making the announcement in 1930, he was setting fire to the stick of political dynamite; it harmlessly burned and sputtered its way out long before the 1932 campaign. Thus Roosevelt brought to a successful conclusion the studied policy he had followed all through the 1920's, the de-emphasis of Prohibition. Even as early as 1930, the depression was becoming serious enough to divert attention from it, and whiskey mattered little to those who could not afford food for their children. By 1932, few would be left to argue with Roosevelt's slogan, "Bread not booze."

* FDR wrote privately that he regarded local option as a solution. Many rural areas which had been genuinely Dry under local option were supporting speakeasies of the worst sort under the Volstead Act. "Public opinion cannot close them today," he pointed out, "but I think it would be able to close them if we had better local option." [33]

CHAPTER XI

The First Roosevelt Landslide

> I ask the electorate of the State of New York for their support. I ask this as a rebuke to those Republicans, national and State leaders, who substituting false charges and deliberate misrepresentations, have had the cowardice to ignore the great problems and issues before the whole State.
>
> — FDR, *November 2, 1930.*

IN the early fall of 1930, a depression winter lay ahead. People were becoming increasingly disgruntled over the collapse of Republican prosperity, and Democratic prospects nationally seemed bright. Nevertheless, Republicans faced the New York election with some optimism, for they thought they had finally found an issue they could pin upon the elusive Roosevelt: the sins of Tammany. They did not have much expectation of defeating him with it, but they did hope it would furnish a knife to pare down his margin of victory drastically enough so that his political glamour and his good name would emerge from the election tarnished.[1]

Obviously Roosevelt could expect re-election; by the end of September odds were three to one in his favor. But neither the depression nor his own political dexterity during his two years as governor guaranteed him any overwhelming victory. He had a strong incentive to fight hard, for he was well aware that with the politicians and newspapermen throughout the country watching him, the degree of his success as a campaigner in 1930 would have a direct bearing upon his chances for the presidential nomination in 1932. It was vital for him to roll up a big majority, to prove himself a brilliant vote getter. It was equally important for the Republicans to stop him. For this reason, the election of 1930 in New York seemed to center more on national than state issues and seemed in some ways a test run of Governor Roosevelt against the Hoover Administration.

This was the emphasis Roosevelt wished; the Republicans tried hard to make it otherwise. Opening skirmishes of the campaign centered around each party's effort to force the other to play on its own home field. The Republicans sought to build their case against Roosevelt upon his failure to clean up the spreading cancer of Tammany wickedness in New York City. In the first eighteen months that they had fenced with him over Tammany, they had made little headway. Nevertheless, since they were weak on positive issues, they had no choice but to concentrate upon crime and corruption in New York City in the hope that they could drive a wedge between Roosevelt and his largest block of sure votes, the Tammany constituency. It was a strategy that they pursued with relentless optimism as gradually more and more noisome facts began to bubble to the surface of the steaming Tammany mudpot.

Since Roosevelt was clinging to the narrow constitutional position that he was responsible solely for the government of the state, not the city, of New York, Republicans seemed to have an opportunity if not to force him into a fight against Tammany, at least to picture him as something considerably short of the relentless crusader he had led upstate and nationwide voters to believe he was. Republicans had built Tammany into such a bugaboo during the Smith campaign of 1928 that they could almost certainly hurt Roosevelt's public stature by incessantly crying "Tiger."

For Roosevelt himself there was the irritating irony which Walter Millis pointed out: "The Governor, like many other American politicians who arose to prominence by making the organization seem blacker than it really is, now finds that if he is to go on (and the issue is the same whether the motive be personal ambition or public service) he must make the organization seem whiter than the facts permit. The Governor is caught." [2]

By the summer of 1930, a serious Republican opponent made his appearance. This was the United States Attorney for the Southern District, the New York City area, Charles H. Tuttle, who won a heroic place in the headlines by exposing and indicting an unsavory group of rascals. Most notable among them were a Brooklyn judge who had received $190,000 for obtaining a city pier lease for a steamship company and a fixer who was obtaining building permits for building construction below legal standards. The exposures were so damaging that Tammany began belatedly to sweep its own halls, but nevertheless the Socialists, Republicans, and many newspapers joined in the hue and cry for a state investigation.[3]

At this point, the Republican legislative leaders, Knight and McGinnies, fumbled again. During the spring of 1930 they had made little headway by passing a bill giving Roosevelt the authority to investigate the city government. When he vetoed it, he urged the legislature to conduct its own investigation; it did nothing, and thus left itself open to the accusation of having played politics. In July, the leaders repeated the identical mistake: they asked Roosevelt to call a special session which would grant him the power he claimed he lacked. Roosevelt parried politely with a lengthy, careful homily on home rule, convincing in view of Tammany's current self-disciplining. He added the assurance that if the local machinery already in operation broke down and it became necessary to call a special grand jury or session of the legislature, he would act promptly and use his executive power to the full. Even the rather unfriendly New York *World* defended Roosevelt's counterthrust, since it was all too obvious that once again Knight and McGinnies were pursuing political rather than reform goals. Roosevelt gloated privately that his reply made them "look more like mother geese than ever." [4]

Roosevelt had not settled the issue that simply, for Tuttle dug out even more shocking evidence that city judges were buying their offices from Tammany, or at least making suspiciously generous donations to the machine. The wife of one of these magistrates, George F. Ewald, had brought ten thousand dollars to a Tammany district leader, Martin J. Healy, at the time her husband was appointed. Tuttle was unable to carry the investigation further because Tammany men successfully invoked the Fifth Amendment to protect themselves from self-incrimination before the Federal grand jury. The task of digging deeper fell upon the Tammany District Attorney for Manhattan, Thomas C. T. Crain, himself a former magistrate. Mrs. Ewald explained to Crain that the sum was an unsecured loan; she had lost the note. Mayor Walker testified that he had appointed Ewald upon the recommendation of prominent German-Americans; obviously service to Tammany was the main criterion for appointment. In mid-August, Crain announced that the grand jury had found no indictments. Reformers furiously proclaimed that this proved the spuriousness of Tammany's investigations of Tammany.[5]

The moment had come when Roosevelt must take action if he would prove that he did not condone Tammany corruption. At this point he moved in three directions at once with such explosive energy that if anything he acted too precipitately for his own political good. Although the Tammany District Attorney, realizing his mistake, moved to reopen the case, Roosevelt, who had ordered the minutes of the grand jury sent to Albany, took it out of his hands and assigned it to the Republican Attorney General, Hamilton Ward. He supplemented this by asking a state Supreme Court justice (also Republican) to convene a carefully selected Extraordinary Grand Jury, or so-called blue-ribbon jury, before which Ward could present evidence. In addition, most notably of all, Roosevelt requested the Appellate Division of the State Supreme Court to undertake a general inquiry of the city magistrates' courts. It chose an eminently suitable referee to run the investigation — a choice which according to Lindley was actually Roosevelt's. This was Samuel Seabury, an authority on the magistrates' courts, a Democrat who was so distinguished and so zealous a reformer that no taint of Tammany could cling to him. Roosevelt had slipped in only one respect in suggesting him. Seabury was intensely ambitious politically. Before long this caused trouble for Roosevelt. But the whole performance gave an impressive picture of Roosevelt the reformer reaching the end of his patience with the bad boys of his own party when they would not, as his strictly constitutional principles told him they should, clean up their own back yard.[6]

Attorney General Ward caused Roosevelt much more immediate political discomfort; the Governor had erred in turning the Ewald bribery case over to his adversary. It did not seem to make sense in September, 1930, to accuse Roosevelt of condoning corruption or coddling Tammany, since he had ordered two vigorous investigations in place of District Attorney Crain's single ineffectual one. But that was exactly what the Republicans did on the grounds that Roosevelt expected Seabury to conduct a general investigation and ordered Attorney General Ward to limit himself to the Ewald case. Naturally Ward, who was ambitious to beat Tuttle for the Republican nomination for governor, did no such thing. Instead he and his special assistant, another Republican, Hiram C. Todd, publicly called for information on the buying and selling of offices, and daily made newspaper sensations with anonymous evidence. Even Boss Curry and other Tammany leaders granted that all these exposures would be very damaging politically, that they would cut Roosevelt's plurality in New York City by at least one hundred thousand votes, and make the election a tight one. Later in the month, Roosevelt's own advisers lamented to newspapermen that the scandals might well cut Roosevelt's lead as low as fifty thousand.[7]

Once again it looked as if the Republicans had run their foxy Governor to earth. They nominated Tuttle for governor, thus committing themselves to a campaign of exposure. Moreover, they nominated him on a Wet ticket, even though this cost him the open endorsement of cautious President Hoover. This, Republicans felt, would further cut the ground out from under Roosevelt, since they reasoned that quantities of well-to-do conservatives in New York City had voted for Smith on the Democratic ticket solely because his platform promised they might eventually buy their liquor legally again. At the same time, with Democratic Roosevelt publicly damp, there seemed no danger that they would thus lose an upstate block of Dry votes. In addition to their own clever strategy, they could count upon the continued floundering of bemired Tammany in New York City.

Tammany's troubles seemed to come to a dramatic climax on September 24, just before Roosevelt left for the convention at Syracuse, when Attorney General Ward's assistant, Todd, brought Tammany leader Curry and sixteen of his subordinates before the blue-ribbon jury and asked them to sign waivers of immunity. They had previously successfully blocked Tuttle before the Federal grand jury with the Fifth Amendment, but ordinarily testimony before a county grand jury carried immunity. Hence the demand for waivers. Again they balked.[8]

Roosevelt at once sent a stern letter to Mayor Walker declaring that whether or not these defendants were within their legal rights, for him to refuse to waive immunity was contrary to sound public policy. He asked, and his precise words were important, that "pleading of immunity by public officers in regard to public acts shall cease." Walker called in his Tammany leaders and gave them twenty-four hours in which to sign waivers of immunity, or resign. The leaders complied, but in a way which further hurt Roosevelt, for they interpreted his letter narrowly. When they appeared again before the jury they offered to sign waivers of immunity but, in keeping with Roosevelt's words, only to discuss their official acts. Todd indignantly refused to accept their limited waivers, since obviously he wanted to investigate their machinations as party leaders, not office holders.[9]

While this maneuver was under way, the Democratic convention met at Syracuse to nominate the state slate. Prominent among the display of flags and bunting the Roosevelt posters waved, dominating the auditorium as Roosevelt himself, not State Chairman Bray or Boss Curry, dominated the convention. The lethargic Bray, despite a vigorous fight on his behalf by a number of upstate county chairmen, was forced to resign as state chairman without even the sop of being nominated for attorney general. Roosevelt exchanged with him the customary public letters of deep regret, and unregretfully replaced him with the indefatigable Jim Farley. The act left no doubt as to Roosevelt's rule over upstate political leaders, and his continued pre-occupation with the campaign north of Bronx. More spectacular but less important was the way in which Roosevelt also demanded, and obtained, complete subservience from Tammany leaders.

Governor Roosevelt, not John F. Curry, was actual boss of the convention, Lindley wrote in the New York *World*, customarily so highly critical of Roosevelt's trimming his sails to the fetid air from Tammany. Roosevelt tailored the platform to fit his political strategy, which meant an emphasis upon his constructive program as governor, and a plank calling for Prohibition repeal without qualification. This last was calculated to show that the Democratic party in New York State was decidedly more Wet than the Governor or the Republicans. Al Smith, who was at outs with the city organization, put on one of his best shows in extolling Roosevelt and his program, and in drawing howls of derision against the Republicans in Washington for failing to beat the depression. He pulled from his pocket and displayed to the delegates a Hoover lucky piece from the 1928 campaign, "Good for Four Years of Prosperity." And while Smith denounced corruption, and another city Democrat, Senator Wagner, called for the ouster of bribers, the smile stayed fixed to the face of the Tiger even though it curdled a little around the edges. Tammany had, at least, the satisfaction of contributing to what was outwardly a magnificent display of Democratic harmony.

For this the Republicans had only themselves to thank. What they had overlooked in nominating Tuttle was that they had thus forced the Tammany leaders into Roosevelt's camp. Tammany men were furious over Roosevelt's letter to Walker, but they had to accept his program whatever it might be, cheer him to a fare-you-well, and scour the precincts for the votes which would re-elect him – it was their only chance to save their own skins. So while voters in Republican rural areas were apathetic and registration went up only five per cent, in New York City Tammany bore down and registration went up a spectacular seventeen per cent.[10]

The political mudpot boiled just as noisomely after the nomination as before. The Republican judge had advised the blue-ribbon jury to go beyond the Ewald affair into related matters, and it responded with enthusiasm. It called upon Roosevelt for an extension of powers, which he refused. Actually he did so because he wanted to prevent political fishing; ostensibly because he did not wish to exceed his authority as governor. He said he was following the advice of his counsel, Rosenman, and of former presidential nominee John Davis. All the red tape he could wind around the Republicans' investigative powers, in order to throw more authority to the Seabury investigation, succeeded no further than to block their funds. It was logical, then, for civic cleanup groups to campaign for private funds with which to continue the probe. They raised plenty, and consequently the jury was able to call witnesses in ever-widening circles and to create the bad impression that Roosevelt once again was hindering the cleanup.[11]

Three more judges were dragged into the investigation, one an anonymous Bronx judge, ultimately completely exonerated, the other two Roosevelt appointees. General Sessions Judge A. A. Bertini allegedly had made a large contribution to Tammany; aided apparently by Tammany's greatest criminal lawyer, Max Steuer, he made such a brilliant and confusing defense of himself that during the campaign nothing happened to him. Finally, there was a highly respected Fordham law professor Roosevelt had appointed the previous spring, Judge Joseph F. Crater, who was investigated because he had mysteriously disappeared. He was never found.[12]

While Roosevelt alternated an occasional publicized crackdown with long spells of shilly-shallying, reformers became increasingly irritated and baffled over his failure to follow up his forceful blows with sustained purposeful action. One of Roosevelt's distinguished Harvard classmates, the Reverend W. Russell Bowie, pastor of Grace Church, echoed accurately the feelings of scores of them when he chided Roosevelt for failing to go beyond his expedient statement that officials should waive immunity and testify as to their official acts:

"It is of the judgment of the whole country and of tomorrow rather than today that I am thinking. I believe that the innate idealism of America is hungering for a leader who in some conspicuous crisis such as this will cut through the entanglements of expediency and stand in the open as the unquestioned assailant of corruption in politics no matter where it is found. This great distinction I covet for you. And the time has come when it seems to me that you must either win or lose it."[13]

Bowie was correct to a degree. As Walter Lippmann in the New

York *World** and other ardent advocates of clean government carped at Roosevelt for taking a legalistic view of his powers as governor, Roosevelt lost stature among thousands of well-educated, well-informed Americans in search of a champion. This is why a great many of them regarded him as a weak governor, and to this extent his political pirouetting hurt him.

In terms of votes within New York State, the results were somewhat different. Tuttle, who appeared to better advantage in courtrooms than on village bandstands, streaked through upstate New York like an avenging angel, calling upon voters to pass judgment at the polls against their dilatory governor. Even in this Tuttle fumbled, as Arthur Krock pointed out, for while Roosevelt would not make political speeches on corruption, he did act when he had to do so. At the very time when Tuttle was denouncing him for not telling how Judge Bertini came to be appointed, Roosevelt was doing just that. Further, Roosevelt expressed his willingness to call a special session of the legislature.[15]

At Watertown, a Democratic leader reported to Farley, "Tuttle discussed none of the issues except the New York City Judges. The people here were very much disappointed, as they expected him to talk on prohibition, agriculture, and water power in this vicinity." In Malone, a disgusted Republican remarked after hearing his candidate that "if New York City was so full of corruption and needed cleaning up so bad why didn't Mr. Tuttle stay there and see what he could do instead of coming way up north to tell us all about it." [16]

Tuttle's crusade failed to pick up momentum partly because voters were more concerned with positive issues, partly because he was an ineffective campaigner, and finally because the corruption issue became so complicated that only a very small minority of the best informed readers could keep straight the tangle of charges and countercharges, demands and rebuttals, that accompanied each new disclosure. Keeping straight the status of each of the disclosures became more difficult than keeping up with the batting averages of the big-league baseball players. The New York *Herald Tribune* on the eve of the election tried to clear up the confusion for its readers by publishing a box score covering eleven of the men involved.† Unfortunately for the Republicans, the

* Secretary of State Henry L. Stimson after his radio broadcast against Roosevelt wrote Lippmann that he had obtained most of his ammunition from the *World*.[14]

† Some of the cases listed by the *Herald Tribune:*

"*Albert H. Vitale*, former magistrate, removed March 13, 1930 for accepting a $30,000 loan from the slain Arnold Rothstein.

average reader was more excited over baseball than corruption; the scandals lost much of their political impact through their very complexity, and the dragging out of the investigation.

When an inquiring reporter asked Kingston retailers what effect the issue would have on the vote for Roosevelt, a very few replied they thought it would be considerable. The consensus ran about as follows:

Henry Schultz, clerk: "No noticeable effect at all. Nobody voted upstate for Governor Roosevelt because of New York City and there was corruption there long before he had office and there will be corruption there when we are all dead and buried."

George Lewis, store manager: "I'm an enrolled Republican but I think Tuttle is using a low-down argument. I don't think it will gain him any votes."

Louis Kantrowitz, merchant: "That argument is a bunch of ——. What I want to know is what happened to the Hoover prosperity — let New York run its own city." [18]

As for Roosevelt, he campaigned almost as though the corruption issue did not exist. Tuttle stung him at the outset by asserting that the campaign would show whether New York would have a governor bigger than Tammany Hall. Roosevelt retorted in his informal acceptance address before the Democratic state convention that he was puzzled as to whether Tuttle was "running for Governor of the State of New York or for District Attorney of New York County." When Tuttle remarked a few days later that the Governor had armed the blue-ribbon jury with only a wooden hatchet, Roosevelt snapped, "Permit me to inform him that I did not give the Grand Jury a hatchet of any kind, wooden or otherwise. Their weapons are the scales of justice and the sword of justice, to protect the innocent as well as to punish the guilty." With these ringing words on behalf of fair play,

---

"*George F. Ewald*, resigned magistrate, indicted by Federal Grand Jury July 7 for using the mails to defraud in connection with the sale of stock. Later indicted by the extraordinary grand jury, accused of paying $10,000 for his magistracy, as was his wife . . .

"*Martin J. Healey*, Tammany district leader and Deputy Commissioner of Plant and Structure, indicted . . . for receiving $10,000 in connection with the appointment of Ewald to the bench. . . .

"*Thomas J. Tommaney*, former chief clerk in Sheriff Farley's office . . .

"*Amadeo A. Bertini*, Judge of the Court of General Sessions . . .

"*Joseph F. Crater* [disappearance being investigated] . . . "

and three others with similar identifying tags and brief explanations.[17]

Roosevelt fell silent on the corruption issue and remained so for weeks.[19]

Instead, Roosevelt put his entire emphasis upon the positive program that he was trying as a hard-working and efficient executive to achieve for the people of his state. He had never the slightest intention of campaigning on anything so negative as corruption. As he pointed out to Rosenman, he never believed in allowing his opponent to pick the battlefield upon which to fight; if the opponent picked one, let him fight upon it alone. Roosevelt followed this policy meticulously in 1930. He not only ignored Tuttle's choice of issues, but avoided mentioning Tuttle's name in speeches.

Rather, Roosevelt chose to emphasize the concrete achievements of his governorship. In part he utilized novel techniques to publicize them. One was the talking motion picture, still relatively new in 1930. He made a film, *The Roosevelt Record,* for exhibition at political rallies. Howe made a survey of radio reception in each county of the state and another survey of theaters willing to rent for rallies, their seating capacity, and their charge. Through the outlets that Howe arranged, Roosevelt's voice came pouring forth listing his fine gubernatorial achievements. It was a successful sortie into technological political warfare.[20]

But even this came later, for during the first week after his acceptance, Roosevelt professed not to be campaigning at all. He could not spare the time, he said, from one of his most serious tasks as governor, the preparation of the executive budget. He was spending his every minute, he wanted it known, conferring with financial experts. A shrewd newsman for the Kansas City *Star*, E. G. Pinkham, who visited Roosevelt's Sixty-fifth Street house during the week of budget preparation, reported this dedication to higher things with somewhat less than the desired reverence:

"That budget is an engrossing thing. By count there were, within an hour, 156 men going up the stairs . . . to help him with it. While waiting in the broad hall, the walls of which are hung with pictures of ships — hundreds of them . . . — they stood in groups shoulder hugging and exchanging budget information in low hissing whispers. . . . The 156 slowly budget their way upstairs and down again, while a new 156 or more come budgeting in the front door. I never saw so many financial authorities in one place before. I am struck with awe. If I had seen them in Madison Square Garden I would have taken them for politicians."

The budget would take two weeks to prepare, Roosevelt told the *Star* reporter. "I will give Mr. Tuttle that time in which to tell the people of New York all he knows about Tammany," he declared. "I am being liberal I think. Probably he could tell all he knows in two hours. But I give him two weeks. By that time I predict the state will be ready to hear about the real issues of this campaign."

As always, Roosevelt faced the campaign with keen anticipation. "He has a tremendous zest for things, especially for a fight," Pinkham reported. "He exhibits a joyousness of spirit in everything he does; its manifestations are an animated countenance, a snapping of fingers, a jerking of the head, and an explosive and infectious laugh." [21]

Although he was full of animal vitality, Roosevelt again worried about the possibility that Republicans might try to whisper votes away from him because of his nearly useless legs. There was some basis for alarm, since an anonymous canard of the vilest sort was being mailed around the country, to the effect that the cause of Roosevelt's incapacity was not polio but syphilis.* Roosevelt's assistant secretary sent a copy of the circular to Howe with the explosive comment, "No one has seen this but myself. Honestly I could murder for much less." [22]

Through his first term as governor, Roosevelt had been careful to correct newspapers which printed misstatements about his health. When the Elmira *Advertiser* had declared that the office was severely taxing his strength, he had written a lengthy protest, not for publication, to the editor. With the campaign about to begin, Roosevelt acted dramatically to forestall both decorous editorials and indecent rumors about his poor physical state. He did not trust that it would be enough to display himself dynamically on campaign throughout the counties, or to let his record as a vigorous, hard-working governor speak for itself. He obtained proof positive that he was in splendid condition by having himself examined in New York City by a group of physicians representing insurance companies. This was on October 3, when he had just returned from the Syracuse convention, where he had done much politicking and very little sleeping. He passed so successfully that, despite the state of his legs, twenty-two companies granted him policies totalling $560,000 at the normal rates, and offered him a

* The Fort Worth lawyer who sent a copy to FDR's secretary remarked that while he had given no especial thought to the next convention, the circular had the effect of enlisting him as one of FDR's active supporters for the presidential nomination.

million dollars' worth if he wanted it. The Georgia Warm Springs Foundation was to be the beneficiary.

Before assembled newspapermen, Roosevelt accepted the policies on October 18. On behalf of the physicians, Dr. Edgar W. Beckwith, Medical Director of the Equitable Life Assurance Company, publicly told Roosevelt that it had rarely been his privilege as an examining physician for life insurance to see such a splendid physical specimen. Dr. Beckwith told the newspapermen that Roosevelt passed a better examination than the average man. Insurance companies would not grant policies above fifty thousand dollars except to extraordinarily good risks. Roosevelt's physical condition at forty-eight was comparable to that of a man of thirty.*

When the doctor pointed out that Roosevelt's chest expansion was five and a half inches compared with an average of three and a half, a reporter inquired how that compared with Jack Dempsey. "Better," replied Dr. Beckwith. Roosevelt grinned and added, "Dempsey is an 'ex'; I'm not." [24]

Remaining a champion, as Roosevelt knew, meant attention to a multitude of details while preparing for the main bout. Roosevelt had neglected none of them. In his two years as governor, he had kept attentive toward voters' interests, and had through crisscrossing the state kept himself in their eyes. He had continued diligent in his fight for a favorable press. Several of the New York City papers favored him, and a scattering upstate. The circulation of the Republican ones north of the Bronx was 712,000, of Democratic ones only 77,000; but Roosevelt noted among the independent ones, with a total circulation of 834,000, several which were favorable toward him.[25]

Under Roosevelt's eye, Farley had done his work well in organizing Democratic workers upstate. There were nine thousand election districts in the state, which meant, as Farley liked to point out, that if a diligent worker in each got only ten additional Democrats to the polls, it would add 90,000 votes to the margin of victory.[26]

Finances, always a headache for Democrats, were doubly so in a

* FDR weighed 182 pounds, normal for his height of six feet one and one half inches; his waist measured 37 inches. His blood pressure was 128, "a little better than gilt-edged for a man of forty-eight." He had originally had paralysis of the lower abdomen, both thighs, and legs; the abdominal muscles were entirely recovered, and the thigh muscles to a considerable extent. He had no internal weaknesses. Dr. Beckwith wrote FDR privately, "Frankly, I have never before observed such a complete recovery in organic function and such a remarkable degree of recovery of muscles and limbs in an individual who had passed through an attack of infantile paralysis such as yours." [23]

depression year. Howard Cullman, Commissioner of the Port of New York, who already was spectacularly combining the cigar business with Broadway theatricals, again as in 1928 faced the problem of fund raising. As early as June, Roosevelt called upon him to raise forty or fifty thousand dollars in order to print a considerable quantity of campaign literature that was being prepared. Cullman set about raising the money reluctantly, for he feared that it would interfere with obtaining substantial contributions in the fall. He estimated that it would take three to four hundred thousand dollars to finance a successful campaign.[27]

Surprisingly, campaign contributions came in much better than Cullman expected. In the end he had collected more money for the gubernatorial campaign than he had in any other year except 1928. Since it came into various committees, it was difficult to estimate the total. The Democratic party officially reported expenditures of $128,000 and a deficit of $27,000 compared with an official Republican report of $276,000 in expenditures and a $103,000 deficit. However, through other committees, the Democrats gathered more money. Cullman reported to Howe after the campaign that he had spent $167,000, and had contributed another $30,000 to the state committee. Of the total, $25,000 was for radio time. With the stakes so high, Roosevelt himself contributed liberally from his comparatively modest personal resources. He gave $2500 to the Independent Citizens' Committee for Roosevelt and Lehman, an additional $1300 to the Democratic party, and $500 to the Dutchess County Democrats. His mother contributed an additional $2000.* Gauged by election results, it was money well invested.[28]

Some of the funds went into the women's work, which Mrs. Roosevelt earlier in the '20s had done much to help make effective in New York. Roosevelt and Farley both recognized the substantial contribution women could make in getting out the vote. They placed Mary (Mollie) Dewson, a hearty bundle of energy, in charge of women's activities. Roosevelt armed her with issues that would make a special appeal to housewives. He assigned to Rosenman the task of writing a handbill or flier which graphically illustrated how much it cost to operate stoves, irons, and other electrical appliances in New York cities

* Herbert Lehman and his family were again the heaviest contributors, followed by the Morgenthaus. Other notable contributors were: Alfred E. Smith, Gordon Rentschler, President, National City Bank, Vincent Astor, John Raskob, Cleveland Dodge, Mrs. Caspar Whitney, August Heckscher, Nathan S. Jonas of Manufacturers' Trust Company, William H. Woodin, Ralph Pulitzer, Felix and Paul Warburg, Samuel Seabury ($250), and Archibald B. Roosevelt, son of Theodore Roosevelt ($100).

compared with Canadian cities. Miss Dewson put three stenographers to work writing personal letters to every woman whose name she received from the state committee, requesting each one to take the handbill to all the women in her community who were not strong Republicans or Democrats and explain to them Roosevelt's proposals to reduce electric rates. The Democratic women liked the flier, and put it to such effective use that in some women's circles the 1930 election came to be known as the "waffle-iron campaign." [29]

With equal care, Roosevelt courted another interest group, organized labor. His and Lieutenant Governor Lehman's effective mediation in several strikes had earned commendation from both labor and management. In the summer of 1929, the state Federation of Labor had placed in its record strong approbation of Roosevelt. Only at one point did he slip, and this was relatively unimportant. At the Salt Lake City Governors' Conference, in pursuing his states'-rights position, he had asserted strongly that he regarded a Federal bill to bar prison-made products from interstate commerce as being unconstitutional. President William Green of the American Federation of Labor hauled him up short, and he quickly recanted with equal vigor. This cleared up, Green and the American Federation of Labor endorsed Roosevelt for re-election before the end of August. "Labor has very seldom secured the enactment of so many measures," Green wrote, as under Governor Roosevelt's "personal inspiration and leadership." [30]

While Roosevelt was getting all these details well in hand, he was shaping painstakingly the keystone of his campaign, the speeches. He set Howe, his law partner, Basil O'Connor, and his counsel, Sam Rosenman, to work drafting them. Rosenman, the principal work horse of the drafting team, had come to grasp Roosevelt arguments and phrasing so well during his two years' seasoning that he was able to turn out drafts which required fewer corrections than those prepared by others. As with the "waffle-iron handbill," Roosevelt sought the concrete and telling detail with which to smite the Republicans. That spring, in sending some material to Professor Frankfurter for checking, he had explained, "Unfortunately, in politics one has to use illustrations that are simple and appeal to the average citizen." Furthermore, Roosevelt emphasized to Rosenman, the speeches must attack Republican leaders rather than voters, since if he were to win he must lure hundreds of thousands of normally Republican voters to his ticket.[31]

As for the ground upon which he chose to fight while Tuttle was thrusting his anticorruption lance into empty air, on the negative side it involved an attack upon Tuttle's sincerity on Prohibition, and, far more important, a major sally against the Republican administration in Washington. This use of the depression issue could not only be effective in New York State, but could attract to Roosevelt the kind of attention he wanted in journals throughout the United States. On the positive side, Roosevelt developed again and again graphic expositions of the program for which he had been fighting in New York State: power development and regulation, public works and construction of hospitals and prisons, labor legislation and old-age pensions, and, always, aid to the farmers.[32]

Prohibition seemed to give Roosevelt the greatest delight because the Dry vote was more of a menace to Tuttle than to him. Republican Drys were angry at Tuttle, who had been in effect the chief Prohibition prosecution officer in New York City, for his switch to a Wet position. In retaliation for his betrayal, they threatened either to vote for Roosevelt or nominate a bone-Dry third candidate. The Republican chairman of one of the Prohibition groups, the National United Committee for Law Enforcement, urged Roosevelt to force Tuttle to commit himself on local option. "We plan to have part in the New York campaign, opposing both old party Wet candidates, if there is a Dry one," the chairman wrote frankly to Roosevelt, "and many if not most of us voting for the Democratic candidate if there is no independent Dry one, providing he does not weaken and wobble on the investigations." Roosevelt replied eagerly that he would certainly find out where his distinguished opponent stood, and warned the chairman not to believe the misleading statements in New York newspapers attacking his stand on corruption. Whether or not Roosevelt's blandishments brought him many Dry votes, they certainly failed to drive them to Tuttle. After much pulling and hauling, the Drys nominated Professor Robert Paris Carroll of Syracuse University, granting that it would aid Roosevelt, but feeling nevertheless that the Republicans deserved punishment for nominating a Wet. Carroll announced that he would ignore Roosevelt during the campaign in order to expose the sinister forces around Tuttle.[33]

Beginning with his informal acceptance of the nomination, Roosevelt took sharp advantage of the Republican discomfort over Prohibition with a gay sally against the leaders for trying to make their party in New York "an *amphibious ichthyosaurus* equally comfortable whether wet or dry, whether in the sea or on the land or up in the air." The following week, in his second acceptance speech (the formal one)

Roosevelt again prodded Tuttle, asking him the absurd question whether he would sign a state Prohibition-enforcement act — absurd because there was practically no chance the legislature would ever pass one. "Who is hedging now?" Roosevelt inquired. "Oh yes, 'wet to the wets and dry to the drys.' * The same old story of Republican hypocrisy." [35]

These digs were embarrassing to Tuttle as he journeyed about rural New York, trying to pacify the Dry wings of the Republican party. At first he attempted this through quiet talks with leaders while in his speeches he maintained silence on Prohibition. By mid-October, because strategy of this sort laid him open to a Wet defection from the party, he abandoned this line of approach and during a radio broadcast at Rochester came out strong for repeal.[36]

While Tuttle squirmed about the state, pronged on the horns of the Prohibition dilemma, Roosevelt drove ahead rapidly with the campaign issue of his own choosing: the depression. In the peroration of his acceptance address, a part of each speech that he always wrote himself, he deliberately threw down the gauntlet to Hoover: "Lack of leadership at Washington has brought our country face to face with serious questions of unemployment and financial depression." In subsequent speeches he elaborated upon the challenge. He blamed the Republicans for not having put a damper on the flames of speculation in 1928 and 1929, for having after the crash concealed its seriousness with falsely optimistic statements, and for failing to undertake swift, decisive action — "nothing happened but words." [37]

It was a weighty gauntlet, but with Roosevelt well out in front, it was one which Hoover's political angel should have advised him to ignore. No President needs to accept the challenge of an ambitious governor; to do so can only enhance the governor's cause. Thanks to the Republican split upstate and the damping effect of the Prohibition issue, Roosevelt was certain of re-election whether or not Tuttle

* In one respect there was validity to FDR's jibe. The Republicans had tried so hard to hedge on Prohibition that, while nominating the Wet Tuttle for governor, they had paired with him as nominee for lieutenant governor Caleb Baumes, militant Dry and author of an act heavily penalizing habitual criminals. FDR egged on the New York *Times* to make Baumes commit himself during the campaign. After the election, Howe turned out a little jingle:

Should dear old Baumes be forgot,
Who did so much for crime,
Who though he tried to be half dry
Was all wet all the time? [34]

could make the corruption charges pay at the polls. By throwing the weight of his administration against Roosevelt, President Hoover would only lend heightened importance to the New York contest, and make the coming defeat appear a loss for his administration, not just for an ambitious Federal attorney. Yet this was the trap into which Hoover fell.

New York Republican leaders, well aware of Tuttle's sad bogging down and fearful that too thorough a lambasting would wreck their organization, pressured Hoover into sending Henry L. Stimson to the hustings. The Olympian Secretary of State carried with him the prestige of the Hoover Administration. Hoover also sent Secretary of War Patrick Hurley, Assistant Secretary of War Trubee Davidson, and Under Secretary of the Treasury Ogden Mills. In unlimbering these big guns from his cabinet Hoover may, as he told Stimson, have been simply giving in to the strong urging of the New York leaders. Beyond this, however, the President regarded the fight in New York as critical. He was thoroughly angry over what he considered to be deliberately political bear raids on the stock market, causing loss and distress throughout the country.* Quite possibly the question of Roosevelt's re-election was beginning to assume the proportions of a moral issue in Hoover's mind, and in this area he would never hesitate to act, regardless of consequences.[39]

Each of the cabinet speeches followed a significant pattern; each was divided between praise of the Hoover Administration and criticism of Roosevelt's failure to cope with Tammany. These high-level attacks worried Roosevelt and his advisers, who feared they would carry weight with voters. Roosevelt decided the way to counter them was with ridicule. He instructed Rosenman and O'Connor to develop the issue of Federal interference in a state election for the last speech in New York City, the one which would receive the most newspaper attention.[40]

Then, on November 1 at Carnegie Hall with the Tammany greats seated on the platform, Roosevelt addressed himself strongly to the charges of condoning corruption which Republicans had been making against him from within the state and from Washington. From start to finish, charged Roosevelt, they had tried to cover up their miserable

* Stimson's speech at least seemed more important to Washington leaders than to New York Republicans. Mills had to talk strongly to them over the telephone, comparing Stimson's intervention to what Chief Justice Hughes's would be, in order to get Stimson's address scheduled at a good radio time.[38]

failure to support a positive program like his in the realm of power, agriculture, and social welfare by misrepresenting and distorting a local situation in New York City. They had tried, he claimed, to make the people of New York City think that the greater part of their 220 judges were corrupt, that the judiciary were no longer worthy of their confidence, and that neither Roosevelt nor the Democratic party in the city or state would lift a finger to punish the guilty. Roosevelt asserted:

"I, as a citizen of the State and as Governor, resent this campaign, as every person in this State who knows me, and who believes in honest and decent government, resents it. . . .

"If there are corrupt judges still sitting in our courts they shall be removed. They shall be removed by constitutional means, not by inquisition; not by trial in the press, but by trial as provided by law." [41]

As for the statesmen from Washington who were airing these charges, Roosevelt wove a crisp and caustic attack upon them through the warp and woof of his speech. What qualified these "men of the finest character" to come from the Republican national administration to instruct the people of New York how to manage their state affairs? One, Hurley, was from Oklahoma and knew nothing about New York State, Roosevelt pointed out; the other two, Stimson and Mills, had both run for Governor of New York, campaigning with the same kind of tactic, and had been defeated. Roosevelt next inquired, were they then qualified by success in Washington to instruct New Yorkers? He answered his rhetorical question emphatically:

"They and their party, this present national administration, came before this State two years ago soliciting the votes of its people on representations, promises, and prophesies. They were the originators of sound business; they were its protectors. Under them prosperity had always prevailed, and only under them could prosperity continue. Poverty was on its way to be abolished. There is no need for me to demonstrate to you how false were those representations. . . .

"I say to these gentlemen: We shall be grateful if you will return to your posts in Washington, and bend your efforts and spend your time solving the problems which the whole nation is [bearing] under your administration. Rest assured that we of the Empire State can and will take care of ourselves and our problems." [42]

And as Roosevelt left the cheering mob, he himself could rest assured that victory at the polls would be his by a substantial margin, and that the ballots would establish him as the major contender against the Republican administration in Washington.

It had been an easy campaign for him; Eleanor Roosevelt remembers it as one of the least demanding. Farley, after canvassing the state, wanted to predict victory by a margin of more than six hundred thousand votes. Roosevelt demurred because he did not want party workers to become overconfident and let down in their work for Democratic assembly candidates. Further, he warned Farley that if the estimate proved wrong, the public would never again believe a political prophecy coming from him. So Farley scaled it down to 350,000, still a startling figure. Farley's private prediction was too optimistic even for Roosevelt, who put the highest figure he himself could estimate into a pool he formed for some twenty correspondents who traveled with him on the campaign. It was 437,000. But when the votes were counted and the margin of victory exceeded not only his guess but even Farley's, Roosevelt eliminated himself from the pool and awarded the prize he was donating, a Brooks Brothers suit, to the next highest guesser, James Kieran of the New York *Times,** whose estimate was 300,000.[43]

As for President Hoover in Washington, he kept his guesses to himself, but they were not making him happy, for he seemed to Stimson "anxious and nervous to have the election over." † And he well might be, for when the count was complete, it showed the Republicans had lost heavily throughout the country; the House of Representatives seemed slipping out of their grasp. Nowhere was the debacle as overwhelming as in New York State. Roosevelt won re-election by the staggering plurality of 725,000 votes, almost twice that of the peerless vote-getter Smith in his best year. Moreover, he had achieved the seemingly impossible by carrying Republican upstate New York by a plurality of 167,000 votes.

* FDR sent Kieran to his old friend and Harvard classmate, Owen Winston of Brooks Brothers, with a note requesting, "Will you please see that your tailor does a very good job on a very good suit for him?"

† On the very day that FDR delivered his attack upon the Hoover cabinet, Stimson deplored in his diary "the ever-present feeling of gloom that pervades everything connected with the Administration." He wrote, "I really never knew such unenlivened occasions as our Cabinet meetings. When I sat down today and tried to think it over, I don't remember that there has ever been a joke cracked in a single meeting of the last year and a half, nothing but steady, serious grind, and a group of men sitting around the table who apparently had no humanity for anything but business. . . . How I wish I could cheer up the poor old President and make him feel the importance of a little brightness and recreation in his own work." [44]

An analysis of the 1930 vote indicates several interesting things: While only 70.6 per cent of the registered voters upstate went to the polls, 91.1 per cent did in New York City. This would seem to indicate that because of Prohibition and the depression, some Republican voters upstate stayed home, while in the city Tammany fought for its existence by getting out nine voters out of ten. The depression, being more sharply felt in the city among wage earners, made it easier for Tammany to get out the Democratic vote.

Roosevelt's achievement in carrying upstate New York was on close examination not as spectacular as it seemed, for the Prohibition ticket had pulled 181,000 votes there, almost all of them presumably from Republicans. Without this diversion of votes he probably would not have carried upstate New York, for the combined vote of Tuttle and Carroll there was 875,000 compared with his 843,000. He had carried forty-three upstate counties compared with fourteen for Tuttle, but in twenty-six of his counties, the Republican-plus-Prohibition vote for governor was greater than the Democratic. Singularly enough, while Roosevelt's managers during the next two years made his upstate victory one of their strongest claims for support throughout the United States, almost no one pointed to the Prohibition party's assistance.

Even without this assist from the Drys, Roosevelt had established himself as a truly formidable vote getter. In 59 of the 62 counties of the state, his vote had exceeded the total Democratic assembly vote; in every county outside of New York City he had received a larger vote than his party enrollment. Here was proof positive that Governor Roosevelt could win Republican votes.[45]

The depression, Prohibition, the Democratic positive program, the deficiencies of Tuttle and the Republican party,* Farley's new upstate organizations and Tammany's Herculean efforts in the city – all these plus Roosevelt's magnetic appeal had contributed to the result. Whatever the weight of each contributing factor, the end was already clear: the Democrats seemed likely to capture the presidency two years hence, and their most probable leader was Roosevelt. For Roosevelt, heading back to Albany for two more years as a depression governor, this was a splendid challenge and a serious liability.

* Howe celebrated Tuttle's debacle in an unkind jingle:

Should Charlie Tuttle be forgot,
To history left unknown,
He banked on the reformers' votes,
And they all stayed at home.[46]

CHAPTER XII

A Fast Start

I am not in any sense a candidate for 1932 — partly because I have seen so much of the White House ever since 1892, that I have no hankering, secret or otherwise, to be a candidate.

— FDR TO MRS. CASPAR WHITNEY, *December 8, 1930.*

THE Democrats nominated their President yesterday, Franklin D. Roosevelt," Will Rogers commented on the day after the 1930 election. This was not just another cowboy wisecrack, as it would have seemed two years earlier. Rogers was voicing the sober view of countless Americans; hundreds of them from all over the country sent their congratulations to the man they hoped and expected would become the next President.[1]

Newspapers throughout the country, which had followed Roosevelt fairly closely during the campaign, predicted his probable nomination, although not all of them relished the prospect. In Charleston, South Carolina, the *News and Courier* admonished its readers amidst the hullabaloo about Roosevelt not to forget the steadfast states'-rights merits of conservative Governor Albert Ritchie of Maryland.[2]

Even in far parts of the world, journals took garbled notice of Roosevelt's rising presidential star. From India, Kermit Roosevelt wryly clipped and forwarded to his distant cousin an article reporting that "Franklin Roosevelt, son of Mr. Theodore Roosevelt . . . is regarded as certain to be Democratic candidate." [3]

All this excitement came as no surprise to Roosevelt. Before the 1930 campaign had really begun, Roosevelt was already prominent as a prospective Democratic nominee. He did not try to disguise the fact when Jouett Shouse, by no means friendly to his cause, invited him to be one of four Democrats to broadcast nationally for the party during the campaign. Roosevelt declined on the grounds that he did not wish to say anything national until after the election. He said he expected one of the Republican pleas to be "that a vote for F. D. R.

will only build him up as an opponent of friend Hoover later on." Roosevelt added with the modesty expected of him, "– all of which is pure rot but will catch some Republican voters if I show the slightest sign of national participation." [4]

With his overwhelming election majority under his belt, Roosevelt was the prime target not only of the Republicans but also of all rival Democratic contenders for the nomination. He could also be certain of undercover opposition from the conservative managers of the Democratic national headquarters, Shouse, Raskob, and their talented publicity writer, Charles Michelson. Already before the end of November, Roosevelt was fearful that Democratic National Committee publicity was being subtly aimed against him.[5]

The danger was that if Roosevelt continued in deed as well as outward appearance the reticence that the American political tradition seems to demand of candidates for the presidency, his opponents might well destroy him before he could openly announce himself a candidate. If he followed custom, he could not announce his candidacy until the beginning of 1932. Since it took a two-thirds vote to nominate in the Democratic convention, his rivals, both open and covert, needed control only one third plus one of the delegates. This was an undertaking far from impossible against even a highly popular candidate. Roosevelt, when he was a political tyro, had seen Governor Woodrow Wilson of New Jersey enjoy the same wide popularity yet nearly lose the nomination. Like Wilson, Roosevelt could not avoid being a conspicuous target, but unlike Wilson he was so experienced in politics that he knew what to do about it: get further out in front, and get there quickly.

This called for no change in Roosevelt's public position. He continued personally to dictate dozens of charming little letters, imaginatively sketching all sorts of reasons why he would find sitting in the White House an unthinkably distasteful task. He seldom admitted to anyone that he was seeking the candidacy, even among his intimate advisers, with the single obvious exception of Howe. This was true even on the jubilant day after the 1930 election. On the rainy afternoon of that day, in the train taking Roosevelt back to Albany, the atmosphere was as radiant within as it was dismal without. The people round Roosevelt, including Missy Le Hand, Grace Tully, Sam Rosenman, and Doc O'Connor, joked merrily with him about the presidential nomination. Roosevelt, sharing their mood, laughed heartily at their witticisms, but even among these trusted followers at no point did he ever say yes or no.[6]

They all assumed that Roosevelt was actively running. Indeed, he had already made his decision to begin an aggressive campaign for convention delegates. Presumably he did so with Howe at a conference so secret that even Farley did not know of its existence. There must have been such a conference, for even Howe would not have dared take such a momentous step without thrashing out all of the pros and cons with Roosevelt in advance. But when Howe sat down with Farley on the morning after the election, he managed to give Farley the impression that the two of them were making a great policy decision on the spot without consulting Roosevelt. Together they drafted a statement which Farley gave to the reporters in his own name on his own responsibility. Farley proclaimed:

"I fully expect that the call will come to Governor Roosevelt when the first presidential primary is held, which will be late next year. The Democrats in the Nation naturally want as their candidate for President the man who has shown himself capable of carrying the most important state in the country by a record breaking majority. I do not see how Mr. Roosevelt can escape becoming the next presidential nominee of his party, even if no one should raise a finger to bring it about." [7]

Not sure just how Roosevelt would feel about the statement, Farley telephoned him long distance from New York as soon as the train reached Albany. It was, amazingly, the first time Farley had mentioned the presidency to Roosevelt. Amused, Roosevelt replied in effect, "Whatever you said, Jim, is all right with me." [8]

As for Roosevelt, he rode through the streets of Albany, accompanied by a brass band, bombs, and redfire, waving to rain-drenched crowds who hailed him as the next President. It remained only for him to write out for reporters his own statement:

"I am giving no consideration or thought or time to anything except the duties of the Governorship. I repeat that now, and to be clearly understood, you can add that this applies to any candidacy, national or otherwise, in 1932." [9]

Thus Roosevelt faultlessly went through every step of the political minuet. Even the New York *Times* correspondent accepted outward appearances by writing that Farley's statement came as a considerable surprise to Roosevelt.[10]

This left Roosevelt free to pursue his great goal with increased vigor. On his own level from the Executive Mansion he had to continue in crayfish fashion: a suggestion (even before the election) to Governor Harry Byrd of Virginia that he come to Warm Springs to confer on taxes along with youthful Governor-elect Richard Russell of Georgia; quantities of invitations to Democratic dignitaries to attend Roosevelt's second inaugural in Albany; and large numbers of requests to political leaders interested in his candidacy that they come visit him at the Executive Mansion. When a Kansas City friend of Boss Tom Pendergast offered his services, Roosevelt replied by inviting him to Albany. More than a year later the friend arrived—with Pendergast.[11]

At the same time, in New York City, Roosevelt's chief of staff, Howe, took this as the strategic moment to shift to a somewhat more open position. As always he remained the main adviser on political strategy and the master political letter writer. For him, as for Roosevelt, the landslide meant a shift in tempo, a beginning of large-scale operations. He was no longer able to operate ostensibly as Secretary to the National Crime Commission; he could no longer finance his correspondence on a shoestring. Many of his letters should from this time on go out from an organization avowedly devoted to Roosevelt's cause, yet they should not bear Roosevelt's signature. Further, an organization could solicit funds; Roosevelt obviously could not. Consequently, Howe rented a few rooms on the seventh floor at 331 Madison Avenue across from the Biltmore Hotel and hired back a few of the most efficient girls who had worked for him in the gubernatorial campaign. Thus equipped, in mid-January he opened a letter-writing and publicity factory of a scope and efficiency new to American politics. This was the "Friends of Roosevelt."

While Howe could plan clever political tactics and conduct a prodigious correspondence in Roosevelt's name, he was no better fitted than before to appear publicly in Roosevelt's behalf. His protégé Farley affectionately remembers him as he was in this period, wearing trousers that had no more crease than burlap sacks, the ultimate goal for ashes that drifted down his shirt front from his Sweet Caporal cigarettes. Nor had his tongue become better tailored with the years. He terrorized the girls in his office, but through long experience they had come to appreciate his fairness and wit. Consequently they rather savored his outward roughness, and worshiped him nevertheless.

Lela Stiles listened with awe one day while Howe argued loudly and profanely over the telephone with Roosevelt in Albany. Roosevelt was about to go for a swim, which gave Howe the opportunity for a crowning epithet. "Well, go ahead, dammit," Howe yelled, "and I hope to God you drown!"

A few political insiders could appreciate this sort of forthright treatment, but strangers at times regarded him as unpredictably rude. At best, he would look them over critically, Farley remembers. If he approved of them, he would tell them in substance, "You make a good appearance and you seem to know something about politics and to have some influence. I think you can be useful to Franklin." If he did not approve he could be devastating. Frank Walker has told Miss Stiles that he once pleaded in advance with Howe to be nice to a wealthy potential contributor, Joseph P. Kennedy. But when Walker brought Kennedy in, Howe sat behind his desk, his head on his arms, his eyes closed. Walker coughed politely, but Howe did no more than open one eye and glare at Kennedy. It was several minutes before he would even sit up and take part halfheartedly in the conversation.[12]

The surprising thing was that Kennedy contributed liberally in spite of Howe. Since others might not take so well to Howe's acid treatment, and since the asthmatic little man was overworked anyway, Roosevelt needed additional lieutenants who could raise funds and conduct an open fight for delegates. No one was readier to acknowledge this need than Howe.

Roosevelt's first choice for commander in the field seems to have been Edward J. Flynn, his secretary of state, and boss of the Bronx. According to Flynn's recollection, he was invited to spend the night at the Executive Mansion shortly after the 1930 election. After dinner, with only Howe present, Roosevelt told Flynn, "Eddie, my reason for asking you to stay overnight is that I believe I can be nominated for the Presidency." Flynn offered to help any way he could. Later he recalled what happened:

"Roosevelt suggested that I should go through the country, making contacts with [his] friends and acquaintances, and begin to line up delegates. I did not agree with this suggestion, for I realized my own limitations. I was not an 'easy mixer,' indeed, found it quite difficult to move about with facility among strange people. I was no 'greeter' or hand-shaker. I felt I could do nothing effective by merely going into a state in which I knew no one, relying on the introductions Roosevelt and Howe would be able to give me. I told Roosevelt that I preferred to remain in the background, doing such work as I knew

I could do well. As a 'front man' I was not to be considered."[13]

It took still another conversation for Flynn to convince Roosevelt that he was not the man. Had he accepted, the preconvention fight might have taken somewhat different turns, since Flynn as a boss might have had some success in negotiating with other bosses for their blocks of votes. This factor and Flynn's nimbleness of mind were probably what prompted Roosevelt and Howe to make the offer. Thus far Flynn's advice on how to handle Tammany had been good; Tammany had remarkably turned out the vote for Roosevelt. Yet there were debit factors as well which emerge more clearly in hindsight. In making the offer to Flynn, Roosevelt was apparently assuming that Southern and Western delegates would come into his camp almost without persuasion. Among many of them Flynn would have been a serious liability to Roosevelt because he was openly and avowedly a political boss, which to editorial writers west of the Catskills meant "Tammany boss." Also, he was personally as well as politically Wet. His obvious skill in negotiating with brother bosses would not offset his distaste or ineptitude for gladhanding small politicos and reporters. In total, Flynn's liabilities were so serious that it seems entirely possible that Roosevelt's offer was somewhat less than sincere — a maneuver to prevent Flynn from being jealous and to obtain his wholehearted support.

In any event, Flynn did work zealously behind the scenes, helping to map policy and assisting in raising funds. He and Frank Walker themselves contributed generously; at times when the bank balance was low, Flynn personally met the payroll of the "Friends of Roosevelt." With Walker he was successful in obtaining money from a few well-to-do Democrats.* These contributors, who helped early when the need was great, so thoroughly won Roosevelt's devotion that in most instances they ultimately received substantial returns in public offices and honors.[15]

With Flynn properly placed in a most useful niche, the choice of a front man inevitably fell upon the most logical candidate, James A. Farley. Even Flynn urged Farley upon Roosevelt. As for Howe, he

* Flynn lists the following who contributed two thousand dollars or more: James W. Gerard, Guy Helvering, Colonel E. M. House, Joseph P. Kennedy, Herbert H. Lehman, Eugene Lorton, F. J. Machette, Henry Morgenthau, Sr., Dave Hennen Morris, Mrs. Sara Delano Roosevelt, Laurence A. Steinhardt, Frank C. Walker, Harry M. Warner, William H. Woodin, and Flynn himself. Farley mentions also as important preconvention contributors: William A. Julian, Jesse I. Straus, Robert W. Bingham, and Basil O'Connor.[14]

had been grooming Farley for the position during the previous two years. In almost every respect, he seemed the ideal choice. Farley had a passion for politics matched only by Roosevelt's and Howe's, yet he was not likely to debate seriously the policy decisions which they and they alone wished to make. Policies were not his specialty or even to any great extent his concern, except that he reported useful information on issues from the field. Rather he had a remarkable knack for making political friends, and inspiring them with such enthusiasm that they were willing to work hard for Roosevelt's cause.

Farley had learned his craft not in Manhattan but thirty-five miles upstate in Rockland County, where at the age of twenty-two he had been elected Democratic town clerk in Republican Stony Point. There he had mastered many of his later famous political techniques, especially the granting of small favors and the prolific writing of letters. Farley's letters, unlike Howe's, derived their significance not through their clever exposition of political questions, but as tokens of political friendship. They were as brief and personal as a hearty backslap, and the signature in green ink was as distinctive as its tall, smiling writer.

As a building-materials salesman, and as an active Elk, Farley had obtained so intimate a knowledge of Democratic politics in New York State that he had become one of the most useful workers for Al Smith. In 1923, Smith appointed him a boxing commissioner, a position which carried no salary but more than ample reward in publicity for a politically ambitious man. He was so notably successful in his work as secretary of the Democratic state committee between 1928 and 1930 that he had made his elevation to chairman inevitable. By the campaign of 1930, Farley was already enough of a celebrity in his own right for the American Tobacco Company to advertise prominently in newspapers his endorsement of Lucky Strike cigarettes.[16]

For political ends he was ready to advocate smoking Luckies and the repeal of the Eighteenth Amendment, but personally he did not smoke or drink.* He was an Irish Catholic, but he was not a city politician, and he had never been a member of Tammany. He was honest, reliable, and ready to work doggedly to the point of near exhaustion. When he ventured beyond the boundaries of New York State into relatively unknown political territory, he was humble enough to accept readily the careful preliminary coaching of Howe. There could have been no better choice of a traveling salesman to market Roosevelt among Democratic leaders from coast to coast. The building

* The cigarette advertisement did not state or imply that Farley smoked.

materials he had to sell were the bricks and mortar for the construction of an invincible Roosevelt organization. He found ready takers.[17]

Roosevelt was well aware that in Farley he had a manager competent to sell him to the nation. A few days after the 1930 election he sent Farley a warm letter expressing appreciation for Farley's achievements in the campaign. "As I went through the State," Roosevelt wrote, "I got expressions everywhere showing that no man since the days of David B. Hill has such hearty backing and enthusiastic cooperation from the organizations as you have." And Roosevelt added an analogy, the significance of which was not lost on Farley: "I have an idea that you and I make a combination which has not existed since [Governor Grover] Cleveland and [State Chairman Daniel S.] Lamont." * He invited Farley to come to Warm Springs and roll up his sleeves. Farley accepted with a will. "I will bring with me all the correspondence I have," he promised Roosevelt, "so that I may go over them with you and clear up a number of matters that require attention." A few days later, Farley entrained for Warm Springs and national politics.[18]

Henceforth, Farley was field commander. Rather typically, Roosevelt wrote in April to an ally in Seattle, "I hope you will keep in touch with Mr. Farley, who has proved to be an exceptionally able organizer." [19]

Even while the new organization was taking shape, the aggressive campaign for delegates began. Here and there Roosevelt clubs came into existence in states as widely separated as New Jersey and Arizona. They were no indication of interest on the part of professional politicians, so Roosevelt ignored these clubs. An exception was the "Warm Springs and Meriwether County Roosevelt-for-President Club" with its fifteen hundred members. Because of its folksy flavor representing Roosevelt's Southern home town, it was an excellent engine to advertise his availability. Despite his frequent disavowals of candidacy, he attended a dinner the club gave in his honor and sat blandly at the table while Governor-elect Russell declared, "Georgia is happy to have a favorite son to present to the next Democratic National Convention." Roosevelt, grinning broadly, felt he could sufficiently protect his position with a weak statement that a lot of water would go over the dam in the next two years and that the convention might nominate some candidate no one was as yet even mentioning.[20]

* Farley in his *Story* states that he treasures the letter as the only formal thanks he received from FDR for managing two gubernatorial and two presidential campaigns.

This was an isolated instance; in subsequent months he stayed free of any direct participation in Roosevelt-for-President clubs. The only outward sign he gave that he was running was his prompt personal attention to newspapers and magazines he considered unfair. He reacted especially vigorously when they warmed up charges that he was not sufficiently severe toward Tammany. The enormous New York City plurality that the machine had rolled up for him in 1930 did not increase his stature or Tammany's. As for Tammany, the New York *Times*, mild in comparison with many critics, asserted after the great victory that it was "First in war, first in peace, and first in the pockets of its countrymen." As for Roosevelt, *Time* magazine, under the guise of objective reporting, tried to smear him with the Tammany pitch: "Critics . . . openly charged that his ambition to become President had sapped his moral courage, that he did not dare break with Tammany." Roosevelt was so outraged that he had two firm letters of protest sent to the publisher, Henry Luce.* He would not even give Luce the satisfaction of signing his own name to them. Rather, although he personally dictated at least one of them, he had them sent over the signature of his secretary, Guernsey Cross.[22]

Apparently Roosevelt had no hope of converting Luce and was simply expressing his strong distaste for *Time* techniques. The magazine continued to plague him. His tactics were quite different toward George Fort Milton, who in addition to being a skillful historian was an influential Chattanooga editor. Milton, at the time an ardent Dry, had published a spirited diatribe against Roosevelt attacking him for his tie-in not only with Tammany but also with Raskob and the Wets. But Milton was allied with Roosevelt's friend Cordell Hull, and Roosevelt had hopes of winning Milton over. So he wrote blandly:

"I am wondering if you are to be in New York sometime this spring? If so, I should much like to have a talk with you. I have been reading an occasional editorial in the Chattanooga News and have deferred correcting some of the statements with the thought that it would be much easier if you and I could have a friendly chat. Do let me know if you can run up to Albany at any time." [23]

While Roosevelt personally belabored or cajoled editors, Howe and his aides were acquiring political pen pals throughout the country.

* FDR was so fearful that he might be identified with Tammany that he even wrote a letter chiding the editor of the San Jose (California) *Mercury-Herald* for declaring editorially that "Governor Roosevelt received a tremendous vote of confidence from Tammany Hall." [21]

Within a few weeks, from the new letter-writing factory on Madison Avenue, they were answering the hundreds of letters that had come in after the election. Many were from persons who might be useful in the future; they received letters encouraging them to write fully on political and economic conditions in their localities. Thus Roosevelt was able to increase the roster of his allies and improve the political intelligence system he and Howe had operated on a lesser scale since the campaign of 1920.

To increase the quantity of useful correspondents, Howe resorted to a variation of his old device, the political form letter. He used invitations to the inauguration as excellent bait to attract favorable letters from prominent Democrats. Few of them came, as Raskob and his followers noted with some joy, but many of them took the opportunity to begin a friendly correspondence, which Raskob did not take into account. In addition, Farley sent out a correspondence opener of his own, a rather dull but uncontroversial promotion piece entitled "Officers and Members of the Democratic State Committee of the State of New York." It was just as its name indicated, nothing but an organizational roster. Even this provided Farley with letters of acknowledgment from all over the country, which he followed with personal replies. Howe and Farley next mailed out a more effective pamphlet, a statistical study of Roosevelt's phenomenal vote getting in upstate New York compared with the former feeble showing of the Democrats. It was an object lesson as well as a correspondence opener.[24]

Roosevelt's lieutenants were wise to maintain as great a semblance of neutrality as possible while they built up a national correspondence. They had to avoid injuring the feelings of numerous favorite sons and, more important still, prevent open warfare with the national organization. Roosevelt tried to cooperate with the party headquarters, even though he did not always find it easy. He acted fittingly grateful toward Raskob for the heavy donations to Warm Springs, and was friendly toward Shouse. But on many policy matters there never had been, and never could be, any real agreement between the basically conservative Raskob * and the frequently progressive Roosevelt. Each fought for national leadership.[26]

* Raskob was so stamped with the General Motors and Du Pont labels that even the Republicans tried to make political capital out of it during the 1930 campaign. They issued a poster which quite untruthfully inferred that Raskob had caused the stock crash by selling short in 1929. Further, it was widely whispered (again untruthfully) that he was leading Democratic bear raids to

Even before Roosevelt took office as governor this was clear. Raskob in December, 1928, proposed a party grand conference; Roosevelt covertly fought the idea among his Democratic friends in Washington. After the election of 1930, the difference immediately became more sharp and open. With newspapers ballyhooing Roosevelt, Raskob at once undertook to demonstrate to the rank and file of Democratic politicians that leadership lay elsewhere. He even tried, despite the blackening depression, to establish as the policies of the party those of big business. He prepared an open letter to President Hoover pledging the Democrats to cooperate in the forthcoming Congress toward the end of business recovery, even to the extent of not seeking revision of the highly protectionist Hawley-Smoot Tariff. The tariff, which had gone into effect the previous June, almost doubled the average ad valorem rate of duties, and was being widely blamed by economists for a deepening of the depression.* Southerners, traditionally low-tariff in politics, and worried about the dwindling overseas markets for their cotton and tobacco, especially disliked the letter. Western Democrats fumed because it said nothing about farm relief or public-power development; city Democrats deplored the lack of any pledge of labor reform or unemployment relief. The surprising thing was that Raskob obtained on his letter the signatures of the three previous Democratic nominees for the presidency, Al Smith, John Davis, and James M. Cox, and of the two Southerners who were the Democratic leaders of the House and Senate, John Nance Garner and Joseph Robinson.[27]

Roosevelt's name was conspicuously absent. Not only was he not asked to sign, but he would not have signed if invited. Publicly he held his tongue, but privately he deplored Raskob's maneuver. "The great majority of Democrats were displeased at the method and text of that joint statement," he confided to a former secretary. "You will notice that I am keeping a most discreet silence." [28]

Raskob's success in obtaining such an impressive array of signatures gave grounds for the feeling in the party national headquarters that

---

drive the stock market downward before the 1930 election. With more justification but little point, the Republicans quoted from a *Ladies' Home Journal* article to prove that Raskob had encouraged people to buy stocks in the summer before the crash.[25]

* On dutiable imports, the average ad valorem rate of duties was 25.9 per cent in 1921–1925, and 50.02 per cent in 1931–1935 under the Hawley-Smoot Tariff. Critics of the tariff blamed the increase for at least a part of the 35-per-cent drop in customs receipts in 1931.

he and the conservatives were thoroughly in control of the leadership. Charlie Michelson, who was one of the insiders, has reminisced, "Smith probably felt that, with the Democratic organization in Raskob's hands, he had little to fear from the amateur efforts at Albany." It was in this confident atmosphere that Raskob planned his next maneuver against Roosevelt, aimed at forcing him to choose between the urban and rural wings of the Democratic party over the threadbare issue of Prohibition. His device on February 10, 1931, was to call for a special meeting of the Democratic National Committee to be held the day after Congress was to adjourn, March 5. Ostensibly, Raskob was planning "to discuss plans and policies to govern our activities during the next fifteen months." Actually, as newspapers speculated in the two weeks that followed, he was plotting to pass resolutions to commit the 1932 Democratic convention to Prohibition-repeal and high-tariff planks.[29]

What motivated Raskob in part was his thoroughgoing opposition to Prohibition. In part, according to Michelson, he wished to embarrass Roosevelt. Raskob and his followers seemed to think that Roosevelt, because he had been recently re-elected on a repeal plank, would have to accept their repeal resolution, and would thus lose the South. "The idea conveyed," Michelson wrote later, "was that the Southern delegates to the coming convention – bound to be against Smith – would not go along with Roosevelt if Roosevelt was put forth as another antiprohibition candidate. The theory was that the Raskob crowd did not care for whom the South voted as long as it was kept out of the Roosevelt column and so diminished the majority which Farley was already claiming for his entry."[30]

It is strange that Raskob, Shouse, and Smith could have arrived at such a foolish notion, since Roosevelt needed only to cling to his damp "states' rights-local option" compromise position of the previous September. That had hurt him very little in the South. Indeed, the few attacks upon him came from misinformed editors like Milton or hostile politicians like McAdoo,* who chose to lump Roosevelt with Raskob and Smith as another wringing Wet. The National Committee meeting, far from being the occasion for forcing Roosevelt into the Raskob-Smith camp, gave him a splendid opportunity to take a public

* As late as the end of March, 1931, McAdoo was privately claiming that FDR was tied in with Raskob and Smith, and was denouncing FDR as an impossibly Wet candidate who if nominated would be badly defeated, though not as badly as Smith.[31]

stand with the opposition. Furthermore, if Raskob and Smith intended the meeting as a testing of strength they were making a grievous tactical error, for each state had two votes, and the South and West could heavily outvote the populous East. All that remained was for Roosevelt to assume leadership and ally himself with the outraged Southerners. This he did quickly.

Outwardly, Roosevelt continued his calm, conciliatory demeanor. He too thought there was amateurishness – but not in Albany. He wrote Woodrow Wilson's former secretary, Joseph Tumulty, who had always been closely allied with the conservative Eastern wing of the party, "If I did not have a sense of humor I should sometimes be out of patience with some of our so-called friends – especially when without background or knowledge they attempt to play a large part in national affairs." This was the position Roosevelt chose for himself – that of the statesmanlike conciliator, ready to fight for the good of the party by working against a destructive rift.[32]

As soon as the maneuver began to take shape, Roosevelt warned his long-standing friend and ally, Senator-elect Hull. By some means not entirely clear, Roosevelt consistently got wind of Raskob's activities even in advance of the fast-spreading rumors and newspaper reports. Shouse once told Michelson that Roosevelt had a spy in the national headquarters; probably he did, because his sources of information were so numerous. In any event, Hull immediately began whipping up anti-Raskob sentiment among numerous Senators and Representatives. He allied himself with a strong group of Southerners, including former Governor Harry Byrd of Virginia, vice-chairman of the National Committee, and Senators John S. Cohen of Georgia, Joseph T. Robinson of Arkansas, and Claude Swanson of Virginia. Privately Hull warned Roosevelt that Raskob was gathering proxies for the meeting ahead; publicly he issued a series of statements denouncing it. If Raskob's course were followed, he declared, the party might as well dispense with the formality of a national convention.[33]

Hull and the Southerners around him fought with a grim seriousness, seeing more involved in the battle than just the Wet-Dry issue. Senator Tom Connally of Texas denounced Raskob's plan as an illegal usurpation of power, but went on to declare that by splitting the Democratic party it would continue the Republicans in power, and thus postpone solving the depression. Hull in one of his statements warned publicly that Raskob was trying to commit the Democrats to a high tariff, and this to Hull was almost as frightening as the Wet issue. He confided to Roosevelt, "I am thoroughly confirmed in the belief that the paramount purpose of the meeting thus far has been to make a strong wet recommendation to the next national convention and to invite all those seeking important special privileges from the government to join the Democratic party on a wet issue alone, by virtually merging the two parties on economics, including special privileges." [34]

Cautious Democratic politicians hungry for victory in 1932 widely shared Hull's fears that disaster would result from Raskob's scheme. Senator Pat Harrison of Mississippi, certainly far from a radical, expressed these worries to one of Roosevelt's agents in Washington and at the same time added that he would gladly back Roosevelt's candidacy. Harry Byrd appealed to Roosevelt to fight Raskob's dangerous move, and added that Governor Max Gardner of North Carolina shared his views. Gardner had added reason for trepidation, for Al Smith was in North Carolina at about that time, making the sort of stereotyped noncommittal statements that the public had come to expect of a politician seeking the presidential nomination.[35]

Roosevelt was only too anxious to get directly into the fight; his one worry was whether he rather than Smith could dominate the party in his own state during the forthcoming test of strength. He had already cautiously sounded out Senator Royal S. Copeland with an ingratiating, sentimental letter reminding Copeland how he had aided in the 1926 Senate campaign. Copeland responded in gratifyingly warm fashion that he also was distressed by Raskob's maneuver. Roosevelt seemed able to persuade Norman Mack, the national committeeman for New York, that in the interest of party harmony, he should leave Raskob's camp for Roosevelt's.[36]

Already Roosevelt had made a direct effort to stop Raskob, but received only a polite, noncommittal reply to his protest. He tried to talk first to Raskob and next to Al Smith on the telephone; neither would accept a call from him. Next he sent a letter of protest to Smith. Having thus done all that politeness required of him, he laid aside amenities and opened fire.[37]

The first shot was a special meeting of the New York Democratic Committee in Albany on March 2, three days before the national meeting in Washington. That morning, Roosevelt, at a meeting with Howe, Flynn, and Farley in his bedroom at the Executive Mansion, drafted a resolution. In the afternoon at the meeting, Flynn introduced the resolution; the committee quickly adopted it. They thus put

By permission of the Director of the Franklin D. Roosevelt Library

Governor and Mrs. Franklin D. Roosevelt with their son John at Albany. c. 1930?

Photo by Wide World. By permission of the Director of the Franklin D. Roosevelt Library

FDR with Louis McHenry Howe and James A. Farley, in Chicago, Illinois, July 4, 1932

By permission of the Director of the Franklin D. Roosevelt Library

FDR in the pool at Warm Springs, Georgia. c. 1930?

themselves on record as backing Roosevelt's stand that the National Committee had no authority to pledge or advise the party on any issues arising between national conventions.[38]

Immediately Roosevelt wired the text of the resolution to National Committeeman Mack and several others it might influence or abet. He sent Farley bearing a copy to Washington, and called Hull at his apartment at the Lafayette Hotel in Washington to tell him that Farley and the two New York committeemen would back him in the fight. Roosevelt's phone call was bracing news to Hull and the Southerners — that Al Smith's own state would fight behind Roosevelt against Smith and Raskob. To Hull and other Southerners who might previously have had some slight reservations, it was a token that Roosevelt was genuinely breaking away from Smith.[39]

At once Roosevelt and his staff in Albany went to work vigorously telephoning and telegraphing throughout the country to line up the proxies of committeemen who would not be present at the meeting. Before Farley took the train to Washington, he announced that he held enough proxies to defeat Raskob's motions two or three to one. Thus even before the meeting, Roosevelt was able to claim the promised victory as peculiarly his own.[40]

In Washington, Southern Democratic leaders, catching their first glimpse of Farley, found him modest and affable, thoroughly to their liking. He registered at an out-of-the-way hotel, avoided reporters, and went into conference quickly with Hull, Byrd, and the others. Together they decided upon a number of speakers to oppose the Raskob faction. Together they went to the meeting, where Farley openly called attention to the new alignment by sitting beside Hull.[41]

It was a formidable array. So thoroughly outnumbered, the Raskob forces at the meeting could do little but fire a few harmless shots in the air and abandon the field. They, like most of their opponents, dared not disrupt the party. Raskob delivered a compromising speech full of orotund Jeffersonian generalities with which most of his listeners could find no fault. On Prohibition, he proposed no more than a states'-rights compromise position, but he did recommend that the National Committee advise the party to include this as a plank in the next platform.

Despite Raskob's conciliatory stand, the Southerners were in no mood to accept from him even what they no longer found objectionable in their ally Roosevelt. Hull counterattacked cautiously, but Senator Robinson of Arkansas proclaimed as violently as though Raskob had made no concession, "You cannot write on the banner of the Democratic party . . . the skull and crossbones emblematic of an outlawed trade." It seemed as though a serious split might develop, but Al Smith, speaking in a semijocular vein, tried to restore harmony. Smith ridiculed as bunk the charges that Raskob was trying to influence the convention, and pleaded for the right of any Democratic leader to express his opinions freely. With Smith on the defensive, Raskob did not dare even submit his mild recommendation as a resolution to be put to a vote. Rather, after nothing more than party oratory, the meeting adjourned. The victory was thoroughly one-sided, and its great beneficiary was Roosevelt, who was not even present.[42]

From this time on, Hull has written in his memoirs, the Southern leaders took Roosevelt seriously and rallied around him as the one candidate who could deliver them from the Smith-Raskob menace. Hull considered the victory over Raskob the most significant turning point in the ultimate defeat of Smith and nomination of Roosevelt. While this may be something of an overestimate, clearly in this first skirmish between the Roosevelt and Smith forces, Roosevelt's lines held so strongly that the Smith side had to retire without much battle. The issue between the two men was far from settled; a real testing of strength in New York must inevitably come. But Roosevelt had convinced his temporary Southern allies that this was real war against Smith and Raskob, not a mess-hall mutiny in the Smith camp. Thus assured that they would not lose their Northern general, many of the Southerners were ready to contract permanent alliances for the duration of the conflict ahead.[43]

Roosevelt was well aware of the magnitude of his victory and what he must do with it. He wrote Norman Mack, "I think on the whole that largely thanks to you and Jim Farley the meeting did no harm, — and indeed I am inclined to think that in the long run the result will be beneficial to the party. . . . The thing we must work for now is the avoidance of harsh words and no sulking in tents." [44]

CHAPTER XIII

Depression Governor

> I cannot truthfully inform you that all is well with the condition of citizens of the State for, during the past year, in common with the rest of the nation, many of them and many of our industries have experienced a decline in prosperity which often has brought about suffering and hardship.
>
> — FDR, MESSAGE TO LEGISLATURE, *January 7, 1931.*

WELL before Roosevelt's re-election in November, 1930, circumstances made him painfully aware that he was a depression governor. In his second term he increasingly had to battle against the same economic problems within the State of New York that on a larger scale were menacing the entire nation. By the winter of 1930–1931 he had begun a long struggle with two of those which still menaced the nation two years later when he went to Washington — catastrophic unemployment and bank failures.

Before cold weather came in the fall of 1930, the state and the nation had sunk into the trough of depression. Despite cheery predictions of an upswing by Republican business leaders like Charles M. Schwab of Bethlehem Steel and Democrats like John Raskob of General Motors, the portents for even greater distress were frightening. The business index had been declining steadily since the latter part of August, and was dropping at the rate of a half point a week. Altogether it had dropped eighteen per cent in the year since the stock crash; steel production was down more than thirty per cent, and automobile production well over fifty per cent. Hundreds of thousands of unemployed in New York had run through their savings; there was nowhere to turn, and they were becoming desperate. At first, many people had taken the crash and ensuing depression rather lightly; it had been the topic of many a joke on the radio and on Broadway. Rapidly it was deepening into one of the worst calamities in the history of the nation.[1]

As a gesture to demonstrate his realization that the depression was no longer a joking matter, Roosevelt ran his second inaugural with the utmost simplicity and economy. By leaving a ceremonial regiment in New York City and paring such items as printing, amplifiers, reviewing stand, and official pictures, he cut the cost of the inaugural from twenty-one thousand dollars to thirty-five hundred dollars. The saving he applied to public works which would employ the needy. In addition, Roosevelt ordered the Inaugural Ball run with a minimum of decorations and flowers in order to pile up a profit from the sale of tickets for the Albany Unemployment Relief Fund.[2]

Roosevelt made economy more than a gesture throughout his second administration. From his inauguation until he left office at the end of December, 1932, he continually pressured his cabinet to cut costs drastically. This hit all departments hard, but for some of them which had to undertake extra work because of the depression, this was especially difficult.

The Insurance Department, for example, operated under a considerable handicap because the depression increased sizably the problem of regulating insurance companies. Federal regulation did not exist and the greatest concentration of companies was in New York. Roosevelt was determined that his administration should regulate them in an honest and efficient fashion, but at the same time he pared the Insurance Department budget.

Because of Roosevelt's own experiences, and indeed his own practices in the twenties as vice-president of Fidelity and Deposit Company, a bonding insurance company, he was well aware of the dangerous interrelationships between insurance companies and politicians. As an insurance man he had played this game himself by putting two sons of New York City Democratic leaders on the payroll of his firm. As governor, Roosevelt soon decided to take no chances mixing insurance and politics. His first appointee as Superintendent of Insurance had been a man of high character but a member of the Brooklyn Democratic organization. In June, 1930, Roosevelt persuaded him to accept appointment as a Kings County judge, and in 1931 elevated him to the state Supreme Court. Nevertheless, Boss McCooey of Brooklyn was confident that he could persuade Roosevelt to appoint another of his organization men to the position. Indeed, McCooey was so confident that he allowed a testimonial dinner to be given his candidate. Meanwhile the Insurance Department was nominally being run by an interim superintendent who was a dying man.

When the time came for a replacement, Governor Roosevelt gave Boss McCooey a rude jolt. In February, 1931, he turned to a Rochester man, George S. Van Schaick,* who he believed could rebuild the run-down department. He warned Van Schaick bluntly that there were two departments in his administration in which politics were taboo, the Banking Department and the Insurance Department.[3]

Despite Roosevelt's warning, Van Schaick's pressing problem as Superintendent of Insurance was not politics but the departmental budget. He found it difficult to heed Roosevelt's demands for economy yet bolster his department so it could effectively police the insurance companies. Van Schaick has recalled:

"At the budget hearings the Governor would preside, assisted by the heads of the Senate and Assembly Committees having to do with state expenditures. The policy was to cut and cut drastically. I rebelled and pointed out that my department needed more not less. In some respects I was able to economize by leaving vacant certain positions not of essential importance, but I insisted on strengthening the department with a considerable number of additional examiners. The Governor backed me up and eventually the legislative leaders acquiesced in my recommendations and I was able to get them. Strengthening a department of government is something more than overnight action after authorization for an augmented force. Proper choice of personnel is laborious and painstaking work. The crisis was then upon us; however, the strengthening should have been done ten years before. Even the augmented force needed to work night and day in face of the increasing problems." [4]

Roosevelt kept Van Shaick on the alert against trouble. He warned his new Superintendent at the Executive Mansion one day that while the economy was bumping along on the bottom it might strike a few potholes. In October, 1931, this happened to the insurance companies when the market prices of the securities they held again seriously slumped. Many of the companies, Van Schaick alerted the Governor, on the basis of these extremely deflated values, were on the ragged edge. He proposed, after consulting the companies and Roosevelt's financial advisers, to substitute an average of market values of stocks over five quarters in place of determining the worth of insurance-company holdings by the stock quotations for a single day.

* Van Schaick, a lawyer of high repute, had no previous insurance experience, but subsequently became vice-president of the New York Life Insurance Company.

In a period of wild fluctuation, when the market was little more than an auction block, this seemed to Roosevelt a more equitable procedure, and he readily acquiesced. The companies remained solvent.[5]

Altogether, Roosevelt was most fortunate in the Insurance Department. Van Schaick warned the companies that they would be penalized if they did not abandon various malpractices, and checked upon them as closely as he could. This sufficed.

In the Banking Department Roosevelt was less fortunate, although he had an able Superintendent of Banks, because the economic onslaught against banks was more severe than against insurance companies. There too, Roosevelt's over-all demand for economy came at exactly the time when the department needed to hire more bank examiners to give the banks more careful scrutiny than during the prosperity years. Again Roosevelt backed down; where it was essential, he was ready to put efficiency ahead of economy. Superintendent Broderick sent him such an emphatic and detailed plea for more examiners that he forwarded it to the legislature; in time Broderick got the examiners.[6]

This solved only a small part of the problem. The basic difficulty was that Governor Roosevelt tried to run the Banking Department in keeping with the wishes of the big conservative bankers in a period of crisis when their cautious policies could not prevent, indeed might foster, the collapse of weaker banks. Partly because Roosevelt had continued to heed the advice of the men he had respected when he was on Wall Street, the Banking Department could do little to protect depositors from the severe consequences of the depression. Although the City Trust scandal of 1929 had led to the imprisonment of Superintendent Broderick's predecessor, it had not led to a drastic reform of banking laws in the state. Neither bankers, Republican leaders, nor Roosevelt had been interested. The existing banking laws, under which many banks quite legally engaged in speculation, had sufficed in the '20s, when profits were easy to make. In the year and a half after the stock crash, when the nation plummeted into what Broderick considered "the most drastic and disastrous nationwide banking depression . . . in the history of this country," the New York laws tragically failed to suffice. They were hopelessly inadequate to protect depositors, and a quarter of the nation's bank deposits, some seventeen billion dollars altogether, were in the state of New York.[7]

This became all too apparent when the Bank of United States crashed shortly before Christmas in 1930. It was the worst bank failure since the founding of the republic; it directly affected some four hundred and fifty thousand depositors and indirectly hurt perhaps a third of the people of New York City. A large part of them, moreover, were those who could least afford to have their deposits frozen and in part lost irretrievably.* Some four hundred thousand of the deposits were sums of four hundred dollars or less.[9]

One of the most shocking things about the Bank of United States failure was that it was a somewhat less corrupt counterpart of the City Trust fiasco. Both were little people's banks; both had been built on the good faith of rather credulous immigrants; both had boards loaded with Tammany politicians who received special favors. Worst of all, both had played speculatively with funds in hundreds of thousands of thrift accounts not subject to the legal safeguards that protected savings accounts.† The biggest difference, and an unimportant one, was that City Trust had been the Italians' bank, and the Bank of United States that of the Jews, especially those in the garment trades. Wall Streeters had referred to it scornfully as the "pants-pressers' bank." Its depositors, impressed with its marble façades and the pictures of the Capitol adorning the walls, regarded it as being as solid as the government itself. Some of them thought it part of the government.

Why had Governor Roosevelt ignored Robert Moses's emphatic warnings in the report on City Trust? Why had he failed to fight through reform legislation which would have prevented the Bank of United States debacle? These are the sharp questions that critics of Roosevelt asked at the time and later.[10]

The answer seems to lie less in Roosevelt's marked dislike for Moses than in his own personal confidence in the banking community, a

* This letter from an immigrant who had four hundred dollars in the Bank of United States is typical of scores FDR later received from distressed depositors:

> "I have received your most welcome favor of March the 29th 1932. I thank you for your valuable information about the BANK OF UNITED STATES, but I am sorry to inform you that I remain jobless yet.
>
> "My wife, she will have soon her first born baby: though she is sewing machine some days now, she very soon will become unable to do nothing. . . .
>
> "If I would be able to get my money the Bank of United States, holds me, we surely go back to our country because we hardly suffer here on account of having fall to the ground at this City, and on consequency I trusted the Bank of United States, as the best institution of this kind in THE UNITED STATES, as people say previously to Bank's crash." [8]

† Unwary depositors did not understand this crucial difference between thrift accounts and savings accounts.

confidence which he retained to a considerable degree well into the New Deal. His own lieutenant governor, Herbert Lehman, was one of the soundest as well as politically the most liberal of Wall Street leaders; in banking matters Roosevelt seems to have followed Lehman's lead, and that was to cooperate as far as possible with the banking titans.

This is probably the best explanation why Roosevelt had not sent Moses's drastic recommendations to the legislature, but instead had appointed another commission. This commission, which did not even include Moses, but had among its members a director and the counsel of the Bank of United States, ultimately reported a mild set of recommendations.* These were about the maximum that bankers (including the soundest ones) were ready to accept at this time, but they were far more than the Republican legislature was willing to pass. When the 1930 session put into law only provisions for regulating private banks and a few very minor matters, Roosevelt publicly rebuked the legislators. Broderick for his part seemed remarkably pleased with the over-all result because he could now regulate private banks. He wrote Roosevelt, "The new legislation is wonderful, it gives us even greater responsibility than we dreamed of." [12]

This was admirable, but the new legislation did not give Broderick authority to deal drastically with the shaky Bank of United States. For many months before its ultimate collapse, the banking community, Roosevelt, and the Superintendent had all been well aware of its precarious condition and had tried to bolster it by any means possible. Even had there been new legislation it would have come too late. It can be said on behalf of Roosevelt and Broderick that had they earlier demanded and received legal authorization to prevent speculation with thrift-account moneys, they could have done little except close down the bank. The damage had already been done, although largely within the law.

In October, 1930, Roosevelt interrupted his campaign for re-election to hold a secret meeting at his New York City home, to try to negotiate a merger to save the bank. Lieutenant Governor Lehman and

* Moses at the time blamed bankers for the failure of both FDR's and the legislature's investigating commissions "to bring forward a single constructive suggestion for the preventing of similar conditions in other institutions" to those in the City Trust Company. He declared, "The banking profession is not easy to regulate. It prefers to go along on the caveat emptor theory. Little and big, all banks and bankers naturally hang together in opposition to public control. Strike one link and the whole chain shivers." [11]

representatives of J. P. Morgan and Company, the National City Bank, the Central Hanover Bank, and the Bankers Trust Company conferred with him, and in the weeks that followed carried on lengthy, painful negotiations. For a considerable time it looked as though they would succeed. At first the heads of the Bank of United States tried to drive a hard bargain; later in desperation they lessened their demands while the great bankers with whom they dickered became more and more skittish. The large banks did not want to allow the Bank of United States to go under because they would suffer indirectly, but in the end balked at a merger which would have cost them serious direct losses.

Rumors of the bank's shaky condition filtered through New York City; gradually, during the fall, more and more depositors withdrew their accounts. Before it closed they had taken out a total of sixty million dollars. On December 10, frightened people began a frantic run on all the branches; at one, fifteen thousand depositors queued up, waiting hours in the rain. The next day, Broderick closed the bank.

The calamity had immediate economic repercussions. Depositors could borrow up to fifty per cent of their accounts from the clearing house at five-per-cent interest, but the freezing of the other half of their assets frightened them. Many depositors in other banks withdrew their savings. Small depositors stormed the City Hall seeking redress; more well-to-do ones formed a protective association to begin a legal search for the villains responsible for their troubles. The familiar pattern for ferreting out Tammany corruption began again to unfold as desperate depositors tried to punish the bankers. They demanded an investigation, and one began under Tammany District Attorney Crain; once more newspapers and reform leaders pressured Governor Roosevelt to take extraordinary steps, and once more he refused. Ultimately several of the bank officials were tried and convicted for some of their manipulations. One reversal, fascinating to tabloid readers, was that a brilliant lawyer, Isidor J. Kresel, who had helped lead the onslaught against Tammany in the Seabury investigation, now switched sides with his hated opponent in that battle, Max Steuer, the gifted Tammany attorney. Steuer ran the investigation; Kresel as counsel for the bank was on the defensive.

Political reactions to this soon extended to Albany. Although one crusading liberal writing for the *New Republic*, John T. Flynn,*

* Rather, Flynn enumerated Broderick's proposals for reform, then criticized the bankers for ignoring them.[13]

did not condemn Governor Roosevelt; a crusading Socialist writing for the *Nation*, Norman Thomas, did. Thomas granted that Broderick was honest and that the fundamental problem was the way in which the bankers had blocked reform, but he pointed to the Governor's failure to appoint Moses to his commission on banks, and his far more serious failure to protect thrift-account depositors.[14]

Under the pressure of circumstances, Roosevelt hastily proposed the bold, positive action from which he had previously held back. After Thomas had twice written him urging him to initiate a special investigation, he continued to decline, but wired Thomas early in January, 1931, "Confidentially, for your information I was greatly disappointed that [the] last legislature did nothing about thrift accounts. I expect to recommend such action to this legislature." [15]

Roosevelt was sincere in his proposal if not in his claim that he had previously advocated action. He spend an evening at the Executive Mansion discussing it with Frank Altschul of Lazard Frères. Altschul's advice was like that of most bankers. He agreed in principle that if thrift depositors were led to believe that they had the same protection as savings depositors, they should in fact receive that protection. In practice, Altschul warned Roosevelt that even to bring up the subject publicly might send thrift depositors in a rush to withdraw their savings. Consequently he counseled establishment of still another commission which would undertake another lengthy study of the entire state banking law.[16]

For the moment, Roosevelt readily agreed that he was in an impasse:

"You have exactly expressed my own thoughts. There is no question that something must be done either to give thrift depositors the same protection afforded savings banks depositors or else make it perfectly clear to the public that thrift accounts do not have the same protection as savings bank accounts. Either of these courses may mean the raising of real concern at the present time." [17]

In the weeks that followed, Roosevelt tried to work out something that would be satisfactory to the bankers, the Republican legislative leaders, and his critics. Of the three groups, his critics, who quite possibly included the great mass of voters, worried him the most. Huge numbers of them held thrift accounts. There were nearly two million such accounts in New York State, he pointed out to his uncle, Frederic A. Delano, which affected at least five million of the twelve and a half million people in the state. He confided to a Republican friend on the Federal Reserve Board, "Frankly I am concerned that the Legislature will do nothing in the way of legislation this year and am very much convinced that the people as a whole feel that something should be done along constructive lines." Late in March, he added as justification for the course he had decided upon, "My complaint is that the bankers so far have merely thrown cold water on every plan suggested to protect thrift accounts. I am not a proponent of any one plan, but I do think something ought to be done before the Legislature goes home. This thing has been going on for two years without any action." [18]

What Roosevelt did was to send a special message to the legislature on March 24, pointing out in simple language the appalling distinction between protected savings accounts and unprotected thrift accounts, and demanding that the legislature reconsider its arbitrary action in defeating any and all plans to safeguard thrift depositors. For Roosevelt thus to attack the Republican legislature was commonplace, but now he added to it a direct rebuke to the bankers:

"If the banking interests themselves had some substitute plan to correct the evils and dangers which lurk in our banking laws, more reliance might be placed on their wisdom. By merely blocking all reform, as they appear to be doing this year . . . they discredit any claim that their efforts are accompanied by any sincere desire to protect the depositors of the State." [19]

Despite these strong words, Roosevelt was ready to accept a most moderate plan which Broderick devised, which would gradually segregate the thrift accounts over a five-year period. Only a very few bankers would accept even this; one of the notable exceptions was the Republican Felix Warburg. A thrift-account bill was introduced into the state senate on March 31, and there it died. At the end of the session, Roosevelt denounced the legislature for this dereliction. The following year he renewed his demand for legislation and again the legislature failed to act. Thus the legislature served once more as a political lightning rod for Roosevelt. However derelict he might have been in not pushing for drastic banking reform after the City Trust crash, the Republican legislators had been far more derelict in refusing to act after the Bank of United States failure.[20]

What all this meant was that in a crisis Roosevelt tended to be cautious and conservative until no other course was open to him except bold action. The City Trust scandal had signified no more to the respectable bankers than that the state Banking Department must be cleaned up and made efficient. This Roosevelt had largely achieved through his appointment of Broderick. The Bank of United States crash posed a rather different problem. Any drastic revision of the state banking laws would have forced it to close sooner; public interest strongly dictated that it be kept open if at all possible. The fact that depositors even in this period of acute deflation ultimately received all but about a quarter of their deposits has led Lehman in retrospect to feel that it should never have closed. Broderick agrees. Except for the intransigency of its managers and the big bankers, and the lack of a Federal agency to help, the Bank of United States too could have weathered the financial storm.[21]

After the damage was done, Roosevelt, ignoring banker counsels, demanded that the legislature act firmly to reform banking law, at the same time that he still took a fundamentally conservative view toward banks.

The frantic search for a scapegoat led ultimately to Broderick, who was forced to stand trial for his role in the failure. Roosevelt stood firmly by his Superintendent of Banks until he was acquitted, and later as President appointed him to the Federal Reserve Board. During the remainder of his term as governor, Roosevelt continued to accept Broderick's advice and looked with disfavor upon both public and private schemes to insure bank depositors against loss. Ironically, in the New Deal, deposit insurance was to prove the final answer to the problem of protecting thrift accounts, and the scheme was to rebound to Roosevelt's credit. What takes a bit of the edge off the irony is the twofold attitude toward banking that Roosevelt carried to the White House: a willingness to follow the lead of conservative bankers as long and as far as he could, and also a readiness when politically necessary to cut loose and castigate the bankers for their conservatism.[22]

In trying to cope with the far more grievous problems of unemployment, Roosevelt demonstrated the same insistence upon exhausting conventional expedients before he would turn to more drastic measures. He brought to the problem little prior knowledge, but a continuing warm, sympathetic interest in people and their troubles. His thinking continued to be in terms of the human beings he had known and met, and those who scrawled pathetic letters to him. He was ready to learn new expedients for dealing with the problems of unemployment, an area in which Frances Perkins served as a skilled, tactful schoolmistress.

From his commission on the stabilization of employment, which had functioned during the less critical months of 1930, Roosevelt had learned the desirability of spreading work to avoid seasonal unemployment. During the winter of 1930–1931, he proceeded to the next step and became a student of unemployment insurance. It logically grew out of the findings of his commission, but was still something daring and untried in the United States. Although several European nations had maintained unemployment insurance for decades, not a single state legislature in this country had enacted it. By 1931, the change was in the air, and although not a state established unemployment insurance, bills providing for it were introduced into seventeen legislatures.* Beginning in 1930, Roosevelt was ready to consult every authority on the subject. He invited Sir William Beveridge, the great English expert, to consult with him in Albany in September, 1930, and sought data from the Metropolitan Life Insurance Company and other firms. He even obtained statistics on insurance in other countries from Harold B. Butler of the International Labor Organization.[24]

At only one point was Roosevelt ready to break away toward the left from the mild proposals then current in the United States. He felt that contrary to the model Wisconsin bill authored by John R. Commons, employers should not be the sole contributors to whatever sort of system was established. He wished employees to contribute too in order that they would feel a responsibility for the program. Later, Roosevelt felt that this had an additional advantage in that it would also give them a vested interest which could not be voted away from them. Otherwise, Roosevelt's thoughts were very cautious. Throughout the winter he leaned toward working out some sort of scheme to finance unemployment insurance through the existing life-insurance companies. Even this struck some critics of his as going too far; they pointed to the difficulties in England as grounds for ignoring the subject entirely.[25] Roosevelt retorted to one insurance man:

"Tell your friend . . . that for eight long years I was in the insurance and surety business myself, — that I am not a wide-eyed radical, — that I am just as much opposed to the dole as he is and that the little tin god I worship is called 'actuarial table[.]' [I]n spite of the ghastly mistakes of the fifty-seven other varieties of nations in installing the old age pension insurance, we might profit from their mistakes and

* In 1921 a Wisconsin bill came within one vote of being adopted, but it was not until January, 1932, that Wisconsin enacted the first state unemployment-insurance law. It was alone in doing so.[23]

discover something which an actuarial table fits. Tell him further that hard-boiled insurance men like us can at least not object to a highly conservative study of the whole subject." [26]

By March, 1931, Roosevelt's thinking had sufficiently crystallized for him to set forth his views in a special message to the legislature. He called upon it to establish a commission to investigate unemployment insurance. In future times of depression, men and women who could not find work should receive some sort of relief, he declared. This should not be a dole – relief to which they had not contributed. This was contrary to every principle of American citizenship and sound government. Rather, Roosevelt expounded:

"The relief which the workers of the state should be able to anticipate, when engulfed in a period of industrial depression, should be one of insurance, to which they themselves have in a large part contributed. Each industry itself should likewise bear a part of the premium for this insurance, and the State, in the interest of its own citizens, and to prevent a recurrence of the widespread hardship of these days, should at the least supervise its operations." [27]

Roosevelt succeeded in obtaining the commission from the legislature, but not, during his term as governor, an unemployment-insurance law. At least he had helped initiate serious discussion and consideration of the problem, for beginning with his remarks to the Governors' Conference in the summer of 1930, he had been the first major political figure in the United States to advocate unemployment insurance.[28]

At best, insurance was only a segment of the whole bleak problem of depression, and one that would help in future crises, not the existing one. This Roosevelt grasped readily as the days shortened and the bread lines lengthened toward the end of 1930. Government machinery for alleviating suffering was almost nonexistent throughout the United States; most states were still functioning on a basis of poor-relief legislation of a sort originally devised in the reign of Queen Elizabeth I. New York was not much better off. There was not much Roosevelt could do on his own authority as governor except to stretch existing public-works projects to the utmost, and to authorize the use of the state-controlled national-guard armories, late at night after drills, to house destitute men. At the same time, private relief organizations and hastily improvised city agencies were staggering under the burden. Roosevelt wanted to act, but was not as yet certain just what he should recommend.[29]

His first major step was to follow a precedent already established in other areas. He called a conference of governors from nearby Eastern states, which contained nearly a third of the nation's population, to study fundamental causes of unemployment and possible remedies. For fear he would diminish the stature of his fellow governors, who, he kept in mind, were equal heads of sovereign states, he had Miss Perkins sound out the labor commissioners of the states before he sent the governors formal invitations. In order to plan carefully for the conference, Miss Perkins sent for a dynamic young economist who was an expert on employment and wages. This was Professor Paul H. Douglas of the University of Chicago, at the time in charge of an unemployment study for Swarthmore College. Douglas came, immediately established a warm relationship with Roosevelt, and within a few days had assembled and digested a large quantity of data into usable form for the conference. By the time the governors assembled, Roosevelt was able to demonstrate an easy working knowledge of the subject. Miss Perkins has recalled:

"Roosevelt understood that his first problem was to disarm these governors, to present himself to them as truly disinterested, a public official charged with a grave duty, honestly trying to find an answer and asking their help and co-operation. . . . He was master of the material which we had piled up in such quantities that it was almost too much to expect him to know what was in the report. . . . He simplified every question that I raised and every point that I made in the outline I had prepared for him. He raised questions himself in a modest and inquiring way. He illustrated and illuminated some of the problems for the governors by referring to concrete cases, always in a graceful, consultative manner which indicated to the governors that he wanted to hear from them, not just to tell them." [30]

At the conference, Roosevelt and the other governors discussed broad questions of industrial and governmental responsibility for the relief and prevention of unemployment. They listened to papers by economists on the subjects of public works, public-employment exchanges, and, above all, on various aspects of unemployment insurance. When they adjourned, they had agreed upon nothing concrete, but for Roosevelt at least there were certain achievements. He had, as Miss Perkins points out, impressed himself upon his fellow governors; but more important, he had acquired some new ideas. He began to think less exclusively in terms of what New York could achieve by itself, and to some extent began to consider interstate compacts as a means of solving those economic problems which so perplexingly crisscrossed state lines. He penciled a press release on January 23, 1931, in which he asserted: "The Governors discussed the problems of uniformity of certain laws of their several States, especially laws relating to labor and workman's compensation and laws relating to corporate taxes." Roosevelt's position was that "industry and workers as a whole would be benefited by a greater uniformity in the laws of those of industrial states which include 47% of all the wage earners in the U.S." [31]

This was a slight step away from Roosevelt's strong states'-rights stand as governor toward his later nationalist position as President.* The conference also marked some shift in Roosevelt's economic thinking. Paul Douglas, Leo Wolman, William Leiserson, and other liberal economists who participated seriously jolted his preconceptions. This is apparent in a lengthy and most revealing exposition of the depression that Roosevelt wrote his brother-in-law Hall Roosevelt a month after the conference. In it he was freed from the caution which marked his public utterances during this period when his aspiration for the presidency colored almost everything he said or wrote. Hall Roosevelt in Detroit had suggested to him that any satisfactory unemployment-insurance plan must prevent abuse in good times by curbing abnormal consumption and abnormal production.

"You have hit the nail on the head but the difficulty is to apply the principle," Governor Roosevelt replied. For his own part, he was ready to "go back to the old law of supply and demand," apparently to achieve balance through some regulation of industrial output. He wrote:

> There are, of course, certain industries which, with a little more organizing, can put the rule into practice[.] [I]t is even easier to do so with raw materials, such as oil, coal and copper. The copper producers are all working it out pretty well and the oil and coal producers are almost ready to follow suit. I am inclined to think that the same methods can be extended to the production of crops, such as wheat and cotton, during the next decade.
>
> These raw material industries, however, while they can restrict or increase production, have very little control over consumption. It is, therefore, the manufacturing industries on whom the

* Miss Perkins points out that as President, FDR would have fallen back upon interstate compacts if he could not have found a constitutional way to frame Federal labor legislation.[32]

real task falls. That brings up the big question of how far the credit system should be extended to the consumer himself.

Personally, I felt from 1922 on that the terrible campaign in favor of installment buying by the individual consumers was the most dangerous thing we had to contend with, but I must be honest in saying that the present depression has not thrown back as many installment wares into the hands of the sellers as I had expected. By the way, a very interesting economist made the suggestion to me last week that there should be definite laws whereby installment buyers could on any installment period, return the goods to the seller, thereby closing the transaction. That would make for much more careful installment selling.

I suppose the automobile industry is one of the best examples of overproduction and over consumption. You know a lot more about that than I do. Would it be possible for the automobile manufacturers to present a plan to prevent both dangers, and at the same time make it a part of an unemployment insurance plan[?] [33]

Here in an early stage was the kind of thinking which led Roosevelt later to accept the extensive government regulation of the National Recovery Administration. As yet his thinking had not advanced to the government-regulation stage, as was apparent from his interest in insurance-company-sponsored unemployment-compensation plans which the state would do no more than foster. Roosevelt was still drawing upon his personal experience in industrial self-regulation as he had known it as head of the American Construction Council in the '20s. He would use this sort of self-regulation to prevent future busts and booms. This stage of his thinking was not much different from President Hoover's, but unlike Hoover he was ready rapidly to move to the next stage: government enforcement of the self-regulation.

In 1931, despite national distress and privation, many an industrial mogul continued to cling somehow to a laissez-faire optimism that America could muddle out of the depression without government interference. "Just grin, keep on working," Schwab had recommended. "Stop worrying about the future and go ahead as best we can. We always have a way of living through the hard times." Roosevelt would no longer have any of this. He was ready to push New York into the vanguard of the states by taking a direct responsibility for coping with the depression. In June, 1931, he proclaimed this strongly before the Conference of Governors at French Lick, Indiana.[34]

With national attention focused upon him as a probable presidential nominee, he took a firm position. Reminding his listeners that Lord Bryce had described the forty-eight states as experimental laboratories, Roosevelt stated his intention to make New York a leading one of them. "Frankly, I cannot take the Pollyanna attitude as a solution of our problems," he asserted. "It is not enough to apply old remedies. A new economic and social balance calls for positive leadership and definite experiments which have not hitherto been tried."

Roosevelt set forth his new credo:

"More and more, those who are the victims of dislocations and defects of our social and economic life are beginning to ask respectfully, but insistently of us who are in positions of public responsibility why government can not and should not act to protect its citizens from disaster. I believe the question demands an answer and that the ultimate answer is that government, both state and national, must accept the responsibility of doing what it can do – soundly with considered forethought, and along definitely constructive, not passive lines."

What some of these lines were, Roosevelt outlined at French Lick: readjustments of tariffs and taxation, insurance for illness as well as unemployment, and the creation of a proper balance between urban and rural life. He was not very explicit, but what this new attitude could mean for both the State of New York and the American nation, the public was soon to see.[35]

CHAPTER XIV

Magic in the Name

> Theodore Roosevelt would make [a clear call] were he alive today, to the people of this whole nation, and especially to the young people of this nation, for their active participation in the solution of pressing problems which affect our national life and our very national existence.
>
> — FDR, *October 27, 1931.*

IN November, 1944, a Lancashireman sent Franklin D. Roosevelt an old picture postal of Theodore Roosevelt at his desk. On the back he wrote, "I am sending you this card to let you see you have not changed much hard at work then as you are now. Old Soldiers never die just fade away." By 1944 it is hard to believe that even the most ignorant of American voters could confuse the two Roosevelts,* but certainly as early as 1931 some of the glamorous aura of Theodore was lending a mystical charm to Franklin.[1]

This was a logical result of the despair of that blighted year. More and more people were disposed to turn toward a leader, toward someone who could propose firm, clear solutions to their problems, and who could propose them with assurance and optimism. As yet, the Roosevelt who spoke before the governors at French Lick could not entirely make good on his claim to this leadership; he was still not well enough known or sufficiently respected. Yet to increasing numbers of Americans, turning from their troubles toward an earlier, happier age, here was the man who seemed most fully to represent the optimistic dynamism of the progressive political leaders before the First World War. Here was the man who could most inspire their confidence, combining as he did the name of the great militant Republican President, Theodore Roosevelt, and the tradition of the Democratic one, Woodrow Wilson.

* Nevertheless, one woman, upon being informed that the President had frequently ridden in the elevator at the Roosevelt Library at Hyde Park, patted the elevator wall and exclaimed, "Good old Teddy!"

In his fight for a following, Franklin D. Roosevelt vigorously appealed to the millions of Americans who cherished a great nostalgia for one or both of these leaders of fifteen years earlier. He sought to capitalize upon the name of one and the tradition of the other to create for himself a new and exciting role as a leader who could guide them up a sure and direct path out of the economic morass.

It was Franklin Roosevelt's good fortune that at the beginning of the '30s the Theodore Roosevelt legend was still in full bloom. T. R. remained the unblemished ideal of almost every Boy Scout, every virile young man, every middle-aged political leader who had battled under his banner in the Bull Moose campaign of 1912. Better still, T. R. was a Republican hero; if Franklin Roosevelt could attract his following, he would be tapping a large source of normally Republican votes. This was fine politics, but it was more than mere calculation on Franklin D. Roosevelt's part, for there was no more enthusiastic believer in the Theodore Roosevelt tradition than he.

Roosevelt took pleasure as governor in fighting for appropriations for the Theodore Roosevelt Memorial Hall at the Museum of Natural History in New York City. On T. R.'s birthday in 1931, when he laid the cornerstone, he asserted that of all the public events in which he had participated during three years as governor, this thrilled and interested him the most. When an author asked permission to dedicate a biography of Theodore Roosevelt to him, he replied that he would feel much honored. The dedication read: "To Franklin D. Roosevelt[.] In Appreciation of His Distinguished Public Service and for the Added Dignity and Honor which He has Brought the Roosevelt Name." [2]

Although Franklin D. Roosevelt cherished the tie, he no longer as openly aped Theodore Roosevelt nor as self-consciously tried to follow in his footsteps as he had at one time. He candidly warned the author, "I feel sure that you are well aware that while I always had the highest admiration for President Roosevelt, he was only a distant cousin. My wife is his niece." [3] There remained the remarkable parallel between the two careers: first the state legislature, then Assistant Secretary of the Navy, then (out of Theodore Roosevelt's order) candidate for Vice President, and Governor of New York. The parallels were no longer of much interest to Governor Roosevelt or to the public, but the emotional pull of the name Roosevelt was. A sophisticated observer, Isaiah Bowman, President of the American Geographical Society, wrote Roosevelt in the spring of 1931 after touring the West:

"Elections are won in part on very simple ideas. The progressive spirit of T. R. is thought by Westerners to be reincarnated in you. The name being the same, the difference in party labels means less. It will be easier for a Republican to vote on the other side because of the name." [4]

Throughout the drive for political supporters, Jim Farley, acting with the Governor's knowledge, endlessly pointed out that there was magic in the name Roosevelt. Roosevelt himself in one of the most important of his national speeches, his Jefferson Day address in 1932, paid the required vigorous tribute to Jefferson, mentioned Franklin, Jackson, and Lincoln, then quoted at unusual length from Theodore Roosevelt as the guide in a crusade away from crass business materialism toward higher moral values.[5]

In the same speech, Roosevelt also cited Wilson, but with less emphasis. Wilson's popularity was still in relative eclipse. Roosevelt's strategy required not a public appeal to the limited numbers of Wilsonians, but a private bid for the support of the old leaders who still wielded influence within the Democratic party.

The key to them was Wilson's Warwick, the elderly Colonel E. M. House, who was already well disposed toward Roosevelt. House saw in Roosevelt a politically available man whom he could perhaps shape and direct as he thought he had once influenced Wilson. There is more than a hint that House did not think Roosevelt capable of arriving at correct policies on his own. He confided to a friend that he thought Roosevelt could beat Hoover in 1932 "if we can keep [him] from making any mistakes and get him to take the right view of national and foreign affairs." Later, House suggested to his Southern ally, Daniel Roper,"What we must do is to confer as to the best position for him to take not only on the question of Tammany but also on the question of prohibition and the economic issues which are so vital at the moment." [6]

It well suited Roosevelt's purposes to nurture House's notion that he could again be a President maker. Nothing could demonstrate more clearly how little intention Roosevelt had of giving power to House than the fact that he sent Louis Howe to court the Colonel. Howe would have been blind with jealous rage if he had thought House in reality could become top adviser. Howe's attitude was so different from rage that at the conclusion of their interview Howe left the Colonel puffed up with importance and full of enthusiasm for the Roosevelt cause.

Roosevelt's device was a foolproof one. In March, 1931, he sent

Howe on the short walk from his New York house to House's winter residence, bearing the draft of an important letter to ask House's advice. It was not Howe's first visit, but it was the first upon which he directly asked House's aid on a problem relative to Roosevelt's candidacy. The question was how Roosevelt could give his encouragement to the many Roosevelt-for-President clubs beginning to spring up throughout the country without frankly proclaiming himself a candidate. Already there were approximately fifty of them, ranging from Massachusetts to the state of Washington. For as skillful a pair of manipulators as Roosevelt and Howe to work out a formula was not difficult. They drafted a letter in which Roosevelt declared that while he was concentrating completely upon his tasks as Governor of New York, he had no objection to organizations which spread information about their candidate's fitness for the presidency.[7]

House, delighted at being consulted, suggested cuts in the letter – which indeed was all it needed. Henceforth it was the formula letter sent to any and all who wrote inquiring if they could found clubs. More important, House had swallowed the bait. He wrote Roosevelt with enthusiasm after his session with Howe, "It is a joy to cooperate with him for the reason that he is so able and yet so yielding to suggestions. We never have any arguments and have no difficulty in reaching conclusions satisfactory to us both. I congratulate you upon having such a loyal and efficient lieutenant."[8]

It is Farley's recollection that House's advice upon policies and issues received careful, thoughtful consideration from Roosevelt and others in the inner circle, but that House never occupied a key policy-making position. At the same time, Roosevelt found it profitable for the time being to let House believe that he had resumed his old Wilsonian role. What was valuable to Roosevelt was that House back in harness worked energetically, gathering useful political intelligence and negotiating powerful support. He entered into an extensive private correspondence on Roosevelt's behalf in the spring of 1931. In these letters, he wrote as a shrewd, experienced politician, appealing to the keen desire of his political allies to pick a winner. The Hoover Administration was trying to prevent the nomination of Roosevelt, he pointed out, because Roosevelt could carry the West as Wilson did in 1916. "No matter what our personal preference is," he insisted, ". . . I hope the Democrats will not aid the Republicans in their efforts to defeat the one man they fear."[9]

House sent a barrage of letters into the South and Southwest, where Roosevelt already had much appeal as a candidate. These went in many instances to former members of the Wilson Administration, like Daniel Roper of North Carolina, who had been Commissioner of Internal Revenue. Many of them had been in the McAdoo wing of the Democratic party during the 1920's. In addition House sent an emissary to the annual Texas Roundup at Austin to boom Roosevelt there. The result was a gratifying harvest of recruits. House sent copies of their letters to Howe, who wrote them follow-up letters and added them to his growing list of correspondents.[10]

All this was of help to Roosevelt in an area whose delegates he must capture if he were to win the nomination. It brought him many useful political friends whom he would have had difficulty courting later after the emergence of favorite sons. He was able to establish himself for the time being as the first choice of many hardheaded politicians less interested in his policies than in his capacity to win. Many of them, as in Texas when John Nance Garner emerged, were to switch their allegiance to a favorite son, but to retain a secondary loyalty to Roosevelt.

Next House tried to maneuver a far more difficult and important political coup for Roosevelt: to win for him the politicians of Massachusetts, who had been so ardently for Smith in 1928. The first step was for House to come out in the open. He admitted to Ernest K. Lindley of the New York *Herald Tribune* that he was back in politics for the first time since 1916, and that he was behind Roosevelt. This created a flurry of interest, and attracted public attention to the next step, a luncheon on June 13, 1931, to bring Roosevelt together with the Massachusetts Democratic leaders. House hoped thus "to discourage Smith and his followers, and to show them how hopeless it was to oppose our man." He reasoned that if Smith saw that he could not count upon Massachusetts, which had been his strongest state in 1928, he would realize his cause was lost and defer to Roosevelt.[11]

Outwardly, House seemed to achieve his aim, and was jubilant over the results. In addition to a group of Wilsonian intellectuals like Ellery Sedgwick, editor of the *Atlantic Monthly*, he entertained the hard-bitten Democratic professionals: both the Democratic Senators from Massachusetts, David I. Walsh and Marcus A. Coolidge, and Mayor James M. Curley of Boston. There were several score newspapermen and photographers present to record their conviviality with the beaming Roosevelt. As a result, House and Roosevelt's other New England friends felt they could safely count upon Massachusetts. They were sadly in error.

Roosevelt profited from House's overestimate of himself as an intimate adviser; he suffered from House's equally inflated view that he could manipulate the Massachusetts organization Democrats. First, last, and always, the Wet city dwellers of immigrant background who made up the backbone of Massachusetts Democracy looked upon Smith as their great hero. Senator Walsh, himself a conservative Irishman, blurted out this fact realistically after the luncheon. "If 'Al' Smith desires to have the nomination, then of course Massachusetts will be for him and none can prevent such a development," he asserted. "Next to Smith, of course, I am for Roosevelt." [12]

If Roosevelt could indeed have been second choice after Smith, as in Texas, he would have furthered his political fortunes. But on his way to the luncheon, he was the victim of an unfortunate political accident. On the train to Boston he encountered Mayor Curley, Irish and Democratic, recently the victim of a sound drubbing from another Irish wing of the party, that of Senator Walsh and Governor Joseph B. Ely. Curley, seeking to regain control of the state organization, hitched his cause to Roosevelt's. Far from being an aid, this mired down Roosevelt by tying him to the minority faction. House in advance had tried to avoid this by not inviting Curley to the luncheon; but after Curley's overtures he belatedly issued an invitation.* Only later did what appeared at the time as a triumph appear in its true perspective as a setback inflicted by an unwanted guest.[14]

Roosevelt should have known he could expect no love feast in Massachusetts, because a poll of the delegates and alternates to the 1928 convention showed that he trailed Smith there. This poll, unfavorable toward Roosevelt in Massachusetts, elsewhere was exceedingly favorable to him. More than half of those who listed presidential preferences named Roosevelt.† He led in thirty-nine out of forty-four states, and, except for favorite sons, was rivaled only by Smith in

* Later House became so sold upon Curley that in 1933 he strongly but unsuccessfully backed Curley to be Ambassador to Italy.[13]

† Of the approximately two thousand delegates to the 1928 convention, 942 answered Straus's inquiry, 844 listed a presidential preference, and of these latter, 478 named Roosevelt, 125 Smith, 73 Owen D. Young, 39 Governor Ritchie, 38 Senator Robinson, 35 Newton D. Baker, 15 James M. Reed. The remaining votes went to thirteen favorite-son candidates. The poll covered every state except New York, which was not canvassed, and Oregon, Wisconsin, and Wyoming, from which no replies came.

Massachusetts, Connecticut, and Delaware. Despite his Wetness he was ahead in every Southern state except Senator Robinson's Arkansas. There could have been no more striking evidence of Roosevelt's availability among Democratic professionals. In this era when the scientific public-opinion poll was still unknown, this was spectacular political news, and a powerful invitation to climb aboard the Roosevelt bandwagon.

The poll was a magnificent gift to Roosevelt from Jesse I. Straus, president of the R. H. Macy and Company department stores. Straus, a businessman and philanthropist of finest repute, was one of the most active of the "Friends of Roosevelt." He did not let this appear when he polled the delegates, and purportedly he polled them without Roosevelt's knowledge. When the poll was made public at the end of March, Roosevelt was able blandly to refuse comment and reap the benefit.[15]

Two weeks later, Straus announced a second poll, which showed Roosevelt as popular among Democratic business and professional men as he was among the politicians. This covered twelve hundred men in every state but New York. Among them, Roosevelt led Smith five to one, and even that industrial statesman Owen D. Young, idol of Democratic businessmen, by a margin of two to one.* This was especially surprising to political analysts because Roosevelt had identified himself so strongly with the progressive rural wing of the Democratic party rather than with the supposedly more conservative business interests.[16]

Both polls gave Roosevelt strong reason for optimism. They seemed to confirm his strategy of taking the lead early, for he had a majority, or almost a majority, against the field. Had he been a Republican this might have been enough, but he was a Democrat, and in the convention he must muster two thirds of the delegates' votes in order to win a nomination. Consequently, favorable as the polls were, there were ill portents in them too. The most ominous was the strength of Smith in the Northeast. What it was in New York State, the polls did not indicate, since Straus wisely omitted New York, supposedly in order not to overweight his figures. It would have been bad policy to have tampered with an exceedingly delicate situation, since the Tammany organization, occasionally harassed by Roosevelt, was beginning to whisper that Smith was a lesser evil. Smith still could be a powerful

* The more important preferences were: 562 for Roosevelt, 256 for Young, 115 for Smith, 95 for Robinson, 85 for Ritchie, and 16 for Baker.

factor, indeed a decisive factor combined with the favorite sons. The combination could easily form an anti-Roosevelt bloc which could hold more than a third of the votes at the convention. Out of a deadlock could come a stampede toward a dark horse, and the Straus polls pointed to an eminently respectable, conservative dark horse, Owen D. Young. Clearly, the Raskob-Smith strategy was to promote Smith and the favorite sons, and also quietly to groom Ritchie, Baker, or Young.

Behind their public rejoicing, the Roosevelt forces prepared for another burst of effort to put their candidates even more decisively in the lead. In June the "Friends of Roosevelt" announced another survey that showed Roosevelt well in front of the ruck of favorite sons, but the time to rely alone on the bandwagon effect of polls and upon voluminous correspondence was past. With the convention not more than a year away, Roosevelt needed to secure as many commitments as possible from state organizations.

Some of this work Roosevelt could do cautiously himself by conferring with leaders who chatted with him at Albany or on his trips to and from Warm Springs. A little of this even got into the newspapers when he went to French Lick early in June to attend the Governors' Conference. While he publicly struck an ideological blow by declaring himself ready to experiment to end the depression, he privately engaged in deep conversation with many a Democratic governor ready to take him seriously as the party's most likely candidate. At French Lick he received assurances from the Indiana organization that it was favorably considering his candidacy; in Ohio on the way back, he conferred with practically every powerful Democrat in the state except Newton D. Baker. He carefully avoided offending any of Ohio's three native sons, Baker, Governor George White, and James Cox, whose running mate he had been in 1920. These conversations, he informed newspapermen, added up to "two days of very pleasing social visits . . . with absolutely nothing political in it." [17]

For Roosevelt thus to confer very often within eyesight of reporters was politically dangerous. Also it was unnecessary since he could send out a well-trained, skillful emissary, Jim Farley, to undertake the task. Farley, who for some months had been planning to attend an Elks' convention in Seattle in early July, could combine politicking with conviviality. From Farley's own accounts it is not clear whether he or Howe first hit upon the scheme; in any event, Roosevelt quickly fell in with it.* On Sunday, June 21, 1931, Farley went to Hyde Park, equipped with a map of the United States, train schedules, and lists of Democratic organizations. For two hours he, Roosevelt, and Howe pored over this data in Roosevelt's tiny office in the front of his home. Roosevelt, with his sense of political geography, took the lead in working out the itinerary, deciding what states Farley should visit, what ones he should avoid. Howe, drawing upon his years of correspondence on behalf of Roosevelt, helped determine the key organizational Democrats in each state whom Farley should visit. Most of these were national committeemen and state chairmen, selected on the theory that they could carry their organizations with them. As from the beginning, the Roosevelt strategy was to appeal to the masses through his speeches and policies, but to negotiate with the key regular politicians.[19]

On June 29, Farley departed upon his junket, armed with names and detailed instructions. Howe had telegraphed and sent airmail letters in advance to the leaders; he had sent copies of the itinerary to House and to Joseph E. Davies, chairman under Wilson of the Federal Trade Commission, in order to obtain further key names. Thus, Howe, like a meticulous promotion manager who has been conducting a vigorous direct-mail campaign, sent out his talented traveling salesman, Farley, to clinch the sales.[20]

Farley has liked since to think of himself as having been a political drummer. He was that indeed, and a good one; thus he must have appeared to almost everyone who felt his hearty handshake. But he preferred to travel through the West in a rather curious twofold disguise — as a visiting Elk, and as the impartial chairman of the Democratic party in a state which had three favorite sons, Roosevelt, Smith, and Young. He made his calls upon leading Democrats ostensibly to confer with them upon organizational matters. It is a thing of wonder that Farley, who had issued a public manifesto on behalf of Roosevelt the previous November, and who had already put his green signature to thousands of pro-Roosevelt letters, actually thought he could fool anyone with this mild bit of dissembling. Apparently he did think so. "I never talked to individuals about the presidential nomination unless I was certain of the other fellow's position," he has written. "Usually, I sparred around a bit by suggesting that we had

* Farley, writing in *Behind the Ballots* in 1938, credits Howe with the idea; by 1948 in *Jim Farley's Story,* he had revised his memory to recall that while others, including FDR, had taken credit for it, the original suggestion was Farley's own.[18]

three outstanding potential candidates for the Presidency in New York State." At least this subterfuge did no harm, and was no more transparent than Roosevelt's "social visits." It did serve the purpose of preventing open irritation when Farley conferred with an occasional politician cool or hostile toward Roosevelt.[21]

Since the Middle Western and Western politicians were well aware of Farley's role as Roosevelt's salesman, his ingratiating appearance and exemplary habits, so in contrast to the stereotype of the tough, hard-drinking Tammanyite, did much to disarm them. He was, as Howe felt, "temperamentally and physically the ideal man to use in the Western States." Howe explained to Colonel House, who had been a bit dubious, "He has a wholesome breeziness of manner and a frank and open character which is characteristic of all Westerners. In addition I think he gives a distinct impression of being a very practical and businesslike politician." Farley repeated the success he had enjoyed when he had first met the Southerners in Washington earlier that year. After he had left South Dakota, the national committeeman wrote, "Our boys all liked you very much. . . . If you make as good an impression everywhere as here there will be no question but that Roosevelt will be nominated." [22]

Wherever Farley established this good impression, he immediately dropped his simulated neutral air and worked hard for his candidate. He stressed Roosevelt's availability and physical fitness, and tried to discourage sentiment for other candidates. He also sought firm pledges of delegates. These were remarkably easy to get. The South Dakota committeeman had exclaimed to Farley, "I'm damned tired of backing losers. In my opinion, Roosevelt can sweep the country, and I'm going to support him." [23]

Farley reported to Roosevelt:

> In my travels throughout the States, I have visited, I have done everything I possibly could on the desire on our part to have an early convention [in each state] and to instruct [national convention] delegates for you.
>
> Have indicated that they must all get away from the favorite son idea, on the theory that it is only used for the purpose of typing up blocks of delegates to be manipulated. . . .
>
> Governor, the presidential job must be a great one, judging from the way they are all anxious to have it.[24]

In nineteen days, Farley covered eighteen states, shaking hands, lunching, and conferring incessantly despite stifling heat at times, and the weariness that must have come from trying to snatch rest night after night on a sleeper. He even found time to dictate some eighteen detailed reports to Roosevelt and Howe. On his way to Washington, he stopped in Indiana, Wisconsin, Minnesota, North and South Dakota, and Montana. It was at Seattle he announced to reporters that "the name of Roosevelt is magic." Privately, he wrote Roosevelt that if he continued to find such overwhelming sentiment, when he reached New York he would make a statement so enthusiastic that "those who read it will believe I am a fit candidate for an insane asylum." On the return jaunt, Farley visited in Oregon, California, Nevada, Utah, Wyoming, Colorado, Nebraska, Kansas, Missouri, and Illinois. With a few exceptions – California was one of them – he continued exuberant over prospects.

Where complications showed signs of developing, Farley handled them deftly. At Kansas City, he attended a touchy political luncheon in his honor, at which he was introduced by Missouri's favorite son, Jim Reed.* Farley warmly praised Reed, did not even mention Roosevelt's name, and somehow managed to extricate himself without having offended either the Reed or the anti-Reed faction in the state organization. Howe, much impressed, felt that Farley was winning his political spurs.[25]

Upon his return to New York City, Farley did indeed give an exuberant report to the press, and it seemed well grounded in fact. No serious signs of opposition were appearing as yet; even favorite sons, like Reed of Missouri and J. Hamilton Lewis of Illinois, had assured Farley of their friendliness toward Roosevelt, and most of the organization men had at least hinted that they would favor him.† The Washington national committeeman, Scott Bullitt, brother of William Bullitt, an ardent friend and supporter of Roosevelt, wrote Farley, "The Governor had made the way easy for us but your visit has made it a lot easier and smoother." With justifiable pride, Farley went to Hyde Park on July 20 to brief Roosevelt and Howe upon his trip. The Roosevelt sun was beating down hot upon the Middle West and West; there were only fluffy clouds on the distant horizon.[27]

* One of the guests at the luncheon was a relatively unknown Pendergast man, Harry S. Truman.

† Farley did have some tendency toward overoptimism. He reported that Arthur Mullen, Nebraska committeeman, had promised at the proper time to guarantee that Nebraska would be in the Roosevelt column. Mullen later wrote in his memoirs, "I was . . . friendly but unpledged. . . . He asked me, pointblank, if I'd be for Roosevelt. I said I wasn't interested yet in any one candidate."[26]

One of these clouds, which irritated Roosevelt as much as it alarmed him, was Farley's report that wherever he went, he still had to assure politicians that Roosevelt was physically fit enough to be President. Even Roosevelt himself ran into this and naturally was upset by it. Several years later he reminisced to a friend that on his way back from French Lick in 1931, he had stopped at Dayton, Ohio, to see James Cox, who was invalided after a very serious operation. "His whole attitude during the two hours I spent with him alone was the same – that it was marvelous that I could stand the strain of the Governorship, but that in all probability I would be dead in a few months. He spent the greater part of the time asking me solicitously how I was, though he was a much sicker man than I was." [28]

Personal pride was involved, but the political considerations were serious. Even before Farley's swing West, Roosevelt worried about the whispering.* "I find that there is a deliberate attempt to create the impression that my health is such as would make it impossible for me to fulfill the duties of President," he confided to a friend. "To those who know how strenuous have been the three years I have passed as Governor of this State, this is highly humorous, but it is taken with great seriousness in the southern states particularly. I shall appreciate whatever my friends may have to say in their personal correspondence to dispel this perfectly silly piece of propaganda." [30]

Fear of this whispering campaign led Roosevelt to work out one final spectacular stunt to publicize his fine health. Earle Looker, a professedly Republican writer who had been one of the White House playmates of Theodore Roosevelt's children, contrived it. He issued a challenge to Roosevelt, which the Governor accepted. The Director of the New York Academy of Medicine was asked to select a committee of eminent physicians, including a brain specialist, to examine him.†

* Some of it was getting into print. *Time* magazine quoted a prominent woman: "This candidate, while mentally qualified for the presidency, is utterly unfit physically." [29]

† The technical part of their report, first published in John Gunther, *Roosevelt in Retrospect,* was:

> *Heart:* Regular; rate, 80; no increased cardiac dullness; no murmurs; aortic dullness is not widened. Blood pressure 140/100.
>
> *Pulse:* Regular 80 – after examination by three physicians rate is 84, returning to 80 after 3 minutes. Electrocardiogram – left preponderance. Inverted T_3. PR and QRS intervals normal.
>
> *Lungs:* No dullness, no changes in respiratory murmurs, no extraneous sounds or *râles;* no abnormalities in voice sounds or fremitus. Chest expansion good.

They emphatically reaffirmed his fitness. "We believe," they wired Looker, "that his health and powers of endurance are such as to allow him to meet any demands of private and public life." [32]

In addition to allowing the medical examination, Roosevelt told Looker that he could come unannounced to observe him at the Governor's office, to see for himself whether Roosevelt was competent to carry out his duties. Three times Looker came. He reported the medical findings and what he himself observed in *Liberty* magazine, July 25, 1931. "I had noted the alertness of his movements, the sparkle of his eyes, the vigor of his gestures," Looker stated. "I had seen his strength under the strain of long working periods. In so far as I had observed him, I had come to the conclusion that he seemed able to take more punishment than many men ten years younger. Merely his legs were not much good to him." [33]

Farley read the article on the last day of his Western trip. He thought it a "corker" which "answers fully the questions . . . put to me many times during the past three weeks." Howe purchased thousands of reprints in order to send a copy to every county Democratic chairman in the country, and to any correspondent who expressed doubt over Roosevelt's health. The "Friends of Roosevelt" broadcast further thousands to prominent Democrats. Joseph Davies reported to Howe after making a trip to the Pacific Coast "reviving and renewing the old Wilson ties and associations for the Governor," that the *Liberty* article had helped a lot. It seemed to minimize the danger that the health issue could grow from a minor cloud into a menacing thunderhead.[34]

In both his public and private life Roosevelt's energies drove the engines of state, and, not exhausted by this strenuous living, expressed their surplus in sparks of high spirits and vivacity. Few of the millions who walked free while he sat chained to his chair could boast such an enviable standard of furious vitality.

The only serious question that could be raised was whether he had

---

Abdomen: Liver and spleen, not enlarged, no pain, no masses. Abdominal muscles show slight bulging on left. No hernia. Umbilical excursion upward.

No evidence of columnar degeneration of spinal cord. Both optic nerves normal. A false Babinski reflex is present on both sides (old "polio" symptom). Right knee jerk absent. Left shows responses in upper and outer portion of quadriceps extensor.

Some coldness of feet below knees; cocktail makes them right. The lower erector spinae are slightly affected. Gluteus medius partial R. and L.

Wassermann – negative with both alcoholic and cholesterinized antigen. No symptoms of *impotentia coeundi.*[31]

any of this energy left over for quiet family life, or whether it entirely went into his public enterprises. Bit by bit the public saw into more and more of what went on behind the doors of the Executive Mansion and on the no longer secluded acres at Hyde Park. Not only Roosevelt himself but even the members of his family had to undergo the penalties as well as the pleasures of incessant publicity.

Partly because of his preoccupation with the question of his health, Roosevelt kept few secrets about his daily routine. When a Butte, Montana, editor asserted he had not dispensed with a wheel chair, he declared, "As a matter of fact, I don't use a wheel chair at all except a little kitchen chair on wheels to get about my room while dressing . . . and solely for the purpose of saving time." [35]

Roosevelt did not invite the Butte editor to come and see for himself, but he might just as well have done so, he lived so public an existence. Several writers did come to observe Roosevelt's every move from the time he awoke until he went to bed. He was seldom alone, and seldom even alone with his family. His former Groton master, George Marvin, described two of these typical days, one at Albany and the other at Hyde Park.

At Albany, his white-coated Negro valet came into the bedroom at eight on the dot every morning, drew the curtains aside, and placed a big bundle of newspapers on the bedside table. Roosevelt pulled himself to a sitting position, drew on a white sweater, and while eating breakfast glanced through the papers. He especially studied the editorial pages. By the time the meal was over, business was beginning. In would come a house guest of the night before at whom Roosevelt wished to fire a parting query, or Rosenman with a legal matter. At the same time, while talking, Roosevelt was going through his mail and taking phone calls. His granddaughter, "Sistie" Dall, would run in and scramble onto the bed and kiss him good morning.

Only after all this, Roosevelt would shave, dress with his valet's assistance, and, using crutch and cane, walk to the elevator to go downstairs. There political visitors would be awaiting him, who might even continue their conversation in the automobile to the Capitol. After a crowded day there, Roosevelt would finally return home after six o'clock for an interlude with his family. Marvin reported:

"When we reach the mansion tea is served in Mrs. Roosevelt's living room upstairs and there about her are gathered the two Groton boys, Franklin, Jr., and Johnny, and with their colored mammy, the two grandchildren – Anna's little girl and boy, 'Sistie' and 'Buz.' Political or governmental talk is banned, except now and then a humorous incident or echo. After this . . . we disperse to dress for 8 o'clock dinner."

That might be a state banquet for the justices of the Court of Appeals, with family and the secretaries, who were practically members of the family, present along with the dignitaries. The guests would not leave until midnight.

At Hyde Park on week ends the tempo was only a little slower. On Sunday morning, Roosevelt might talk crops and politics with his tenant farmer, about old Dutchess County records with Helen Reynolds, and about the site for a new Hyde Park school with a local Democratic committeeman. The flow of visitors continued until dinner. At the table, according to Marvin, "On Franklin Roosevelt's right sits the American wife of an English peer. On his left is a well known novelist [Fannie Hurst], who is playing with the idea of becoming a Dutchess County farmer. The Governor's mother, Mrs. James Roosevelt . . . presides at the far other end of the table, giving occasional directions in French to the butler. In between . . . a secretary and a handsome, husky sergeant detailed from the State troopers; the daughter and son-in-law from Tarrytown; knickerbockered neighbors from Hyde Park manors and fox hunting friends from Staatsburg; a somewhat bewildered biographer from Boston, seeking copy is wedged between an Assemblyman and a stenographer from Albany. The Titian-haired leader of the Women's Labor Union hobnobs with the bob-haired manager of Mrs. Roosevelt's furniture factory."

At four o'clock whoever was talking with Roosevelt at the time was likely to be invited to ride along in the Ford while Roosevelt drove about his estate inspecting his Guernsey herd and his trees. Afterwards Roosevelt might play fan tan in the library, interrupting the game to deliver a short radio talk into a microphone on the table. After supper, Mrs. Roosevelt would take the train to New York City, and Roosevelt, warmly wrapped, would sit beside the chauffeur in the front of an open car and return to Albany.[36]

In all of this incessant oral interplay with people, Roosevelt demonstrated almost unfailingly high spirits and good humor. Among his guests he showed no especial sensitivity because he could no longer as once bound around the house and his fields. His literary agent at this time, Nannine Joseph, remembers how startled she was when she heard a sound like the click of a pistol being cocked when she prepared to leave a car with him. He laughingly reassured her that it was only his braces, which had to be locked before he could get out.[37] Again, Nicholas Roosevelt, standing on the porch, watched Elliott Roosevelt and Gus Gennerich, his bodyguard, lift him into his roadster. As they turned away, he fell onto his back on the seat. Nicholas Roosevelt recalled:

"I doubt if one man in a thousand as disabled and dependent on others would have refrained from some sort of reproach, however mild, to those whose carelessness had thus left him in the lurch. But Franklin merely lay on his back, waved his strong arms in the air, and laughed. At once they came back and helped him to his seat behind the wheel, and he called me to join him. For a moment I had seen the true spirit of the man. He was not putting on an act. Rather it was the instinctive reaction of a brave and gallant gentleman – as illuminating as it was moving and inspiring." [38]

Fortunately, much of his recreation required no physical effort. He would relax with his stamps or whittle at a ship model. The walls of his office in Albany, as in his home at Hyde Park, came to be covered with naval pictures and prints. Despite his fairly tight financial condition, he continued to make purchases, and obtained one magnificent acquisition. This was a book of watercolor sketches of naval operations in California during the Mexican War. "I am fascinated by it," Roosevelt commented when he first saw it. "The pictures are not only of great naval and marine corps interest, but are, I imagine, the only existing sketches of the occupation of California which were done literally on the spot. I cannot afford to buy them, but I am doing it nevertheless." He sent a check for nine hundred dollars. Several years later, he published the sketches.[39]

Roosevelt's collector's instinct combined with hero worship as he followed the exploits of his old Navy friend, Richard E. Byrd, who was in the Antarctic. After Byrd's return he wrote, "By the way, as you had already given me the envelope which you carried over the North Pole and the little silk Flag which you took over the ocean, I wish much that you could send me a scrap of something which you took over the South Pole flight – even if it is a piece of your sock – as I much want to have all three framed together to hang in my office." Byrd replied, "You poor old son of a gun, don't you know that I carried an American flag for you over the South Pole? I will get it out and send it to you with a little inscription." Roosevelt obtained his memento, and presided over a gala reception for Byrd at Albany.[40]

Thus even in his hobbies, Roosevelt functioned in part as a public figure. Family affairs inevitably spilled over into the news. When Elliott Roosevelt decided he did not wish to go to college, a commendatory editorial apeared in the New York *Telegram.* Letters poured into Albany about Elliott's choice, and Roosevelt wrote, "I feel that a college education is a tremendous help but my son Elliott preferred starting out on his own and Mrs. Roosevelt and I feel he is the one to decide." [41]

When James Roosevelt prepared to marry Betsy Cushing, daughter of the renowned Dr. Harvey Cushing, the forthcoming event was splashed across the pages of newspapers. Roosevelt, as the father of the groom, wrote a facetious note to Dr. Cushing, which though full of whimsy had an undertone of the way family matters could become entangled with political life:

> My better half has made a demand that within three days I give her a complete list of all political and business associates whom I have shaken hands with during the past twenty-five years, in order that they may be invited to your wedding! I want to go on record as expressing my gratitude to you for paying for the event! I think you will find it better in the long run to hire Mechanics' Hall. Perhaps Jim Curley can introduce you to a good caterer. A shore dinner should prove the least expensive but for heaven's sake get the best brand of beer!
>
> I am making arrangements with the New Haven for two special trains leaving New York the week before the wedding and have told them to bill you.[42]

Mrs. Roosevelt, during the years when her husband was governor, worked diligently to preserve her private life and personal interests. While she functioned as official hostess at most Albany functions, she could depend upon Roosevelt's charming secretaries, Marguerite Le Hand and Grace Tully, to ease part of her burden there. She continued to spend the first three days a week in New York City, where she was vice-principal of the Todhunter School, taught classes in American history and modern history, and lectured on current events and the biographies of famous Americans. She also maintained her interest in the furniture and handicraft manufacturing at the Val Kill industries. And she was in constant demand as a speaker. She had not much more time than her husband to give to purely family concerns.[43]

Yet for all the hustle and publicity of their lives, the Roosevelts were a devoted family. Sara Roosevelt at Hyde Park was a stately but tender matriarch. She was proud of her son, and at times perhaps even fathomed too well the political mysteries swirling about the estate. Once when Huey Long was at lunch she whispered audibly, "Who is that horrible man?" Within the family, she continued her rather exasperating habit of undermining the Roosevelts' authority by spoiling the children. When one of the boys wrecked his car in a lark, they decided to punish him by forbidding him to have another. A few days later he returned home in a newer and finer one his grandmother had purchased him. On the whole, she gloried in the excitement around her. Once while her son was governor, she wrote him that over a half century before she had first come to Hyde Park to visit. "If I had not come then," she commented, "I should now be 'old Miss Delano,' after a rather sad life!" [44]

When she fell seriously ill with pneumonia in Paris in the spring of 1931, Roosevelt, taking Elliott with him, hurried to her. Fortunately, she was convalescing by the time he arrived. But the crisis served to remind Eleanor Roosevelt poignantly how much the family ties meant. She wrote her husband in Paris after their leavetaking, "I think I looked tired chiefly because I hated so to see you go though I knew it was the best thing for you to do and the sensible thing for me not to go. We are really very dependent on each other though we do see so little of each other! I feel as lost as I did when I went abroad & I will never do that again!" [45]

Unfortunately for the family, the magic that was gathering around the name Franklin D. Roosevelt was removing him more and more from their circle. It is one of the most remarkable things about him that as his preoccupation with public life grew, he lost none of his magic for those closest and dearest to him. This must have mightily reinforced his self-confidence as he moved ahead to meet repeated political and economic crises.

CHAPTER XV

Pioneering Relief

> The . . . responsibility of the State undoubtedly applies when widespread economic conditions render large numbers of men and women incapable of supporting either themselves or their families because of circumstances beyond their control which make it impossible for them to find remunerative labor. To these unfortunate citizens aid must be extended by government – not as a matter of charity but as a matter of social duty.
>
> – FDR TO LEGISLATURE, *August 28, 1931.*

LONG before the end of the summer of 1931, statisticians were predicting that the coming winter would bring grimmer human deprivation than any previously known in American history. Private and municipal aid came close to foundering as the relief burden, which had increased 32 per cent in 1930 over the year before, in 1931 climbed 80 per cent over the high mark of 1930. Governor Roosevelt feared that in another twelve months the number of destitute might double.

As early as June, Roosevelt felt that the time for long-range planning was past, that for the moment he must concentrate upon immediate and effective relief measures. He warned Governor Gifford Pinchot of Pennsylvania, who was planning a governors' conference on unemployment, that it should limit itself to practical plans for the coming winter in order to focus attention upon immediate relief.* It was only after Pinchot's sharp objection that Roosevelt joined in a call for a conference which would include basic planning, but his thinking remained

* FDR obviously also feared to become politically associated with Pinchot in what might be considered radical schemes. He wrote Pinchot, "Everybody frankly doubts if [the] call [of] a new conference by you and me alone would result in real cooperation on a national scale by those concerned with relief either in industrial, social or public fields. Many people would feel either political motives on our part or else fear of some crackpot plan and would stay away. These people include many of our real friends, who are essential to success of [the] conference and who would cooperate in a conference called in a different way."[1]

unaltered.[2] On the back of Pinchot's letter calling the conference, Roosevelt jotted:

"Ask each State & each of the larger municipalities to tell situation *&* plans & ask them how to coordinate against next winter's emergencies — Problem to have a single leadership [and] Whether this can be done by joint effort or by federal gov. Cut out all reference to long range." [3]

Within New York, Roosevelt moved rapidly in this direction. There is the possibility that he did not wish Pinchot to overshadow him; there is the certainty that he did not wish Pinchot to hamstring him with a commitment to concepts that more conservative Republicans would not swallow. It was essential that Roosevelt limit himself to the immediate problem if he were to gain the support of the Republican-dominated state legislature. Here obviously was an immediate crisis, and, unlike the long-drawn-out unemployment-insurance controversy, it was one which demanded instant solution. Roosevelt would not dare get into a deadlock with the legislature over a matter so urgent.

First, Roosevelt wanted the facts. Early in August, he addressed a letter to the mayors of each of the twenty-four cities in the state with a population of twenty-five thousand or more. He warned them that according to statistics gathered by the state Department of Labor, employment in New York had declined three per cent in May and June, and that many more people would have exhausted their resources by winter. He inquired, therefore, whether there was a local committee in each city to raise and distribute private relief funds, and whether the committee was raising or would be able to raise adequate funds. He added that as governor he would join in a general appeal to people to contribute generously, and would continue to insist that public-works projects give as much employment as possible. But Roosevelt had no intention of stopping at this point if it was not adequate.

"If private relief funds are not raised in sufficient amount, public relief must be given," he declared. He pointed out that New York City was spending about a million dollars a month for special employment under authorization from the state legislature. If additional legislation was necessary for the forthcoming winter, Roosevelt wanted the mayors to recommend it so that he could make plans for it.[4]

When the legislature met in special session later in August, Roosevelt quickly turned its focus to relief problems. This had not been the intention of Republican leaders, who as always were preoccupied with the struggle to clean up Tammany. They had persuaded Roosevelt to call the special session to pass legislation which would enable the New

York City investigating committee to grant immunity to witnesses.* Presumably this would be embarrassing to Roosevelt, but he called the session and sent it a message recommending the legislation. Two days later he turned the tables on the Republican leaders by commending them for their legislative investigation of local government, and urging them to extend it to a number of Republican-dominated local governments outside of New York City. The next day he completely overshadowed all questions of corruption by sending a special message recommending a comprehensive relief program. It would be easy to interpret this, as did outraged Republican leaders at the time, as a wily political maneuver to counteract the Tammany investigation. Certainly Roosevelt was not averse to achieving this end, but the relief problem was paramount in his mind.[5]

In the spirit of his June address before the governors, Roosevelt asserted the obligation of the state to care for those of its citizens who were victims of the depression. "Modern society, acting through its government," he declared, "owes the definite obligation to prevent the starvation or the dire want of any of its fellow men and women who try to maintain themselves but cannot." He went on to present evidence that private charities and communities could no longer handle the relief burden unaided; the state must supplement their contributions. Therefore, he recommended the establishment of a new state agency, the Temporary Emergency Relief Administration, which should distribute twenty million dollars through local subsidiary commissions. Significantly, Roosevelt wished to distribute relief on a pay-as-you-go basis. He recommended raising the funds not by borrowing, but by increasing the state income tax by fifty per cent.[6]

Through using the rather redundant words "temporary" and "emergency" as a prefix for his relief commission, Roosevelt was trying to emphasize that this was not a permanent system of unemployment insurance like the British dole. The dole, the handout of direct relief pittances, was under a broad and continuous attack in many influential American publications for tending to undermine the character of recipients and to bankrupt the British Government. Roosevelt proposed to protect the moral fiber of the unemployed through expending the funds in wages for work relief rather than direct charity. "I have tried to outline my program in such a way that the dole will be avoided,"

* The legislature in authorizing an investigation had provided for immunity in a resolution, but the state courts had ruled that the resolution was not sufficient. A special law must be enacted.

he wrote a few days later. "The important thing is to provide any kind of useful public work for the benefit of those who are now unable to find employment and to furnish the necessaries of life only when useful employment cannot be found." [7]

There was nothing in the proposal to rile Republicans. Quite the contrary was the case, since President Hoover was asserting in Washington that states and local governments must shoulder the responsibility for relief.* While Republican Governor Pinchot was attacking the President for not calling a special session of Congress to vote relief funds, Democratic Governor Roosevelt in contrast was carrying out the President's wishes in New York.[9]

By calling for heavier taxes to meet the relief costs, Roosevelt seemed soundly conservative. This was more than a pose. In a private letter, he contrasted his pay-as-you-go recommendation with Hoover's deficit financing. "I can tell you frankly," he wrote on September 2, 1931, "that I am disturbed by this morning's news that the President's policy seems to be to borrow money, over one billion dollars, to pay the current treasury deficit because this merely puts the burden of this unemployment cycle on future generations." [10]

The best politics for Roosevelt was to avoid any appearance of politics. Even Republican newspapers like the Washington *Post* were ready to hail his declaration of independence of Federal bureaucracy as an indication of his qualifications for the 1932 Democratic nomination. Bainbridge Colby wrote a complimentary editorial which appeared from coast to coast in Hearst newspapers. It was entitled "Roosevelt Acts." [11]

More important, Roosevelt carried this air of nonpartisanship to the legislature. When it took up his proposal, he told reporters he had no pride of authorship, and would welcome constructive suggestions from the Republican legislative leaders. Acting with their customary shortsightedness, the Republican leaders refused to cooperate with Roosevelt in a spirit of moderation. Although the new Republican state chairman, Kingsland Macy, warned them not to do so, they

* President Hoover had declared in February, 1931: "This is not an issue as to whether people shall go hungry or cold in the United States. It is solely a question of the best method by which hunger and cold shall be prevented. It is a question as to whether the American people, on one hand, will maintain the spirit of charity and mutual self-help through voluntary giving and the responsibility of local government as distinguished, on the other hand, from appropriations out of the Federal Treasury. . . . If we start appropriations of this character we have not only impaired something infinitely valuable in the life of the American people but have struck at the roots of self-government." [8]

insisted upon squeezing through their own unemployment-relief bill containing two provisions unacceptable to the Governor. They would put the administration of relief under the state Department of Social Welfare, which had a Republican head. More important, they provided for an unlimited matching of local funds with state funds.[12]

This immediately put the legislature in the wrong and the Governor in the right. Roosevelt threatened to veto the measure because of its blank-check provision, which he said might put the state into bankruptcy. He opposed putting administration under the Department of Social Welfare on the grounds that it might lead to bureaucratization and create fear that relief might become a permanent function of the government. When the leaders were adamant, he threatened to call them back into special session and keep them there indefinitely until they passed an acceptable relief bill. He so obviously meant what he threatened, and the likelihood of public outrage was so great, that the Republican leaders capitulated. All they had succeeded in doing was once again unnecessarily to make themselves the villains and Roosevelt the hero.[13]

Roosevelt crowed self-righteously:

"You will have seen that at the eleventh hour the legislative leaders discovered their mistake, came downstairs, conferred, and in less than twenty-four hours the whole trouble had been straightened out, the bill passed and the Legislature gone home. It may interest you to know that in my judgment all of this talk and by-play could have been avoided if the leaders had come to see me two weeks before. The net cost of that extra two weeks was about $50,000. to the taxpayers of this State." [14]

Compared with Senator Robert Wagner of New York, Roosevelt lagged in his thinking on relief. Wagner as early as the spring of 1930 had demanded a large-scale long-range Federal public-works program to smash the depression. Compared with most other governors, however, Roosevelt was in the vanguard. His state committee on stabilization, which he established in March, 1930, had been the first official state body of its sort; the Temporary Emergency Relief Administration was the first new state relief agency.* It became a model for state organizations, and the prototype of a Federal agency. It was the forerunner of the New Deal alphabetical agencies — newspapers called it the T.E.R.A.[15]

* New Jersey followed the next month, Rhode Island in November, and Illinois in February, 1932.

As Roosevelt developed the system, he hoped to utilize the voluntary services of high-caliber civic leaders who would be less likely to assume positions in the old state welfare organization. He obtained as chairman an outstanding businessman and powerful political supporter, Jesse Straus, who had engineered the very favorable opinion polls for him. Only a few weeks earlier, Straus had declined Roosevelt's invitation to join the old Board of Social Welfare. Straus, a Democrat, was one of Roosevelt's most valuable helpers in the preconvention maneuvering; with the same capacity and enthusiasm he threw himself into the task of organizing relief in New York. He received hearty support throughout the state.[16]

Straus had practically a free hand in organizing the T.E.R.A. The other two members of the administration were cooperative; they were Philip J. Wickser of Buffalo, a Republican insurance man and banker, active in many philanthropic organizations, and John L. Sullivan, President of the State Federation of Labor. As for Governor Roosevelt himself, he went to Warm Springs on vacation, leaving it to Straus and his colleagues to establish the relief agency. Straus, experienced in such matters, went to the professional welfare workers in the private organizations in search of an executive director. He could not obtain his first choice, William Hodson, director of the Welfare Council of New York City, who was recommended by Lieutenant Governor Lehman. He then turned to a second choice, suggested by Hodson. This was Harry L. Hopkins, an intense and shrewd young man of great capability, who was executive director of the New York Tuberculosis and Health Association.[17]

Thus Hopkins, who later became such an intimate and powerful adviser to Roosevelt, entered the Governor's service without Roosevelt having in any way participated in the selection or even having seen him except for a casual handshake during the 1928 campaign. Nor did Roosevelt become particularly well acquainted with Hopkins during the year that followed. Hopkins's role was almost completely nonpolitical, and he had few direct dealings with Roosevelt. He had little to do with the 1932 campaign — just enough to identify himself firmly as a member of the Roosevelt camp. His contributions were to organize a group of social workers on behalf of Roosevelt, and to contribute a paragraph on relief for a draft of one of Roosevelt's speeches. He did so with enthusiasm, for he believed President Hoover was making a mess of relief work.[18]

Within New York, Hopkins tried to avoid a similar mess. He labored diligently to build a smooth-running agency. By borrowing right and left from private welfare agencies, he quickly recruited a capable staff of professional welfare workers. Roosevelt was pleased with the results they obtained, but worried over a Civil Service Commission warning that the hundred supervisors were being overpaid. They were receiving two thousand dollars a year, which was a good bit more than was being paid to individuals doing the same kind of work in many localities. Hopkins was so successful that in the spring of 1932 when Straus resigned, Roosevelt appointed Hopkins chairman of the administrative committee.[19]

The task of the new T.E.R.A. was huge. Within a short time it was providing relief to nearly ten per cent of the families in the state. The sums were sparing, averaging about twenty-three dollars per month, but in the acute deflation of the time, that was sufficient to keep families from starving. In Rochester, arrangements with wholesalers made it possible to feed people for fifteen cents per day. New York's relief program was munificent compared with that in some areas; in southern Illinois, the Red Cross was able to give families of coal miners only a dollar and a half for food once every two weeks; relief payments in Detroit dropped to five cents per day per person. By November, 1932, New York had spent twenty-five million dollars on relief.[20]

The T.E.R.A. demonstrated Roosevelt's willingness to experiment and his sensitivity to suffering. As a practical solution, it did at least impose a flimsy barrier between destitute New Yorkers and the raging wolf of starvation, but it was a temporary makeshift, and a costly one.* Many people felt that despite its defects it threw a favorable light upon Roosevelt. In the fall of 1932, Harry Hopkins privately expressed his belief that Roosevelt would make a better President than Hoover, "chiefly because he is not afraid of a new idea," and Hopkins was not alone in this belief.[21]

Although Roosevelt's new ideas did not seem particularly adequate to the relief problem and did comparatively little to lessen the harsh distress behind the appalling statistics, at least he kept continuously canvassing possibilities. As late as March, 1932, he maintained a flicker of faith in voluntary self-help. In a radio address, he called attention

* In the ensuing six years, the T.E.R.A. aided, at one time or another, about five million people — forty per cent of the population of the state — at a cost of approximately $1,155,000,000. By 1937, seventy per cent of these were no longer dependent upon government aid.

to a block-aid drive being launched in New York City, and urged other cities to observe what was happening there: "Let us see how quickly it can attain its purpose of breaking down a city with seven million people into many thousand small communities, each of which can help provide the money necessary to make jobs for people who are experiencing hardship and tragedy because of unemployment." If the plan succeeded in New York, Roosevelt asserted, it should sweep like wildfire across the country.[22]

A barter scheme which came to Roosevelt's attention indicates the way that he went about sifting proposals, scuttling most of them. It was drafted supposedly by several highly respected economists; a legislator brought it to him. It proposed that unemployed men should be put to work in idle plants and on unused lands, where they would produce goods and foodstuffs, not for the open market, but for exchange with each other through state and local relief agencies. It was a comprehensive plan bearing marked similarity to the later "End Poverty in California" program upon which Upton Sinclair campaigned in 1934. What Roosevelt did with it was to submit it to John Sullivan, President of the New York State Federation of Labor, who obviously would be sharply hostile. Sullivan consulted with state labor leaders, and reported back to Roosevelt that the plan was impracticable. Roosevelt forwarded this formidable negative report to the legislator; that was the end of the scheme.[23]

While barter may never have captured Roosevelt's imagination, he did throughout these years cling to an old dream of his, that city workers could be moved back to the land, where they could raise some of their own produce. This was partly the earnest interest of Roosevelt's agricultural advisers in sound rural planning, partly the Governor's sustained enthusiasm for his Uncle Ted's "Country Life" movement, and partly Roosevelt's romantic faith in the Jeffersonian ideal of the independent yeoman living in bucolic abundance. Certainly Roosevelt was under no illusion concerning the plight of the New York farmers, but while with the one hand he was drawing up schemes to reforest abandoned worn-out farms, with the other he was plotting to send unemployed urbanites to the country.

To many Americans this made good, common sense. Henry Ford, a great industrialist with pretensions to being a homespun sage, remarked, "No unemployment insurance can be compared to an alliance between a man and a plot of land." Ford envisioned the decentralization of industry into smaller communities, and the placing of workers on subsistence acres. This in part was in Roosevelt's mind. It was at the heart of an address he gave in August, 1931, before the American Country Life Conference at Ithaca, New York. For industry, relocation in smaller communities would bring advantages, such as cheaper power, he argued. For the worker it would bring a more wholesome life, away from the grime and misery of city slums. "There is contact with earth and with nature and the restful privilege of getting away from pavements and from noise," he elaborated. "There is an opportunity for permanency of abode, a chance to establish a real home in the traditional American sense."

Here too, Roosevelt declared, was new opportunity for the unemployed. He quoted a conversation with a discouraged raiser of relief funds:

> "Suppose," I said, "one were to offer these men an opportunity to go on the land, to provide a house and a few acres of land in the country and a little money and tools to put in small food crops . . . what proportion of them do you think would accept such a proposition?"
>
> "All of them," he said promptly.[24]

This colloquy was undoubtedly close to the mark. Thousands of unemployed would have jumped to share Roosevelt's romantic dream. Unfortunately, there seemed no immediate means to put it into effect. In the summer of 1930, Roosevelt had created an Agricultural Information Bureau in the state Department of Agriculture, to serve as a clearing house of information for prospective buyers of farms. He proposed attaching to it representatives of the Italians, Poles, and Jews in New York City. But unemployed people had no money with which to buy farms, nor could they borrow any. The following summer, in his Ithaca speech, Roosevelt announced he had established a Commission on Rural Homes. He charged it with drafting legislation on rural zoning and canvassing means for relocating people in the country. No matter how much this might be in advance of future trends, it could achieve little during the depression but the preparation of reports which would ultimately wind up in legislative pigeonholes.[25]

Meanwhile, many an unemployed man, stirred by Roosevelt's optimistic words, wrote to Albany to find out how he could obtain a subsistence farm, only to have his hopes dashed by an empty reply. Nevertheless, Roosevelt, in a speech in November and in his message to the legislature in January, returned to his theme. Finally in May he announced a program. He ordered the T.E.R.A. to place as many families as possible on subsistence farms—to pay the rent of small farms, and to provide them with tools, seed for planting, and household necessities. Thus, said Roosevelt, "they may secure through the good earth the permanent jobs they have lost in overcrowded industrial cities and towns." [26]

A few days later Roosevelt boasted that T.E.R.A. had already placed 244 families on farms, and that he expected to propose this program on a national scale. But this was a pitifully microscopic number among the million on relief in New York, and it was a program repugnant to farmers already buried under crop surpluses.* To stave off farmers' criticism, he announced early in June that it was by no means a "back to the land" movement, but rather an economical means of caring for those on relief. Nevertheless, fear of antagonizing the national farm vote led Roosevelt to jettison his beloved hobby in the 1932 campaign after he had suggested it to some farm editors at Columbus, Ohio.[27]

Throughout the remainder of his governorship, Roosevelt continued to canvass other means of coping with the depression, leaning for advice usually upon well-qualified experts. In the winter of 1931–1932, he considered establishing a commission to work out a plan to save small-home owners in danger of foreclosure, and thought of proposing in his 1932 message that no interest on any mortgage should exceed four per cent, and that there should be no amortization. He decided against both steps.[28]

Before the end of the winter, Roosevelt gave way before harsh economic facts upon two principles to which he had previously clung. Within New York, the state could not possibly continue to meet the mounting relief burden on a pay-as-you-go basis. Reluctantly he proposed to the legislature that a thirty-million-dollar bond issue be submitted to the people of the state in the November election. Reiterating his belief that relief expenses must be met out of current revenue whenever possible, he confessed he could not blink the fact that the heavy existing tax burden, and the even heavier burden that the depression was imposing upon business, made this impossible. "In such extraordinary times," Roosevelt concluded, "I believe that extraordinary measures, otherwise not to be considered, are justified." In the same

* FDR wrote privately, "The wheat farmers and a few others may complain but I am trying to explain at the same time that people who move to small farms will not raise all their food supply and, because of the fact of being nearer the source, will actually purchase more milk, vegetables, etc. than in the city."

spirit, Roosevelt abandoned his firm states'-rights position that relief was a state and local problem. He wired Senator Robert F. Wagner his endorsement of the $750,000,000 unemployment relief bill pending before Congress. It should not be the permanent policy of the Federal Government, Roosevelt reaffirmed, but it was "the definite obligation of the government to prevent starvation and distress in this present crisis." [29]

In the spring, Roosevelt decided to call another unemployment conference for early June, to work out further relief plans before politics obscured the issues. "Conventional remedies have been honorably tried both by State, municipalities and private charity," he pointed out. "They have been well carried out but have proved insufficient. What next?" What he wanted was for a broad and representative committee of experts, operating on practical, simple, and nonpolitical lines, to investigate the moral and ethical considerations growing out of two years of continued unemployment, and its new and unforeseen problems. What they must formulate were proposals "progressive, new and fearless, without being radical." [30]

In preparation for the conference, Miss Perkins and Henry Bruere invited Harry Hopkins and twenty outstanding economists to dinner. There they canvassed proposals, and came to the disappointing conclusion that those which could be considered immediately on a state level were only three: more public works, transplanting city dwellers back to the farms, and the stimulation of some housing projects. The economists gave their general approval to all, but felt a laymen's conference such as Roosevelt planned would find insuperable difficulties surrounding each. Moreover, Senator Joseph Robinson, Owen D. Young, Alfred E. Smith, and President Hoover were all making statements on unemployment relief on the national level.[31]

If Roosevelt were now to act again on a state level, he would no longer be in the vanguard, but to the rear. He acted upon the recommendation of Bruere and Miss Perkins, and canceled the conference. The time for him to use New York as an experimental laboratory for solving unemployment had passed; his thinking and his political fortunes were carrying him into the vast national laboratory. But before he could get there, he had several challenges to meet, and one pre-eminent challenger.

CHAPTER XVI

Break with the "Happy Warrior"

What a queer thing that was for Al to fight so bitterly!
— FDR, *Election day, 1931.*

FROM the day in November, 1928, when Roosevelt was elected Governor of New York while Smith went down in defeat, it became almost inevitable that the two men would clash sooner or later over Roosevelt's presidential ambitions. The outward amenities between them scantly covered Smith's deepening distrust of Roosevelt's ability and his festering hurt because he could not run the Roosevelt administration in Albany. Added to this must have been Smith's growing disappointment as the worsening depression made it evident that any Democrat who received the nomination in 1932, whether Catholic, Wet or what, would probably win the election. Given these factors, and given the failure of any other outstanding anti-Roosevelt leader to appear, it became unavoidable that the "Stop Roosevelt" movement of the moneyed and the machine Democrats should coalesce behind Smith. The one bitter last-ditch fighter who might be able to block Roosevelt's trail to the nomination was the man Roosevelt, nominating him in 1924, had dubbed the "Happy Warrior." The warrior was not happy now and he was showing unmistakable signs of going after Roosevelt's scalp.

In the fall of 1931, Roosevelt was well aware of Smith's unhappiness; he and his advisers did not yet take the matter too seriously since Smith still seemed to be in no mind to run. All the news that came in from almost every part of the country was so uniformly optimistic that Roosevelt felt no need for the time being to sanction any official organization to promote his candidacy. He was prone to take the advice of his friends in both the South and West and let things drift, since the state organizations were so friendly toward him.[1] Howe confided to an Illinois Roosevelt man:

"It is a long way to Convention time, and many things may happen, but at the present moment, I think all of the Governor's friends who have been in touch with the various state leaders feel that were the Convention to be held tomorrow, the Governor would be elected on the first ballot with not more than three states out of line." [2]

Roosevelt began to sound in some of his letters as though he were past the convention and drafting campaign speeches. He sent Colonel House his tentative ideas on a national overhaul of the credit system,[3] and to William E. Dodd, the American historian, he wrote concerning agriculture:

"There is no doubt but that we have lost the proper balance between the agricultural and industrial elements of this country and I am beginning to think more and more that the solution of our present difficulty lies in the restoration of that equality which existed before the manufacturer became, very largely through the Republican Party, a master of our Nation." [4]

Issues were, of course, the proper provender of the letters Roosevelt and his organization sent out in such huge quantities, just as information which could be collected, collated, and filed for future use was the product of the incoming mail. Roosevelt kept in close touch with the policy statements that went into the outgoing letters, and kept them, like the one to Professor Dodd, lofty in tone and vaguely agrarian in leanings. Most of these Howe and his staff could handle alone; Roosevelt ordinarily corresponded only with the leading figures.[5] Some of the interchanges were simplicity itself, as in the instance of the penciled scrawl of a South Carolinian:

"Your Honor: Should you ever be a President of America please do the best you can."

Howe ghosted this reply on behalf of Roosevelt:

"Replying to yours of October 9th, you may take this as my assurance that if I should ever be President of America, I will certainly do the best I can." [6]

Sometimes the answers were not so easy to prepare. Howe sent one from Nebraska to Farley in October, 1931, with the notation:

"Around and around and around goes the buck — from you to Franklin, from Franklin to Sam, from Sam to me; and as this letter is addressed to you I promptly wish it off on you. If you are not a farmer you ought to be by this time, and you must learn and read all you can about the great throbbing, agricultural heart of the West." [7]

Occasionally a real sticker went to Roosevelt himself, such as the letter from a South Dakotan inquiring what Roosevelt had learned in his trip abroad about French protection for farmers. Howe was baffled, but Roosevelt rose to the challenge and replied that since production of wheat was less than consumption in France, a protective tariff aided the grain farmers. What worked in France, Roosevelt added obliquely, would not suffice in the United States. He dodged comment upon McNary-Haugenism and all such schemes, but remarked that the French felt that if they produced even a small amount of surplus wheat for export, their tariff would be valueless.[8]

Conversely, Roosevelt sometimes sought information from his correspondents. He inquired of the business editor of Amon Carter's Dallas *Times Herald* whether a protective tariff would help raise the price of domestic oil. Would not an outright embargo on foreign oil be better? [9]

Out of these interchanges, Roosevelt was beginning to arrive at positions for the campaign ahead. Certainly it was none too soon to do so. But he took one further step in order to try to steal a march upon Raskob and his supporters. Raskob, he heard, was planning another Democratic National Committee meeting for the fall in which he would try to force through a resolution to commit the Democrats to his policies. "Raskob is apparently so angry with me that he does not even want to discuss matters," Roosevelt reported. "I do not particularly care but I do want to avoid a row."

Probably more as a means of thwarting Raskob than as a measure of his own self-confidence, Roosevelt accepted Hull's suggestion that he begin work quietly with his leading congressional supporters, Hull, Thomas J. Walsh, Pat Harrison, and a few others, to construct a platform. This, as Howe frankly stated, was predicated upon the consensus that Roosevelt would be the candidate.[10]

At first, Roosevelt went about this informally, querying Hull on the tariff, and sending word to Walsh that he would appreciate a complete platform draft. In October, 1931, he decided to work out a platform on a systematic basis, even if he risked a leak to the opposition. He sent Howe to Washington with a memorandum of instructions for his three allies. Although Roosevelt himself wrote it, it was unsigned, made use of the plural "we," and emphasized that this was to be a harmony move involving "a confidential interchange of tentative views relating to the platform, and not in any way to candidates." Roosevelt wanted a crisp, readable platform, perhaps only a quarter of the usual six-thousand-word length. He asked each recipient to state in a short, general way what he thought the party position should be on the tariff, economic relief, agricultural relief, and Prohibition. Finally, he asked them to list some proposed subjects for planks in the order in which they should be emphasized in the platform, and to add others. The topics were:

Economic Reform
Agricultural Relief
Tariff
Regulation of Public Utilities
Prohibition
Foreign Relations
Currency Reform
Unemployment Relief.[11]

Significantly, Roosevelt was soliciting counsel at this point from two Southerners and a Westerner. He had casually mentioned his project to one Middle Westerner, Senator Lewis of Illinois, and to another Southerner, Governor Byrd of Virginia. Both of them were favorite sons. Walsh planned to bring Senator Carter Glass of Virginia into the project later. Perhaps it was this emphasis which caused Roosevelt to turn in the final stages to a Pennsylvanian who had been Wilson's Attorney General, A. Mitchell Palmer. It was Palmer who ultimately incorporated the principal beliefs of Roosevelt's senatorial leaders into a concise, succinct platform.[12]

The preliminary drafting of a platform was not an extraordinary enterprise; Smith, sure of the nomination in 1928, had enlisted Senator Key Pittman well ahead of time to rough out his. In Roosevelt's case, there was certainly something to gain. His avowed purpose was carefully to set forth the views of the dominant wing of the party well in advance. Not avowed, but implicit in his choice of advisers, was his strategy to crystallize behind him the leaders of that wing – even if they were favorite sons, like Byrd, or conservatives, like Glass – to make of them a group united in its opposition to the Raskob-Shouse-Smith faction.

Roosevelt was, in effect, laying down a challenge; his opponents were quick to pick it up. In New York State, Smith personally engaged in a test of strength with Roosevelt. He was unwilling to allow his name to be used as a presidential candidate, but he did pick a relatively obscure issue in the 1931 off-year election. This he used as a public test of his drawing power at the polls compared with Roosevelt's. The issue was a proposed amendment to the constitution of the State of New York to empower the state to reforest submarginal farmlands. At two successive sessions, the legislature had voted to amend the constitution. Next it had to come before the voters. The amendment would provide for a bond issue of nineteen million dollars, to be spent at the rate of one to two million dollars per year to purchase poor land, strip it of scrub trees, and plant seedlings on it.

This was a favorite scheme of Roosevelt's. For more than a score of years he had planted trees on his own Hyde Park lands, and had advocated forest control of one sort or another. In 1931 it would have the added advantage of taking submarginal lands out of agricultural production at a time of acute surplus. If nationwide attention were to focus upon the proposal, and it were to be identified with Roosevelt, it might bring him additional prestige among farmers, conservationists, and progressives in general.* Moreover, the amendment had the support not only of conservation and sportsmen's organizations, but of the lumbering interests, and of the Republican as well as the Democratic parties.[13]

On the surface, it seemed a quixotic ground for Smith to choose for a tilt with Roosevelt. Expediency must have dictated his choice at least in part, for in the two years that the measure had been pending, he had never said a word against it. The time had come when, if he were to rally his following, he must make a public stand against Roosevelt and deal a blow to his leadership within the state. Smith had an enormous statistical advantage in fighting a constitutional amendment, since in the previous decade the voters of the state had defeated every one which came before them by an average of half a million votes. This was an off year, a depression year, and the amendment involved a substantial bond issue.[14]

While Roosevelt was resting in Warm Springs, Smith opened a surprise attack upon the amendment at a Tammany rally in New York City. It was a scathing onslaught, which he followed up with an even more vehement press statement and further speeches. Both the newspapers and Roosevelt instantly gauged the purport and danger of the attack. The New York *Times* editorially speculated that the cleavage between Al and Frank concerned the presidency more than it did conservation.

As for Roosevelt, immediately upon his return from Warm Springs he threw Farley's elaborate and smooth-functioning party machinery

* The Shenandoah (Iowa) *Sentinel* of October 31, 1931, declared: "There is one thing about Governor Roosevelt of New York that we heartily approve. That is the advocacy of reforestation, the planting of trees in the waste places of New York, and it might well be extended to all other states."

behind the amendment. He personally dictated a strong letter to go over Farley's signature to every Democratic worker in the state. At once he rallied behind him every conceivable pressure group from the Isaak Walton League to the State Federation of Labor. And he obtained the hearty cooperation of Republican State Chairman Kingsland Macy, who sent a letter to Republican workers and warmly defended the amendment in a radio address. Macy indicted Smith's attack as being sheerly political, aimed at wrecking Roosevelt's drive for the presidential nomination. Tammany for the moment was observing an uneasy truce with Roosevelt, and chose to deliver its votes to him rather than to Smith. To have done otherwise would have been to court a vigorous gubernatorial investigation. Finally, Roosevelt himself, in a cogent radio address, answered Smith's charges one by one, and persuasively argued for the amendment.[15]

With logic and the political organizations of both parties behind him, Roosevelt could feel certain by election day that he had overcome the weight of Smith's statistical advantage. He had indeed, by a safe margin of 778,192 to 554,550. Within the state and throughout the nation, he had enhanced his prestige. "Hurrah for Trees!" wrote Governor George H. Dern of Utah.[16] Even before the polls had closed on election day, Roosevelt mused:

"What a queer thing that was for Al to fight so bitterly . . . ! I cannot help remembering the fact that while he was Governor I agreed with almost all the policies he recommended but I was against one or two during those eight years. However, for the sake of party solidarity, I kept my mouth shut. I could readily have taken a public position in opposition to the Governor but, frankly, I did not think the issue was of vital enough importance to cause a party dispute." [17]

Roosevelt was not this naïve; he was busy preserving the fiction he and Smith shared that they were still good friends, and that there was no injection of personalities into the fight over the reforestation amendment. This was technically true. And, of course, neither would mention that there was a presidential campaign in the offing. Realistically, the only queer thing about Smith's foray was that he had chosen such an unpromising target upon which to break his first lance.

A few days later, Roosevelt invited Smith to lunch at his house in New York City to discuss state finances. Both Smith and the hovering reporters assumed that this would be the showdown conference between the rivals. Not so. Roosevelt, who had blandly assumed from the outset that Smith had meant what he said when he had asserted

"Never again" after the 1928 debacle, kept the conversation firmly on budgetary matters.

"What did you talk about?" a reporter asked Smith when he emerged from the house.

"We talked about state finances," Smith snapped. "That makes four words, don't it?"

Another inquired if they had not discussed politics.

"Not a word. Politics went out the window." [18]

So also had any but the most perfunctory relationship between Smith and Roosevelt. Smith was thoroughly hostile toward Roosevelt's candidacy, yet had little grounds for charging Roosevelt with disloyalty. After all, Smith had given no indication either publicly or privately that he was planning to run again. Sometime earlier, Boss Flynn had consulted Smith about this. Like so many New York Democratic leaders, Flynn was torn between allegiance to Roosevelt and Smith. Flynn had committed himself to Roosevelt's candidacy on the basis of Smith's earlier public statement, but his conscience bothered him a bit, and he wished to smooth out relations between the two men. Roosevelt gave his blessing to the diplomatic mission.

When Flynn explained his position, Smith emphatically told him he was completely through with politics. Opening a desk drawer, he spread before Flynn a number of papers representing heavy family indebtedness, and explained it would probably take the rest of his life to liquidate these obligations. Later Smith told Lieutenant Governor Lehman substantially the same thing. Both Flynn and Lehman had then publicly announced their support of Roosevelt; they had felt their obligation to Smith discharged. Certainly there was no reason why Roosevelt himself should feel obligated.[19]

Thus Smith turned away support at the critical time, and left one after another of his former followers, like Flynn, free to pledge allegiance to Roosevelt. In keeping with his emphatic statements, Smith and his friends Raskob and Shouse had spent the fall of 1931 not in whipping up support for Smith's own candidacy but in promoting favorite sons wherever possible, and in quest of a candidate who would have national appeal. Cynical political correspondents saw in this quest the search for a stalking-horse – someone who could, together with the favorite sons, tie up the convention. Then at the proper moment, both the stalking-horse and Roosevelt would be forced to retire to make ready for the real candidate, perhaps even Smith himself.

Rumors were persistent that this group, together with conservative Wall Streeters and utilities men, had first pinned their hopes upon Owen D. Young. But Young refused them. Next they approached Newton D. Baker of Ohio, who had been Wilson's Secretary of War. Baker, who earlier had possessed a fine administrative record and had been notable in his progressivism, was a favorite among many intellectuals. He was less emphatic than Young in his refusal; there were some indications that if he were to be in the race, he would prefer to be a dark horse rather than a stalking-horse. Nor was Baker hostile to Roosevelt. He had written a friend in June, 1931, that he hoped a natural leader would emerge around which all Democrats could rally with enthusiasm. "At present it looks as though Governor Roosevelt . . . had a very distinct lead in popular favor," Baker added. "As I know and admire him, I am hoping that this favor will grow steadily." [20] A copy of this letter found its way to Roosevelt. Nevertheless, in September Farley worried sufficiently about Baker to send a circular letter to pro-Roosevelt leaders throughout the country asking if they found indications that the Raskob forces were trying to start an artificial boom for Baker. They replied that there was no evidence of such a development.[21]

The Smith-Raskob forces, the reports were, then settled upon a political unknown, Melvin Traylor, President of the First National Bank of Chicago. They made rather ineffectual efforts to promote him in Kentucky and Texas, where he had formerly lived, as well as in Illinois. Publicity depicted this multimillionaire banker as a barefoot boy who had been in his teens before he even saw a railroad train. It seemed merely to make Traylor look rather ridiculous. At about the same time there were similar political rumors about former Governor Cox of Ohio, and Governor Ritchie of Maryland.[22]

Of these only Ritchie seemed promising, since there were signs immediately after the 1931 election that he would receive the backing of both the Smith-Raskob group and the big-city machines. Ritchie, who started with the slight advantage of being Maryland's favorite son, was a handsome and ingratiating politician, Wet enough for the organizations, conservative enough for the big-business interests. There were indications that he might be the candidate of a new alliance of the organizations.

Mayor Anton J. Cermak of Chicago, up to this point benevolently neutral toward Roosevelt, came East to confer with Raskob, Smith, and Boss Frank Hague of New Jersey. Ominously, he called for a candidate who would not pussyfoot on Prohibition, someone of the Al Smith type. Next Ritchie came to visit Smith and Raskob. While he was in New York, Ritchie told newspapermen that the two leading issues in the campaign would be unemployment and Prohibition. He did not know which would come first, but was strongly opposed to subordinating Prohibition. This was a position directly challenging Roosevelt's. At this very time, Bernard Baruch, former Chairman of the War Industries Board, praised Ritchie at a banquet as the man "to whom the finger of fate seems to point as being perhaps destined to move" into the White House.[23]

Reporters interpreted Baruch's speech to mean that he had joined Smith and Raskob in support of Ritchie. This dismayed Baruch, who wrote Roosevelt that his words were merely in praise of Ritchie's work for the War Industries Board, and that he did not have any favorite candidate for the nomination.[24] Roosevelt firmly replied:

"I do not need to tell you that I know you yourself would not engage in any surreptitious methods because you, too, realize that the situation from the national and party viewpoint is too serious to engage in such tactics — and also because you personally are above them. But I cannot, of course, help knowing of the conversations of some people who profess friendship but nevertheless emit innuendos and false statements behind my back with the blissful assumption that they will never be repeated to me."[25]

During the weeks that followed, Roosevelt and his advisers continued to feel that Baruch was backing Ritchie. And the story was prevalent that Baruch was referring to Roosevelt as "that Boy Scout." * This was serious, because Baruch had great prestige and influence as well as much money. When an ill-informed supporter suggested to Roosevelt that he might tap Baruch for preconvention funds, Roosevelt laughed and replied that Baruch was a sure-thing better; he would provide money all right, but not until after Roosevelt had won the nomination.[26]

Even more serious was the question of what Smith would do. In times as desperate as the winter of 1931–1932, an economic conservative like Ritchie could win no overwhelming Democratic support. If the bosses really wished to pull their organizations with them, they could do much better with Smith. Consequently, Roosevelt and the

* In talking to Morris L. Cooke, Baruch referred to FDR as "the Boy Scout Governor," and told him he was for Owen D. Young for President.

men around him wondered increasingly if Smith would abandon his behind-the-scenes role to throw his own hat in the ring.

Several more intermediaries went to Smith, as had Flynn and Lehman, and with rather similar results. When George S. Van Schaick, Roosevelt's Superintendent of Insurance, visited Smith at his apartment, Smith mixed old-fashioneds, then launched into a lengthy cataloguing of grievances against Roosevelt. Most of them were minor matters, but as he went on, his voice got louder and he pounded his fist.[27]

On another occasion, Clark Howell of the Atlanta *Constitution* told Smith he could guarantee Democratic victory by supporting Roosevelt, that indeed the nation expected it of him and would not believe he could do otherwise.

"The hell I can't," Smith retorted, but added that he would put the party above any man and support the man best for the party.

"Governor," Howell inquired, "is there any ground for personal hostility on your part against Roosevelt?"

Howell reported to Roosevelt a few hours later what Smith replied:

" 'No,' he said — 'socially we are friends. He has always been kind to me and my family, and has gone out of his way to be agreeable with us at the Mansion at Albany, but' — then he arose, stamped his foot, and said — 'Do you know, by God, that he has never consulted me about a damn thing since he has been Governor? He has taken bad advice and from sources not friendly to me. He has ignored me!' And then with increased fervor, and slamming his fist on the table, he said — 'By God, he invited me to his house before he went to Georgia, and did not even mention to me the subject of his candidacy.' "

In his talk with Van Schaick, Smith seemed basically upset because he blamed his 1928 defeat on the religious issue, and therefore believed he merited vindication in 1932. Speaking to Howell, he claimed that millions of people in the Northeast resented the way he had been treated, and that no Democrat had ever polled as many votes as he had. In conclusion, Smith told Howell that he was not committed for or against Roosevelt, and was going to take his time before saying what he was going to do.[28]

Roosevelt betrayed his nervousness about Smith at this delicate time when *Collier's* printed a rumor which had been circulating widely since the Governors' Conference at French Lick. The story was that Roosevelt had confided to someone, "Smith was a rotten Governor. I didn't know it until I got into the governorship myself." Roosevelt was furious out of apparent proportion to the incident. He hotly told newspapermen, "Any man who circulates a story of that kind is not only a liar but is a contemptible liar." The president of *Collier's* sent a conciliatory telegram pointing out that the story was clearly labeled as only a rumor, and *Collier's* was glad to give Roosevelt the opportunity to deny it. Roosevelt retorted that he doubted whether it was "good ethics, good morals or good journalism to publish articles based on falsehood with the happy thought that it gives the victim an opportunity to deny the authenticity of the story." [29]

Certainly the report had angered Smith, who took great pride in his achievements as governor. And Roosevelt was equally upset over the rumor that Smith had referred to him as "crackpot." Both stories had probably grown in the repetition, but there was a ring of truth to both of them. The rift between the two men seemed far too broad and deep to close; the question was how much Smith would make of it.[30]

While Smith was making up his mind, Roosevelt could only hope no more ugly stories would crop up to create additional trouble. In coping with his other major opponents, the militant Raskob and Shouse, he was able to take firm countermeasures. When Shouse went to Alabama, purportedly to secure anti-Roosevelt unpledged delegates to the convention, Howe wrote Shouse frankly that he construed this as a deliberately unfriendly act. To Shouse's disclaimer, Roosevelt smoothly replied that many of his friends had jumped to the conclusion that Raskob and Shouse were trying to "stop Roosevelt" through the unethical tactic of backing favorite-son and uninstructed delegations. Roosevelt concluded that he felt confident that Shouse and Raskob as the directing officers of the Democratic National Committee would maintain a correct neutrality.[31] It was Roosevelt's hope that because Shouse had made overtures to be continued in office if Roosevelt were nominated, this firm tone would produce results.

Instead, Raskob launched a new, naïve program to undermine Roosevelt on the issues. He was obsessed with the notion, which his idol Smith seemed to share, that Prohibition was the paramount question as 1932 approached. Smith had told Howell that Roosevelt was dodging on Prohibition, and should speak out for a national referendum. Raskob at the end of November announced that he was polling the ninety thousand contributors to the 1928 campaign on what the party platform should be on Prohibition. He seemed to be going on the assumption that to have contributed to the party funds should give one a voice in policy — something politicians frequently admitted in private, but seldom made so obvious to the public. In addition, he called a meeting of the Democratic National Committee for January 9, 1932, to select the convention site, and to consider once more Raskob's liquor plan.[32]

In effect, Raskob was stirring up for a second time the same fight that had rocked the National Committee the previous March. Drys protested that he was again trying to steamroller the committee into endorsing a Wet plank. Roosevelt's friends accused Raskob of trying to embarrass Roosevelt in the Dry South, and charged that to poll the contributors would be unfair, since half of them came from the Wet Northeast and Illinois. Again, Roosevelt remained personally silent while Farley worked with his Southern allies to rebuild the coalition so triumphant in March, 1931. Again, they worked not on the basis of Roosevelt's candidacy, but on the principle of building a Southern and Western combination, including favorite sons, against Raskob and the Wets. Raskob was threatening a party split; Roosevelt was still trying to straddle. But if he were forced to choose, clearly his power and support were overwhelmingly in the rural camp.[33]

From New York, Howe sent wires to all of Roosevelt's supporters on the committee, requesting them to help either in person or by proxy. Hull and Byrd worked vigorously in Washington. At first, it appeared that the Roosevelt forces would have no more than a bare majority, but by the end of December they could count sixty-five votes out of one hundred and nine; on the eve of the meeting, Farley claimed over ninety. The Roosevelt coalition was so far ahead that once more Raskob had to compromise. He proposed that the committee merely refer, not recommend, his plan to the convention, and submit to it the results of the poll. Farley accepted, and proclaimed that Raskob had evidently "become convinced of the impropriety of attempting to make the national committee an official voice for the Democratic party as regards . . . matters of policy." [34]

Despite this victory over Raskob on Prohibition, Roosevelt took a decided setback at the meeting on the choice of a convention site. This was not the result of Raskob's prowess, but of the necessity for Roosevelt to go along with a majority of his followers. Four cities, Atlantic City, Chicago, Kansas City, and San Francisco, were bidding for the convention. Roosevelt preferred Kansas City, because Boss Tom Pendergast was friendly toward him, and did not object to San Francisco, where he had been nominated for Vice President. He wished to avoid Chicago or Atlantic City, where the wringing Wet bosses Cermak or Hague might pack the galleries with hooting, hostile mobs. Farley could not override the geographical loyalties of his supporters, nor the additional fifty thousand dollars that Chicago bid at the last moment. So Chicago was chosen. In addition to the possibility of trouble there, it was a psychological reverse for Roosevelt, since newspapers incorrectly interpreted the choice as a victory for Raskob.[35]

The inescapable fact was that a majority of the members of the national committee were for Roosevelt, as Senator Walsh pointed out afterwards. As a result, Farley came out of the meeting with the one small plum obtainable there. He won for an ardent Roosevelt supporter, National Committeeman Robert H. Jackson of New Hampshire, the position of committee secretary. This would be of some significance at the convention.[36]

Raskob charmingly tried to spike newspaper reports of a combination against Roosevelt by asserting, "There is not a single member of this committee who knows of one thing that any of us has done to try to defeat or deter in any way those who, very properly, are promoting Mr. Roosevelt for the Presidential nomination." [37]

There was no need for an answer to this, for the hostility of Raskob and Shouse was all too apparent to everyone. It was growing into the proportions of a genuine menace, but in one respect that continued to be more help than hindrance. It was solidifying behind Roosevelt the support of the South and West. Even in areas plumping for favorite sons, behind the local candidate was a friendliness for Roosevelt, and an unalterable opposition to Raskob, Shouse, and Smith.

As for Smith, he tried to maintain the outward semblance of a friendship with Roosevelt. He wired Roosevelt on January 30, his fiftieth birthday, "Hearty congratulations on the half century." Roosevelt replied on February 8, "I was sorry you could not be with us at the Hyde Park party." Two days before this reply, Smith had announced he was available for the nomination.[38]

At last Roosevelt knew what his opposition was to be. Smith would be a powerful adversary, for despite his conservative views and wealthy associates, he was still the darling of the city millions. The time was past for intricate maneuvering and preliminary tilts for position. The season of state primaries and state conventions was opening; they would determine the relative strength of the minor candidates, and of Roosevelt and Smith. The cold war between the two leading Democrats had thawed into a hot and open battle.

CHAPTER XVII

Hat in the Ring

It is the simple duty of any American to serve in public position if called upon.

— FDR, *January 22, 1932.*

AT the end of January, 1932, Roosevelt dropped his lengthy masquerade as a public servant interested in nothing beyond his job as New York's governor, and formally opened his fight for the presidential nomination. His means of doing so was to authorize his name to be entered in the primary election in North Dakota, a state where under the law a candidate had to announce his availability before he could run in the primary. Accordingly, Roosevelt on January 22 wrote to Fred W. McLean, Secretary of the North Dakota State Democratic Committee, "I willingly give my consent, with full appreciation of the honor that has been done me."

In his statement, Roosevelt made only a general reference to his policies. "One who believes in new standards of government for meeting new problems in the translation of forward looking thought into practical action," he declared, "must welcome a chance to do his share toward that end." [1] He explained to Homer Cummings a few days later why he had not been more concrete: "It seemed to me not only unwise from the political point of view, but also contrary to my real obligations here as Governor for me to go into a long dissertation on national affairs, and I sought to pursue the honest and honorable course." [2]

Thus simply, Roosevelt announced his candidacy. The choice of North Dakota disappointed Roosevelt's ardent and effective supporter in the state of Washington, A. Scott Bullitt. He had planned with Roosevelt for Washington to launch the candidacy through county conventions which would meet on Roosevelt's birthday, January 30, to select pro-Roosevelt delegates for the state convention on February 6. Roosevelt switched to North Dakota because he wished to appear more democratic. He thought it looked better to enter a primary rather than to win delegates, as in Washington, at an organization-controlled convention. The public did not realize that the organization would determine the outcome in either instance. In North Dakota, backing was so strong that Roosevelt had no cause to fear he would lose in the primary on March 15.[3]

Actually the first delegates Roosevelt won were six from Alaska, the first to pledge to any candidate. These six were somewhat more significant than the number indicated, since territorial delegates usually aligned themselves with the leading contender. On February 7, Roosevelt acquired his first delegates in the United States, sixteen from Washington, instructed to vote for him under the unit rule.[4]

To this point, Roosevelt's strategy had worked perfectly, and, as he had planned, he was out in front — far ahead of any opponent. It had every sign of being a runaway campaign for Roosevelt until Smith entered the race. Indeed, Smith and other serious contenders entered so late that they were hard pressed to try to catch up with Roosevelt. Farley and Howe, with their letter writing, traveling, and telephoning, had won over a remarkable array of professionals, many of whom might well have supported Smith or others if these contenders had joined the contest earlier. Roosevelt had gained particularly critical support during the few days between his own announcement of candidacy and Smith's belated and apparently hesitant flip of his brown derby.

When Roosevelt became an avowed candidate, he did not expand his campaign organization, as many of his supporters had expected. Rather he wished to lean, as he had up to this point, upon Howe, Farley, Flynn, and a small coterie of others in New York. To House's disappointment, Roosevelt chose to keep him and his cohorts in secondary positions. From New York, he could send out newspapermen like Cornelius Vanderbilt and Marvin McIntyre to scout rumors and gather political opinion, or envoys to cement deals with state organizations. By keeping his organization small he could keep it tight, and thus discourage leaks and inefficiency. By keeping it highly centralized he could himself maintain close control over almost everything going on.

The one major addition at this time was a Washington representative, Homer Cummings of Connecticut. Since the turn of the century, Cummings had been a member or chairman of the National Committee; he had been a McAdoo leader in 1924 and was closely allied to

Colonel House and Roper.* His association with Roosevelt dated back to 1919, when he had accompanied the then Assistant Secretary of the Navy on a demobilization junket to Europe. His acquaintance among congressmen was enormous, and his powers of persuasion upon them were gratifyingly great. In the critical days in mid-February after Roosevelt's announcement and Smith's, Cummings, with the aid of Senators Dill and Hull, conferred with over a score of Democratic senators, most of whom had not openly expressed any presidential preference. He persuaded twenty-four of them from twenty states to announce themselves for Roosevelt. In addition, he enticed a number of prominent Democratic congressmen onto the Roosevelt bandwagon. After attending one of the Roosevelt meetings, Senator Walsh wrote a friend, "I was surprised to learn how nearly unanimous the sentiment is in his behalf." [6]

The bandwagon technique — the reiteration that Roosevelt was a sure winner — worked not only with congressmen and other political professionals, but among voters as a whole. While Roosevelt was deliberately leaning upon the professionals and organizations for his support, he was well aware of the pressure of public opinion upon them. The impressive array of opinion polls, which seemed to indicate widespread support for Roosevelt among the voters, had done much to win wavering politicians to him. By this time, Straus had conducted a total of five polls, including one among small businessmen. Each one had shown Roosevelt well in the lead. These had attracted so much interest, since they were something of a novelty at the time, that they led newspapers and magazines to conduct further polls, which tallied similar results. They showed not only a Democratic preference for Roosevelt but also a general voter preference for Roosevelt over Hoover. One of the most important, a poll conducted by twenty-five Scripps-Howard newspapers, led to the prediction that Roosevelt not only would be nominated but would win in November. It is hard to say to what extent these polls measured opinion, and to what extent they molded it. Undoubtedly they did much to create the bandwagon spirit which Farley encouraged further with his periodic predictions that Roosevelt would have an enormous lead at the convention.[7]

Thus Farley fortified Roosevelt's formal entrance into the presi-

* Colonel House was keenly disappointed when FDR stood by Farley and refused to appoint Cummings his campaign manager. This left House in the second echelon.[5]

dential race by claiming that Roosevelt could already count upon a certain 678 votes on the first ballot, only 102 short of the 770 required to nominate.* And Farley listed 286 of the remainder as being doubtful. This runaway lead impressed most tough-minded old-timers.[8] One of Roosevelt's backers, Breckinridge Long, Secretary of State at the end of the Wilson Administration, reported to the unfriendly McAdoo at the end of January:

"Roosevelt is 'way out in front again. When I saw you it was my impression that he had lost some ground, but when the men met here from over the United States at the Jackson Day dinner, I talked to a good many of them from everywhere and almost every one of them were for Franklin Roosevelt. I was quite astonished at the unanimity of opinion. New England, the Northwest, North Central, Middle West, South, and Atlantic Seaboard – were practically every one of them for Roosevelt. There were exceptions, of course, like your friend Frank [Hague]." [9]

Nevertheless, this bandwagon spirit and Roosevelt's first few simple victories did not obscure the fact that he was going to have a fierce fight. If Farley were to be correct in his prediction, Roosevelt would have to enter the convention with more than two thirds of the delegates, since the time-honored Democratic rule dating back to the Jackson period persisted, that a candidate must receive two thirds of the votes to be nominated. Smith's task was far simpler, since he had to secure only a third of the delegates in order to exercise a veto over Roosevelt's nomination. Professionals throughout the country were well aware of this too. They knew perfectly well they could deny the nomination to Smith also, but if he were able to deadlock the convention, it might create a miraculous opportunity for a compromise candidate. Consequently, many a favorite son who had held back now began an active canvass for delegates in the hope that he might fish the nomination out of the muddied waters of a tied-up convention.

Through February, Raskob and Shouse continued their flimsy pretense of neutrality but openly encouraged these favorite sons. Three days after Smith announced his candidacy, Shouse publicly recommended that state Democratic conventions not instruct delegates in order that they might come to the nominating convention unfettered.

* Farley's estimate was fairly realistic, especially since at the time he made it Smith had not formally entered the race. He was wrong mainly in his claims in the pivotal states of New York, Massachusetts, Indiana, and California, but FDR picked up sufficient delegates elsewhere to be only twelve votes below this estimate on the first ballot.

Roosevelt indignantly proclaimed that this was contrary to the principles of the party. It would enable a handful of party leaders to select the nominee through trade and barter, he declared, and might block entirely "the popular choice of the rank and file of the party." [10]

Shouse made no headway with his plea for uninstructed delegations, but he lent further encouragement to the favorite sons. Most of them had little appeal outside of their own states or were harmful to Roosevelt only in their collective denial of the votes he would need to win nomination on the first ballot. Senator Hamilton Lewis of Illinois, in spite of his notable ability, was handicapped by his pink whiskers, toupee, and eccentricities. Thus he could claim only an Illinois favorite-son vote. He was friendly toward Roosevelt, who hoped the delegation would swing to him after a complimentary vote for Lewis. Unfortunately for Roosevelt, Illinois had also Mel Traylor, the barefoot boy who became a millionaire. Throughout the country, Governor William H. "Alfalfa Bill" Murray, the darling of the poverty-stricken Oklahoma farmers, demonstrated a marked ability to win public attention with his slogan, "Bread, Butter, Bacon, and Beans." But Murray, a rather unkempt-looking elderly man with an erratic past, could not transform the headlines into votes. He gave Roosevelt no cause for concern.[11]

Rather, Roosevelt had reason to worry over John Nance Garner of Texas, who appealed to exactly the same Western Democrats who previously had rallied around Roosevelt. "Cactus Jack" Garner, with his beetling brows and ten-gallon hat, had started as a banker and real-estate operator in the small West Texas town of Uvalde. Through long years of able service and party regularity in Congress he had risen by December, 1931, to the position which represented the pinnacle of his political ambitions, Speaker of the House.[12]

On New Year's Day, 1932, William Randolph Hearst, publisher of a powerful national chain of newspapers, delivered a vehement nationalist tirade over the radio against all those men, like Roosevelt, Baker, Young, Smith, and others, who were internationalists fatuously following the visionary policies of Woodrow Wilson. He urged his listeners to elect a President whose guiding motto would be "America First." The man Hearst visualized as thus symbolizing the nation's hope was Garner. The next day Hearst splashed his nomination of Garner across front pages of his newspapers in an editorial entitled "Who Will Be the Next President?" [13]

It was not Garner's anti-League bias or his feeling that Europe must pay its war debts which won him an immediate enthusiastic following. Rather it was his Western background and his stand in favor of strong measures to fight the depression. Interestingly too, although he frequently rejoiced in "striking a blow for liberty" by downing a bourbon with his cronies at the Capitol, he became a rallying point for Drys who distrusted Roosevelt's Prohibition straddle. In addition to Hearst, Texas politicians backed him, and soon also McAdoo in California, but there was no possibility he could cross the party rift to win Eastern Wet or conservative support. He was anathema to Smith followers, and he knew it.

Garner had a keen desire to be an effective Speaker, but as a major political figure he had no illusions about himself. After the 1930 election he had confided to Bascom Timmons that Roosevelt looked like the Democratic candidate for 1932. When Timmons inquired about Roosevelt's health, Garner replied, "For the Presidency you run on a record and not on your legs." As late as November, 1931, Garner confided to Howe that he thought Texas would probably instruct for Roosevelt, but as Speaker he felt he should not come out openly for the Governor. He even requested that Howe find how Roosevelt stood on a number of issues to come before the House Democratic caucus, since he felt that the probable candidate for President should have a voice in policy.[14]

When the Garner boom got under way at the beginning of 1932, he refused to comment upon it to newspapermen, and did nothing to solicit support among his many friends in Congress. He wrote, "There are no presidential bees buzzing around my office." The story reached Roosevelt that Garner, after locking the door, had told a delegation of Texans that while he appreciated the honor of being mentioned for President, he was not a damned fool; nobody was kidding him and he was not kidding himself. He said he was just a country fellow who knew his own limitations, and did not expect to be nominated.[15]

This attitude gave Roosevelt cause for continued optimism, since Garner, unlike Smith, had no fierce determination to stop Roosevelt. It did make Roosevelt look vulnerable, since it meant the immediate loss of forty-six Texas delegates, and a contest over forty-four in California, where Garner's backing was potent. This cut by a possible ninety votes the strength with which Roosevelt would enter the convention. Roosevelt countered by trying to build secondary support in Texas, and by sending five thousand dollars to the friendly

California Democratic organization to help finance the fight against Garner.[16]

At the same time, Roosevelt and his lieutenants were careful to do nothing to offend the Garner men. Indeed, this was Roosevelt's strategy in dealing with all factions. He carefully avoided entering primary contests against favorite sons in their own states, at the same time that he was ready to do battle against Smith, Alfalfa Bill Murray, or anyone else, in neutral states. Farley even went so far as to pay his personal respects to Smith only a week before Smith openly entered the contest. The strategy was to try to avoid any animus that might make negotiations impossible at the convention or create a split in the party which could throw the election to Hoover.

Fortunately for Roosevelt, almost everyone within and without the party remembered how the deadlocked 1924 convention had wrecked any remote chances for victory. They were disposed to cooperate with Roosevelt in maintaining at least a semblance of cordiality.

To do so on a smile-and-handshake basis was easy enough, but issues were beginning to intrude. There Roosevelt faced a critical problem in that he must say enough on national affairs to justify his candidacy without alienating supporters. With considerable success, he had been able to pursue a studied policy as governor of not commenting upon national affairs. In the summer of 1931, he had even bested the astute New York *Times* columnist Arthur Krock, who was critical because Roosevelt would not comment upon President Hoover's moratorium upon war-debt and reparation payments. He pointed out to Krock that previously newspapers had been ready to criticize him if he did comment upon national affairs.*

Actually, Roosevelt had his clear-cut programs as governor, to which he could point, in the areas of agriculture, conservation and power

* FDR sent Krock a little fable: "Once upon a time an unfortunate individual was elected Governor of the State and found there was Much To Do running the State without dipping into National Problems. One day he foolishly did discuss a National Problem because he thought it had something to do with the Progress and Prosperity of his own State. Thereupon, an All-Wise Press hopped all over him and said that he was obviously seeking national honors.

"Having learned his lesson he stayed within his State. A little later a great international problem arose and the Press and the President of his country made an excellent suggestion. The Governor, however, having learned his lesson, said nothing. Thereupon, an All-Wise Press chided the said Governor for not commenting on National and International Affairs."

Krock flatteringly replied that Roosevelt could gain fame as a political Aesop.[17]

development, social welfare, and unemployment relief. He had taken a compromise position, but a clear one, on Prohibition in the fall of 1930. The only area of his administration where his position was seriously equivocal was in his attitude toward Tammany corruption in New York City. He had said nothing on foreign policy, on the firm grounds that it was not in his province as governor to do so. In January, 1932, when the editor of a London paper wired for his attitude toward the Manchurian crisis, he replied, "I have very definite views but please read the Federal Constitution." [18]

Despite Roosevelt's tangible policies as governor, his silence on foreign policy and on some vital national issues, and especially his backing and filling toward Tammany, threatened him with loss of support from several vital directions, and undermined the confidence of intellectuals in him.

Walter Lippmann in his columns in the New York *Herald Tribune* summed up the misgivings of the intellectuals toward Roosevelt. Roosevelt's faction, he had pointed out at the end of December, 1931, was saying a lot about economic issues being paramount, but was not specifying just what these issues were. He concluded tartly, "Governor Roosevelt belongs to the new post-war school of politicians who do not believe in stating their views unless and until there is no avoiding it." To Lippmann, the game of gathering delegates first and stating policies afterwards was ignoble. To Roosevelt, it was sound politics. Nevertheless, there were many thoughtful people who shared Lippmann's distress.

Some of Roosevelt's supporters were sooner or later going to feel let down, Lippmann pointed out in a famous column on January 8, 1932. Some were as far to the left as Senator Wheeler of Montana, who stood for inflation; others as far to the right as the editors of the New York *Times*, who felt no upsetting plans or socialistic schemes could attract Roosevelt. Above all, Lippmann felt, Roosevelt had demonstrated himself a master of the art of carrying water on both shoulders; he was deliberately trying to straddle the whole country. Which Roosevelt was most deceiving, the left or the right, Lippmann could not decide. "The reason is," he asserted, "that Franklin D. Roosevelt is a highly impressionable person, without a firm grasp of public affairs and without very strong convictions." To Lippmann he seemed "an amiable man with many philanthropic impulses, but he is not the dangerous enemy of anything. He is too eager to please." During Roosevelt's three years as governor, Lippmann charged, he had been so cautious that not a single act of his had involved political risk. His water-power policy was safe because capitalists had become enlightened and were ready to accept state financing. In his relations with Tammany, he was not popular but had a working arrangement, so that he exposed corruption only reluctantly, and received Tammany votes at elections. This meant, charged Lippmann:

"Franklin D. Roosevelt is no crusader. He is no tribune of the people. He is no enemy of entrenched privilege. He is a pleasant man who, without any important qualifications for the office, would very much like to be President." [19]

This was the most penetrating attack upon Roosevelt in all the months leading up to the convention. It appeared in newspapers from coast to coast, and was reprinted and circulated as a telling piece of ammunition against Roosevelt. Through Lippmann's columns ran a thread of praise for Newton D. Baker, but it was the "Friends of Smith" who capitalized upon his attacks on Roosevelt.[20]

Roosevelt writhed. He and Jim Farley wisecracked over one of the earlier attacks. Farley had suggested he not read it until late at night; Roosevelt replied he had done so. "The result is that this morning I am somewhat exhausted as I never closed my eyes!" This may have come close to being the truth later. Howe reported, "I do not think there is anything we can do about it." As for Roosevelt, he encouraged Morris L. Cooke to refute Lippmann's slur upon the power policy. "In spite of his brilliance," Roosevelt asserted, "it is very clear that he has never let his mind travel west of the Hudson or north of the Harlem!" [21]

Lippmann's criticisms, although much too harsh, came uncomfortably close to the mark. Roosevelt was far too shrewd a political poker player to reveal his hand unless he could gain rather than lose support. In the early months of 1932, he was forced to state his position in some areas in order to avoid serious defections. This was painful and dangerous; Roosevelt proceeded in a gingerly fashion. He had before him the rather unfortunate example of Newton D. Baker.

By January, 1932, Baker was obviously clearing his way to be the compromise candidate, should Roosevelt and Smith block each other. He had two handicaps. One was the rather minor one that he had recently been representing one of the major utility corporations in a lawsuit. This, Senator Walsh and others granted, should not be held against him. The other was far more serious in an era when the public temper was extremely opposed to war, or to any contribution to collective security that might possibly lead to war. Baker was the generally recognized heir to Wilsonian internationalism; his pronouncements, which from time to time made the front pages of the respectable dailies, kept alive the hopes of the League enthusiasts. But Baker was so anxious to make himself available that a few weeks after Hearst's "America First" pronouncement for Garner, he made a statement quite out of keeping with his record. He declared that if it were in his power, he would take the United States into the League, but only if "an enlightened majority of the people favored the step." The statement was a failure. As Stephen Bonsal, Wilson's interpreter at Versailles, pointed out to Howe, "League of Nations fanatics are hurt and distressed by what they regard as a crawl, while the Anti Leaguers are by no means mollified." [22]

Roosevelt took no such chance. As long as possible, he continued to maintain his silence on the League, but Hearst made this more and more difficult. He attacked Roosevelt in his papers as an internationalist. When Senators Wheeler and Dill defended Roosevelt from this charge, Hearst ran another front-page editorial in his newspapers, quoting several of Roosevelt's strong statements on behalf of the League in the campaign of 1920. Hearst amplified his attack by instructing his editors to exploit local anti-Roosevelt political sources. The editor of the Atlanta *Georgian-American* was especially energetic in appealing to Tom Watson's following on the grounds that Roosevelt was pro-League. Several of Roosevelt's supporters warned that the attacks were sharp and telling. "This is bad ball," Howe told Roosevelt. "You may have to make a public statement before we get through, if this thing gets any more violent." [23]

Hearst forced just this step. Howe had recommended that Roosevelt telephone Hearst, which would have been no unusual step, since Roosevelt had been in touch with Hearst several times during the previous year.* Before Roosevelt could do this, Farley went to the editor of Hearst's New York *American* to assure him that Roosevelt indeed was no internationalist. Hearst immediately reported this on his front pages and retorted, "If Mr. Roosevelt has any statement to make about his not now being an internationalist he should make it to the public publicly, and not to me privately." [24]

So it was that Franklin D. Roosevelt, who as vice-presidential can-

* FDR had written in March, 1931, "W.R.H. is still in California, and I have exchanged a number of messages with him."

didate in 1920 had fought so earnestly for the League, in 1932 ate his words. He wasted no time doing so; he chose an occasion only three days after Hearst's challenge, a meeting of the New York State Grange on February 2. And he wafered these words between two more palatable international themes. First, he attacked the Republican Smoot-Hawley Tariff in terms that he knew would bring pleasure to Senator Hull — as a tariff fence so high that it cut off the exchange of goods. As a result, American farmers were buying manufactured goods in the protected American market, and having to sell their produce in the competitive world market. The remedy, said Roosevelt, was a reciprocal trade program.*

After thus placating liberal believers in economic internationalism, Roosevelt turned to the difficult task at hand. American participation in an international trade conference would, he asserted, in no way involve the United States in political controversies in Europe or elsewhere, or in any way renew the question of American entrance into the League. He declared:

> In common with millions of my fellow countrymen, I worked and spoke, in 1920, in behalf of American participation in a League of Nations, conceived in the highest spirit of world friendship for the great object of preventing a return of world war. For that course I have no apology to make.
>
> If today I believed that the same or even similar factors entered into the argument, I would still favor America's entry into the League; and I would go so far as to seek to win over the overwhelming opposition which exists in this country today.
>
> But the League of Nations today is not the League conceived by Woodrow Wilson. It might have been, had the United States joined. Too often through these years its major function has been not the broad overwhelming purpose of world peace, but rather

* In this first statement of his on reciprocal trade, FDR declared, "It is time for us to sit down with other nations and say to them 'this tariff fence business, on our part and on yours, is preventing world trade. Let us see if we can work out reciprocal methods by which we can start the actual interchange of goods. We do not ask you to buy our goods for cash because we know you have not got the cash, but we do suggest that it would be good for us and for you if we could send to you each year a large volume of American products in exchange for your products. But we do recognize the fact that we can probably use many of your articles and at the same time we can start our own wheels of industry going in manufacturing the things you need and want — all with adequate safeguards for the American standards of labor.' "[25]

> a mere meeting place for the political discussion of strictly European political national difficulties. In these the United States should have no part.
>
> The fact remains that we did not join the League. The League has not developed through these years along the course contemplated by its founder, nor have the principal members shown a disposition to divert the huge sums spent on armament into the channels of legitimate trade, balanced budgets and payment of obligations. American participation in the League would not serve the highest purpose of the prevention of war and a settlement of international difficulties in accordance with fundamental American ideals. Because of these facts, therefore, I do not favor American participation.

There it was, as strong a statement as even Hearst could desire. Roosevelt finished off his speech with words that must have been equally pleasing to Hearst and his followers. He castigated the European nations for indulging in an orgy of spending and not meeting their just obligations to the United States, the payment of war debts. He might as well have repeated the words of Calvin Coolidge which he had earlier mocked, "They hired the money, didn't they?" Apparently Roosevelt saw no inconsistency between his plea for an increase in international trade and his demand that European nations state when and how they would resume war-debt payments.[26]

Altogether, the speech was a tour de force of exactly the sort that inspired scorn in Lippmann and despair in some of Roosevelt's most devoted followers. How inconsistent was it with Roosevelt's thinking at the time? Probably not greatly. During the League fight in 1919–1920 he had been privately impatient with President Wilson for not accepting various Republican-proposed changes in the League covenant.* In 1928, he had hedged as spokesman for the Democrats on foreign policy by proposing cooperation with the League on matters involving general welfare, "without entering into European politics." Apparently he was convinced that his view had long been one of opposition to American entrance into the League. He ordered a search of newspaper files for the previous six years, hoping to find a public statement of his that he could quote back to Hearst, and thus avoid the charges of opportunism.[27]

* In 1924, FDR had drafted a charter for a new international organization, pointing out that a League by any other name would be more acceptable to the American public.

This was a serious matter for Roosevelt to be selling out his Wilsonian heritage of internationalism in order to stop Hearst attacks upon him. It did, no matter what Roosevelt's earlier thoughts about the League may have been, indicate a considerable degree of political cynicism, or perhaps of desperation. Proof of this lies in the fact that Roosevelt was ready if need be to switch his stand on the World Court. Both publicly and privately, like Republican Presidents Harding, Coolidge, and Hoover, he had urged American adherence. As recently as the previous August, he had written, though not for publication, to the head of the National World Court Committee, "I approve American membership in the World Court." Fortunately, Hearst did not force him into a disavowal of the World Court.[28] When Howe confided to Colonel House what Roosevelt intended to say, House warned Roosevelt:

"In view of your attitude on the League of Nations I do not think such a reply would satisfy many of your most ardent and influential friends. What you said about the League has already strained their loyalty, and many of them have told me that if you take the same position on the World Court they cannot support you. This has come from some of those close to you." [29]

Indeed, Roosevelt was stretching the loyalty of many of his internationalist followers almost to the breaking point, even though it could be argued that by 1932 there was not the remotest possibility the United States would enter the League.* He had, as House wrote Farley, "created something akin to panic among the devoted Wilson followers." Josephus Daniels, Roosevelt's old chief in the Navy Department, complained to Hull that Roosevelt had gone entirely too far, and that the speech had reacted against him. Hull himself was disappointed. A family friend mourned, "It was all unnecessary and

* FDR sought privately to mollify outraged Wilsonians with what Howe used to refer to as "soothing syrup." As in 1928, he took the view that the end justified the means:

> "I had hoped you would understand. Can't you see that loyalty to the ideals of Woodrow Wilson is just as strong in my heart as it is in yours, — but have you ever stopped to consider that there is a difference between ideals and the methods of attaining them? Ideals do not change, but methods do change with every generation and world circumstance.
>
> "Here is the difference between me and some of my fainthearted friends: I am looking for the best modern vehicle to reach the goal of an ideal while they insist on a vehicle which was brand new and in good running order twelve years ago. Think this over! And for heaven's sake have a little faith." [30]

savors of Hearst. I am devoted to Franklin but he ought to be spanked." Roosevelt had confirmed the suspicions of intellectuals who opposed him; he had shaken but not lost his idealistic Wilsonian followers. But these followers were few in number and influence compared with the multitudes in the hinterland who were acutely suspicious of Europe and Europe's quarrels, and whose grinding poverty at the beginning of 1932 focused their attention completely upon the depression. These people cared very little whether or not Roosevelt had switched. Indeed, they knew very little about Roosevelt, unless he were attacked in front-page editorials in type so large they could not avoid seeing them. To them, Roosevelt was a name, a symbol of a way out of their troubles. It was important that these people not be turned away from Roosevelt, and indeed Hearst ceased his attacks.[31]

Thus, although the speech left Roosevelt open to scorn, it had achieved its purpose. Senator William E. Borah, that archisolationist, murmured sarcastically, "Repent ye, for the kingdom of heaven is at hand." But the Borahs in both parties were ready to accept Roosevelt's confession of faith. Senator Dill, a Democrat, predicted that the Roosevelt Administration would have "the interests of America first." What was still more important, it meant that whatever block of votes Hearst was able to assemble behind Garner in the West would not at a crucial point in the convention swing to the internationalist Baker, any more than to the Wet leader of the city masses, Smith. This in the light of subsequent events became the most vital factor in the entire preconvention period. Roosevelt had come in sackcloth and ashes and prostrated himself before Hearst. The humiliation was an essential step toward the ultimate triumph.[32]

Other maneuvers that same month of February, 1932, emphasized what an intricate course Roosevelt was following. After placating isolationist Democrats in the South and West, Roosevelt tried to appease Eastern Wets, especially those in New Hampshire, where he shortly faced a primary fight. He went to the Wet city of Buffalo on February 20 to address some thirteen hundred people who, despite the depression, spent three dollars for a dinner in order to hear him. In his talk, he easily met the challenge of the Smith-Raskob forces, which were accusing him of being secretly Dry. All he needed to do was to reiterate his formula of September, 1930, which, as he well knew, had done him no harm in the South. It was necessary for him to repeat it because, as Norman Mack pointed out to him, very few people remembered what he had said eighteen months earlier. He called for the repeal of the Prohibition Amendment and the return of the liquor-control problem to the states. His only new addition was a proposal more likely to help than to hinder him with Drys, that states establish liquor-control plans which would bring them new revenue.[33]

Again, as earlier, a few die-hard Southern Wets were upset. Daniels, pulled as he was all spring between personal liking for his former assistant and repugnance toward some of his policies, complained to Hull that the Buffalo statement made many of Roosevelt's friends lose heart and hope. How could they call upon people to make a fight against Smith and Raskob against a candidate advocating an almost identical policy?[34] Hull had already pointed out that the Smith-Raskob forces, once they had destroyed Roosevelt, would destroy all other candidates who differed from the Republicans except on Prohibition. He concluded:

"I am unable to see what alternative there is except chaos and anarchy. It is in the light of this situation that I feel justified in driving ahead in an effort to be of some aid in organizing the right-minded and right-thinking forces around Roosevelt. I, of course, appreciate very fully the points of reservation to which you refer. It is now or never with the Democratic party, and so far I see no feasible or available course open without the serious risk of gravitating in behind the leadership of the DuPont-Raskob-Smith Forces."[35]

Thus it was that Roosevelt was able to pull along with him a following by no means delighted with his every action. This was what saved him despite the miserable botch he made of his relations with Tammany during the early months of 1932.

All of this, the first part of Roosevelt's intricate maneuvering for the nomination, was intended to win, not wound, the great mass of Democrats suspicious of Tammany and the outraged intelligentsia who thought he was being soft toward the organization. He was forced to maneuver next in an opposite direction. What he had done already had lent considerable truth to Lippmann's charge that Roosevelt was leaning over backward to keep his hands off of New York City affairs. Had he been too vigorous there, he not only would have jeopardized the huge block of ninety-six New York votes at the convention, but would have risked crystallizing against himself the machine votes of Illinois, Indiana, and New Jersey. As with the Garner supporters, Roosevelt wanted their votes if possible, and if not possible, at least did not want their undying opposition. The rift between the two factions in the party was growing wider day by day, but Roosevelt, uncomfortably leaning on the rural side, was still precariously reaching out to keep a continued grip on the urban side of the chasm.

Reformers in New York City were making it increasingly difficult for Roosevelt not to lose his grasp entirely. Certainly there was no love lost between Roosevelt and Tammany; theirs was a marriage of convenience. Nor had Roosevelt any illusions about New York's fun-loving mayor, Jimmy Walker. "Our little Mayor can save much trouble in the future by getting on the job, cleaning his own house and stopping wisecracks," Roosevelt commented in March, 1931. "If he does not do all this he can have only himself to blame if he gets into trouble." [36]

Had Walker done so, he would have saved Roosevelt infinite difficulties too. As it was, Roosevelt had looked less than courageous at this time when he ignored the formal charges requesting removal of Walker sent to him by the Reverend John H. Holmes and Rabbi Wise for the City Affairs Committee. Despite Walker's feeble reply, Roosevelt said that he saw no justification to their demands for removal or further investigation. Nevertheless, Roosevelt signed a bill providing a half million dollars and wide powers for a legislative investigation. In June, 1931, the investigation got under way with the indefatigable Samuel Seabury as chief counsel, backed by a youthful and vigorous staff. Altogether in the next fourteen months they gathered an enormous and appalling mountain of evidence and some sixty-nine thousand pages of testimony.

Perhaps Roosevelt had hoped that because the investigation was the work of the Republican legislature, headed by a Republican state senator, Samuel H. Hofstadter, Republicans could achieve the cleanup on their own and divert the wrath of Tammany from him. Certainly through the fall of 1931, Roosevelt had succeeded in giving limited aid to the reformers without losing the grudging support of Tammany. At the special session of the legislature in August, 1931, he had approved legislation recommended by Seabury to grant immunity to witnesses, yet in November had obtained Tammany aid in his reforestation-amendment fight with Smith.[37]

By February, 1932, with Smith an open candidate, it was all too clear that the New York City leaders felt stronger political and emotional ties to Smith than to Roosevelt. At the same time, Roosevelt's inaction against the offenders that Seabury was uncovering was worrying Roosevelt supporters throughout the country. At stake on the one hand were those New York delegates Roosevelt still hoped to secure, and on the other, a considerable measure of his national prestige.

In this crisis, beyond much question Roosevelt would not face up to himself as the wily opportunist reformers charged him with being, but was in his own mind convinced that he was a moral man determined to do justice. He may well have toyed with throwing caution to the winds and scourging Tammany with his righteous gubernatorial wrath. Colonel House, who granted that several cities in the United States were worse governed than New York, warned Roosevelt that he must reckon with the feeling against Tammany throughout the nation. House suggested an alluring course: "You could get the nomination and be elected by taking an unjust stand against Tammany, but you could not be nominated and elected if you were considered a wholehearted supporter of that organization." [38] Roosevelt nevertheless refused to follow a course which from the start he had considered immoral.

This he best illustrated in the flagrant case of Sheriff Thomas M. Farley of New York County. In October, Seabury had proved that Sheriff Farley, whose salary and legitimate income for a seven-year period totaled $87,000, had made bank deposits totaling $396,000. Where had he obtained the remaining money? Farley charmingly explained that he had accumulated it earlier and kept it in a tin box, a "good box I had . . . a wonderful box," containing over $100,000. Into this he had dipped from time to time. Even if true, this left $200,000 unaccounted for.[39]

At the end of December, 1931, Seabury sent Governor Roosevelt a transcript of the testimony, requesting that Roosevelt remove Farley. Roosevelt moved with deliberation, giving Farley an opportunity to reply to the charges. On February 16, Governor Roosevelt examined Farley at a public hearing, and on February 24 finally ordered him removed.[40]

While this slow process was under way, one of Roosevelt's Harvard classmates, the Reverend J. Russell Bowie, wrote Roosevelt it would be a disaster to public morale in New York City to allow Farley to remain in office. He called upon Roosevelt to demonstrate the new leadership in political life that Roosevelt had been talking about in a recent speech. Roosevelt retorted with a small sermon, asking Bowie if he remembered "the action of a certain magistrate by the name of Pontius Pilate, who acted upon public clamor after first washing his hands." He added, "When I re-read a certain poem, entitled 'IF' I am strengthened in my resolution not to let politics interfere with my decisions as Governor, nor to deny the right to be heard even to the meanest criminal in the State." [41]

This noble pose probably masked from Roosevelt himself, but not from many other people, his almost hysterical fear that the continued efforts of the reformers to force him to act against Tammany might cost him the presidential nomination. Certainly their communications to him and his devious replies were being circulated against him in pamphlet form on behalf of that product of the Hall who had maintained a complete silence concerning Tammany corruption, Alfred E. Smith. Probably too, Samuel Seabury was gunning not only for Tammany and Mayor Walker, but also for Governor Roosevelt.* It became increasingly apparent that Seabury, a conservative Democrat, also had presidential aspirations. All this hurt Roosevelt and justifiably irritated him, but did not in the slightest excuse his bad conduct in the spring of 1932.

In the aftermath of the Farley removal, Holmes and Wise moved to take advantage of the excellent dictum that Roosevelt had handed down during the hearing. This was that public servants had a responsibility to explain their private sources of income during their terms of office. "Democracy is a just but jealous master," he declared.† On the basis of this ruling, Holmes and Wise asked Roosevelt to remove two more New York City officeholders who could not explain their fat bank accounts. These were the chief clerk of the surrogate's court of Queen's County and the sheriff of King's County, James A.

* At Cincinnati Seabury in veiled reference to FDR said that the power of Tammany was a menace not only to New York City but to the nation as well: "It drives public men, whose instincts would lead them to speak out in protest against the corruption that has been revealed, to a solemn silence. . . . Where they hold public office and are forced on given occasions to rule adversely to Tammany Hall, they soften their opposition so that while the public will not regard them as pro-Tammany, Tammany Hall will not regard them as opposed to it." [42]

† FDR had asserted, "As a matter of general sound public policy . . . where a public official is under inquiry or investigation, especially an elected public official, and it appears that his scale of living, or the total of his bank deposits far exceeds the public salary which he is known to receive, he . . . owes a positive public duty to the community to give a reasonable or credible explanation of the sources of the deposits, or the source which enables him to maintain a scale of living beyond the amount of his salary."

Moley drafted this paragraph for FDR. It was one of the first of his important services.[43]

McQuade, who was engaging in fantastic and irrelevant explanations that he was supporting thirty-two relatives. Here were unmistakable parallels to the Farley case.[44]

Instead of acting upon these two cases by holding hearings, as was clearly indicated, Roosevelt petulantly charged the two reformers with urging him to an unconstitutional course, to punish the accused without due opportunity for them to be heard in their own defense. In the case of Sheriff McQuade, he asserted, they were recommending a course repugnant to representative government, because since McQuade had committed his alleged peculations, he had been overwhelmingly re-elected sheriff. Upon Wise and Holmes themselves, rather, he vented his fury:

> It would perhaps be easy for me to question the good faith in which these letters were written, or to assume that you care more for personal publicity than for good government. . . .
>
> Let me tell you two gentlemen straight from the shoulder, that I am becoming convinced from your letters that corruption in public office and unfit servants in public office are both far less abhorrent to you than they are to me. A rushing into print early and often, with extravagant and ill-considered language, causes many of our decent citizens to doubt your own reliance on law, on order and on justice. . . .
>
> The time which you two gentlemen now spend in bringing charges and asking your Governor to perform unconstitutional functions and to ignore the principles of representative government could be more profitably spent. If you would exert yourselves patiently and consistently in pointing out to the electorate of New York City that an active insistence on their part would result in better qualified and more honest and more efficient public servants, you would be rendering a service to your community which at the present time you are not performing.[45]

The tirade proved nothing so conclusively as that Roosevelt, ordinarily so affable and genial, was not bearing up well under the strain of the battle for the nomination. His middle course, a success in so many areas, was an utter failure when applied to Tammany, for it enraged the machine men and nauseated the intelligentsia. He had erred seriously, as Lippmann relentlessly pointed out, in not leading in a thorough, fearless cleanup of Tammany much earlier when it would not have had implications for the presidential nomination. Far too many influential leaders were supporting Roosevelt not so much out of firm faith in him as because he represented a lesser evil.

The point had come when he must formulate clear-cut public positions on many a crucial issue, positions he could use as weapons in the fight for dominance. Avoiding negative reactions was no longer sufficient; he must win enthusiastic positive support. He could expect the sort of difficulty he was encountering over foreign affairs, Prohibition, and Tammany to spread into many another critical area as convention time approached. The man who once delighted in piloting a destroyer through treacherous waters had now a far trickier course to steer between the whirlpools of evasion and inaction and the craggy cliffs of positive commitment on controversial matters.

CHAPTER XVIII

A Champion for the Forgotten Man

> These unhappy times call for the building of plans that rest upon the forgotten, the unorganized but the indispensable units of economic power, for plans like those of 1917 that build from the bottom up and not from the top down, that put their faith once more in the forgotten man at the bottom of the economic pyramid.
>
> — FDR, *April 7, 1932.*

IN the spring of 1932, Roosevelt needed a Brain Trust. Just as he had long since put into operation a smooth organization to obtain delegates, by April he had reached the point of needing a staff to formulate for him appealing campaign statements on national issues. There was far more to be done than he himself could master, occupied as he was with the intricate political battles for delegates, and the heavy burden of being chief executive of the State of New York during the depression crisis. As in every March, more than eight hundred bills were piled high on his desk, awaiting his signature or veto. At the same time, he must prepare several major national speeches.

Roosevelt came naturally and easily to the idea of recruiting a group of policy advisers. Smith had done so in the campaign of 1928. Roosevelt had depended upon professors in developing almost every one of his important policies as governor; it was not only logical but almost inevitable that he should turn to them in 1932. Undoubtedly during the first months of 1932 he thought more than once about establishing such a group. Recruiting it would be easy, but it was not so clear who should organize and lead it.

During his years as governor, Roosevelt had leaned constantly upon his young, indefatigable, and shrewd counsel, Samuel I. Rosenman. But Rosenman, who had served Roosevelt with a selfless devotion, had little time or energy to waste on charming new converts. Certainly he had not succeeded in winning over Howe, who had always prided himself upon being Roosevelt's idea man. Howe had a nagging fear that Rosenman might upset things in Albany. There was a further possibility that academic men might chafe a bit over working under a lawyer younger than they were — he was only thirty-six. As for Rosenman himself, he was fearful that he would get beyond his depth. While he expected Roosevelt to retain the same basic philosophy, he knew that many national problems would call for solutions different from state ones. Little that Roosevelt had done for agriculture in New York State would help nationally. Rosenman did not feel qualified to advise as he had on state matters, and very much hoped for appointment to the state Supreme Court.[1]

Thus it was that Rosenman suggested to Roosevelt one evening in March, after they had finished some state business, that Roosevelt should go to the universities to recruit some advisers who would strike out on new paths. And Rosenman suggested to Roosevelt that he head the group with a man both Rosenman and Howe admired, Professor Raymond Moley of Columbia University.

Roosevelt puffed on his cigarette and nodded, but Rosenman felt by no means sure as he wheeled the Governor into his bedroom that Roosevelt was sold. On the contrary, Roosevelt, as was so often the case, was not tipping his hand. As with Flynn's suggestion of Farley to head the campaign, so Rosenman's of Moley eased Roosevelt out of a difficult spot.* He had no intention of abandoning so loyal and valuable an assistant — he gave Rosenman the appointment to the Supreme Court — but Moley could perform a most useful service in assembling speeches.[2]

Moley was tried and trusted, and apparently sympathetic with Roosevelt's political philosophy. He had come out of the Ohio of the dynamic progressive reformers, Tom Johnson and Newton D. Baker, to become a specialist on politics and criminal law at Columbia University. Avowedly a conservative in his basic outlook, he wished to see practical reforms like those of Johnson in Cleveland extended to the entire nation. He had advised Roosevelt since the campaign of 1928 on questions involving criminal law and the administration of justice. Since 1931, he had performed excellently as the leading member of a commission to recommend reforms in the judicial system.

In January, 1932, Roosevelt had talked again tentatively to him about aid in the campaign, but he had been more immediately concerned with advice on the removal of Sheriff Farley. Moley's work on the removal order, and upon a speech on judicial reform that Roosevelt

* Long after Farley and Moley were gone, Roosevelt still leaned upon Flynn and Rosenman.

delivered in March, were in both instances effective. He was not a flashy or especially original man, but he possessed a remarkable knack for clear analysis, combined with a succinct and pungent style of writing. He had what anyone close to Roosevelt needed, a great capacity for endless work, and a talent for organizing both ideas and men. He possessed, as he has written, a technique which no one then around Roosevelt (except Rosenman) seemed to have, the knack of working on speeches so as "to help crystallize [Roosevelt's] own ideas and inclinations, reflect them accurately, and extend them where necessary, and present them congruously – in brief, to relieve him of a good deal of personal drudgery." [3]

At the beginning of March, Roosevelt had lamented to Moley that he was falling behind in his efforts to prepare policy speeches, and that they were out of Rosenman's sphere. Consequently, it came as no surprise to Moley when Rosenman called him up and invited him to gather a council of advisers. Roosevelt had felt that it would be good to assemble New York City professors; it would be easier to consult with them as a group. Since he chose Moley as their leader, it was logical that they should be from Columbia University. Rosenman, together with Roosevelt's law partner, Doc O'Connor, and Moley met shortly thereafter in New York City. Moley prepared a tentative list of subjects and men who might advise upon them.

First, there was agriculture, which practically held the key to the nomination and election of Roosevelt. Roosevelt had emphasized farm problems in New York State; he must now broaden his appeal to the distressed farmers of the entire nation. For this crucial spot, Moley suggested a neighbor of his on Claremont Avenue, a handsome and delightful economics professor, Rexford Guy Tugwell. Moley knew him only slightly; their ideas were by no means in agreement, for Tugwell was advocating drastic overhauling of the economic system. But Moley recognized him for a first-rate economist with an original mind. "Rex was like a cocktail," he has reminisced, "his conversation picked you up and made your brain race along." Tugwell had had some slight experience in advising on agricultural programs; he had assisted Alfred E. Smith early in the campaign of 1928.[4]

On credit and corporations, Moley chose Adolph A. Berle, Jr., who with an economist, Gardiner C. Means, had prepared an influential analysis, later published during the summer of 1932, *The Modern Corporation and Private Property*. Berle, who had early attracted attention as a child prodigy at Harvard, had caught Moley's eye in meetings of the Columbia law faculty. He had a scintillating mind, an intense spirit, and wrote prolifically and prodigiously. In retrospect, he seemed to Moley a bit alarmist in his point of view, since he made strong statements about remaking the economic order. But Moley felt that Berle was probably talking to hear himself talk. When Moley invited Berle to join the group, Berle informed him that he already had another candidate. Moley knew this to be Newton D. Baker, but told Berle that that did not matter.

In the months before the convention, Berle made some decided contributions. He presented a memorandum on debt which Moley considered of the utmost importance. Moley had been influenced by the historical writings of Charles A. Beard to feel that the basic political problem in the United States was the struggle between debtors and creditors. Consequently, he had Berle prepare a compilation of the debt structure in the United States of agriculture, railroads, cities, real estate, and the rest.[5]

There were others recruited in the first few weeks. For advice on tariff, Moley obtained a memorandum from Lindsay Rogers, another outstanding Columbia professor, who had advised Smith in this field in 1928. On administrative reorganization there was Schuyler Wallace, and on questions of constitutional law, Howard Lee McBain. Many men prepared memoranda on single subjects for Moley and otherwise were not used; others went with him to see Roosevelt, and were of assistance again and again.[6]

By trial and error a group came into existence. At its nucleus were two nonacademic men, Rosenman and O'Connor, and Professors Moley, Tugwell, and Berle. Many another was on the periphery. Some of the candidates fell by the wayside. One was too pedantic, and kept saying the same thing over and over again, Moley later wrote. Another irritated Roosevelt with his stuffy manner. For it was Roosevelt himself in the final analysis who made the selection. "The routine was simple enough," Moley has explained:

> Sam, "Doc," and I would take one or two men on the late-afternoon train to Albany, arriving in time for dinner. The talk at the table would be pleasant, casual, and generally inconsequential. But once we had moved out of the dining room to the study which adjoined it . . . random talk came to an end. Roosevelt, Sam, or I would throw a question at the visitor, and we were off at an exciting and exhausting clip.

> The Governor was at once a student, a cross-examiner, and a judge. He would listen with rapt attention for a few minutes and then break in with a question whose sharpness was characteristically blurred with an anecdotal introduction or an air of sympathetic agreement with the speaker. Sooner or later, we would all have at the visitor, of course. But those darting questions of Roosevelt were the ticks of the evening's metronome. The intervals between them would grow shorter. The questions themselves would become meatier, more informed — the infallible index to the amount he was picking up in the evening's course.
>
> By midnight, when the time came to dash for the train to New York, Sam, "Doc," and I would be done in; the visitor (who would not realize for some days, in most cases, that he had been squeezed dry) would look a trifle wilted; and the Governor, scorning further questions, would be making vigorous pronouncements on the subject we had been discussing, waving his cigarette holder to emphasize his points.[7]

All this was essential to Roosevelt's education, since he must be able in the months ahead to extemporize quickly and correctly on any issue about which newspapermen or politicians might quiz him. Thus, the advisers served not only as drafters of speeches but also as teachers. Tugwell became especially skillful at the process. He discovered Roosevelt almost entirely lacking in knowledge of economics, and undertook to fill the gap. His technique was to reduce what he had to say to the most simple and graphic terms, until he could present it in about five minutes. He would try it out on noneconomist friends to see if they would grasp it. Then, when he was sure what he had to say was absolutely clear, he would pop it on Roosevelt. Usually, he had the satisfaction within a few minutes of hearing his gifted pupil expound to someone else with emphasis and feeling what he had just acquired from Tugwell.[8]

Roosevelt took to the professors at once. To them he must have seemed a bit baffling at times, but he represented an incredible opportunity at a time of great national crisis for them to carry their ideas from the classroom to the hustings. Theodore Roosevelt too had liked professors, and Robert M. La Follette had leaned upon them heavily in developing a state program in Wisconsin, but never in American history had academic men possessed such an opportunity. They brought, as Rosenman had hoped, a freshness of viewpoint and a willingness to break with the past. They suggested new solutions at a time when tried and true ones seemed hopelessly inadequate. Roosevelt was rather startlingly receptive to what they had to say, and, somewhat to Moley's dismay, amazingly uncritical. He displayed a facile eclectic virtuosity, but little depth or precision in handling ideas. To him the irreconcilable could always be reconciled.

The professors, on the other hand, lacked his sense of political realities. This was true to some extent even of Moley, a remarkably shrewd student of politics in most respects, when he had to face up to Roosevelt's knack of making a speech say several contradictory things at once. To Moley, as to Lippmann, this was most unpleasant. To other of the professors it might be more tolerable, but repeatedly they demonstrated their political innocence.

How Roosevelt appeared to a keenly analytical academic mind is clear in Moley's private exposition at the time:

> One thing is sure — that the idea people get from his charming manner — that he is soft or flabby in disposition and character — is far from true. When he wants something a lot he can be formidable — when crossed he is hard, stubborn, resourceful, relentless. I used to think on the basis of casual observation that his amiability was "lord-of-the-manor" — "good-to-the-peasants" — stuff. It isn't that at all. He seems quite naturally warm and friendly — less because he genuinely likes many of the people to whom he is pleasant (although he does like a lot of people of all sorts and varieties) than because he just enjoys the pleasant and engaging role, as a charming woman does. And being a born politician he measures such qualities in himself by the effect they produce on others. He is wholly conscious of his ability to send callers away happy and glowing and in agreement with him and his ideas. And he particularly enjoys sending people away who have completely forgotten (under his spell) the thing they came to say or ask. On the whole, his cordiality and his interest in people is, to all appearances, unfeigned. . . .
>
> The man's energy and vitality are astonishing. I've been amazed with his interest in things. It skips and bounces through seemingly intricate subjects and maybe it is my academic training that makes me feel that no one could possibly learn much in such a hit or miss fashion. I don't find that he has read much about economic subjects. What he gets is from talking to people and when he stores away the net of conversation he never knows what part of what he has kept is what he said himself or what his visitor said. There is a lot of autointoxication of the intelligence that we shall have to watch. But he gets a lot from talking with people

who come in. A typical approach to a big problem is "so-and-so was telling me yesterday." Another is "now *we* found in dealing with the *state* so-and-so that we had to deal with such-and-such." . . .[9]

At first Roosevelt teasingly referred to his tutors as the "privy council," a term which made Moley wince as he speculated on what unfriendly newspapers could do with it. For a long time the very existence of the group was secret. Before deciding to recruit them, Roosevelt had confided to Rosenman his fear that they might talk about their work and thus do damage through premature newspaper reports. As late as the end of May, when Rosenman arrived in Warm Springs as a courier from them, they were still operating confidentially. The New York *Times* was so far off the scent that it speculated whether Rosenman had made his trip to report to Roosevelt on Tammany's latest maneuvers. It was not until September that James Kieran of the New York *Times*, reporting on the group, which by that time was quite well known, tagged it the "brains trust." By then, Roosevelt was glad to accept the new title.[10]

The first task of the "brains trust," or, more specifically, of Moley, was to draft a ten-minute address for Roosevelt to deliver over a nation-wide radio network on April 7. This was under the sponsorship of Lucky Strike cigarettes, and in theory Roosevelt spoke under the auspices of the Democratic National Committee, but it gave him an opportunity to address a national audience upon his own behalf. This was his chance to answer his intellectual critics by laying down the outlines of a positive progressive program. Moley wove skillfully for Roosevelt a pattern incorporating in general terms much that they had been discussing in their conversations, and upon which the Brain Trust was working.

In this speech, Roosevelt asserted that he considered the depression a graver emergency for the United States than the First World War. But during the war, the leadership had mobilized the entire nation from bottom to top. In contrast, the Hoover Administration had either forgotten or ignored "the infantry of our economic army." Roosevelt asserted that upon these, upon "the forgotten men," plans must be built.* What were these? Roosevelt said that of ten or a dozen aspects

* Moley had taken the phrase "forgotten man" from an essay by William Graham Sumner first published in 1883, and was applying it more broadly to encompass the lower as well as middle class.[11]

of an over-all program, he had time only to mention a few. He declared that public-works expenditures running into the billions would not completely solve unemployment; they would be only a stopgap. Instead, he emphasized what he felt were more basic remedies. He would raise the purchasing power of the farmer, since the employment of every city worker was tied in with the farmer's dollar. "No nation can long endure half bankrupt. Main Street, Broadway, the mills, the mines will close if half the buyers are broke." Along with this, the government must not loan money just at the top, as it was doing through the Reconstruction Finance Corporation, but should assist the farmer and the small homeowner in preventing mortgage foreclosures. Finally, it must stimulate the sale of goods overseas through a reciprocal trade program.[12]

In retrospect, this seems a most mild and rather vague speech. At the time it was received as a bold challenge to the conservatives, giving heart to those impatient for change, frightening those wedded to the status quo. Western and Southern Democrats expressed their delight over Roosevelt's open attack upon the Republican theory that R.F.C. loans to large corporations would trickle down to the masses, and his demand for aid to farmers. A Minnesota leader wired that it met with "the hearty approval of the people of our state," since it "expresses conditions exactly as they exist with our farmer[s]." To the wealthy and conservative, on the other hand, it was nothing short of demagogic.* Again and again they used the term. A prominent Wall Street Democrat, Thomas Chadbourne, charged it in an open letter. The New York *Times* blushed editorially that its candidate should indulge in talk which coming from another would be judged demagogic claptrap. Lippmann joined in the hue and cry on the grounds that Roosevelt had misrepresented the R.F.C., and had not explained how he would increase the purchasing power of the "forgotten man."[13]

The opportunity seemed too good for Alfred E. Smith to miss. A few days later he chose the occasion of the annual Jefferson Day dinner in Washington, D.C., to join the conservative onslaught against Roosevelt. Almost every powerful conservative in the Democratic party was there, but not Roosevelt, who had been warned by Washington friends to withdraw his acceptance of Raskob's speaking invitation. Even as

* Before making the speech, FDR had asked Baruch's advice on an economic program. Baruch recommended balancing the budget, slashing it from four billion dollars to three and a half, and raising funds through bonds for two billion dollars' worth of self-liquidating public works.

he had been led to expect, the gathering was "packed . . . and packed the wrong way!" Certainly Smith, who had made himself famous as the champion of the urban masses, attacked in the wrong direction. While many of those present tensely followed advance copies of the speech, he laid down a vehement challenge to Roosevelt, slashing into him from the right.[14]

"I will take off my coat and vest," Smith declared, "and fight to the end against any candidate who persists in any demagogic appeal to the masses of the working people of this country to destroy themselves by setting class against class and rich against poor." [15]

After the dinner, he disclaimed that he had Roosevelt or anybody else in mind. Outwardly Roosevelt accepted the disclaimer at face value. He had listened to the address over the radio, Earle Looker observed, "making no comment whatever, nor allowing his expression to change." When newspapermen queried him about it, he joked, "Wasn't that a terrible attack Al made on Alfalfa Bill Murray?" [16]

Roosevelt had no need to be dismayed. Republican newspapers, such as the Des Moines *Register* and the San Francisco *Chronicle*, cheered Smith; a Republican congressman from Kansas cried, "Hit him again, Al!" Their hope was that Smith's defiance of Roosevelt would lead to another split convention and Democratic debacle. All they were demonstrating was that they were beginning to look upon Smith as one of their own. And this was what Smith himself was making clear to those discontented Democrats in the farm areas. It did not alienate his tried and true following in the Eastern cities, who were so emotional in their support that they cared little what he said, and were impervious to reports that he had discarded his brown derby for a high silk hat. It did confirm the suspicions of the others, and strengthen their opposition to Smith or their support of Roosevelt. Those who supported Garner, or Murray and other Western favorite sons, were never likely to switch to Smith or his group.[17]

Smith and the other conservative Democratic leaders had shown themselves almost bankrupt of positive ideas for ending the depression. The exception was that Smith had advocated heavy public-works spending, in which he was in advance of Roosevelt, who labeled it a stopgap. At the Jefferson Day dinner, Smith had talked about a continued moratorium on war-debt and reparation payments and revision of the tariff to stimulate foreign trade. And, as always, he advocated Prohibition repeal. Governor Ritchie of Maryland also talked of lower tariffs and flayed Hoover for not cutting government expenses in order to balance the budget. Former Governor Cox of Ohio called for a spiritual awakening among public men. Governor White of Ohio demanded heavy horizontal cuts among Federal departments, bureaus, and commissions to weed out all but the strictly necessary and essential.[18]

It was against this backdrop of the programs of his conservative rivals, not against what they ideally hoped could be done, that Western Democrats judged Roosevelt. The contrast between his "forgotten man" speech and the Jefferson Day addresses heightened their support for him. National Committeeman Arthur Mullen of Nebraska wrote, "Our friends who are complaining about arraying class against class, ought to realize the fact that we have reached a point in this country where it is the mass against a class. Those who think that the south end of Manhattan can direct the policies of the United States have a wrong concept of the public mind at this time. The ordinary man in this State believes that these so-called captains of industry and big business institutions are largely responsible for the present deplorable conditions that exist." [19]

Smith had in effect repeated his blunder of the 1928 campaign, when he had conspicuously arrayed behind him Raskob and General Motors, and had created the impression among some progressives that he was a big-business candidate. In 1928 it made no difference; in 1932, when the depression was the big issue, it hurt. A newspaper survey indicated that Roosevelt's "forgotten man" speech had strengthened his progressive following.[20]

Nevertheless, Roosevelt picked up Smith's challenge with caution. He was anxious not to alienate any more seriously than necessary either Smith or his following. Nor did he wish to alarm his Eastern supporters. Internecine warfare could not only prevent him from winning the nomination, but even if he did win it, it could wreck him during the campaign. Consequently, when Roosevelt spoke at Saint Paul at a Jefferson Day dinner five days after the one in Washington, he clung firmly to his progressivism, but couched it in the words of Jefferson, Lincoln, Wilson, and Theodore Roosevelt.

As Roosevelt traveled out to Saint Paul, news came that the great Insull public-utilities empire was cracking. He had Moley, who had worked on the speech, meet him on the train at Detroit and help devise some last-minute changes. In the speech, he detailed at length his New York State power program, adding something new and different. He had become convinced that because power transmission crossed state lines, control could not be effective through state or even interstate compacts. There must be a firm national control. In addition, he elaborated upon the need for tariff revision,* and in terms fairly vague, as they must be if he were not to lose supporters.

The tone of the speech, rather than the contents, impressed the political observers. He had not picked up Smith's challenge. Instead he had redefined some of his remarks in the "forgotten man" speech. "I am not speaking of an economic life completely planned and regimented," he explained. He talked instead of the need for a real community of interest in the economic regulation he felt imperative. "In much of our present plans there is too much disposition to mistake the part for the whole, the head for the body, the captain for the company, the general for the army. I plead not for a class control but for a true concert of interests." He interpolated that if this was treason, "make the most of it." [22]

Even Lippmann had to grant that the speech was thoughtful and free from demagogic appeal, and that on power policy and the tariff Roosevelt had demonstrated a firm grasp of fundamentals. This was because Roosevelt, in keeping with the counsel House, Hull, Roper, and others had given him, had phrased his speech in such conservative and historic terms that newspaper critics did not see that he was maintaining the position he had assumed in the "forgotten man" speech. "I certainly tried to keep my temper," he wrote Senator Walsh, "and at the same time I took back nothing!" [23]

While Roosevelt placated the East, he had been encouraged by his reception in a Middle West which seemed again ripe for political insurgency. "What impressed me most," he commented upon his return, "was the general expression of opinion that if I am nominated it will do more than anything else to solidify the party, — to bring in many Progressives, Farmer-Laborites, and Republicans and to bring many former Democrats who strayed away." [24]

This emphasis upon progressivism carried over into one more important speech that spring. This was the address that Roosevelt delivered before the graduating class at Oglethorpe University on May 22. It was almost entirely ghosted for him, and under rather

* In the tariff section he had the misfortune to state word for word a passage identical to that Smith had used in his Washington speech. Lindsay Rogers had submitted the same memorandum to both men. Newspapers made much of the duplication — although the tariff policies Smith and FDR proposed were quite dissimilar. FDR stood by Moley amidst the furor, but Rogers withdrew from active participation in the Brain Trust.[21]

unusual circumstances. One day while he was picnicking at Warm Springs, the newspapermen with him began good-naturedly criticizing his speeches. He retorted that if they did not like his speeches, why didn't they draft one for him? Ernest K. Lindley, one of the group, picked up the challenge. He was well qualified to do so, for he had recently published a remarkably moving and penetrating campaign biography of Roosevelt. Lindley well understood his subject, and in the Oglethorpe speech, which received little trimming and revising, he put into Roosevelt's mouth emphatically progressive words.[25]

At Oglethorpe, Roosevelt called for the control through adequate planning of the production and distribution of the vast quantity of goods the American economy was capable of turning out. Insufficient buying power, not insufficient capital, had led to the depression; the way out would have to come through thinking less about the producer and more about the consumer. The rewards for speculative capital must be less; for a day's work, greater. These were objectives. Methods must come later through true leadership. Roosevelt concluded:

"The country needs and, unless I mistake its temper, the country demands bold, persistent experimentation. It is common sense to take a method and try it: If it fails, admit it frankly and try another. But above all, try something. The millions who are in want will not stand by silently forever while the things to satisfy their needs are within easy reach." [26]

The words might be Lindley's, but the spirit of the address was one which Roosevelt had already been demonstrating in the State of New York. Behind it also was a reservoir of more concrete recommendations into which the Brain Trust was busily pumping fresh data. Throughout the spring of 1932 it was busy working on memoranda.

These memoranda were in constant process of development, subject to modification as times or pressures changed. Some could fit the needs of immediate preconvention speeches, others the campaign later. One significant recommendation, the recognition of Russia, Roosevelt never mentioned during the campaign but did implement when he reached the White House. Thus what Rosenman carried to Warm Springs on May 19, 1932, was a ten-point memorandum covering what Moley considered "the really important economic problems that ought to form the basis of a political campaign, or, at least, a pre-Convention statement." The items that Moley particularly noted were the tariff, agriculture, Russia, power, and economy in government.[27]

The most important of these in terms of both political urgency and long-range effect was agriculture. Here the Brain Trust did its most significant piece of policy formulation in the weeks before the convention. Above all Roosevelt must possess a winning formula which would at least promise a solution of the country's most critical problem. This would not be easy to find, since in the early months of 1932, the leading farm organizations could agree only upon the most general sort of plan. They formed the National Farm Conference, which proposed that the government accept one or another scheme to dump the surplus, that it legislate some sort of tariff equality, and that it sponsor rather mild inflation to restore an "honest dollar" to the farmer.[28]

These vague generalizations Roosevelt could and did readily accept for his position on agriculture. He talked and wrote in terms of subsidizing the export of the surplus, and did so with such pleasant generalities that he was able to correspond cordially with the right-wing George Peek, who had been head of the Moline Plow Company, and confer warmly with John A. Simpson, president of the militant Farmers' Union.[29]

Within a few months it was no longer enough to endorse some sort of McNary-Haugen export scheme, for at exactly this time a new farm plan was brewing. It was an indication of the notable effectiveness of the Brain Trust that Roosevelt almost immediately became aware of it. This was the Voluntary Domestic Allotment plan. A number of economists had contributed to developing it; among them were Milburn L. Wilson, W. J. Spillman, John D. Black, and Beardsley Ruml. By April, 1932, Wilson, a professor at Montana State College, who looked and talked like a farmer, was rallying so many strong farm leaders behind the plan that it was becoming politically potent. On April 10, Wilson held a conference with Henry A. Wallace, editor of *Wallace's Farmer*, Peek, and a number of others. They arrived at the basic principles of acreage restriction to cut farm production, and benefit payments for those who accepted a limited "domestic allotment" of their crops, to be financed through taxes on the processors of agricultural commodities.[30]

Roosevelt's agricultural expert, Tugwell, was already predisposed toward some sort of crop-control program. He had written a number of scholarly articles proposing planned farm production, and, although he had not met Wilson, was immediately favorable toward Wilson's ideas. When Roosevelt demanded that Tugwell and the Brain Trust devise a plan which would unite the farmers, Tugwell turned to

Wilson and the domestic-allotment scheme. Thus it was that Roosevelt and Moley sent Tugwell to Chicago to attend the final meeting of the domestic-allotment advocates on June 23, 1932.[31]

Tugwell returned to New York so full of enthusiasm over Wilson's ideas that he and Moley persuaded Roosevelt to make a sudden switch of farm plans. While at Warm Springs, Roosevelt in his own hand had written a telegram to *Collier's* once again endorsing an export scheme. "We must at once take the Farm Board out of speculation in wheat & cotton, [and] try out a new plan to insure getting surplus crops out of the country without putting the government in business," Roosevelt had asserted. But a few days later, he put into the draft of his acceptance speech a general proposal for the domestic allotment. He suggested planning farm production by voluntary means in such a way as to reduce the surpluses and "make it unnecessary in later years to depend on dumping those surpluses abroad in order to support domestic prices." The actual wording of the bill he would leave to the responsible farm groups.[32]

Thus, through the Brain Trust, even before his nomination, Roosevelt had accepted the formula which was to become the basis of the Agricultural Adjustment Administration. Agricultural relief was the most striking example of the way in which Roosevelt and the Brain Trust in area after area were ready to maintain flexibility of thinking and willingness to explore new solutions.

Out of this spirit grew the substance for the theme that ran through all of Roosevelt's speeches — the dynamic challenge to Smith and other conservatives within the Democratic party, and to President Hoover and the Republicans. The details might not yet be spelled out, but Roosevelt's general position was clear enough. He had said sufficient to stake out a strong claim to liberalism. After the convention he would be ready to fill in requisite details from the Brain Trust memoranda.

CHAPTER XIX

The Fight for Delegates

I am inclined to think that everything is going all right and that the keynote must be to avoid deadlock and if possible bitterness.

— FDR, *March 11, 1932.*

ARMED with public pronouncements encouraging to a depression-weary nation, Roosevelt made an early and impressive start in the battle for convention delegates. His greatest weapon was his positive though vague program, which every survey indicated appealed widely to the electorate. His general staff, headed by Farley in the field and Howe at headquarters, was compact and on the whole efficient. His shock troops in the majority of instances were the state Democratic organizations. Ideologically, Roosevelt was progressive, in step with the dominant public mood; organizationally, he was regular, in keeping with political realities.

For several years, Roosevelt and Howe had conducted a correspondence with Democratic leaders large and small in every one of the forty-eight states, the District of Columbia, and even to some extent in the territories. Although Roosevelt was an Eastern governor, he had met with his greatest success in the South and West, and it was to these sections that he had especially aimed his public statements. If he were to hold two thirds of the delegates at the convention, he must win these two sections almost solidly, and augment them with a substantial showing in the East.

In the South and West, Roosevelt could count upon die-hard opposition to his main opponent, Smith; in the East he could hope that Smith had started so late that he would not be able to pick up much organization support. Many an organization Democrat, hungry for a winner, had come out publicly for Roosevelt before his old favorite Smith had announced his availability. Smith, in addition to starting late, had further hampered his cause by making his candidacy somewhat equivocal. He had declared that while he was receptive, he would not put on an active fight for delegations. This confusion during precious weeks in the early spring contributed to Roosevelt's advantage.

Nevertheless, Roosevelt did not find it easy to be the contender against the field. Even in the South, where he was so strong, he had to conduct numerous careful campaigns state by state in order to secure the delegates. His trips to Warm Springs increased in number; it was an ideal locale for many a swim or picnic with Southern politicos. He played to perfection the role of favorite son of Georgia, even entering with zest into a public controversy over how to eat corn pone with potlikker. Huey P. Long, the Louisiana Kingfish, claimed it should be dunked. "Because I am at least an adopted Georgian," Roosevelt wired the Atlanta *Constitution*, "I am deeply stirred by the great controversy." And he sided with the *Constitution* in contending the corn pone should be crumbled into the potlikker. More important to Southerners, still hostile to the Wets, was Roosevelt's relative Dryness, his unwillingness to allow Prohibition to become a major campaign issue. He appealed to them more than Ritchie, or even the also Wet Baker, because of his slogan, "Bread not Booze." [1]

In the South especially, where every state had an all-powerful Democratic organization, Roosevelt was determined to work with the regulars. The alternative would be factionalism and disaster for Roosevelt. To his great irritation, a pair of amateur promoters appeared on the Southern scene at the end of 1930 to organize Roosevelt Southern Clubs. They worked independently of the professionals, and seemed primarily interested in soliciting memberships through agents at a dollar apiece. Because of the overwhelming Roosevelt sentiment in Dixie, they achieved remarkable success in organizing clubs, and consequently became embarrassing. For a long time, Roosevelt refused to deal with them directly, which they regarded as tacit endorsement. Finally he had an interview with them at Warm Springs, at which they interpreted his customary smiles and nods as warm approval. Howe had early favored sending professionals into the clubs to take them over, but it was not until early in 1932 that Farley flatly told the promoters that he would not reimburse them for their expenses.[2]

"I know of no way to get out an injunction against these people who are trying to make a money racket out of my candidacy," Roosevelt wrote angrily to Senator Pat Harrison of Mississippi. "The only thing possible is to spread the word in Mississippi, as has been done in Alabama and Georgia, that they have no connection with the Demo-

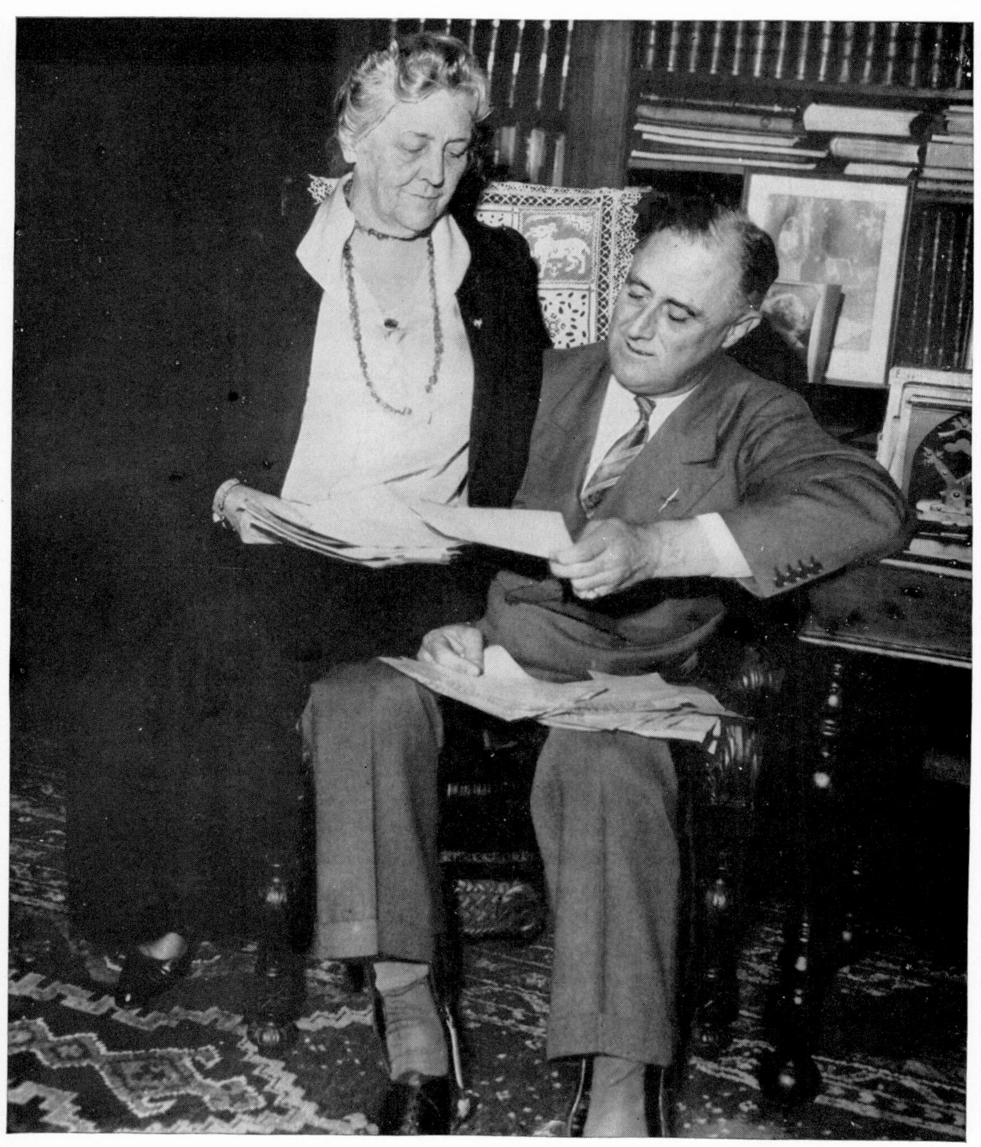

By permission of the Director of the Franklin D. Roosevelt Library

FDR and his mother at Hyde Park, November 6, 1932

Photo by Wide World. By permission of the Director of the Franklin D. Roosevelt Library

FDR at Seattle, Washington State, on a campaign trip, September 22, 1932

Photo by I. N. By permission of the Director of the Franklin D. Roosevelt Library

FDR and a miner, at Elm Grove, West Virginia, en route from Pittsburgh, Pennsylvania to Wheeling, West Virginia. October 19, 1932 cratic organization or with any people who are working for me." [3]

Farley followed this with form letters to Democratic chairmen throughout the South, disavowing the clubs. In retaliation, the promoters sued Roosevelt for expense money, swung their support to Alfalfa Bill Murray, and published an exposé of their dealings with Roosevelt. The exposé was remarkable only because they revealed that at the outset they had received the backing of the Atlanta Ku Klux Klan headquarters and tried to tie Roosevelt in with the Klan. Although a Wisconsin Smith backer spread these charges against Roosevelt throughout the nation, they seemed to do him no harm. He had erred in not nipping the promotion scheme at the outset, but his natural luck held and he did not suffer from it.[4]

By working with the regulars, Roosevelt managed to tie up all but four of the delegations from sixteen Southern and border states — and one of the others was actually for him. First came Georgia in March. His friends were so enthusiastic that they paid his thousand-dollar primary entrance fee; Roosevelt, saying he was deeply touched, contributed a like amount for the treatment of Georgia polio victims at Warm Springs. Roosevelt's popularity was so great in the state that Garner's manager, Representative Sam Rayburn, did not want to challenge it. Nevertheless, a Georgian filed as proxy for Garner, backed aggressively by Hearst's Atlanta newspaper. Because of Georgia's unusual system of selecting delegates by counties rather than for the state at large, there was a good opportunity for Garner to win a few delegates. But on March 23 Roosevelt won a victory even beyond the expectation of his managers, crushing the Garner candidate by a popular vote of almost eight to one, and winning all twenty-eight delegates. To Roosevelt's especial delight, Warm Springs voted for him 218 to 1.[5]

Six days later, Roosevelt won a most valuable victory when Tom Pendergast of Kansas City, the only one of the big bosses to line up with Roosevelt in 1932, saw to it that a nominally Reed delegation from Missouri actually should support Roosevelt. "Pendergast assured me," one of Roosevelt's scouts reported before the Missouri convention, "that he had informed Senator Reed that he might have the Missouri delegation as a complimentary vote until it was needed by Roosevelt, but that when Reed was out of the picture, he reserved the right to cast his vote as a unit for Roosevelt." Moreover, Senator Harry B. Hawes assured Roosevelt that most of the delegates were personal friends and old supporters whom he hoped to keep in line for Roosevelt. Thus it was that Roosevelt acquired vital hidden reserve strength among the thirty-six Missouri delegates, upon which Farley could draw at a critical point in the convention.[6]

Maryland, as was a foregone conclusion, pledged its delegation to its favorite son, Ritchie, on March 30. Roosevelt followed a policy there as elsewhere of not challenging favorite sons. But the next day Roosevelt was the beneficiary of the reluctant favorite son of Arkansas, Senator Joseph T. Robinson, who had no wish to be a party to a deadlocked convention. He withdrew the day before the state convention; Arkansas politicians, who had long looked upon Roosevelt as a second choice, picked an uninstructed delegation of eighteen, a majority of whom were Roosevelt backers. The Governor and other Roosevelt supporters were ready to work valiantly to keep the delegation in line at the convention, but it was a skittish group.[7]

Kentucky was more critical because there the minority faction in the party, including most notably Judge Robert Bingham, publisher of the Louisville *Courier-Journal*, was supporting Roosevelt. The majority faction under Governor Ruby Laffoon was trying to make Senator Alben Barkley a favorite-son front for the anti-Roosevelt forces. Barkley, who privately leaned toward Roosevelt, was reluctant to enter into this maneuver, which might jeopardize his otherwise certain renomination to the Senate. Roosevelt and his lieutenants worked out a scheme to capitalize upon Barkley's reluctance and win the Kentucky delegation. They had been casting about for someone to oppose Shouse as Temporary Chairman of the National Convention, a post which Shouse would use to try to destroy Roosevelt. Barkley would be an ideal man. They offered him their support, which would be the equivalent of election, since they expected to control a majority of delegates. Homer Cummings went to Louisville early in March, came to an understanding with Barkley, and managed to win the support of both factions of the party. Governor Laffoon and Senator Barkley both come out resoundingly for Roosevelt. "Instead of attempting to confuse and clutter up the situation and waste our energy and opportunity," Barkley declared, "we ought to be uniting all our forces behind a man who can appeal to the imagination of the people." Roosevelt, pleased, wrote a friend, "It was a very fine statement, and I am sure will have a wholesome effect . . . around the country generally."[8]

In May and June, Roosevelt reaped a rich harvest of Southern delegates. On May 3, he won Alabama after lengthy and complicated political infighting, which involved sending several envoys to repudiate amateurs trying to speak on behalf of Roosevelt, and undermining a hostile professional, the state chairman. When the chairman tried to call a convention to select delegates, the Roosevelt forces on the state committee overrode him forty-two to six. Roosevelt won in the primary by a three-to-one ratio. The top delegate was former Governor William W. Brandon, who had begun 103 roll calls at the 1924 convention with the cry, "Alabama casts twenty-four votes for Underwood." At Chicago he was ready to cast them for Roosevelt.[9]

In West Virginia, Roosevelt had the backing of the state organization, led by Senator Matthew Neely and former National Chairman Clem Shaver. He crushed Alfalfa Bill Murray, his only opponent, by a primary vote of almost nine to one. In South Carolina, the state chairman and both Senators, especially James F. Byrnes, had long been for Roosevelt. Although the delegation was, in keeping with custom, uninstructed, both the state chairman and Byrnes assured Roosevelt that it would be with him first, last and always. In Tennessee, with Hull and almost every other Democratic leader of importance behind Roosevelt, the state convention on May 20 instructed its delegation to cast all twenty-four votes for Roosevelt under the unit rule. In Delaware likewise, the organization was behind him, and he acquired six delegates.[10]

Huey Long finally decided early in May to bring his uninstructed Louisiana delegation over to Roosevelt. In January and February he had been unfriendly toward Roosevelt and seemed inclined toward Garner. Senator Wheeler reported he had succumbed to the power interests, but it seemed more likely he was influenced by anti-Roosevelt gossip around the national Democratic headquarters. Wheeler, who was Long's best friend in the Senate, tried hard to convert him to Roosevelt, but when Long switched he gave the credit to Republican Senator George W. Norris of Nebraska. Norris had told Long he would not support Hoover, that Roosevelt was the only hope of the country. Long announced for Roosevelt, and by the time he arrived at Chicago had strong motivation for staying within the Roosevelt camp. His Louisiana enemies sent a contesting delegation (he himself brought a second contesting delegation which turned the situation into a runaway Louisiana hayride), and this meant he must depend upon the Roosevelt majority to get his delegation seated.[11]

Mississippi gave Roosevelt some cause for worry because it adhered to tradition and on June 7 picked a delegation uninstructed but supposedly favorable to Roosevelt. It was not entirely loyal, so that Roosevelt had to fall back upon his supporter, Senator Pat Harrison, to keep it whipped into line. "Good for old Mississippi. I am delighted," Roosevelt, who was anything but delighted, wired Harrison. Through the unit rule, Harrison hoped to control the delegation, but he had only a one-vote margin.[12]

On the same day, Roosevelt defeated Murray in a Florida primary by better than five to one. The victory was really another over Shouse, who as in Mississippi had counseled against the primary and in favor of an uninstructed delegation. North Carolina Democrats in convention on June 16 instructed the delegation of twenty-six for Roosevelt. Roosevelt wired his old Navy chief, Josephus Daniels, one of the many Democratic leaders firmly behind him, "Perfectly delighted with good old North Carolina's action." This time he really was delighted.[13]

Indeed, he had reason to be thoroughly pleased with the over-all results of his preconvention campaign in the South. When he made a brief appearance from his train at Greenville, South Carolina, on his way north from Warm Springs at the end of May, someone in the crowd shouted, "Dixie is with you." Roosevelt replied, "That's right. I'll have every State below the Mason and Dixon line except Texas and Virginia." [14]

Roosevelt had forgotten about Maryland; otherwise his statement was correct.* Texas had gone to Garner, but Roosevelt's agents had been busy in the state insuring that if Garner failed, his friends would not take a die-hard stand against Roosevelt. The only real disappointment was to come in Virginia, where Governor Harry Byrd, who had left the Roosevelt camp to become a favorite son, took his candidacy seriously. And Roosevelt, with a misplaced optimism, expected that the Virginia votes would ultimately come to his standard.[15]

In the East, Roosevelt had a much more serious fight, since there he could not count upon friendly organizations. His first major battle was in New Hampshire, important because it held the nation's first presidential primary. Hence he could count upon national attention. Further, the Democrats there had previously been warmly for Smith, and Smith forces were ready to battle with Roosevelt for the delegates.

Before the Smith men began operations, National Committeeman

* FDR also had the six District of Columbia delegates under the unit rule.

Robert Jackson * committed most of the regulars to Roosevelt, carefully balancing the ticket of delegates geographically, and among rural Protestant supporters and urban Catholic French-Canadians. Howe sent Jackson a total of twelve thousand dollars, reputedly the largest amount spent in any state, to line up key workers. The money was well spent; the Roosevelt lines held firm when the Smith onslaught began. In order to fill a slate of delegates, the Smith men had to depend almost entirely upon the city of Manchester, and were under a further disadvantage that the primary would be on town-meeting day when there would be a heavy rural turnout. Nevertheless, Roosevelt expected to lose two delegates to Smith.

The results exceeded Roosevelt's expectations. Although there was a heavy snowstorm in the northern part of the state, which cut the rural vote, Roosevelt defeated Smith 14,500 to 9000. The victory was impressive. Roosevelt was elated but refused to comment; Farley issued a statement predicting Roosevelt's nomination on the first ballot.[17]

One unfortunate result was overconfidence in the Roosevelt camp. Howe confided to Marvin McIntyre that Farley's statement represented "the general attitude we are taking against the whole Smith movement, which so far as we can see is largely a fake movement." Indeed, there seemed some possibility that if Smith would not assert himself as an aggressive rather than a merely receptive candidate, his movement might collapse. Consequently, Smith, in retort to Mayor Curley's gibes that he was not really a candidate, announced to his Massachusetts partisans that he welcomed their support.[18]

This meant, after Roosevelt had won a notable victory in Maine thanks again to clever maneuvering by Robert Jackson, that he headed into trouble with Smith throughout the East. Up to this point, at the end of March, Roosevelt had won seven victories in every section of the country. April was to be a sobering month.[19]

The first of the setbacks was in New York, where Roosevelt, for all of his hedging on Tammany, could not count upon its support at the convention. In February, Tammany and its upstate allies decided upon an uninstructed delegation. This meant pro-Tammany delegates where it controlled, pro-Roosevelt delegates throughout the rest of the state. The only primary contest over district delegates was in Buffalo, where two Smith delegates challenged the pro-Roosevelt

* Not to be confused with the later Supreme Court Justice from New York. Charles Michelson has wisecracked that the New Yorker was called the "Good Bob Jackson," the New Hampshire man simply "Bob Jackson." [16]

Buffalo organization, and lost. At the convention in Albany on April 15 to choose delegates-at-large, Tammany Boss Curry completely dominated. Roosevelt had declined nomination as delegate-at-large, hoping that political delicacy would lead Smith likewise to decline. Smith did not, and was elected. To emphasize his pro-Smith leaning, Curry, without consulting Roosevelt, pushed through a wringing-Wet resolution calling for immediate repeal of the Prohibition Amendment. There was nothing for Roosevelt to do but force a smile and tell newspapermen, "Everything was lovely and harmonious. The wet resolution is in absolute accord with my views." [20]

Tammany, it seemed to many political observers, was trying to dangle the bait of its votes before Roosevelt to keep him from pursuing too harsh a policy toward it. He had removed Sheriff Farley, but failed to remove Sheriff McQuade. What would he do if, as seemed logically the next step, the ambitious Samuel Seabury demanded the removal of Mayor Jimmy Walker? Was a horse trade imminent? One New York congressman commented, "Tell me about Walker and Seabury, and I'll tell you about Roosevelt and Hoover." But no matter what reformers did to the Hall, New York would not be a complete loss to Roosevelt, for he could pretty well count upon thirty-nine to forty-five delegates from Boss Flynn's friendly Bronx northward.[21]

Roosevelt's second great botch, indeed the largest single error of his preconvention campaign, was in Massachusetts. There he had been maneuvered into cooperating with Curley's minority faction against the dominant organization led by Senator David I. Walsh and Governor Ely. Curley saw in Roosevelt the means of winning back control over the organization, and egged him on with overoptimistic predictions. Roosevelt, flushed with his New Hampshire victory over the Smith forces, happily entered the fray. He should have stayed out. When, too late, it became apparent that Walsh and Ely were far too strong, and Smith still the idol of the Massachusetts Democrats, efforts at compromise failed. Curley and his young lieutenant, Roosevelt's oldest son, James, continued to the end to issue exuberant statements, but by the close of the campaign, insiders at Albany told reporters Roosevelt would be happy to win five of the thirty-six Massachusetts delegates. Even this was too optimistic. Smith ran over Roosevelt three to one, and took every delegate in the state.[22]

Thus by a single cataclysm the Smith candidacy gained vitality and that of Roosevelt was thrown into doubt. "I am not the least bit downhearted," Roosevelt wired Curley. "You are right that a skirmish does not win a battle." But most of the rest of New England promptly crumbled. Rhode Island, which State Chairman J. Howard McGrath had proclaimed to be a Smith state as early as the previous December, followed Massachusetts. A pro-Roosevelt resolution in the state convention was downed 172 to 23. And by failure to compromise in time, the Roosevelt forces lost all sixteen delegates in Connecticut. Cummings under the unit rule had to vote for Smith at Chicago, even though he seconded Roosevelt's nomination. Only Vermont resisted the Smith tide and chose a Roosevelt delegation on May 18.[23] Outside of New England, Boss Hague placed New Jersey's thirty-six delegates behind Smith.

In explaining Roosevelt's mistake in fighting Smith in Massachusetts, Howe declared that it was essential to maintain the morale of Roosevelt workers in Pennsylvania. Without the contest in Massachusetts, he rationalized, Roosevelt would not have won seats in Pennsylvania. Even there, Roosevelt only won a limited victory against Smith. Again he had only a faction, and the weaker one, of the Democratic organization behind him. They were almost too far behind him. His leader there was former National Committeeman Joseph Guffey, who had predicted the previous July that Roosevelt would capture 66 of Pennsylvania's 78 delegates. Both the national committeeman and state chairman were closely allied with Raskob, and fought Guffey stoutly. The split throughout the state was as elsewhere rural-urban, with the country strongly pro-Roosevelt, and Philadelphia, Pittsburgh, and the hard-coal area as vehemently for Smith. The outcome, the same day as the Massachusetts primary, was another disappointment for Roosevelt. He had defeated Smith, but by only twenty thousand votes. He claimed sixty of the delegates, but actually had only about forty-four.[24]

In the industrial areas beyond the Appalachians the solid menace of Smith gave way to the rather vague shadow of Newton D. Baker. Behind that shadow was the concrete figure of Roy Howard and the powerful Scripps-Howard chain of newspapers. Roosevelt tried to court Howard by inviting him to Albany in January, but Howard could not come because of the death of his mother. Howard nominally supported Smith, but worked quietly toward a compromise on Baker. In Ohio, with White, Cox, and Baker, its three favorite sons, Roosevelt could only try to remain on friendly terms with everyone, and so stayed out of the primary. Ohio instructed for Governor George White, but with an off-the-record arrangement with White that if he did not pick up additional support at the convention, the delegation would swing to Baker. Farley hoped down to convention time that he could switch Ohio's fifty-two delegates to Roosevelt.[25]

Howard's undercover work for Baker apparently was effective in Indiana, where National Committeeman Tom Taggart would have none of Roosevelt, despite all the blandishments from Albany. Farley stopped off in Indiana to drop the word that the Democratic candidate for governor, Paul V. McNutt, "would be very pleasantly remembered" with the chairmanship of the Committee on Permanent Organization at Chicago, if Indiana fell into line. The Hoosiers refused, and picked an uninstructed delegation of thirty. Supposedly this was because of an intraparty dispute in Indiana, but actually Taggart, McNutt, and the state chairman were in complete control. Rather, Farley learned, Howard made a deal with McNutt for a minimum of eight Newton D. Baker votes on each of the first three ballots in return for Scripps-Howard newspaper support for the state ticket. Since many of the Indiana delegates were friendly to Roosevelt, Farley claimed twenty-four of the state's thirty votes.[26]

The equivocal situation in Indiana was frustrating to Farley, because he felt that the key to an early nomination lay in securing the votes of Ohio, Indiana, and Illinois – and Illinois was also eluding him. The state was backing its favorite son, Senator Ham Lewis. Farley could only try to secure a second-choice commitment to Roosevelt from the Illinois delegates. Downstate in the agricultural areas he met with enthusiastic support, but in Chicago and environs, Mayor Anton J. Cermak was cooperating with the Smith wing of the party. He was ready, like the Indiana boss, to work for a deadlocked convention.

Early in June, Illinois Roosevelt supporters succeeded in holding a meeting of all delegates at Springfield to try to work out a compromise with Cermak. The boss seemed conciliatory; he agreed the delegation need not be bound by the unit rule but could vote their preferences after the first ballot. This seemed hopeful to Roosevelt, but he watched warily for future developments. Down to the opening of the convention, Illinois with its fifty-eight delegates was one of the biggest and most important of question marks to Roosevelt.[27]

Things went more to Roosevelt's liking in one key industrial state, Michigan. There he was fortunate in having as a vigorous booster Mayor Frank Murphy of Detroit, who had been re-elected in November, 1931. Roosevelt negotiated through his brother-in-law, G. Hall

Roosevelt, who was city controller under Murphy. "Now that you fellows have won, isn't it time for us to get busy delegate collecting?" Howe inquired of Hall Roosevelt after the mayoralty election. "We have done absolutely nothing in Michigan waiting for you people to say when to move!" Murphy and the Michigan Democratic organization did move rapidly in the weeks that followed. They dominated the convention at Saginaw in mid-April. Their thirty-eight delegates were instructed for Roosevelt only for the first ballot, but obviously would stay by him through thick and thin.[28]

In Michigan, Roosevelt also had the quiet support of the Reverend Charles E. Coughlin, already famous as a radio priest. In the spring, Father Coughlin accompanied Murphy on a visit to Roosevelt in New York City. He was ready if need be to speak out discreetly upon behalf of Roosevelt's philosophy of government on his network program, but was not called upon until the fall, when he carefully let his listeners know where he stood.[29]

Throughout the rest of the Middle West, Roosevelt's great success was due to his strong appeal to desperate farmers. On March 10 he began his triumphs in the farm belt by winning all but one of ten delegates in the North Dakota primary, which had occasioned his announcement that he would run. Smith supporters failed, because of snow blocking the roads, to file on time petitions placing Smith on the ballot. But Alfalfa Bill Murray, stronger in North Dakota than anywhere else outside of Oklahoma, stumped the state for three days, winning much applause among old Non Partisan League members and prairie radicals. To offset Murray, Roosevelt, partly at the suggestion of a Non Partisan League Republican, William "Liberty Bell" Lemke, sent Senator Wheeler into the state to make a state-wide radio address assuring farmers Roosevelt was their friend. In addition, Roosevelt himself wired that he favored farm relief, specifying refinancing of farm mortgages at lower interest rates, farm membership on the farm boards, construction of waterways and flood-control projects, and appointment of a Secretary of Agriculture from a farm background. This firm agrarian stand and the united support of Democratic professionals were sufficient. Roosevelt won easily over Murray 52,000 to 32,000, but the surprising thing was that such large numbers of Republicans had crossed into the Democratic primary that the total ballots were almost 85,000 rather than the expected 20,000. In the 1928 primary, only 11,000 voters cast Democratic ballots. It augured well for Roosevelt to carry the prairie states if he won the nomination.[30]

Roosevelt supporters in the neighboring state of Minnesota also won on March 10. They formed a majority of the state convention, and picked a Roosevelt delegation. This so angered a Smith minority that they deserted to hold a rump convention and pick a rival set of delegates. Roosevelt was not in the least disturbed, since he expected a majority at Chicago, which would mean that the convention would seat the twenty-four Roosevelt delegates.[31]

In Iowa, where the state convention was to be held March 29, Farley was sure Roosevelt leaders would secure an instructed delegation. Howe, fearful that Roosevelt's opponents would pressure Iowans into electing an uninstructed delegation, had Roosevelt push Farley into going to the convention. It was well that he did, for it took his most earnest powers of persuasion to talk the Iowans into following the action of Maine that same day. Thus it was that Roosevelt picked up twenty-six more delegates.[32]

On his way back from Iowa, Farley stopped to address a Democratic dinner at Milwaukee, thirsty for legal beer. There the Wisconsin organization was strongly supporting Roosevelt, but the national committeeman was fighting vehemently for Smith. At the dinner, Farley emphasized what Wisconsin Democrats wanted most to hear, that Roosevelt "does not quibble as to . . . prohibition. . . . The present law is a blot on our sincerity." Because Wisconsin Catholic Democrats had so adored Smith in 1928, the organization privately expected to lose five delegates to him, but on April 5, voters elected all twenty-six Roosevelt men. Only two had even a close race. Roosevelt owed his victory not only to the Democratic organization, but also to the large number of Progressives who swung into the Democratic ranks. So many deserted the Republican party that the La Follettes lost control of the delegation to the Republican National Convention for the first time since 1904.[33]

In Nebraska, Roosevelt won the delegates because of the adroit manner in which National Committeeman Arthur Mullen thwarted Governor Charles W. Bryan's aspirations to be a favorite son. Roosevelt himself cleverly parried when Bryan, assuring Roosevelt of his personal friendship, asked Roosevelt not to file in Nebraska. Roosevelt replied he was asking Mullen to take no action without consulting Bryan, but added that he supposed the decision of the Garner forces to file changed the entire situation. Nebraska followers of Hearst's Omaha *Bee* entered Garner's name despite the protests of his manager, Rayburn. The combination of Roosevelt and the organization was disastrous to Garner. Roosevelt won three to one over Garner; he defeated Garner and Murray combined by almost two to one – and he had sixteen more delegates.[34]

In two more prairie states, Roosevelt won easily because of organization backing. On May 3, he ran unopposed in the South Dakota primary to pick up another ten delegates. On May 12, he swept the Kansas convention to obtain twenty more. In Kansas, Governor Harry H. Woodring effectively muzzled the pro-Baker opposition led by Shouse's law partner. Shouse obtained a seat on the Kansas delegation, but suffered the ignominy of being bound by the unit rule to vote at Chicago for Roosevelt.[35]

Further West, where Roosevelt had so much strength in February, he had picked up his first delegates in Washington, and had not contested Murray in Oklahoma. In every other Western state except Idaho, delegates were chosen in May. The month began disastrously for Roosevelt with a serious reverse in California.

Farley had predicted on his Elks survey the previous summer that while Roosevelt sentiment was strong in California, it would be a serious threat to Roosevelt's fortunes if Smith were to enter the primary. This was cause for real concern, since if Roosevelt were to win the nomination on the first ballot, he needed California. As late as February it appeared safe, since the Democratic organization in the state was behind him, with some prominent Smith Democrats on his bandwagon. Then Smith announced his candidacy, the Dry McAdoo came out for Garner, and what seemed a walkaway turned into a stiff three-way fight. Garner received the formidable support of the Hearst newspapers and the Texas Society of California, a hundred thousand strong. McAdoo and southern California Drys fought vigorously for him in order to seize control of the Democratic machinery in the state. Smith was the sentimental favorite on the sidewalks of San Francisco, a city which he had come within four thousand votes of capturing in 1928. Smith leaders declared, "If you are Wet, vote for Smith – if you are Dry, vote for Garner – if you don't know what you are, vote for Roosevelt." [36]

Managers for Roosevelt did their utmost, but the organization was weak, and almost all of the newspapers opposed or ignored Roosevelt. His fortunes were badly squeezed between Los Angeles Drys and San Francisco Wets. The outcome was 216,000 votes for Garner, 170,000 for Roosevelt, and 138,000 for Smith. Garner had piled up a 76,000 lead in Los Angeles County; Smith carried San Francisco and ran ahead of Roosevelt in Los Angeles; Roosevelt led in thirty-six of California's fifty-eight counties. To Garner went the fat prize of California's forty-four delegates.[37]

It was a resounding blow to Roosevelt's fortunes. Coming only a few days after the disappointment in Pennsylvania and the fiasco in Massachusetts, it all but ended Roosevelt's hopes for nomination on the first ballot, and raised serious doubts if he would be nominated at all. Outwardly Roosevelt maintained his optimistic mood. From Warm Springs he wrote Lieutenant Governor Lehman:

"All goes well here. I am not the least bit disturbed by the California Primary result because Garner will, I am sure, not join any mere 'block movement.' I am getting real sun and lots of sleep." [38]

No amount of "real sun" could mitigate the bleakness of that May. The "Stop Roosevelt" movement was gaining tremendous momentum and the Roosevelt camp, with delegates still to be chosen in half the states, was running low on funds if not morale. Even Roosevelt's mother reflected the uncertainties of the moment when she was called upon for more money. She wrote her son:

"I have given Mr. Howe a cheque for $5,000. out of *principal*, as my income is cut down. He said he *might* not need it now, but I think it would be well for you to tell him that if he has any *extra* money it would be well to keep it until you are *nominated*. . . .

"If you are not nominated, I should not *weep*, but it would be money thrown away!" [39]

Sara Roosevelt did not realize that once Roosevelt was nominated his money problems would be slight; the acute problem was to get money with which to battle for the nomination.

The California primary on May 3 turned out not to be the beginning of the end for Roosevelt but rather the low ebb in his tide. There were further disappointments but no more spectacular mishaps. Throughout the West he won state after state, unfortunately most of them with small delegations. On May 9, Wyoming, dominated by National Committeeman Joseph C. O'Mahoney, instructed its six delegates for Roosevelt. In Arizona on the same day, the struggle was solely over whether the delegation should be instructed or friendly but uninstructed. Eleanor Roosevelt's girlhood friend, Mrs. John C. Greenway, the former Isabella Selmes, led the fight — the only woman among all Roosevelt's state leaders. After much maneuvering, she won an instructed delegation of six for Roosevelt. An admirer wrote, "She developed into a political phenomenon if not a political genius." [40]

New Mexico was unusual in that Roosevelt bypassed the state chairman and national committeeman to entrust his fortunes to the governor, who was stronger than they. Thus he acquired the six delegates on May 16. In Montana both Senators Walsh and Wheeler had fought for Roosevelt from the outset; every important Democrat in the state fell into line. With Roosevelt's strength well publicized, the convention pledged Montana's eight delegates to him on May 17. Three days later in Oregon, with the organization backing him, he defeated Murray in a primary by a four-to-one margin, to acquire ten delegates. In Nevada, backed by Senator Key Pittman's faction, Roosevelt acquired six delegates on May 21.[41]

The Colorado national committeeman, with ample aid from Roosevelt headquarters, overrode the more cautious state chairman to obtain twelve Roosevelt delegates, May 28. Governor George H. Dern of Utah had assured Roosevelt in April that he could count upon a Utah delegation. Within the state there was much talk of a "Roosevelt and Dern" ticket; the state convention pledged the eight delegates to it on May 28. If Roosevelt had not needed to use the vice-presidential nomination for bargaining purposes, the ticket might have materialized. On June 11, Roosevelt acquired the last of the Western delegates, the eight of Idaho. Unfortunately, all ten of the states in the West that Roosevelt had carried had a total of only 86 votes at the convention, compared with the 44 Garner had acquired in California and Murray's 22 in Oklahoma.[42]

By the end of June, when the last state and territory had chosen its delegates, the outcome at the convention was still in some doubt. Smith and the "Stop Roosevelt" forces had demonstrated strength in the East; Garner had behind him the large delegations of Texas and California. Roosevelt had rolled well past a majority, but had failed by some eighty votes to acquire the two thirds necessary to nominate on the first ballot.*

* Garner claimed 90 delegates in California and Texas; Lewis, 58 in Illinois; White, 52 in Ohio; Reed, 36 in Missouri; Murray, 23 in Oklahoma and North Dakota; Byrd, 24 in Virginia; and Ritchie, 16 in Maryland. Six of the Indiana delegates were labeled uncertain. Smith claimed 209, and Roosevelt, 690. Some of the claims were overlapping:

Smith — instructed or favorable:

Connecticut	16	Rhode Island	10
Massachusetts	36	Canal Zone	6 (claimed)
New Jersey	32	Philippines	6 (claimed)
New York	65 (claimed)	Puerto Rico	4 (claimed)
Pennsylvania	34 (claimed)		

Roosevelt faced several alternatives. Since he had a working majority of the delegates, he could organize the convention and try to revoke the two-thirds rule. If he succeeded in destroying that century-old tradition, he could then obtain the nomination with his majority. Failing this, he could try to win over "favorite sons," hoping that the dynamiting of one or two blocks of votes would set off an avalanche. Above all, he could hope that the Smith and Garner forces, so antithetical in most respects, would not stand together to stop his nomination. Smith might be a bitter-ender, but Roosevelt was well aware of Garner's earlier friendliness. Farley had assiduously cultivated Garner supporters in both Texas and California. Since the California primary, Roosevelt had seen Garner's block of votes as the key to his nomination. Prophetically, he confided to Daniels that if he could secure them, that "would cinch the matter" of his nomination. Applying the cinch demanded the utmost in energy, resourcefulness, and political intelligence from the team that had been in training so long at Albany.

Roosevelt – instructed or favorable:

Alabama	24	Maine	12	Pennsylvania	60 (claimed)
Arizona	6	Michigan	38	So. Carolina	18
Arkansas	18	Minnesota	24	So. Dakota	10
Colorado	12	Mississippi	20	Tennessee	24
Delaware	6	Montana	8	Utah	8
Florida	14	Nebraska	16	Vermont	8
Georgia	28	Nevada	6	Washington	16
Idaho	8	New Hampshire	8	W. Virginia	16
Indiana	24 (claimed)	New Mexico	6	Wisconsin	26
Iowa	26	New York	45 (claimed)	Wyoming	6
Kansas	20	North Carolina	26	Alaska	6
Kentucky	26	North Dakota	9	D.C.	6
Louisiana	20	Oregon	10	Hawaii	6
Panama Canal Zone	6			Puerto Rico	6
Philippines	6 (claimed)			Virgin Islands	2

Total: 690

CHAPTER XX

Roosevelt or Deadlock?

The drive against me seems to be on. All I can hope is that it will not develop into the kind of a row which will mean the re-election of Brother Hoover.

— FDR TO ROBERT W. BINGHAM, *June 22, 1932.*

WHILE the battle for delegates went on and on, Roosevelt and Farley were carefully planning their strategy for the great culminating struggle at the nominating convention. On April 4, 1932, they fought a crucial preliminary skirmish at the meeting of the committee on arrangements at Chicago.

Although Roosevelt was already well on his way toward a majority of the delegates, he was not entirely sure that he could dominate the convention. Shouse was cleverly using his supposedly neutral position on the Democratic National Committee to build support for himself for temporary chairman of the convention. If he succeeded in winning this post, he would be able to hand down rulings on critical matters which would be damaging if not disastrous to Roosevelt's cause. Yet Shouse and Raskob had succeeded in appointing an arrangements committee friendly to them. Several of the Roosevelt supporters on it had committed themselves to Shouse in the mistaken notion that the temporary chairmanship was only an empty honor involving nothing more than delivery of the keynote address.

Consequently, Roosevelt had to attack obliquely at the meeting of the arrangements committee. He disguised his real reason for opposition to Shouse, explaining to Governor Byrd, "Frankly, as I told Raskob, I am inclined to think that Shouse has become rather an old story throughout the country because of his many speeches, propaganda statements, etc. etc." These were the grounds Roosevelt gave for supporting Senator Barkley.[1]

At the meeting, Roosevelt's position was so weak that he had to authorize Farley to accept in modified form a compromise suggested by Governor Byrd. Originally it provided that the committee recommend Barkley for temporary chairman and Shouse for permanent chairman. This in the end would have been almost as unfortunate to Roosevelt as to have Shouse temporary chairman. When Farley telephoned Roosevelt in Albany for instructions, Roosevelt pointed out that it would be unprecedented for the committee to choose the permanent chairman. But his agile mind hit upon a formula. He told Farley he would not object if the committee were to commend, rather than recommend, Shouse for permanent chairman. This would amount to a gesture of good will, said Roosevelt, and would not bind the convention – at which Roosevelt would control a majority of the delegates. The action of the arrangements committee would be no firm commitment because the committee would be acting outside of its jurisdiction.[2]

Roosevelt, clearly explaining to Farley and to Jackson, the Secretary of the Democratic National Committee, the difference between "commend" and "recommend," dictated to each an acceptable resolution embodying the word "commend." Jackson took Roosevelt's resolution to Shouse and told him what Roosevelt had said. Shouse agreed to it, but asked that Jackson explain the background of the resolution to the arrangements committee. This Jackson did; he told the committee he was proposing a resolution "commending" Shouse, and that Roosevelt had approved it.[3]

Unless Jackson in the report he wrote Roosevelt immediately afterward was untruthful, the Roosevelt forces were not guilty of bad faith as their opponents later charged. It was probably the best compromise Roosevelt could obtain at the time, but it was an unfortunate one because of its ambiguity. Shouse in a press statement at the close of the meeting dropped the distinction between the two words "recommend" and "commend." Roosevelt in a press conference at Albany emphasized them, and the day after Farley returned from Chicago, his headquarters hinted strongly that they would have a choice other than Shouse for permanent chairman. Newspapers and publications unfriendly to Roosevelt, like *Time*, chose from the outset to accept Shouse's interpretation, which subsequently would make Roosevelt appear to break his word. The juggling of words that seemed to mean almost the same yet expressed the opposite intentions of the warring factions placed Roosevelt in a position where he could hardly dodge appearing slippery.[4]

By the end of April, the Roosevelt leaders were openly opposed to Shouse. Several Senators, charging that Shouse had aided in promoting the Roosevelt setbacks in Massachusetts and Pennsylvania, announced they would oppose Shouse as permanent chairman. Rather, they hinted that they would support Senator Thomas J. Walsh of Montana. From the Democratic National Committee came prompt cries of "Unfair, unfair." [5]

As a first order of business, Roosevelt decided definitely upon Walsh when he held a quiet strategy meeting at Hyde Park on June 5. This was the consensus of the sixteen Democratic leaders advising him, including Howe, Farley, Flynn, Hull, Dill, Wheeler, Walsh, Cummings, Roper, Jackson, and Guffey. Walsh's senatorial colleague and friend, Wheeler, told Roosevelt that if Shouse were permanent chairman, he would never be nominated. They decided upon Arthur Mullen of Nebraska for floor leader at the convention, and upon Claude Bowers, newspaperman and popular historian, to deliver the nominating speech. Senator Robert Wagner had already declined because he did not wish to offend his close political associates Smith and Curry. Bowers also regretfully resigned because he did not want to annoy his employer, Hearst. Finally, Roosevelt turned for reasons of sentiment to Judge John E. Mack of Poughkeepsie, who had helped start him in politics in 1910. He chose Hull as candidate for chairman of the committee on resolutions, and Bruce Kremer of Montana to be chairman of the rules committee. He selected no nominees for two other committee chairmanships in order to leave Farley free to dangle them before the coy Indiana Democrats.

The most dangerous problem that the conferees debated at Hyde Park was whether or not Roosevelt should try to end the two-thirds rule.* A majority at the convention could abolish it, and then proceed to nominate him. Could Roosevelt exercise sufficient control over his majority? Could he make this maneuver without its being construed as a sign of serious weakness? The consensus of the conferees was that the rule should be revoked, but they decided to wait for the convention before coming to a final decision.[6]

Here the danger was that the opponents would succeed in convincing a majority of delegates that Roosevelt was acting in bad faith. Immediately after the Hyde Park conference, when Farley announced that the Roosevelt forces would support Walsh for permanent chairman, Shouse vehemently proclaimed that Roosevelt was breaking his

* Sara Delano Roosevelt lent charm to the conference. Senator Wheeler recalls that she remarked she did not want to see her son nominated if he had to be elected on a liquor ticket.

earlier word. During the remaining three weeks until the convention met, this created sufficient furor. Any effort to scuttle the two-thirds rule was sure to lead to even greater uproar.[7]

While Roosevelt and Farley pondered questions of grand strategy, they worked in every small way possible to hold delegates in line and try to lure waverers onto their bandwagon. Farley mailed letters signed in green ink to every friendly delegate; Howe sent each of them an autographed photograph of Roosevelt and a small phonograph record "containing a message especially for you, from the Governor." What Roosevelt said was trivial; it was the warm quality of his voice that made the record important. It was part of Roosevelt's conscious reliance upon the power of his voice to influence the convention even though he remained in Albany. Howe had already ordered an open telephone circuit to connect Roosevelt at the Executive Mansion to a loud-speaker at the Roosevelt headquarters, 1102 Congress Hotel.[8]

In planning for the convention, Howe overlooked no detail. He arranged to send the trustworthy telephone operator from the Executive Mansion, Louise Hachmeister, to run the switchboard in Chicago, so there could be no leak of information. One of his assistants crossed the palms of the attendants at the Chicago Stadium to obtain several locked rooms where Farley could hold secret conferences. And to make sure the opposition would not seize the rooms, Howe insisted that the assistant sleep there until the convention began. He worked on the layout of convention headquarters, assigned tasks to every subordinate, and listed absolutely loyal Roosevelt delegates to put on each convention committee. In this culmination of his planning of many years, he tried to leave nothing to chance.[9]

At the same time Farley was exploring endlessly for cracks in the enemy's fortifications. He continued to predict a first-ballot nomination for Roosevelt, which he hoped to engineer through switching favorite-son delegations before the results were announced. To his dismay, he found on a mid-June trip through the three critical states of Ohio, Indiana, and Illinois that the leaders there seemed more interested in selecting a compromise candidate than in swinging to Roosevelt. Farley's problem was to lure some favorite son into switching a decisive block of votes. The bait was the vice-presidential nomination, and the key favorite sons were White, Byrd, Ritchie, possibly Traylor, and, above all, Garner.[10]

Unfortunately for Roosevelt, any faint chance of lining up a solid block of New York votes had been shattered. In May, Seabury's investigation of Tammany reached its logical culmination when he brought Mayor Jimmy Walker to the stand. Seabury's investigators had found several quite embarrassing matters for Walker to explain. How did it happen that a sixty-dollar-a-week bookkeeper in Walker's old law firm had been able to deposit $961,000 in the bank, out of which he paid many of the Mayor's bills? How was it that the representative of a taxicab holding company had given him $26,000 in bonds? Or that a publisher had split stock profits with Walker, so that while the Mayor did not invest a penny, he received $246,000? Walker readily testified that all this financial good fortune was simply the doing of generous friends. He did little to refute serious evidence against him.[11]

At the conclusion of Walker's evasive testimony, Seabury briefly left the state, while the newspapers howled against Governor Roosevelt for action. Roosevelt complained to the reporters that it was up to Seabury and the investigators of the legislative committee to present him with the evidence. "It is time," he insisted, "to stop talking and do something. It is not the time for political sniping or buck passing." To Colonel House, he expressed his bitterness and chagrin over Seabury's tactics. "This fellow Seabury is merely trying to perpetrate another political play to embarrass me," Roosevelt complained. "His conduct has been a deep disappointment to people who honestly seek better government in New York City by stressing the fundamentals and eliminating political innuendoes." [12]

Seabury immediately accepted Roosevelt's challenge. He sent Roosevelt a transcript of the hearings, an analysis of the testimony, and a list of fifteen accusations against Walker. He made no recommendation as to what Roosevelt should do. Thus neatly Seabury impaled Roosevelt upon the twin horns of a political and moral dilemma. Too strong a stand against Tammany at this time might throw all of the Smith and machine forces, outside of New York as well as within, into die-hard opposition at the convention. Further, although Roosevelt would profit greatly among antimachine Democrats if he punished Walker, from the outset he had assumed, with unquestionable seriousness and sincerity, a moral position of fairness and judiciousness. Lippmann, spokesman for the reformers and brilliant theorist on public ethics, saw clearly the quandary Seabury had created for Roosevelt:

"Governor Roosevelt has lost his moral freedom. He is so heavily mortgaged to Tammany that he must prove his independence of it. Yet at this late date there is no way of proving his independence except by a procedure which must outrage everyone's sense of justice. For to try James J. Walker before a man who stands to profit enormously by convicting him is a revolting spectacle." [13]

Roosevelt did the one thing possible: on June 21, six days before the convention met, he sent Seabury's specifications to Walker and requested a reply. Walker declared he would reply after the convention was over. Thus Roosevelt was forced to go through the convention with the putrefying Walker albatross around his neck, and at the same time was still the target of Tammany fury.[14]

To Roosevelt it seemed all part of a larger conspiracy to flout the will of a majority of the Democrats and wrest away from him the nomination rightfully his. In mid-June he expressed his apprehensions to the Governor of Arkansas:

"Things look to be going well but the Smith-Shouse crowd is using desperate tactics. They will threaten a terrific row and possibly a split in the party. We must not pay any attention to that because if I am nominated they will have to follow in line — and incidentally I am very certain that a large part of the opposition to me is being instigated and financed by the Republicans here in the east." [15]

When the delegates began to arrive in Chicago at the end of June, Roosevelt's apprehensions appeared well founded. The Republicans had just dispersed after an apathetic, defeatist convention in which they had done the only thing possible, renominated President Hoover. They had no enthusiasm for him. The professionals had never liked him, and, since misfortune had hit him, made little effort to disguise their distaste. Not to have renominated him would have been an even worse party calamity, so they did so. Their apathy underscored what was readily apparent to every office-hungry Democratic politician. In this year any Democrat who received the nomination — were he Roosevelt or Smith or even a dark horse — was almost certain to win the election. There was no need to nominate the most popular Democrat, Roosevelt, in order to be sure of winning. Therein lay an added difficulty for Farley in trying to hold delegations in line.[16]

Aware of their difficult task, but still full of confidence, Farley and Edward J. Flynn arrived in Chicago a week in advance to open the Roosevelt headquarters. They confessed to each other that they felt rather green in national politics, but they went to work like veterans. They set up headquarters in the Congress Hotel, and got busy. Farley took over the main reception center, where he began to greet Roosevelt delegates, brief the more important ones on their tasks at the convention, and seek to impress and win over delegates pledged to opposition candidates. Already on his tours he had met a remarkable number of the Democratic leaders who began to arrive in Chicago.

One of Farley's most useful props was a huge map of the United States upon which he had blocked in Roosevelt states in red. It was impressive, for certainly in terms of area the nation's Democrats were behind Roosevelt. It had a sobering effect upon the delegates, for even though certain populous Eastern states were conspicuously not red, they could see that Roosevelt was clearly the choice of far more than a majority. Smith when he arrived commented that Roosevelt had lots of area, but not what was more important, lots of delegates. Nevertheless, it worried the opposition enough that they referred to it at every opportunity as "Field Marshal Farley's Map." [17]

While Farley operated the main reception center, Flynn from his own suite of rooms carried on additional negotiations. A few days later Howe arrived and moved into a still more secluded suite. There he placed the microphone attached to the direct wire from Albany. There he and Farley and Flynn, and the Roosevelt leaders, could confer privately with Roosevelt in his little study at the Executive Mansion. There they could bring the arriving delegates, group by group, to speak to the Governor. Lela Stiles, who helped Flynn usher them in, remembers, "We never knew when we went into Louis' room whether we'd trip over a Senator, a Governor, a farm delegation, a labor group, or a bunch of coils and wires."

Roosevelt's voice would come booming through the microphones. "My friends from Nebraska . . ." or whatever the state was, he would begin, and launch into a personal message. Surprisingly often he called them by their first names, and asked them personal questions. In his warm and friendly fashion, he answered their queries and expounded his views to them. They were amazed, delighted, and, in most instances, impressed. Thus Roosevelt was able to preserve his position as the leading candidate while remaining at home, and through his direct wire electioneer efficiently and participate actively in almost every important decision at Chicago.[18]

As the other candidates and their managers began to converge upon Chicago, the pressure and excitement intensified. Shouse, according to newspapers, said, "We have Roosevelt licked now." Smith's manager, Boss Hague of New Jersey, sneered before the convention began that Roosevelt could not carry a single state east of the Mississippi and very few in the Far West. Smith himself, as he prepared to leave for the convention, scoffed at first-ballot predictions as ballyhoo, or "Farley's Fairy Stories." These were not sober appraisals, but a throwing down of the gauntlet. Hague, who listed every opponent of Roosevelt's as being stronger, in addition invited the others to form a close alliance to stop Roosevelt.[19]

When Farley telephoned Hague's vehement words to Roosevelt, the Governor dictated a dignified reply for Farley to give the press: "Governor Roosevelt's friends have not come to Chicago to criticize, cry down, or defame any Democrat from any part of the country." [20]

The anti-Roosevelt coalition did rapidly take form at Chicago; newspapermen referred to this group of candidates – Smith, Ritchie, Baker, Garner, and several favorite sons – as the Allies. The alliance was energetic in its opposition to Roosevelt, but there was little else to hold it together. The raucous galleries illustrated this, for they were packed with men who hissed and hooted against Roosevelt, but who also cheered wildly for repeal and Smith.* Their wild yells could not have brought much joy to Garner's manager, Sam Rayburn, or to the leader of the California delegation, McAdoo. The fact was that while the Allies were united to work for a deadlock, none was ready to defer to another to throw the nomination his way. This was the weakness of all of them, and the man most seriously suffering from it was Smith.

Many of the Democratic leaders were startled to discover that Smith came to the convention dedicated not only to stopping Roosevelt but to winning the nomination for himself. Some of the Allies had interpreted Hague's statement as a Smith offer to stand aside so that they could coalesce on a compromise candidate. Hague issued a denial. Smith when he arrived said he knew nothing about a "Stop Roosevelt" movement; he was worried about a stop-Smith movement. He told newspapermen, "I am here to get myself nominated." He meant it. He was far from being a happy warrior as he poured out his personal rancor and privately threatened if need be to take to the platform and deliver a personal denunciation of Roosevelt. He seemed to have lost his political perspective, and showed no realization that his fierce determination to get the nomination for himself, his rule-or-ruin attitude, was frightening to cautious Democratic politicians. The fiasco at Madison Square Garden in 1924 and the debacle at the polls in 1928 were too recent for them to overlook.[22]

* The noise and rudeness of the galleries, which Mayor Cermak had packed, may well have reacted in favor of FDR rather than hurt him, through antagonizing Southern and Western delegates.[21]

In the lobby of the Congress Hotel, Smith supporters handed out to delegates handbills reprinting a particularly virulent column by Heywood Broun attacking "Feather Duster" Roosevelt, the "corkscrew candidate." Roosevelt workers quietly took them by the handfuls, tore them up, and dumped them in trash cans. They might better have not bothered, for with his every move, Smith made his own nomination more impossible.[23]

All this created acute nervousness among Roosevelt's relatively untried command. The first crisis arose on June 24 when Farley presided over a gathering of sixty-five pro-Roosevelt leaders. He soon found it was like trying to maintain control over a noisy town meeting. Senator Huey Long, the Louisiana Kingfish, took the floor and offered a resolution to abolish the two-thirds rule. It was not something Farley wanted out in the open as yet; he was still in the stage of cautious conferring, and had been utilizing others at the convention, like Josephus Daniels, to send up trial balloons. Farley tried to persuade the gathering not to act; it would be unfair to do so without consulting Roosevelt. But he made the mistake of allowing discussion to continue, and it turned strongly against the two-thirds rule.* This gave Long his opportunity. He asked and received permission to second his own motion, took off his coat, and with his arms waving launched into a harangue so effective that at its conclusion the gathering voted to fight the rule.[24]

Farley was frightened. "The incident hit me like a blow on the nose," he has reminisced. "My confidence was badly shaken for the first time." Roosevelt and Howe reassured him that he could well let things drift, and if need be back down at the proper time without doing too much damage. The trouble was that to back down would appear to the opposition a sign of weakness, while at the same time throughout the Southern delegation — in which lay much of Roosevelt's strength — there was a gathering current of disapproval of the Long motion. In the past the rule had given the South in effect a veto power over nominations. Many Southerners did not wish to lose it. Senators Josiah Bailey of North Carolina and Harrison of Mississippi and Representative William B. Bankhead of Alabama all were opposed. The Allies took advantage of the commotion to denounce Roosevelt.†

* A formidable group spoke in favor of abrogating the rule: Dill, Kremer, Woodring, Wheeler, Hull, Mullen, Cummings, and Daniels. All these were angry with Hague and fearful that Smith would deadlock the convention.

† FDR's opponents gleefully publicized a statement he had made at the 1924 convention: "I doubt if any rules of the convention should be changed after the delegates are elected." If Roosevelt had gone ahead with the fight against the two-

Smith claimed he was trying to change the rules after the game had started — that it sounded like a cry for a life-preserver. Baker declared that if Roosevelt thus won the nomination, it would have a moral flaw. None of them, as Farley later pointed out, seemed to think they were being unsporting in trying to wrest the nomination from the man who was the choice of well more than a majority of the delegates.[26]

At first Farley had thought he had one hundred votes to spare on the two-thirds-rule issue, but Long's resolution had come so early that the Allies had time to coalesce against it; the Southerners, on the other hand, were becoming increasingly restless. A New York *Times* survey indicating he might lose came to Farley's attention, and loss on this would be fatal. Retreat became imperative, even though it would give great encouragement to the "Stop Roosevelt" forces. Roosevelt himself decided to issue a statement backing down. With the implied reservation that his forces might later try to abrogate the rule to prevent the catastrophe of a deadlock, he asserted he was withdrawing from the fight so that there might be no taint on his honor. "It is true that the issue was not raised until after the delegates to the convention had been selected," he admitted, "and I decline to permit either myself or my friends to be open to the accusation of poor sportsmanship or to the use of methods which could be called, even falsely, those of a steam roller." [27]

Roosevelt had withdrawn his forces intact, but clearly had lost the skirmish. The fault lay with Long's resolution, which brought the issue out in the open in time for opposition to solidify. Had the Roosevelt leaders suddenly popped it upon the assembled convention, they could probably have won. Having lost, they enheartened the Allies, especially Baker's supporters. The Allies began to feel that Roosevelt actually could be stopped.

A second premature move also hurt Roosevelt, though less seriously. This incident looked at first like good luck. Two days before the convention opened, Senator Lewis of Illinois sent a telegram releasing his delegates. Farley was overjoyed, thinking the bandwagon rush was on, not taking into account the resourcefulness of Mayor Cermak,

thirds rule in 1932, he intended to do so by charging that it was the basis for convention deals. He drafted a statement reading: "I refuse to pay Delegates with any promises or concessions whatsoever. . . . There must not be created even the semblance of compromise as to principle or candidate. . . . I am not willing to gain the nomination by the methods of a poker game. My hands are clean, and before God, I intend to keep them so." [25]

who promptly switched the Chicago delegates to a reserve favorite son, Traylor.[28]

Despite all of Farley's enthusiastic predictions to newspapermen, as the convention opened the Roosevelt bandwagon had not yet begun to roll. Neither was there any sign that the Allies had put any permanent chocks under its wheels. When National Chairman Raskob called the convention to order at 12:50 in the afternoon on June 27, the outcome was in doubt, but Roosevelt was still far in front. The Roosevelt forces organized the committees, and in the platform committee they passed upon Roosevelt's platform, which Mitchell Palmer had drafted with the assistance of Hull and his friends. Farley and his lieutenants were still encouraging Roosevelt delegates, probing for weak points in other delegations, and carrying on quiet negotiations in many directions and with infinite duplications. They were aiming these toward winning over a decisive block of votes which would put Roosevelt over the two-thirds mark. That would be essential when the balloting began. Meanwhile, the Roosevelt high command faced a group of critical contests, each of which it must win.[29]

Maneuvering for victory in these contests went on behind the scenes while the excited delegates in the huge, steaming Chicago Stadium listened for two hours to Senator Barkley's exhaustive keynote address. "It had to be a long speech," Will Rogers pointed out, "for when you start enumerating the things that the Republicans have got away with in the last twelve years you have cut yourself out a job." Nor did the delegates spend the entire two hours sitting on their hard chairs. At the mention of the forthcoming Wet plank, they seized standards and paraded up and down the aisles, shouting and yelling while the pipe organ and bands played "How Dry I Am." The reaction gave impetus to a movement to put the Democrats on record for outright repeal.[30]

Away from the bedlam, Farley worked vigorously to persuade the rules committee that it must not drive for a compromise on the two-thirds rule, but must drop the issue completely. And he lined up strength for the test votes at the second session. On all of these trial runs, the Roosevelt leaders performed brilliantly; they made no more blunders. First was the battle over the seating of the Minnesota and Louisiana delegations. The credentials committee recommended that the Roosevelt delegates be seated, but because minority reports were filed, the contests came before the entire convention. Before the committee, Long had engaged in much crude oratory, and a third burlesque delegation he had brought along had indulged in considerable horseplay. In the steaming atmosphere of the committee room, this sent the temperature of some of the delegates still higher. Long's friend Wheeler, his silk suit drenched with perspiration, had difficulty in calming down the committeewoman from Montana, and in persuading Long to drop his buffoonery when the issue came before the assembled convention. Long did, and argued with convincing reasonableness. The Roosevelt forces won, 638¾ to 514¼. The convention seated the Minnesota delegation by an even larger margin.[31]

This did not remove Farley's anxiety when the next fight began on the convention floor, over whether Roosevelt's choice, Walsh, or the Allies' Shouse should be permanent chairman. Clearly, as Press Agent Charles Michelson later declared, Shouse would have been a torpedo under the prow of Roosevelt's craft at the convention. But many a Roosevelt delegate had earlier committed himself to Shouse, and many another might be susceptible to the cries of "Unfair" that arose at Convention Hall over the "recommend-commend" controversy. John W. Davis, who had been the 1924 nominee, spoke strongly in favor of Shouse. Smith had announced he would do so, but changed his mind. As the balloting began, it was touch and go. Farley nervously jotted down figures on long sheets of brown note paper. Michelson carried in one pocket the acceptance speech of Shouse, and in another that of Walsh. It was not until the state of Missouri was reached in the roll call that he gave the press Walsh's speech. The vote was 626 to 528, the narrowest margin by which the Roosevelt forces won any vote at the convention.[32]

Farley could breathe more easily as Walsh, a supple parliamentarian, walked up to the rostrum. For the moment, Roosevelt could feel secure, since he had no cause to worry over the platform. It was precisely what he wanted, concise, readable, and strong in its emphasis upon economic questions rather than Prohibition. His moist Prohibition plank called merely for resubmission of the question to the people of the United States. The Republicans too had gone this far.

Sentiment among the delegates, and behind them among the public, rapidly was snowballing in favor of outright repeal. Had Roosevelt chosen to become involved in this struggle between the formerly Dry, now moist faction and the dripping-Wet faction, he might have gotten into trouble. As it was, he had worked carefully from the outset to eliminate Prohibition as a vital issue in the campaign, and to place the emphasis upon economic questions, where it belonged. He was perfectly ready to be either moist or Wet, whichever the party preferred.

Smith, Ritchie, and the Eastern wing of the Allies were economically conservative, and had only the Prohibition string to their bow. They had pulled it so frequently that it was worn out and frayed, but the more they pulled it, the more they thought it crucial. It was difficult for them to readjust their thinking from Prohibition repeal, which was suddenly becoming a foregone conclusion, to the depression issue.* So they went on showering their arrows into the Prohibition camel, not seeming to realize that the poor beast was dead, while Roosevelt was aiming his shots in the other direction at a quite live elephant he labeled "depression." Farley stood aside to let Roosevelt delegates vote as they pleased. The dripping Wets won overwhelmingly, 934¾ to 213¾, and in so doing eliminated the biggest reason for nominating Ritchie or Smith.[34]

The Allies, conversely, thought they had won another advantage over Roosevelt, and prepared for the balloting for a candidate, full of confidence. They had worked hard on every wavering Roosevelt delegate, had found weakness in Mississippi, and were pressing Iowa, Michigan, and Maine. Farley, well informed on their probing, had tried at every point to shore up his defenses. "The opposition was assailing us at every point," he has recalled, "and we had the longest line." [35]

Smith kept predicting self-hypnotically that Roosevelt's support would crumble after the first ballot. Mencken, in a hostile dispatch, reported that Roosevelt was anything but popular at the convention. "I can recall no candidate of like importance who ever had so few fanatics whooping for him," he asserted. "His followers here are as silent as if they were up to something unpalatable to the police." [36]

Roosevelt's followers, quite the contrary, were as loud as any delegates could be, but sometimes they had trouble making themselves heard over the Smith claque in the galleries. The silent ones, acting

* Henry L. Mencken, the wittiest of the champions of the thirsty, in covering the convention from the Ritchie viewpoint, demonstrated this singular inability to see beyond the speakeasy, that the Prohibition issue was dead in the hinterland. He shouted his hallelujas over the Wet plank, but predicted that as a result the Democrats faced a very difficult if not impossible campaign. The Southern and Middle Western delegates, he reported, were "going home with a tattered Bible on one shoulder and a new and shiny beer seidel on the other, and what they will have to listen to from their pastors and the ladies of the W.C.T.U. is making their hearts miss every other beat." [33]

with the approval of Farley, Flynn, Howe, and in some instances Roosevelt himself, were dangling offers in front of old friends in the Allies' camp, softening them up for the big deal which would consummate Roosevelt's nomination. They were unceasing in their blandishments to the key men in Texas, California, New York, Illinois, Indiana, Ohio, and Maryland. It was a tense time, Farley remembers:

"The nervous strain during this period of suspense was very close to the limit of physical endurance. At a time when clear thinking and cool judgment were needed as they never were before, I was working eighteen or nineteen hours a day, conversing with hundreds of people, constantly consulting with other leaders, receiving reports from every delegation, and meeting at least twice daily with several hundred newspapermen. I ate my meals, usually consisting of sandwiches and milk, off a tray, and slept a few hours just before dawn if the opportunity offered. . . . Hundreds of other men were caught in the same dizzy whirl and were trying to keep up the same maddening pace." [37]

The emaciated Howe in Room 1702 of the Congress Hotel was close to physical and nervous collapse, part of the time lying on a couch panting. But he kept on the phone to Albany, advising Roosevelt and passing on his orders to the workers in the hotel rooms and on the convention floor. As for Roosevelt in Albany, the suspense and the inability to be in the thick of things must have been almost intolerable. "I would have given anything in the world to have been there too," he wrote several days afterward. "It was the most difficult thing for me to sit here with the telephone and get everything secondhand." [38]

While Roosevelt and Howe waited, negotiations went on in every direction. Nothing had been settled when the nominating speeches began on the afternoon of June 30. Alabama yielded to New York. Roosevelt's Dutchess County political mentor, Judge Mack, came to the platform to nominate Roosevelt. He declared that the honor came to him not through any merit of his own, but because of the spirit of friendship of the candidate. His speech did little to disprove this, but it was warm and sincere. Fortunately Roosevelt's nomination did not depend upon perfervid oratory. As Mack concluded, a huge picture of Roosevelt unrolled from the balconies, the organ bellowed "Happy Days Are Here Again," and state delegations poured into the aisles to parade behind their standards. Howe, between coughing fits, over and over again sent orders to the organist to repeat the song.[39]

Nomination after nomination followed. Tom Connally of Texas put in Garner's name; Governor Ely of Massachusetts nominated Smith in the finest of the orations. And each nomination led to endless seconding. It was, as Farley described it, "a merciless and unholy flood of oratory," which washed against the weary, perspiration-soaked delegates for hour after hour.[40]

Both in Chicago and Albany the night seemed endless. At the Executive Mansion, Rosenman was helping Roosevelt revise the acceptance address. In the garage in the rear, the newspapermen had set up their telephones and typewriters. Mrs. Roosevelt sent them out pots of hot coffee, and at one point made them scrambled eggs. Judge Rosenman has vivid memories of the night:

"We presented a strange picture along about three o'clock in the morning here in the small sitting room. . . . The Governor, his wife, his mother and I sat listening to the radio. He was in his shirt sleeves, silent, puffing on one cigarette after another. The phone was at his side, and he used it frequently. He seemed deeply interested in the convention oratory, nodding approval of some parts, shaking his head in disapproval of others, laughing aloud when the eloquence became a little too 'spread-eagle' in tone."[41]

For Farley in Chicago the question was whether to allow adjournment at the conclusion of the speeches or to push ahead immediately for a first ballot. He held a hasty council of war, stretched out on a cot in his rooms at the Chicago Stadium. Everyone urged a ballot, since delay might indicate weakness and be dangerous. Farley reported this over the telephone to Roosevelt, who coolly and firmly advised an immediate ballot. Vainly the leaders tried to shut off the seconding speeches; no politician wanted to give up his few minutes of glory before the microphones. It was dawn, 4:28 in the morning, before the roll call began.[42]

As the drawn-out roll got under way, Farley was still confident that the bandwagon spirit would prevail and that Roosevelt would win on the first ballot. It dragged on for an hour and a half or more. Feeling ran high among the delegations; several of them demanded a poll of each member in order to demonstrate strength for one or another minority candidate. Roosevelt's delegates stood firm and he came out with 666¼ votes — 89 more than a majority, and 464½ ahead of his nearest rival, but 104 short of two thirds. Farley still hoped for a miracle, for a switch before the ballot was announced. But McAdoo refused to swing California, and Cermak told Farley he could not change Illinois without a caucus.[43]

At once a second ballot began. It was necessary for Roosevelt to pick up a few additional votes in order to prevent a fatal decline. Fortunately, Farley was able to acquire six of them from the Pendergast's friendly Missouri organization. Roosevelt's delegates were still holding firm, but so were those of the Allies. The Roosevelt floor leader, Mullen, moved adjournment; the opposition objected, hoping that they could crack Roosevelt on a third ballot. In Albany, Sara Roosevelt was so upset by the bleak turn of events that she announced she was returning immediately to Hyde Park; Rosenman, munching frankfurters as he worked on the peroration of Roosevelt's acceptance speech, wondered if it would ever be delivered. Farley, on the platform at Chicago, his clothes disheveled and his spirits low, remarked that the ballot would show whether he could ever go back to New York.[44]

Disaster almost struck on that third ballot. Mississippi was ready to crack, but through the pressure of Senator Harrison, or, as many insist, because of the pressure of Senator Long upon Harrison, Mississippi held in line under the unit rule by a margin of 10½ votes to 9½. Farley drew upon a bit more of his meager reserve of delegates, and managed to pull the Roosevelt total up to 682.* It was 9:15 in the morning, and the convention finally adjourned until that evening.[46]

The delegates and reporters alike staggered back to their hotel rooms, as Lippmann reported, "so stupefied by oratory, brass bands, bad air, perspiration, sleeplessness and soft drinks that the fate of mankind is as nothing compared with . . . longing for a bath, a breakfast and a bed." They went off with the feeling that Roosevelt had been stopped, and the convention deadlocked. Farley had mustered all possible support

* The results of the first three ballots were: [45]

	First	Second	Third
Roosevelt	666¼	677¾	682.79
Smith	201¾	194¼	190¼
Garner	90¼	90¼	101¼
Byrd	25	24	24.96
Traylor	42½	40¼	40¼
Ritchie	21	23½	23½
Reed	24	18	27½
White	52	50½	52½
Murray	23	—	—
Baker	8½	8½	8½
Will Rogers	—	22	—

and was still 87 votes short; Mississippi and several other Roosevelt states were close to mutiny. Unless Roosevelt could pick up new, decisive strength on the fourth ballot, he seemed through. The rumors were that Baker would be the compromise candidate.[47]

Now if ever was the time when Farley must bring to fruition the negotiations which had been going on so incessantly since before the convention started.* In the retrospect of many years, Farley felt that any one of a number of these would have sufficed to bring the bandwagon break, and that even if Mississippi had slipped he could have held the Roosevelt strength for another ballot or two until one of these materialized. At the time, Farley did not want to take any such chances. He took a cab with a few of his lieutenants to confer with Howe at the Congress Hotel. Howe was lying on the floor, his head on a pillow, under the breeze of two electric fans. Farley motioned the others away, lay down beside Howe, and whispered in his ear that he wanted to stake everything on winning over Texas.† Howe agreed.[49]

Within a few minutes, Farley went to the hotel apartment of Senator Harrison and his intimate, George E. Allen, later famous as President Truman's White House jester, to meet with Garner's manager, Rayburn. Although the nomination seemed to hang upon the outcome, the exhausted Farley snored away on Allen's bed until Rayburn arrived. The meeting lasted only a few minutes. Neither Rayburn nor Silliman Evans, who accompanied him, mentioned the vice-presidency. At the conclusion, Rayburn said, "We'll see what can be done." He made no further promise than that, but Farley left elated, certain that this clinched the nomination for Roosevelt. He recognized that Rayburn had hard work ahead of him. Rayburn did indeed, and there was still more to the story. The nomination was not yet in the bag for Roosevelt.[50]

* Farley had been negotiating with Ritchie through Howard Jackson, Mayor of Baltimore, and even more indirectly through Breckinridge Long. Long suggested Ritchie might be Vice President, but Ritchie declined the night before the nominating speeches. Ritchie, however, only controlled 21 votes. Byrd of Virginia, who had 24 votes, had promised Roosevelt in April that he could have them when he needed them, but Byrd seemed more interested in a deadlock. Farley felt they could always make a deal with Byrd, but by this time FDR was not very fond of him. There was still the possibility of a deal with Cermak, which would bring not only Illinois but Indiana as well — and the nomination for Vice President of some Illinois man.[48]

† Up to this point, Howe had felt the Garner forces would remain adamant to the bitter end, and that Farley should concentrate upon Virginia.

It was too soon to be certain whether success or failure was to be the end product of negotiations which had been going on for days. On the eve of the convention, Cummings, Kremer, Roper, and others had begun work on McAdoo, and the pressure on him had continued. Although the men who most strongly implored him to shift California had been among his most loyal supporters in 1924, he remained firm. Some have reminisced since that he was seeking personal gain, but it is more likely that he was simply in no position to swing the delegation. It was under the influence of Hearst, and it was personally tied to Garner.[51]

As for Hearst, the Roosevelt leaders telephoned him at San Simeon. He had no love for Roosevelt, feeling like many others that Roosevelt was fundamentally weak, but he had a hearty hatred for Smith, with whom he had long feuded in New York. And he had an equal fear of Baker, whom he considered a dangerous internationalist. Roosevelt had at least cleared himself in Hearst's eyes of the internationalist label when he had come out against American membership in the League in February, 1932. So when several of Hearst's lawyers, Joseph Kennedy, who was a business associate, Farley, and other Democratic politicians all argued with Hearst over the telephone, they worked him into an amenable state of mind. But not even Hearst could swing California to Roosevelt. The delegation was pledged to Garner and Garner alone could release it.[52]

Negotiations with the Texans led to the same blank wall. Rayburn was affable and completely honorable as he met secretly on several occasions with Farley. He listened politely the night before the convention when Farley suggested to him that if Texas threw its support to Roosevelt, Garner would receive the nomination for Vice President. Rayburn replied that they had come to Chicago to nominate Garner, but they did not wish to encourage a stalemate. Senator Tom Connally similarly parried offers from Roosevelt's floor manager, Mullen. Texas, like California, was tied to Garner, and Texans had come to the convention determined to win.[53]

The key, therefore, was Garner himself in Washington. Just before the convention began, he had confided to Bascom Timmons that he considered Roosevelt the majority choice, and Baker the most likely compromise candidate. Garner was not too optimistic about the chances for victory of any compromise choice; he felt they had seldom won in the past. If an ugly stalemate developed at Chicago, as Garner feared would be the case, it might shatter public confidence and cost the Democrats the election. He was satisfied with being Speaker, and had no intention of being party to a disastrous deadlock.[54]

Obviously, though, Garner was ready to wait for a few ballots to see whether Roosevelt was really strong and whether the convention was really likely to be tied up. In Washington, the night before the convention opened, Senators Hawes of Missouri and Pittman of Nevada received Roosevelt's permission to work for a Roosevelt-Garner ticket. Hawes sent hundreds of wires to Democratic leaders at the convention and elsewhere, urging it upon them. In addition, he erroneously wired Farley that he was ADVISED WOULD BE SATISFACTORY TO PARTY HERE. Garner early in the morning called Hawes and gave him a tart tongue-lashing for making this unauthorized proposal.

So matters stood until after the third ballot. All that day Smith tried to get through to Garner, and the Speaker would not answer the telephone. He explained later he meant no discourtesy, but that Smith was trying to commit him to a last-ditch stand in which he wished no part. That same day, Hearst, through one of his newspapermen, did get a message to Garner advising him to release his delegates to Roosevelt.[55]

Garner was already of a mind to do so, for he was not pleased with his analysis of the first three ballots. He called Rayburn that afternoon, to tell him he thought it was time to end the balloting. The nomination should be on the next roll call. Rayburn said he would check with his delegations and report back. He did later in the afternoon before the convention reconvened. California, he reported, would swing to Roosevelt if Garner released the delegates, but Texas would not unless Garner took second place on the ticket. Garner was loath to leave his position of power as Speaker of the House to become a vice-presidential figurehead, but feared a debacle would be the alternative. He has reminisced to Timmons: "So I said to Sam, 'All right, release my delegates and see what you can do. Hell, I'll do anything to see the Democrats win one more national election.' "[56]

Thus it was Garner himself who played the really decisive role in guaranteeing the nomination to Roosevelt. Basil O'Connor wisecracked to Roosevelt a few days later, "Of the 55,000 Democrats allegedly to have been in Chicago for the recent Convention, unquestionably 62,000 of them arranged the . . . shift." Certainly a remarkable number were working one way or another for the ultimate compromise, and many of these played notable roles in softening up one or another member of the Texas and California delegations. It is not surprising, therefore, that Mullen, Roper, McAdoo, Hearst, and others, both in print and orally, have claimed credit for the great climax.[57]

Even after Garner had told Rayburn to release the delegates, it was not entirely over. The Texas delegates, cheered by Garner's acquisition of ten additional votes on the third ballot, were hopeful that they could next pick up Mississippi and Arkansas and move ahead to the nomination. Many of the most ardent Garner men in the Texas delegation were out working for him when Rayburn caucused the delegation for Roosevelt. He was able to persuade them to switch by a vote of only 54 to 51; had the die-hards been there,* Rayburn might not have been able to swing them.[58]

On his way to the Texas caucus, Rayburn saw McAdoo in the Sherman Hotel. McAdoo declared, "Sam, we'll vote for Jack Garner until Hell freezes over if you say so." Rayburn instead informed him of Garner's decision to release his delegates. McAdoo, who had apparently already struck a similar bargain with Roper, readily acquiesced, and easily gained the consent of the California delegation.[59]

Friday evening, July 1, 1932, when the convention reassembled, there was an air of tense expectancy as delegates and spectators awaited what they thought would be another full night of balloting. Only insiders knew what was in store. Even some of the Roosevelt leaders had not yet received the word and were still offering the vice-presidency here and there. Farley had informed the Tammany chieftains of the break, but they were incredulous and adamant. The Allies were still in high spirits because they had just won over Mississippi.

Then the fourth ballot began. When California was called, McAdoo jumped up. "California asks the opportunity of explaining its vote to the convention," he declared. He had offered to wait for Texas, but Rayburn felt it would cause less ill feeling among furious Garner supporters like Amon Carter if McAdoo burst the bombshell. Certainly McAdoo was ready to make the most of the moment. There was irony that he should publicly end the hopes of Smith once and for all as Smith had ended his at Madison Square Garden after McAdoo had held a majority on ballot after ballot.[60]

"California came here to nominate a President," McAdoo asserted. "She did not come here to deadlock this convention or to engage in another disastrous contest like that of 1924." Roosevelt delegates went wild with joy; the galleries rocked with hisses and boos so loud that

* One of them on the way home declared the Roosevelt-Garner slate was a kangaroo ticket, stronger in the hind end than the front.

finally Chairman Walsh had to appeal to Mayor Cermak to quiet them. Then, finally, McAdoo cast the forty-four votes of California for Roosevelt.[61]

In Albany at his radio, Roosevelt exclaimed, "Good old McAdoo." [62]

When Illinois was reached in the roll call, Mayor Cermak switched the votes of his state. Indiana immediately followed. Governor Ritchie personally turned over the Maryland vote. At 10:32 in the evening, Walsh announced that on the fourth ballot, Roosevelt had received 945 votes: "I proclaim him the nominee of this convention for President of the United States." [63]

Only Smith in his hotel remained silent, refusing to release his delegates in order to make the nomination unanimous.* The next noon, he and his followers left Chicago before Roosevelt could arrive.

It really made no difference. Roosevelt's victory at the convention had been overwhelming even if there were those who could not help thinking their own candidate would have been stronger. He had the Democrats solidly united behind him at a time when the Republicans were weak. Smith and his loyal cohorts were no more than a dissident splinter in the party. Most of the delegates remained on, eager to see and hear the man they were confident would lead the Democrats back into power after twelve politically lean years.

Not for nothing had Sam Rosenman worked through the night at Albany. The Governor needed that speech accepting his party's nomination of him as "the man who . . . will be the next President of the United States."

* Mencken wrote a sad political epitaph for Smith: "The failure of the opposition was the failure of Al Smith. From the moment he arrived on the ground it was apparent that he had no plan, and was animated only by his fierce hatred of Roosevelt, the cuckoo who had seized his nest. That hatred may have had logic in it, but it was impotent to organize the allies. . . . Perhaps the Al of eight or ten years ago, or even of four years ago, might have achieved the miracle that the crisis called for, but it was far beyond the technique of the golf-playing Al of today. He has ceased to be the wonder and glory of the East Side and becomes simply a minor figure of Park avenue."[64]

CHAPTER XXI

Toward a New Deal

> I pledge you, I pledge myself, to a new deal for the American people.
>
> — FDR, ACCEPTANCE ADDRESS, *July 2, 1932.*

ROOSEVELT'S first act upon winning the nomination was a spectacular break with tradition. He announced what he had decided weeks before to do, that he would fly to Chicago to deliver his acceptance speech in person before the convention. At a time when the formal acceptance of the nomination was a stiff occasion weeks after the event, conducted as though the candidate had been in the dark up to that moment, Roosevelt's smashing of precedent thrilled the nation. Even his decision to fly was something of a novelty in a period when commercial air transport was still in its infancy.* To a country stagnating in depression, Roosevelt's bold dramatic action brought a lift of hope. Nothing could have convinced Americans more effectively that he was a decisive leader coming forward at a moment when the nation was crying for positive leadership.[2]

Roosevelt did not relish flying, but there was no time for him to get to the convention by train. At 7:25 the next morning, July 2, he boarded a new trimotored airplane at the Albany airport, accompanied by Mrs. Roosevelt, their sons, Elliott and John, Rosenman, secretaries, and bodyguards. The convention reassembled at two o'clock to nominate a Vice President, but it was a foregone conclusion that it would be Garner.† Consequently, the attention of the nation focused

* Word was sent out well in advance that FDR would go in person to the convention, but he chose to conceal the means of transportation. He twitted reporters by telling them he planned to go on a five-seat bicycle, himself in front and his four sons behind.[1]

† Garner's nomination was not really in the nature of a deal, since he would be leaving a powerful office for one of relatively little importance. Farley had repeatedly offered the vice-presidency to Garner leaders; they had never made it part of the bargain. Farley felt Garner was entitled to the nomination if he wanted it; Roosevelt approved. Consequently, Farley obtained Rayburn's permission and lined up Roosevelt support for Garner. He parried those urging other

upon Governor Roosevelt as he flew westward. The plane bumped against strong headwinds, gradually falling more and more behind schedule. At the Chicago Stadium, delegate after delegate made seconding speeches for Garner; there was ample time to drag out what could have been done in minutes. One other candidate, General Matt A. Tinley of Iowa, was nominated. From time to time the Chairman read bulletins on the progress of Roosevelt's plane. Finally, when he reported it sixty miles from Chicago, it was time to get to work. Tinley moved that the rules be suspended and the nomination of Garner be made unanimous.[4]

Aboard the plane, Roosevelt and Rosenman put final touches on the acceptance address. For weeks Roosevelt had been working upon it, discussing with Moley the recommendations of the Brain Trusters, revising a speech memorandum Moley prepared early in June, going over Moley's subsequent draft with Rosenman. During the critical balloting, Rosenman in Albany drafted a conclusion in which he picked up from Moley's memorandum the words "new deal." On the plane Roosevelt polished away. Radio messages came in from the convention hall that the delegates were becoming impatient. Some were leaving for home. Hearing this, Roosevelt began cutting. The more the plane fell behind schedule, Rosenman has recalled, the more paragraphs Roosevelt pulled out of the speech. Actually all Roosevelt had to do was make quite minor revisions. He was able to nap part of the way to Chicago. By the time they arrived, the speech was crisp, succinct, and ready for delivery.[5]

Amidst the cheering throng at the airport, the passengers disembarked. First came the family; one member, John Roosevelt, staggered out airsick. Then came Roosevelt himself, beaming and nonchalant. "I was a good sailor," he told Mayor Cermak, who had left Chicago Stadium with its hostile galleries to turn good host. The crowd pressing in around Roosevelt knocked off his hat and sent his glasses awry, but Roosevelt showed no dismay. The campaign had begun, and he was in his element. He warmly clasped Farley by the hand and exclaimed, "Good work, Jim!" Then he climbed with Howe into a big white car to ride to the stadium. On the way, Howe thrust into Roosevelt's hands another draft acceptance speech. Roosevelt protested that he already had a speech in final form, but Howe was

---

Roosevelt supporters, such as Senators Dill of Washington and Wheeler of Montana and Governor Dern of Utah. Baruch spoke to Farley on behalf of Ritchie. Farley refused even to call a conference on the vice-presidential choice.[3]

insistent. He had not liked the version as it had come in over the direct wire from Albany, on July 1, and he had written another. So Roosevelt rode through the streets of Chicago, as he liked to tell with gestures, waving his hat to the crowds, shouting "Hello," and between waves turning the pages of Howe's manuscript in his lap.[6]

At the Chicago Stadium, Senator Walsh introduced Roosevelt amidst thunderous applause.*

"Chairman Walsh, My Friends of the Democratic National Convention of 1932," Roosevelt began, "I appreciate your willingness after these six arduous days to remain here, for I know well the sleepless hours which you and I have had." In the rear of the hall, Moley anxiously began to follow Roosevelt's words on his copy of the address. The ideas were the same, but the words were unfamiliar. Then, in a couple of minutes, the phrases fell into line and they too were the same. Howe's speech was no more than a revision of what Roosevelt and his advisers had worked out in Albany. Roosevelt, not wanting to rob Howe of his supreme moment of satisfaction, had substituted the first page of Howe's draft † for the one he had brought with him on the plane, then had swung into his prepared speech.[9]

With the nation listening, Roosevelt in his clear, confident voice expounded his position in warm, ringing generalities. He pointed to the way in which he was breaking traditions, and pledged his party to the task of destroying foolish ones. One tradition he wished to nurture, that of the Democratic party as the bearer of liberalism. This was the only alternative to a descent into unreasoning radicalism. "Wild radicalism has made few converts," he continued, "and the greatest tribute that I can pay to my countrymen is that in these days of crushing want there persists an orderly and hopeful spirit on the part of the millions of our people who have suffered so much. To fail to offer them a new chance is not only to betray their hopes but to misunderstand their patience."

* Later in the summer, FDR wrote Walsh profuse thanks for his work as chairman. At one point, when the Minnesota delegation challenged the unit rule, Walsh by ruling in favor of FDR had prevented the start of what might have been a debacle.[7]

† FDR dictated a memorandum to accompany the ready copy of the acceptance speech in which he said he had put it into final shape at Albany at 1 A.M. on July 2. "On arrival at the Chicago Airport, Mr. Howe had ten or twelve pages of a suggested speech, based on a review and amplification of the Democratic platform. I discarded all of this except the first page which seemed better than what I had prepared. It worked into the rest of the speech and expressed my ideas. Hence it was used in place of my first page."[8]

What Roosevelt offered to them was in outline what he had been promising during the spring and demonstrating as Governor of New York. He did not spell it out in detail at Chicago; that was not necessary. He talked of domestic causes of the depression and the need for the government to bolster the credit of independent economic groups through rigid governmental economy, Prohibition repeal, regulation of securities sales, construction of self-sustaining public works, and reforestation of marginal and unused farmland. To farmers, he pledged a voluntary crop-control program to cut down agricultural surpluses, and the rediscounting of farm mortgages. To businessmen, he pledged a lower tariff to restore foreign trade; to those in distress, he promised home-mortgage refinancing and Federal relief. In total, he was assuring a distressed nation that he would fight to restore their old standards of living and to give them a more equitable share in the national wealth. In the almost religious spirit of the Progressive movement of twenty years earlier, he concluded:

"I pledge you, I pledge myself, to a new deal for the American people. Let us all here assembled constitute ourselves prophets of a new order of competence and of courage. This is more than a political campaign; it is a call to arms. Give me your help, not to win votes alone, but to win in this crusade to restore America to its own people." [10]

The words "new deal" stuck. There was nothing new about them, and nothing consciously slogan-making in the insertion of them into the speech. Roosevelt was later ready enough to give assent when a nephew of Mark Twain's asked if he had not borrowed them from *A Connecticut Yankee in King Arthur's Court*. But they were so widely in use that no one noticed when several hours before on that very day in that same hall, John McDuffie of Alabama, in nominating Garner, had intoned: "There is a demand for a new deal in the management of the affairs of the American people."

But the appearance of the term in Roosevelt's peroration, and the magic ring he gave it, caused it to catch the imagination of newspapermen and cartoonists. The next day Rosenman saw a Rollin Kirby cartoon depicting a farmer gazing skyward at an airplane. On it was the legend "New Deal." With this for a name the Roosevelt program had taken wing.[11]

So, also, had the campaign. Roosevelt's dynamic acceptance speech brought thunderous applause from the weary delegates and an equally warm response from the American public, tired of the depression.

State and local leaders reported to Farley that it got Roosevelt off to a flying start.[12]

Roosevelt, as full of verve and energy as though he had just returned from a long vacation, plunged into his campaign work before the applause died down. He began shaking hands with delegates as he left the platform, and continued for hours in the Roosevelt headquarters at the Congress Hotel as hundreds of well-wishers crowded up for his greeting. From many of them he solicited information which might be of value during the campaign, as when he asked Governor Dern of Utah to advise him on public land and Western water-power policy.

That evening Roosevelt dined with the Democratic National Committee. At the beginning of the dinner, Raskob presided for the last time; Roosevelt was replacing him with Farley. Roosevelt devoted the major part of his remarks to rubbing ointment into the stinging wounds of "my very good and old friend, John Raskob," and "my old friend Jouett Shouse." [13] He thanked these bitter adversaries of the day before for their great services to the party, and invited them to give assistance during the campaign. "I am very confident," he pointedly declared, "that we shall have a united party to meet the Republican leadership." Had Smith been present, Roosevelt certainly would have lavished soothing words upon him too. As it was, Roosevelt had left Dorothy Rosenman in Albany to arrange for Smith's friends * to dissuade him from issuing a bitter statement which would cause trouble later in the campaign.[14] Roosevelt had no intention of allowing personal rancor to fester into a nasty sore. Farley later observed that, at any rate, the tenseness of the struggle for the nomination at Chicago publicized Roosevelt far more effectively than a drab convention ever could have. It had the happy result of exciting the popular imagination.[15]

After midnight, when Roosevelt signaled Moley to ease the last visitors out of the rooms at the Congress Hotel, Moley was ready to pick up his hat and depart, but Roosevelt was not ready to let him do so. He told Moley that he was not even a little bit tired, and launched immediately into his plans for the campaign. According to Lela Stiles, Howe had months earlier worked out itineraries and speech topics. Certainly Roosevelt had the subject at his finger tips that night. He and Moley talked for an hour and a half, while Moley jotted pages

* Mrs. Rosenman had Justice Bernard L. Shientag board the Smith train at Harmon near New York City. Shientag persuaded Smith to remain silent. Smith's most devoted follower, Mrs. Moskowitz, wired FDR gracious congratulations.

and pages of notes on trips, speeches, and even on speech content.[16]

Organization as well as issues concerned Roosevelt that evening. He authorized Moley to put the Brain Trust to work immediately on the half dozen big issues, and flatly assured him that all drafts, suggestions, and proposals must be cleared through him. This was more than a stricture upon Howe, preventing him from acting separately on policy; it applied also to Farley and to Democratic leaders and politicians. Roosevelt kept his word without exception. Shortly after Moley got back to New York, he had a heart-to-heart talk with Farley. They shook hands on the proposition that Moley's job was issues and Farley's was votes.[17]

Moley had already acquired a valuable recruit to the Brain Trust that day, General Hugh S. Johnson. Baruch, putting party loyalty ahead of his friendship to Ritchie and Smith, had come immediately to Howe, bringing Johnson with him. Howe had been so delighted to greet this prodigious source of ideas and funds that he had shown Baruch the drafts of the acceptance speech. Along with Baruch was General Johnson, who usually roared like a lion, but was a quiet mouse that day. Baruch asked if Johnson could also see the acceptance speech, then donated Johnson to the campaign. Johnson earlier had been cynical about Roosevelt. He had complained to Peek in May, "He answers according to Hoyle and then gets on the radio and says something somebody fixes up for him. He's all wet all right in more ways than one." In July, once he had joined Roosevelt's forces, Johnson, like a loyal soldier, threw all his energies into the cause. He brought to the writing of speeches all the fire that he once had put into boys' adventure stories. "Baruch had dropped him into our midst casually enough," Moley has written, "but once there, he exploded, like an elaborate fireworks display, into a series of enchanting patterns." Baruch himself also began contributing suggestions and memoranda;* Moley soon considered him one of the best of the Brain Trusters.[19]

Moley's policy group continued to have as a nucleus Tugwell, Berle, Rosenman, and O'Connor; Johnson and a few others joined it after the convention; innumerable professors, businessmen and political leaders contributed from time to time. Before the active speechmaking began, Roosevelt wrote key Democrats, asking them to hold themselves in

* On July 6, for example, Baruch wired FDR, "I hope you will not permit yourself to answer such people as [Arthur M.] Hyde and [George H.] Moses who are so thoroughly discredited that nobody will pay any attention to them. Also I hope you will answer no one." This referred to Secretary of Agriculture Hyde's attack upon FDR's reforestation proposal in his acceptance address.[18]

readiness for consultation with Moley. It was a notable group, including Baker, Young, Traylor, House, Pittman, and Robinson.[20]

Altogether, Roosevelt was able during the campaign to draw upon the brains of scores of American leaders. Significantly enough, they represented many shades of economic thought from left to right. The adherence of men like Baruch and Johnson after the nomination marked a decided shift toward the right. Moley, the head of the group, was a middle-of-the-roader; even at this time, he considered himself basically conservative. Berle, Tugwell, and Frankfurter, who was outside of the group but influential, were all pulling and hauling toward the left. For Roosevelt this was ideal, since he sought balance. He wished to win back the disgruntled conservative Democrats of the East without losing the liberal Democrats of the West.

Hence the Brain Trust as it was constituted was perfect for his purpose. It served as a clearing house and testing center for ideas which poured in from everywhere. Farley, Howe, and Roosevelt himself channeled hundreds of suggestions to it. Moley has described the process:

"We were at once working up the material for specific speeches, pushing ahead with the broad economic education of ourselves and Roosevelt, adopting or rejecting thousands of ideas that poured in on us, and trying to observe the elementary political maxim that no one who voluntarily offered suggestions or plans, however silly . . . must be sent away unhappy." [21]

This called for a remarkable combination of traits, Moley has pointed out. One must be an expert in at least one field, and demonstrate writing ability, tact, accuracy, good humor, and an iron constitution. "Consider the difference of opinion and temperament that inevitably cropped up in such groups," Moley has written, "the crucial decisions on policy and political strategy that had to be made, the endless meetings, telephonings, draftings, and checkings it all entailed, and you get a picture vaguely hinting of the swirling chaos, the dizzying turmoil of July and August." All this the advisers had to do for long hours in the summer heat of New York City, and entirely at their own expenses. One had to be truly dedicated to be a Brain Truster.[22]

Meanwhile, Farley was gathering about him an assembly of over five hundred vote-getting experts of similar talents at the Biltmore Hotel in New York. He had no lack of applicants. Before the end of the summer, he complained to Senator Matt Neely that Howe was more bothered by volunteer workers than by those who wished pay.

He could parry the latter easily enough, but the former could eat up scarce office space, supplies, and the time of stenographers who did get paid. He wanted them only if they were effective, but unfortunately many a volunteer was influential enough to get on the staff yet not efficient enough to justify his space.[23]

In time the Roosevelt and Democratic organization became highly complex. Of Raskob's group in Washington, Roosevelt retained the talented publicity man Michelson. Indeed, he had arranged this before he obtained the nomination. Michelson, who loyally had followed Raskob's orders and through the spring of 1932 had blacked out Roosevelt in his Democratic handouts, moved over immediately to the Roosevelt camp.* Roosevelt had known him during the First World War. At Chicago he greeted Michelson cheerily with a nautical "Glad to see you aboard." Michelson spent half of his time at party headquarters in Washington, and half at Roosevelt headquarters in New York.[25]

Most of the Democratic stalwarts took one or another position in the campaign bureaucracy, some displaying talent and efficiency, others riding hobbies, airing their jealousies, or demonstrating an overfondness for liquor. One of the most famous and talented of the senatorial advisers risked a tragic scandal when, in his cups, he tossed a bottle out of the window at the Biltmore. Fortunately it did not hit anyone.[26]

There were all the usual campaign committees and subcommittees. The Women's Division was especially large and effective under the vigorous leadership of the irrepressible Mary W. Dewson. For the first time it was a major campaign unit. Farley realized that a women's organization could increase the Democratic vote by ten to twenty per cent, and gave it his enthusiastic backing. In 1928, the Democrats had brought out the vote of the urban women from poorer homes for the first time; in 1932, Democratic women worked effectively, speaking and distributing literature, to appeal to clubwomen as well. In mid-July, Eleanor Roosevelt planned an organization with Miss Dewson. They used former governor Nellie Tayloe Ross of Wyoming for field work and speeches, and established divisions for field work, clubs, labor, publicity, speakers, files, and mail.[27]

Rather than set up regional committees, Roosevelt and Farley de-

* Michelson put his heart into his service with FDR. When four years later Raskob invited him into the opposition for more money, Michelson found himself no literary Hessian, and declined.[24]

pended entirely upon the state Democratic organizations to get out the vote. This placed the responsibility upon the chairman of each state committee. Since it also gave each of them the prestige and subsequent claim to patronage, this brought screams from the loyal preconvention Roosevelt supporters in state after state where the organization had fought against Roosevelt's nomination. But Roosevelt and Farley were still determined to work with the regulars.

In Alabama, for example, this meant cooperating with Edward Pettus, the state chairman, who had fought Roosevelt before the Alabama primary and had worked within the Alabama delegation at Chicago, trying to get it to break away. Roosevelt's New York friend, Judge Bernard Ryan, pleaded with him on behalf of W. C. Fitts, who had worked brilliantly to secure Alabama for Roosevelt. Roosevelt replied, "Nothing is further from my mind than that my good friend Judge Fitts should in any way be left out of the picture and I have spoken to Jim Farley about it." But he added, "Under the general rule we have to recognize a state organization." * Roosevelt was taking no chances on jeopardizing his opportunities for victory by replacing regulars with Roosevelt men, even though the regulars might cause him trouble later when he was President.[29]

As far as they could, Roosevelt and Farley tried to make their personal influence reach down to the precinct-worker level. Farley collected as complete a list as possible of county and precinct workers in every state so that he could send campaign pamphlets and letters signed in green ink to them. He reasoned that much of the printed matter distributed to regional, state, and then local committees never trickled down to the workers. So he sent it directly, along with letters which the workers were thrilled to receive. Altogether sixty-eight different Dupligraph letters and two hundred and twenty-three Multigraph letters went out – nearly a million seven hundred thousand copies altogether. There were also some four hundred and seventy-five news releases totaling three hundred thousand copies, approximately forty-two million pieces of printed matter, and ten million buttons and pins. All these had their effect. "The fellow out in Kokomo, Indiana, who is pulling doorbells night after night," Farley reasoned,

* Similarly when Hull complained to Farley that FDR's early supporters in Texas were being sidetracked, Farley replied, "To be very frank with you, Senator, I think we will make a terrible mistake if we fail to carry out the campaign through the regular organization in Texas. . . . If we do it otherwise we are going to be in trouble." [28]

"gets a real thrill if he receives a letter on campaigning postmarked Washington or New York." [30]

Even more effective than these were the supposedly personal letters that Howe's hard-working machine poured into the mails in answer to the thousands pouring in to Roosevelt. Most of these had the personal touch, utilizing the "mirror" technique of picking up and repeating various of the phrases or comments in the incoming letter. In the pressure of the campaign, not only the rank and file of writers, but even Senators, governors, and farm and labor leaders sometimes received these machine-made replies. More important ones did at least receive an authentic Roosevelt signature. An occasional troublesome one simply fell by the wayside. On an inquiry from the president of the Allied Patriotic Societies as to whether Roosevelt favored existing immigration restrictions, Howe facetiously noted, "I am sorry this letter was lost in the mail. The Gov. would have loved to have plunged into the hot water that an answer would have involved." [31]

Some of the answers were bold and blunt. To a correspondent who sent an anti-Catholic, anti-Roosevelt paper called *The Rail-Splitter*, Roosevelt's ghost replied, "The scurrilous propaganda which you enclosed is of a type that I will not dignify by answering. I must depend upon such loyal workers as yourself to combat this malicious type of personal attack." Occasionally someone was so pleased with an answer that he would request permission to publish it, as when Roosevelt (Gabrielle Forbush) wrote, "I am a Democrat 'by conviction,' as our Quaker friends say." [32]

On the whole, Roosevelt's ghosts did an excellent job. Only a tiny number of the letters, such as one in which Roosevelt was made to seem opposed to a protective tariff for agriculture, caused trouble. Moley later felt thankful that the Republicans did not gather up any number of them, he was so fearful that they were full of contradictions. Remarkably enough, this was not so. They were so general, so innocuous, and hewed so closely to Roosevelt's speeches that the Republicans could have done little with the entire enormous file – except expose it as a factory product.[33]

The incoming letters continued to serve Howe as an excellent source of intelligence on conditions throughout the country. He supplemented it with vast numbers of clippings of editorials and local political news, at the height of the campaign as many as fifteen thousand a day. Skilled readers condensed all important reports and clippings into daily bulletins for Roosevelt and his campaign staff.[34]

From the outset, the problem of money raising was one of the most difficult facing the campaigners. This was especially true in as bleak a year as 1932. Funds poured in compared with the preconvention period, but the needs were infinitely greater. Frank C. Walker served as treasurer, which meant chief money raiser, as he had before the nomination. On the whole, fund raising did not impinge directly upon Roosevelt. There was one embarrassing episode during the campaign when Roosevelt's longtime friend, the promoter Arthur P. Homer, rather pointedly solicited contributions from businessmen to whom Roosevelt had given Navy contracts during the First World War. Some of Homer's correspondence fell into Republican hands, which made it necessary for the Democrats to disavow him. This permanently concluded Homer's long, sporadic association with Roosevelt.[35]

Altogether, the Democrats made reported expenditures of about two and a half million dollars, compared with approximately two million nine hundred thousand dollars for the Republicans. Although they sponsored campaign books, medallions, tire covers, and other devices to stimulate small contributions, they had, as always, to depend upon a few large donors.[36]

The largest single expenditure of each party was for radio time, which Roosevelt as early as 1928 realized could be the Democratic means of overwhelming the preponderantly Republican press. In 1932, the Republicans bought even more network time than the Democrats, seventy hours compared with fifty hours. But the Republicans had no one to put on the air whose radio appeal could remotely approach Roosevelt's.[37]

As for Roosevelt, he was far more than a matchless radio voice and a ceaseless grin. Despite the size and the ramifications of the campaign institution stretching below him, and despite his willingness to confer endlessly with his leaders and farm out his speeches to the assembly line of brains, he himself remained always in command. In the final analysis, it was Roosevelt who decided what the campaign methods were to be, and at times he went athwart the advice of most of his subordinates. It was Roosevelt who decided how far to veer to the right or the left. He was, in truth as well as in name, the commander in chief of the Democratic forces. It was Roosevelt himself and nobody else who would determine how fast and how far the campaign would move toward a New Deal.

CHAPTER XXII

To Starboard or Port?

> That cruise with the boys was a real rest and now the preliminary organization work seems to be going well.
> — FDR TO JOSEPHUS DANIELS, *July 26, 1932.*

ROOSEVELT'S nomination brought him for the first time into sharp public conflict with his opponent, President Hoover. Previously he had sniped at Hoover like a little boy shying an occasional snowball at a distant dignitary in a top hat. Now Roosevelt had suddenly grown into a formidable adversary who posed a major threat to the President, and in some ways a baffling one. As Roosevelt prepared for his offensive in the summer of 1932, it was not entirely clear whether he intended to deploy his man-of-war against Hoover from starboard or from port. Would Roosevelt campaign as a conservative or as a liberal?

Whatever course Roosevelt might steer, Hoover faced the problem of meeting his attack, for the President personally shouldered the responsibility for the fight against Roosevelt. In this respect, though in few others, the two men resembled each other. Hoover, suffering from low morale if not mutiny among many of the professional Republicans, remained adamantly in command of his forces. At the top, the campaign became a dramatic and bitter personal duel between the two old acquaintances.

Whatever friendship had once existed between these men had eroded into keen antipathy by the summer of 1932. The admiration which had led Roosevelt to advocate Hoover for President in 1920 was largely gone by 1928; there was little in their quite different personalities to draw them to each other. Through 1928 there was not much difference between the ideologies of the two, and even up to the campaign of 1932 there was not a great deal to choose between the President's and the Governor's advocacy of a limited governmental attack upon the depression. The hostility between them had been, up to this point, a clash of politics and personalities more than issues.[1]

Roosevelt was more than willing to match Hoover's dislike for him, as the result of an episode that had taken place in the spring of 1932. President Hoover had invited the governors, who had been holding their annual conference at Richmond, to dine at the White House. At this time Roosevelt was contesting vigorously for convention delegates, and one of his opponents' chief arguments was that this polio victim was not physically fit for the demanding job of President. The Roosevelts arrived a little early, knowing that it would take a while for Roosevelt to make his way down the main hall, one arm clasped to Mrs. Roosevelt, the other gripping a cane. But when they reached the East Room, where they were supposed to stand until the President and Mrs. Hoover appeared, they were forced to wait and wait. Twice Roosevelt was offered a chair, but both times he declined, apparently for fear he might thus give his opponents an opportunity to whisper he was physically weak. Painfully he continued to stand on his braces, perspiration beading his forehead but a smile on his face, for a full half hour until the Hoovers arrived. A man as humane and decent as Hoover could never have resorted deliberately to such a cruel political stratagem, but Roosevelt, who had undergone torture, was suspicious.[2]

Despite his personal animus, Roosevelt at first did not want the Democrats to make personal attacks upon Hoover during the campaign. When Garner informed Roosevelt that he intended in his letter of acceptance "to punch the Administration in the nose, especially Hoover and Mills, at every opportunity," Roosevelt counseled a different course. Personal attacks upon Hoover might not be taken too well by Republicans switching to the Democratic ticket, Roosevelt felt. "Frankly, I think it is best to hammer at the Republican leadership – not the Republican party – " he explained, "and it is all right to talk about Mills, Mellon, Hyde, etc. without too much reference to Hoover himself. He is personally flat and we can safely leave him there." [3]

Hoover could not afford to take the same condescending view of Roosevelt. During the campaign of 1928 he had never deigned to mention Smith, but before the 1932 campaign was over, he was singling out Roosevelt by name. Whatever hope President Hoover and the Republicans may have had that they could easily undermine Roosevelt disappeared with the dramatic flight to Chicago and the flair of his acceptance speech. Secretary of State Stimson could pick flaws in it when he analyzed it, but he had to grant it was pretty good.[4] After he visited the White House on July 5, he wrote in his diary:

"I found the President rather blue on the subject of Roosevelt. The people around him evidently had been rather overconfident . . . and are now awake to the full power which Roosevelt will produce in the field to the radical elements of the West and the South. Roosevelt is not a strong character himself and our hope is that the four months' campaign will develop and prove that he has pretty well lost the confidence of the business elements in the East. But he is making his appeal to the West, and in hard times it is very easy. An inflation campaign and soft money campaign make it look like some of the elements of 1896. But the difficulty is that then it was the Democrats who were in power during the hard times and now it is the Republicans who are in power. That gives us an uphill fight. Also there is no split yet in the Democratic party as there was in 1896, and there is no Mark Hanna in the Republican party to organize a very big educational campaign." [5]

This in essence was the plight of the Republicans in 1932. They faced another great agrarian revolt from the West, but under the leadership of an urbane Roosevelt rather than of a frightening Bryan. To stave it off they had a Hoover rather than a Hanna.*

All the Republicans could hope for was that a sudden, spectacular return of prosperity might save their ticket, or that the Democrats would stumble into some serious error. Since the Democrats for the past decade had demonstrated a remarkable ineptitude and a zest for internecine warfare, there was cause for at least some faint Republican hope. "I fear that only the Democrats will save Hoover," the Republican voice of Kansas, William Allen White, wrote. "How, I don't know. But they are versatile and can find some way in crises." [7]

There were indeed some slight signs of economic improvement in the summer of 1932. The New York *Times's* "Weekly Index of Business Activity," which included car loadings and production of steel, electric power, automobiles, and lumber, rose slowly from about two thirds of normal (66.2) on August 6, 1932, to three fourths of normal (73.8) by January 7, 1933. Hoover in years since has regarded this as the beginning of true recovery, destroyed by the politicking of Roosevelt and the Democrats.† Roosevelt and his supporters were suspicious at

* Many observers noted the parallel to 1896. Lippmann had predicted this sort of campaign even before FDR's nomination.[6]

† This point of view was even more strongly stated by Hoover's secretary, Theodore Joslin, who wrote in *Hoover Off the Record:* "The full force of the depression had been spent. Real recovery had begun in July, immediately after the adjournment of Congress. But it now showed signs of going back. I had definite information before election day that in September and October orders totalling several hundred million dollars had been placed, subject to the election.

the time that it might be an upward turn manufactured by Republican businessmen rather than true economic demands. Claude Bowers, Hearst editorial writer and ardent Democratic historian, warned Roosevelt that the Republicans through manipulating the market would try to run up the price of wheat, then try "through subservient press agencies to create the impression that prosperity is 'just around the corner.' " Bowers cited numerous Associated Press stories on improved business conditions to try to back up his contention. "You are right about the Republican game — " Roosevelt replied, "their strategy is now perfectly plain." [9]

One of the Brain Trusters, Berle, watched the bull market closely, and reported to Roosevelt upon it from time to time. At the beginning of August, he declared that the securities rise was coming from European speculative sources, and that business conditions were worse than before. Through the fall, it was the opinion at Democratic headquarters that the rise in the stock market would have little effect upon the election.[10]

Any upswing toward prosperity was not trickling down to the average voter. Certainly farmers were not feeling it. Prices had not gone up since the spring, when one of Governor Roosevelt's outraged constituents had sent him a voucher indicating that she had received thirty-nine cents net for the sale of a four-weeks-old calf. "With 61¢ a hundred lbs. of milk and 39¢ calves its impossible to live," she had protested. "If you don't help us soon we will be homeless." Early in September, the former editor of the *Iowa Farmer* sent Roosevelt a detailed breakdown * to indicate that, in 1932, the average farmer on one hundred and sixty acres in Iowa would lose $1650.[11]

Nor was the ugly encampment of the Bonus Army in Washington, the nation's show window, any earnest of returning prosperity that summer. Some eleven thousand veterans were encamped in the capital, many in a shanty town by the Anacostia River, trying to pressure Congress into paying them their bonus for service in the First World War. President Hoover signed a bill to pay them their rail fare home,

---

If Mr. Hoover were returned to office, the orders would become immediately effective. If he were defeated, cancellation of the contracts was optional. And every last one of those contracts was cancelled! Business and industry were going to take no chances until they found out what Mr. Roosevelt would do in the way of experimentation." [8]

* The editor figured the farmer's work for the year as being worth $1200.

but only half of them took advantage of it.* Among the riotous remainder, Hoover found, fewer than a third were actually veterans, and many were Communists or ex-convicts. As disorder increased, Hoover instructed the Army to evict them. The Army did so speedily and efficiently, as newspaper and newsreel cameramen shot scenes reminiscent of the rape of Belgium. Chief of Staff Douglas MacArthur, resplendent in his uniform and medals, took conspicuous command against the "insurrectionists" as though he were going to the aid of a beleaguered city. "That . . . was a bad looking mob," he later stated. "It was animated by the essence of revolution."

MacArthur's army behaved in accepted counterrevolutionary style. Tanks rumbled through the streets, and soldiers equipped with gas masks and fixed bayonets advanced on the jeering rabble. Refugees carrying their meager possessions rushed from their burning hovels as the soldiers charged, throwing tear gas ahead of them.

The Army in its enthusiasm had somewhat exceeded President Hoover's directions. He had merely ordered it to drive the men back to their camps. Washingtonians were greatly relieved that the danger was past, and newspaper editorials almost without exception commended the President. It may have been a necessary move, but it was excruciatingly bad politics, underscoring as it did the desperation of masses of Americans, and adding to the personal unpopularity of President Hoover.[13]

Apparently the President saw no broad implications of nationwide distress in the Bonus Army, but rather regarded it as primarily a Communist conspiracy to repudiate him. Similarly in his *Memoirs* he has described the selling of apples on street corners as a device of the apple-growers' association to sell their crop and raise prices. He has asserted that some people left their jobs for the more profitable one of selling apples. This was somewhat less than a realistic approach to the growing canker of depression, but many Republican party leaders and newspapers shared Hoover's attitude.[14]

It led them to try to frighten voters by warning against the radicalism of the Democrats at a time when millions of Americans were far more interested in jobs than in political ideologies. The villain of Republican spokesmen in the summer of 1932 was not Roosevelt, whose only left-wing statements had been exceedingly vague, but the vice-

* In June Governor Roosevelt offered fare to New York veterans wishing to return home, but only a very few accepted the offer.[12]

presidential nominee, Speaker Garner. By the time Congress adjourned in July, Garner had made himself conspicuous as the strong proponent of a large-scale public-works spending program. This made him repugnant to conservatives. Hoover and the Republicans felt that he had been engaging in political obstructionism and pork-barrel tactics; they held him responsible for delaying the tax program and unbalancing the budget.[15]

In effect, what the Republicans would have liked to do would have been to campaign against the Democratic Congress rather than against Roosevelt. Bankers, insurance men, and businessmen focused their attention upon Garner and the congressmen, and emphasized that the question was not so much whether Hoover or Roosevelt would make the better President, but which party could do the better job in Washington. The Washington *Post* took a slightly different tack by suggesting that while Roosevelt hedged on everything, Garner as Speaker was running the Democratic show. "It is an odd and embarrassing situation," the *Post* declared, "in which the tail of the kite becomes more important and influential than the head." Then there were the inevitable renewed whispers about Roosevelt's physical and mental health, with the implication that a vote for Roosevelt was really one for Garner.[16]

This talk was personally embarrassing to Garner. He had his wife forward the *Post* editorial to Roosevelt with the assurance that he was not going to take the initiative in any way, but would be governed by Roosevelt's policies throughout the campaign. Roosevelt, implying that he expected Garner to campaign vigorously throughout the autumn, urged him to come to New York for a visit with him, and said not a word about his supposedly left-wing views.[17]

As more and more Democrats worried more and more audibly for fear Garner would alienate voters, Garner became increasingly sensitive. "I don't know any way but to give the Republicans hell," he protested to Farley, "and that does not seem to be agreeable to the eastern sections of the country." Roosevelt tried his best to placate his running mate. He assured Mrs. Garner, "I want you and the Speaker not to worry one bit about these fool editorials in some of the eastern papers. They are grasping at straws and, because of lack of other material, are building up false impressions against us both."[18]

Garner did come East to confer convivially with Roosevelt and pose for joint pictures before the photographers. But he told Howe in New York, and undoubtedly told Roosevelt also, that he felt the less he had to do with the campaign, the better. His motto became, "Sit down – do nothing – and win the election." What he wanted was for Howe to arrange it somehow so he could return to Uvalde, Texas, and do his sitting down right there with a fishing rod in his hand.[19]

Although Howe and Farley tried to argue Garner onto the hustings, at least in Texas and California, Garner clung to his "poker hunch" that the less he said the better their luck would be.* He sat out the campaign in Uvalde with Charles Hand, a publicity man from New York, who had been sent out to ride herd on his statements. He participated only twice, once when he went to Topeka to appear on the platform with Roosevelt, and once when he delivered a radio speech, largely of his own fabrication, on taxation and the need for government economy. He told the Democratic National Committee that he considered one speech per campaign was enough.[21]

As he settled down in Uvalde to fish, Garner confided to Farley, "Now if I can just be cautious enough to keep up with Governor Roosevelt's viewpoints . . . I will have accomplished something at least." [22]

Roosevelt also went fishing that summer, but in a very public way. On July 11 he set out from Port Jefferson, Long Island, with three of his sons – James, Franklin, Jr., and John – in a forty-foot yawl, the *Myth II*. With reporters hovering nearby in a launch, he slowly sailed three hundred miles up the sound, through the Cape Cod Canal, around Cape Ann, up to Portsmouth, New Hampshire.

"I love to be on the water. It is great fun," he told the reporters. "I like everything on the water but a steam yacht." As he drifted across Massachusetts Bay on a languid day, he seemed to be disporting himself in a huge goldfish bowl, focused in the eyes of the nation through the glass of the omnipresent press. While he and his sons finished up a lobster dinner, he called across fifty feet of water in answer to newspapermen's questions. They told him some good bit of political news; he shouted joyously, and waved his soft white hat in the air. Obviously he was in the pink of physical condition and having a wonderful time, and whether or not the big ones were biting, the political fishing couldn't have been better.[23]

* Garner's silence did not indicate any personal dislike for FDR. He wrote Farley after his New York visit, "Give the Governor and Mrs. Roosevelt my love when you have occasion to talk with them. I learned to like those people with the little opportunity of association I had with them. Mrs. Roosevelt deeply impressed me as a mighty sensible woman." [20]

Newspapermen wondered if perhaps he was trying to dispel rumors about his health with this display of strenuosity. This did indeed concern him and may have dictated some of his activities during the campaign. But, as the reporters found in ensuing years, strenuous living was entirely normal and enjoyable for Roosevelt. If the Governor had any ulterior motive in his sail up the New England coast, it was to placate the Smith Democrats of the area. When his boat anchored at Stonington, Connecticut, and off Marblehead, he conferred with politicians. Upon the conclusion of his voyage, he attended a large Democratic rally at Hampton Beach. As he motored homeward from Little Boar's Head, New Hampshire, he stopped at Beverly Farms, Massachusetts, to talk to Colonel House, and at Swampscott to meet with Massachusetts political leaders. He succeeded in thawing out Smith's loyal lieutenant, Governor Ely, and strengthened his position considerably throughout New England.[24]

While Roosevelt ingratiated himself among Massachusetts politicians, Farley, vacationing at Atlantic City, made peace with Boss Hague. Roosevelt agreed to speak at a Hague political rally at Sea Girt in August. Hague's brother confided to Roosevelt that Hague's full first name, like Roosevelt's, was Franklin. "It is a coincidence," James Hague added, "that you both were called for the finest character in American history." It was no coincidence that Roosevelt now was friendly with the former leader of the Smith forces, the man who one disgruntled Jersey Democrat wisecracked had "been known to steal the starch out of a fellow's shirt." It was politics.[25]

With more dignity, Roosevelt was able to repair friendships with conservative Democrats who had been suspicious of him before the convention. He had to hurry back to Albany from his conference at Swampscott in order to have dinner with Baruch, who had delayed going to Europe in order to give advice. Several days later at Hyde Park, he conferred with Young about the Lausanne reparations agreement and foreign policy. A scion of a wealthy Republican family joined them. This was Averell Harriman, Chairman of the Board of the Union Pacific Railroad and Chairman of the Executive Committee of the Illinois Central. Roosevelt explained to the newspapermen, "We are talking economics." [26]

From Harriman, and from Daniel Willard, President of the Baltimore and Ohio, Roosevelt gathered important suggestions on reorganization of railroads. More significant still, by conferring with them he was making himself look respectable to the wealthy and conservative elder statesmen of the party. Young had written Roosevelt a letter, cordial but candid, explaining that he was withholding his public blessing until he could see how Roosevelt's policies unfolded during the campaign; he was reticent with reporters at Hyde Park.[27]

These maneuvers meant no more than that Roosevelt was trying to avoid a party schism and obtain for himself as broad a base of support as possible. Conservative Senator Millard Tydings of Maryland had delicately hinted to Roosevelt that "it would be unfortunate if there was *too much* opportunity offered the Republicans to present you in a false light" as the spokesman of Long and Wheeler. But to many a liberal Southern and Western Democrat, the news of Roosevelt's conferences with conservatives was disheartening. Governor O. Max Gardner of North Carolina granted that Roosevelt would be wise to keep the base of his policy broad and receptive, but was sure he would make a fundamental mistake if he made his main appeal to the conservatives. "This vote is going to Hoover, and in my judgment it is less powerful today than at any time in this century," Gardner asserted. "If I know anything about the public mind of this country, it is that the people are either going to follow a liberal leadership or they are going to develop it themselves." [28]

Kingfish Long much less delicately asserted that with the trend what it was, he had better be forgotten as a campaign speaker. "I am so sincerely set for the proposition that the rich and powerful must be scaled from their privilege and control over the finances of the country and our resources," he wrote, "that along any other line I would be worthless." * Long, who proclaimed to the press that at Chicago he had held the delegates in line for Roosevelt, phoned him to air his feelings on the way Roosevelt had been consorting with right wingers. Roosevelt, who took the call while eating lunch, did his best to appease Long. When he finally got him off the line, he turned to Tugwell, who was sitting next to him, and remarked, "That is one of the two most dangerous men in America." Tugwell blinked, and after a moment asked who the other was. "Douglas MacArthur." [30]

Roosevelt, having moved toward the right to confound his Republican and conservative Democratic critics, with equal virtuosity and

* Long, nevertheless, tried to persuade Farley to send him about the country on a special train, making speeches promising immediate payment of the veterans' bonus. Farley, regarding Long as something of a political clown, likely to do more harm than good, compromised by sending him into a few states either strongly for Roosevelt or definitely lost. Long campaigned so effectively that Farley decided afterwards he could have swung Pennsylvania to FDR.[29]

fervor swung now to the left. The difference was that while there were campaign funds and some middle-class and machine votes to the right, the great bulk of votes was to the left. Undoubtedly the concept of political balance, of serving all important groups in the American community, was in the forefront of his mind. However, he never lost sight of the votes.

Almost immediately after the convention, Roosevelt called the attention of progressives throughout the country to his excellent power record. He had strong reasons for doing so, since nothing could endear him more to independent and Republican liberal intellectuals. His record on utilities was so correct from their viewpoint that Lippmann had been able to disparage it only by claiming that "the main resistance in New York State was broken before the problem came to him." [31] It was Roosevelt's power stand that secured him the support of Senator Norris and his Republican progressive followers, even before the Democratic convention. Norris came out for Roosevelt so quickly after the nomination that Chairman Walsh was able to read the press bulletin to the still assembled delegates.[32]

Roosevelt chose a dramatic fashion to proclaim his position on power to the American public. He wired President Hoover on July 9 requesting a personal conference with him over the proportion of cost New York should bear in developing Saint Lawrence power. The Federal Government should reach an understanding with New York on this matter before concluding its treaty with Canada, he insisted. The agreement should make it possible to submit a treaty to the Senate for immediate ratification. This, he proclaimed, was a point which the State of New York had a legal right to insist be agreed upon before the President concluded the Canada treaty. Settlement of it should lead to an immediate treaty. He hoped the Senate would act upon it favorably as soon as signed. A treaty would make possible quick initiation of the project, which would mean cheap transportation for Western farm products, cheap electricity from the state-owned and state-controlled generators for homes and industries, and immediate employment of thousands of workers. "I hold myself subject to your call and am ready to go to Washington on forty-eight hours' notice at your convenience," Roosevelt concluded.[33]

As soon as Secretary Stimson saw the telegram in the newspapers, he called up President Hoover, and found him very much excited because Roosevelt was apparently trying to play politics with the Saint Lawrence waterway. At first, Hoover was ready to blame Stimson because Stimson during the preceding year had negotiated quietly with the Power Authority of the State of New York. Stimson was unable to make the President see "how much politics we had saved during the year by our conduct." He shared the President's indignation but urged him not to take too truculent an attitude toward Roosevelt because it would be undignified and would make matters worse. So Hoover wired in reply that it would not be necessary for Roosevelt to interrupt his cruise to come to Washington, since questions between New York and the Federal Government could be settled only through the Congress after the treaty was negotiated. "Having ardently advocated for over ten years the great work of completing this shipway from Duluth and Chicago to the sea," Hoover remarked, "I am glad to know that it will meet with your support." [34]

Roosevelt clearly won out with progressives on this interchange. At the same time that he gave the press his telegram to President Hoover, he released a Power Authority report accusing the State Department of wanting to charge the State of New York so much for construction costs on the American side that it would frustrate the attempt of New York to produce cheap electricity. Sumner Welles complained to Roosevelt that it was President Hoover who was playing politics, that he was making unnecessary concessions to Canada in his eagerness to get the treaty concluded before the campaign got under way.[35]

In Washington, Senators Norris, La Follette, and Edward P. Costigan all agreed that Roosevelt had scored against Hoover. Norris, whom Hoover regarded as a great master of demagoguery, suggested that Roosevelt might reply further that Hoover was taking a highly technical position, and in his refusal was breaking State Department pledges to the Power Authority.* But, for the time being, Governor Roosevelt said no more. He had scored a hit; for the moment he was satisfied, and saved his remaining power ammunition to fire in the Northwest. Meanwhile progressives still did not know exactly how he stood on national power policies.[36]

The liberal intelligentsia worried also about Roosevelt and Tammany. Well into the summer, the great question mark of Mayor Jimmy Walker continued to hang over Governor Roosevelt as Walker continued to delay answering Roosevelt's charges. It left Roosevelt, at the very time that he needed to work on his campaign speeches, still

* The United States and Canada signed a treaty July 18, 1932, but the Senate shelved it after the election, and did not ratify a Saint Lawrence treaty until 1954.

perched on the same uncomfortable dilemma that he had been riding since early June. He was making headway in placating the Eastern machines, yet continued delay over Walker might jeopardize liberal support.

From Chicago, that erstwhile Bull Mooser, Harold L. Ickes, warned, "While many independents and Republicans are favorably inclined toward you at this time I find that they are not prepared to make up their minds finally until you have passed upon the case of Mayor Walker." * Professor William E. Dodd reported to Roosevelt that every man and woman he had interviewed in the week after the convention promptly and positively urged Walker's immediate removal. Professor T. V. Smith, Clarence Darrow, Robert Bulkley, and Herbert Friedman, spending a week end together, all agreed that if Roosevelt could be brought to remove the Mayor, it would tremendously aid the Democratic ticket.[38]

Roosevelt, well aware of this liberal groundswell, let it be known to newspapermen that he was irked over Walker's stalling tactics. When Walker finally on July 28 sent a lengthy and evasive answer, Roosevelt acted promptly. He accepted a rebuttal from Seabury, gave Walker only four days for an answer, and, on August 5, summoned Walker to appear before him in the executive chamber in Albany to answer charges. Roosevelt was determined to see it through. "It may last two days, or two weeks," he commented. "No escape!"

The date Governor Roosevelt set for the hearing was August 11; perhaps it was not entirely coincidence that this was also the date the Republicans had set for President Hoover's acceptance address.[39]

The dramatic opening of the hearings nudged the acceptance speech for top position in the newspapers. Even the conservative New York *Times*, in unusually broad headlines, proclaimed on the right-hand side, "Hoover Admits Failure of Prohibition," and on the left, "Governor Queries Mayor on Sisto Bonds." Mayor Walker, still looking youthful if one did not peer too closely, was in a bitter and defiant mood, ready with his lawyers to circumvent the questions and to seek refuge in every possible technicality. Governor Roosevelt, hardly noticed by the crowds outside, slipped into his secret elevator and up to the executive chamber, where he took personal charge of the hearing with a quiet dignity. He had prepared diligently for the proceed-

* In the spring of 1932, Ickes had tried to organize a movement among Republicans to repudiate President Hoover and nominate Gifford Pinchot.[37]

ing;* flanked and aided by his distinguished counsel, Martin Conboy, he began a brilliant and merciless questioning of Walker.

In the executive chamber, Roosevelt avoided as much as possible any hint of politics, and consciously tried as hard as he could to be objective. Yet to the entire nation, the drama was obvious. More was involved than the potential removal of the playboy Mayor of New York City: the possible loss to Roosevelt of New York State in the election. And so far as anyone knew in August, the loss of his home state might mean the loss of the election.[41]

Day after day, Roosevelt put aside his politicking and speech writing to sit at the hearings, either himself questioning Walker and the witnesses, or listening attentively while Conboy did. The hearing went on relentlessly. Walker tried to stop it with a court order but failed to obtain one. As the time approached for Roosevelt to begin active campaigning, he stepped up the pace by holding additional sessions from eight to eleven in the evening. The hearing was dragging on, Roosevelt complained to Frankfurter, "but I am confident that it is best I should not give them any chance to say that I am railroading the case." [42]

As Roosevelt fired questions over his flattop desk at the fidgeting Walker, his stature grew throughout the country. Many a thoughtful person who had doubted the depth and capacity of this debonair, sometimes compromising governor began to regard him with a new respect. One of his Brain Trusters, Berle, a superb law professor, congratulated Roosevelt on the nature of his accomplishment. "To manhandle a situation of this sort into a proceeding which is both dignified, pointed, and fruitful, is an achievement of the first order," Berle declared. "It is doubly so since you have not the buttress of a codified procedure which supports judges on the bench." [43]

Throughout the hearings, Walker failed to give Roosevelt any better answers than he had given Seabury. At a few points he departed from his earlier testimony. The nation wondered if at the conclusion Roosevelt would find some device for censuring Walker but leaving

* FDR had not only mastered Walker's earlier testimony, but prepared himself for eventualities. He wrote Frankfurter four days before the hearing, "I shall have a bad time if Walker insists on calling and cross examining all the witnesses, etc. . . . I have, of course, complete discretion, but it is my feeling that if Walker gives specific reasons to cross examine definite witnesses on definite points, I must summon them in order to avoid the obvious effort to make it appear that he is about to be convicted after the prosecution has been heard, without opportunity for him to cross examine. I wish you would give me your slant on this." [40]

him in office, or if he would actually remove him. Certainly Roosevelt expected to be exceedingly careful in coming to a decision.* He invited Frankfurter to come to Albany whenever the hearing ended "to talk with me in strict confidence about the ethics and the law involved." Judge Rosenman, who had been his counsel during most of his administration, has concluded, "I am sure that he was becoming persuaded by the testimony that Walker should be removed, and that he was getting ready to do so." [44]

Roosevelt never had to decide. On the evening of September 1, Roosevelt, in his study in Albany, was arguing hotly with a delegation of prominent Democrats who were urging him to let Walker off, when a telegram came. Walker had resigned as mayor.[45]

The resignation was a splendid triumph for Roosevelt. He and his advisers were greatly relieved; he could now concentrate entirely upon the campaign. But in one respect he had never left the campaign. Judge Bingham of the Louisville *Courier-Journal* summed up the consensus when he wrote Roosevelt, "I am convinced you made no new enemies, but, on the other hand, you gave a host of people throughout the country an opportunity to know you. It was a grand job, fearlessly, fairly, nobly done." [46]

As for the Tammanyites, they were, of course, surly and resentful, but not to the point of daring to knife the ticket. Throughout the East, Smith Democrats continued to nurture no love for Roosevelt. Wilson's former secretary, Joseph Tumulty, commented on the indifference and lack of enthusiasm of the Irish voting population in New Jersey. Tumulty even thought it was growing deeper and more menacing, and that the Walker resignation would mean a split in New York State. He was wrong in considering Roosevelt to be in jeopardy, for he overlooked the fact that much as some of these voters might dislike Roosevelt, on the whole they were suffering painfully from the depression and disliked Hoover even more bitterly. Admiration for Roosevelt might not drive them to the polls, but hatred against Hoover would.[47]

The nearest Boss Curry dared come to retaliation was to deny Judge Rosenman what ordinarily would have been automatic nomination for his Supreme Court seat. Roosevelt wired Rosenman, "I have a long memory and a long arm for my friends." Within less than a

* Moley remembers that one day FDR mused to him, "What if I gave the little mayor hell and then let him off?" Then FDR shook his head and added, "No, that would be weak."

year, Rosenman was back on the bench, and Curry was out as Tammany leader. Curry would have liked to carry his vengeance one step further to deny Lehman nomination as Governor of New York. He even managed to line up sufficient delegates to do so, but this had the interesting result of bringing Al Smith to Lehman's rescue. With both Roosevelt and Smith behind him, Lehman boldly faced Tammany and secured the nomination.[48]

For Roosevelt, the outcome was most felicitous. He was happy not only over the nomination of Lehman, whose warm cooperation at Albany he could expect, but also over once again having Smith fighting on his side.

At the state convention, Smith was sitting on the floor as a delegate when Governor Roosevelt came up onto the platform. Smith strode down the aisle and joined him. "Hello, Frank, I'm glad to see you," Jim Farley heard Smith say. Roosevelt responded, "Hello, Al, I'm glad to see you too – and that's from the heart." A newspaperman nearby, unable to hear their exact words, wired that Smith, pumping Roosevelt's hand, had shouted, "Hello, you old potato." The phrase caught the fancy of editorial writers and Smith's followers. The rift was closed, at least for the duration of the campaign. In the weeks that followed, Smith orated vigorously for Roosevelt. Some of what he said may not have helped in the West, but in the estimation of Farley, it did much to bring out the vote for Roosevelt in the East.[49]

In this happy fashion, Roosevelt managed to hold on to the Eastern organization vote without losing that of Western liberals. It was one further example of his skill as a political navigator, as he directed his man-of-war, now to starboard, then to port, throughout the campaign. He shifted course from time to time in a fashion infuriating to his political opponents, and sometimes rather saddening to his supporters, but almost always with calculated intelligence and with profitable results. Though he tacked occasionally to the right, he customarily bore much harder to the left.

CHAPTER XXIII

The Big Trip to the Coast

As you know, I love campaigning.
— FDR TO THOMAS J. WALSH, *July 26, 1932.*

NO matter what the risk of junketing around the United States, Roosevelt never had any intention of conducting his campaign from a rocking chair. Professional after professional warned him that campaign trips seldom won votes and frequently lost them. They reminded him how McKinley from his front porch had beaten the barnstorming Bryan; how Hughes had gone into California and inevitably run afoul of two rival factions of his party; how Harding had beaten Cox in 1920 when Roosevelt himself was on the hustings. All Roosevelt had to do, they reiterated, was to play it safe * and give a few national radio speeches.[2]

What they feared above all was that Roosevelt might collapse on the trip. Farley assured one of the most vehement exponents of the stay-at-home viewpoint that he agreed wholeheartedly. But Roosevelt required more convincing argument. Granting that there were two schools of thought concerning the advisability of a trip to the coast, he asked Senator Walsh's opinion. He assured Walsh that although he loved campaigning, he would do no barnstorming, and make only two speeches on the entire trip. Walsh surprisingly wrote Roosevelt what he wanted to hear, that on reflection he thought a trip to the Pacific Coast would do much to dispel any remaining whispers about Roosevelt's lack of physical endurance. This was all the encouragement Roosevelt needed. Without it, he undoubtedly would have gone anyway on what he referred to as "the big trip to the Coast." [3]

Before he started off, he wrote Josephus Daniels that he was glad

* Senator Dill, for example, warned Farley, "I hope it will be possible for him to avoid making jaunts around the country. The candidates that do are never elected. He has such a fine reason to stay at home since there are so many things to do as Governor. I know how well he likes to barnstorm, but let him do that after he gets into the White House." [1]

he had had the 1920 experience because otherwise he would be worried by the prospect. That was mere bravado, for campaigning was an unending delight to Roosevelt. Moley caught the significance of it when he wrote, "It was broad rivers, green forests, waving corn, and undulating wheat; it was crowds of friends, from the half dozen who, seated on a baggage truck, waved to the cheery face at the speeding window to perspiring thousands at a race track or fairground; it was hands extended in welcome, voices warm with greeting, faces reflecting his smile along the interminable wayside." [4]

As of the end of July, Roosevelt was thinking of going to Seattle, then down the coast to Portland, San Francisco, and Los Angeles, thence East to a big homecoming celebration at Warm Springs, Georgia. He planned later to take two short trips, one to the Middle West and the other to New England. Through August, the plans for the trip grew and grew, but as they grew they necessitated more and more homework, and a few preliminary speeches in the East.[5]

Roosevelt opened his formal campaigning at the end of July when he discussed and amplified the Democratic platform in a radio broadcast from Albany. It was notable mainly for the fact that he now introduced the nation to the quiet, persuasive speaking manner to which the people of New York had already become accustomed from hearing his reports to them on the alleged shortcomings of the legislature. "In the olden days, campaigns were conducted amid surroundings of brass bands and red lights," he began. "Oratory was an appeal primarily to the emotions and sometimes to the passions." And he went on to explain that he was interested in the spread of education through newspapers and radio, and an appeal to reason in the quiet of the home. He spoke to them "in this quiet of common sense and friendliness," more effectively approaching their emotions than he could possibly have done through old-fashioned oratory.[6]

Republican economic policies were Roosevelt's target in his first major address before a political gathering, at the Democratic state convention at Columbus, Ohio, August 20. He attacked the Republican policies in terms which every listener should be able to understand, or at least to find entertaining. The subject was rather dreary as he planned it, "a general indictment of the Hoover Administration, basing it on Hoover's own speeches, promises, and actions," but he enlivened it by planting in the center an *Alice in Wonderland* parody of Republican policies of the 1920's:

A puzzled, somewhat skeptical Alice asked the Republican leadership some simple questions:

"Will not the printing and selling of more stocks and bonds, the building of new plants and the increase of efficiency produce more goods than we buy?"

"No," shouted Humpty Dumpty. "The more we produce the more we can buy."

"What if we produce a surplus?"

"Oh, we can sell it to foreign consumers."

"How can the foreigners pay for it?"

"Why, we will lend them the money."

"I see," said little Alice, "they will buy our surplus with our money. Of course, these foreigners will pay us back by selling us their goods?"

"Oh, not at all," said Humpty Dumpty. "We set up a high wall called the tariff."

"And," said Alice at last, "how will the foreigners pay off these loans?"

"That is easy," said Humpty Dumpty, "did you ever hear of moratorium?" [7]

To Republicans this speech was a monumental folly, but Democrats and many independents were delighted. Sumner Welles reported that it had an amazing effect in Maryland; Claude Bowers called it a humdinger; Colonel House reported that it had won over Norman Hapgood; and the ordinarily critical Oswald Garrison Villard expressed his delight to Roosevelt that he had "handled Hoover without gloves." Robert Woolley suggested the technique was excellent for throwing Hoover off balance. "If there is one thing that Hoover cannot stand it is attack," he reported to Roosevelt.* "He flinches and withers under it. . . . More power to your tongue and your elbow!" [8]

Roosevelt had no intention of repeating himself. Rather he shifted themes completely when he drove into New Jersey a week later. Demonstrating Democrats met him in town after town as he passed through Boss Hague's domain to Governor A. Harry Moore's summer home at Sea Girt. Hague had promised him the biggest political rally ever held in the United States, and to Farley it seemed as though

* Woolley declared: "Every time Jim Reed would lambaste [Hoover] on the floor of the Senate in the days when he was Food Administrator, he would complain to the President; on several occasions offering to resign, so Tumulty tells me. Newspaper correspondents also tell me that he is more sensitive to criticism than ever."

Photo by Acme. By permission of the Director of the Franklin D. Roosevelt Library

FDR and his children on arrival at Chicago, Illinois, by plane, to receive notification of his nomination for the Presidency. July 2, 1932

By permission of the Director of the Franklin D. Roosevelt Library

FDR and Al Smith at a Democratic rally in the Academy of Music at Brooklyn, New York, November 4, 1932

Hague had kept his word. Acres of people, an estimated hundred thousand or more, stretched in front of the speaker's platform on Governor Moore's lawn. It was a typical Hague rally – an exciting Democratic vaudeville performance, with comedians, a band, aerial bombs, and airplanes flying overhead.[9]

Before this thirsty crowd of city dwellers on that rather hot summer day, Roosevelt delivered a reasoned speech in favor of repeal. He charged the Republicans with evasion, and himself took a firm stand as an honest Wet. Republican Representative James M. Beck of Pennsylvania sneered at his careful talk as coming from "Little Lord Fauntleroy," and Representative William E. Hull of Illinois claimed that the Democrats had not broadcast the speech because they did not want it heard in the West and South. Perhaps this was true, but newspapers nationally carried Roosevelt's firm words. He had placated Eastern Wets without arousing animus in the West and South. The editor of the *Oklahoma Farmer-Stockman* had assured him, "The farm people in our section are hardly interested in prohibition as an issue in this campaign. They are still dry and will vote dry. Economic issues take precedence with them." [10]

Roosevelt was far more concerned about the West than the East; he would not have risked saying anything to Hague's minions that might have had unfortunate repercussions in the hinterland. While he had been wooing Easterners and businessmen, he had been paying even more attention to Westerners and farmers. He entertained his old schoolmate Colonel Robert R. McCormick of the Chicago *Tribune;* they were again on "Frank" and "Bertie" terms. McCormick assigned a trusted young reporter, John Boettiger, to cover the campaign; a few years later he became Roosevelt's son-in-law. The implications of this renewed friendship were weighty indeed throughout the corn belt.[11]

Roosevelt, with his eye on the West, was able also to retain the cordiality of the Hearst press throughout the nation. Arthur Brisbane, Hearst's star columnist, came to visit at Hyde Park, and lamented later that he could not describe in his column, "the house in which you live . . . the old furniture, with no concessions to the new, modernistic foolishness." Brisbane, at Roosevelt's request, arranged for Cissy Patterson, who was leasing Hearst's Washington *Herald,* to come to lunch a few days later. And the formidable lord of San Simeon himself wired early in July inviting Roosevelt to stay at his ranch when he came to California.* Roosevelt declined, but arranged to see Hearst in Los Angeles for a good talk. Fortunately for Roosevelt, Hearst and Brisbane had no inkling that Roosevelt might have some new, modernistic trappings in his mind; and throughout the campaign they boomed him with especial effectiveness in the West.[13]

Above all, as Roosevelt prepared for his Western junket, he concentrated upon the farmers. They remained in the forefront of his thinking; they would be the key to his victory. This did not mean that it would be easy to hold them in line, for they varied enormously among themselves in their demands. It was not simple to work out a formula which would appeal to the broad political spectrum ranging from the conservative Board of Trade representatives to the violent followers of Milo Reno. What Roosevelt had to offer to all of them was some sort of vague conglomeration of principles in which those who knew what to look for could see the hazy outline of the domestic-allotment plan.

Roosevelt's eleventh-hour conversion to domestic allotment just before the convention necessitated several disavowals during the summer. There was not only the embarrassing *Collier's* statement, but also a rather clear-cut commitment to McNary-Haugenism and an attack upon easy credit that appeared at the end of July in Roosevelt's book *Government, Not Politics*.† This upset a South Dakota editor who was one of Roosevelt's key correspondents on farm matters. Morgenthau also worried about the inconsistency. But not Roosevelt. He had a letter drafted in reply saying that when he wrote the chapter he had not given full consideration to more recent proposals, and that the statement in his acceptance speech expressed more clearly his present attitude.[14]

Roosevelt's nomination had brought into his camp not only General Johnson but also Johnson's close friend and former business associate in the Moline Plow Company, George N. Peek. It was at the very moment that Roosevelt was abandoning McNary-Haugenism that he acquired the support of the strongest advocate of overseas dumping. When Johnson through Baruch took an advance look at Roosevelt's acceptance address, he wired Peek that it was very hasty, but "We will get what we want. Hold all fire." Peek replied, "My training was

* At about the same time, FDR's friend Richard Crane tried to convince Newton D. Baker, who was lukewarm toward FDR because of Hearst's supporting him, that Hearst had done his best for Garner at the convention until the end.[12]

† The endorsement of McNary-Haugenism originally appeared in one of a series of articles in *Liberty* magazine that Earl Looker ghosted for FDR.

holding the plow not holding fire but will try." What he wanted was for Roosevelt to call upon the Democratic majority in Congress to pass farm legislation immediately, even though President Hoover would veto it. Speaker Garner declined to work for it since it would be a waste of time. Johnson admonished Peek to be patient. "Hold your horses," he wired. "Our man is not yet the boss. He honestly intends to act. The job now is to let us know exactly whom he should consult and whom he should ask to prepare specific plan." [15]

So far as Roosevelt was concerned, the Hope-Norbeck and Rainey-Norbeck bills, which included some aspects of domestic allotment, had not been developed for use in his campaign. But the Republican opposition to them in the summer of 1932 played into his hands. Nor were Peek and others insistent that Roosevelt should take the politically dangerous step of flatly advocating a single plan. "I question wisdom of candidate committing himself to definite plan at present," Peek wired Johnson. "It may be better to cover definite principles and defer setting up of specific plan for opponents to pick flaws in." [16]

What made Roosevelt's task comparatively simple was again the fact that he did not need to satisfy farm leaders in entirety in order to gain their support. He was in their eyes far preferable to Hoover. Peek was not ready to endorse Roosevelt too enthusiastically until he made stronger statements, but explained, "We know that we cannot expect anything from Hoover and I hope we may expect much from Roosevelt. Continuation of the policies of the last twelve years, in my judgment, would spell disaster to the country." Hoover further reduced the pressure upon Roosevelt when in his acceptance speech he defended his unpopular Farm Board, and warned against the dangers of government loans or subsidies to farmers and the extension of bureaucracy to aid them.[17]

Consequently, as Roosevelt received farm envoys at Hyde Park, he was able to avoid promising them much. He used his well-polished technique of querying them on their problems and suggestions, then nodding in sympathetic understanding. Any remarks he made were broadly inclusive, or likely to be specific references to his own problems as a farmer in New York or Georgia. When he invited Representative Hatton W. Sumners to visit him to talk about agricultural exportable surpluses, he commented that while many people thought he should concentrate only upon wheat, he wished to consider cotton also. "As you know," he declared, "I am a cotton grower myself." When the heads of farm cooperatives came to Hyde Park and criticized the grain stabilization activities of the Farm Board, Roosevelt commented sympathetically without committing himself. Conservative Byrd of Virginia, one of the nation's biggest apple growers, came to make his political peace, and Roosevelt asked him to tell the reporters about the iniquities of the tariff, which was leading to overseas retaliation against American apples.[18] On another occasion, Tugwell brought to Hyde Park M. L. Wilson, chief planner of Roosevelt's agricultural pronouncements. Roosevelt listened, smiled, nodded, and at the end threw back his head, made a sweeping gesture with his glasses, and laughingly exclaimed, "Have you been telling me your plan, Mr. Wilson; or have I been telling you mine!"

Roosevelt avoided the political dangers of conferring with the conservative Board of Trade; he sent Morgenthau, his roving ambassador on farm matters, to talk to them instead. In the other direction, he had little personally to do with Milo Reno, whose approach to farm problems was as direct and violent as a punch in the nose. Reno was trying to get farm prices above production costs that summer by stopping milk and produce trucks from going to market. Roosevelt did no more than send him a ghosted letter accepting the principle of equality for agriculture and a price for farm products which would give the farmer the equivalent of a laborer's wage. He warned Reno that the solution would be complicated and could come only through the advice of farm leaders, intelligent unorganized farmers, and level-headed economists.[19]

At the same time, Roosevelt extended the hospitality of Hyde Park to the more safe and important farm leaders. On July 20, he conferred with Edward A. O'Neal, the president of the powerful American Farm Bureau Federation, who brought with him the vice-president and a director of the federation. O'Neal, a Southerner and a Democrat, expressed his pleasure over seeing Roosevelt's "great earnestness and strong desire to help agriculture." Roosevelt was at his most ingratiating, since the federation was the most powerful of the farm organizations, representing as it did the more successful corn-hog farmers of the Middle West and the cotton farmers of the South. While the federation maintained a technical nonpartisanship, O'Neal was obviously ardent in his support. In Washington, Chester H. Gray, the federation's lobbyist, carefully avoided appearance of partisan activity, but helped the Roosevelt cause.[20]

The Farm Bureau leaders helped Roosevelt plan a small conference of farm leaders, which would give him a broader base. He invited former Governor Frank O. Lowden of Illinois, most notable of the Republican farm leaders, to be chairman, in an effort to pull him into active support. Lowden was friendly, but preferred to remain in the Republican ranks, so the coup failed.[21]

In August, Morgenthau did persuade a notable maverick Republican farm leader to come to Hyde Park. This was the Iowa farm editor Henry A. Wallace, who had supported Smith in 1928 but was a registered Republican and the son of Harding's Secretary of Agriculture. Wallace arrived two days after the Walker hearings had begun, expecting to find Roosevelt worn out. To his surprise, he found a man "with a fresh, eager, open mind, ready to pitch into the agricultural thing at once." Wallace found Roosevelt quite skeptical about inflation; at lunch Morgenthau prodded Wallace to tell about the inflationary "Honest Dollar" sentiment in the Middle West. Wallace particularly had the iniquities of the Republican tariff on his mind, but in this line of reasoning he was by no means representative of disgruntled farmers of his section. Antiprotectionism was fine for the South but not the Middle West. Had Roosevelt followed it, he might have found himself in trouble. In any event, Roosevelt was less interested in what Wallace had to suggest than in the fact that he had secured an influential editor of the Farm Bureau persuasion who was ready to work for his cause. He immediately drew upon Wallace for aid on the farm speech.[22]

When Roosevelt was at Columbus on August 20, he conferred with the representative of a very numerous but quite different group of farmers from those for whom O'Neal and Wallace were spokesmen. This was John A. Simpson, President of the Farmers' Educational and Cooperative Union, which appealed to the smaller, poorer, more radical farmers. Roosevelt had seen Simpson in the spring, and at his insistence had included a "cost of production" statement in the Democratic platform. Immediately after the convention, Simpson had come out strongly for Roosevelt and begun vigorous campaigning.[23]

Simpson, talking like an old Populist of the 1890's, afterwards wrote Roosevelt, urging him to state publicly that he favored a cheaper dollar. He pointed out to Roosevelt that it took three bushels of wheat to purchase a dollar, and that those three bushels would make almost two hundred one-pound loaves of bread. Simpson wanted considerably more inflation than the "Honest Dollar" that Wallace was talking about, and behind him was an impressive amount of Western pressure. There were the silver interests, conspicuously present in Roosevelt's campaign entourage in the person of Senator Key Pittman of Nevada, and the greenback advocates, whose representative in the Senate was Elmer Thomas of Oklahoma.[24]

Inflation was the way in which Simpson hoped to get farm prices up above the cost of production. He wanted Roosevelt to reaffirm at Topeka his belief in an ample return for farmers, and in lower interest rates on farm mortgages. This was part of the credo of not only the Farmers' Union but also Reno's farm strikers; if Roosevelt accepted it, Simpson held out the lure of a rich political harvest. "If you will let the farmers know that you approve of the government regulating the marketing of farm crops just like they regulate the marketing of transportation," Simpson wrote him, "then all over this Nation the farmers will rise up like they did one hundred years ago, go to the polls and support you as they did Andrew Jackson in 1832." [25]

The harvest of farm votes became Roosevelt's principal objective as he prepared to travel westward. Early in July, Governor Woodring of Kansas had sent word that Kansans were keenly interested in a concrete program of farm relief, and that the key to the state would be the farm speech at Topeka. Roosevelt asked Woodring for suggestions, then turned to his Brain Trust, to Morgenthau, Wilson, and a score of others to draft him a speech.

The speech making machine went into action. Moley invited Wilson to prepare a memorandum as the basis for the speech. Wilson wrote what was no more than an elaborate outline, sounding the themes of "equality for agriculture" and voluntary domestic allotment. He went over it carefully with his friend and admirer, Wallace, and sent it in. This Tugwell in turn worked over. Morgenthau and his assistant, Herbert E. Gaston, who had once been a member of the radical Non Partisan League, prepared memoranda on the farm debt, oppressive farm taxation, and planned use of land. Hugh Johnson dashed off an exciting speech. Finally, Roosevelt dictated some other material and an introduction portraying himself as a friend of agriculture. All of this Moley then wove into a single draft, which began to go the rounds of the Brain Trust and undergo the knife of revision again and again. Berle contributed the phrase "political skywriting," Wilson the expression "the shadow of peasantry," and Roosevelt himself paraphrased Lincoln, "This Nation cannot endure if it is half 'boom' and half 'broke.' " Several farm editors and senators made corrections. The process of constructing this opus was not much more complex than that of producing many other speeches of the campaign, but

Moley estimated it came off the production line as "the direct product of more than twenty-five people!" [26]

The product of the brains factory was exactly what Roosevelt needed: a speech so broad in implications that it would encompass all the aspirations of Western farmers no matter what their prejudices, and at the same time so vague in its endorsement of domestic allotment that it would not frighten conservative Easterners. "It is the last word on agriculture," Roosevelt wrote, "and at the same time has plenty of punch." [27]

The agriculture address was typical of the speechmaking process in that while Roosevelt drew upon many experts and skilled speech writers like Moley, in most instances he himself made major contributions, just as he took entire responsibility. The speeches conveyed the ideas he accepted, and sometimes did so in his own words.

"My job from the beginning," Moley has pointed out, "was to sift proposals for him, discuss facts and ideas with him, and help him crystallize his own policy. . . . I constantly tried to induce Roosevelt to dictate as much as he possibly could between speeches and appointments. I then spun together the pertinent material, as in the agriculture speech. This new draft Roosevelt would pencil over with comments. The draft would shuttle back and forth, back and forth, between us until the language of the original memorandum prepared by someone or other was almost completely obliterated." [28]

After weeks of this sort of preparation, Roosevelt started out on his Western jaunt, loaded with drafts of speeches and full of enthusiasm. He carried with him the almost incredible news that the Democrats had carried the state elections in Maine. It was a cheering portent, since Republicans had made much of the slogan, "As Maine goes, so goes the nation." Senator John S. Cohen of Georgia wired congratulations and reiterated his prediction that Hoover would carry only eight states. Roosevelt wired back, "Privately, I believe you are not optimistic enough in your forecast." [29]

On the train out to Topeka, Frank W. Murphy of Minnesota got into a hot argument with Moley over several figures in the speech, and over Roosevelt's statement that the farm plan must not be coercive. Moley argued that the speech had already been given to the press, and checked the figures by telegraph with the Department of Agriculture. They were accurate. What really hurt Murphy was the emphasis upon voluntary action. Peek consoled Murphy by agreeing that his first impression was that it was "a gratuitous slap in the face of many people who had done most to bring the farm situation to national attention," but Peek and Murphy both went right on supporting Roosevelt.[30]

This preview rather clearly foreshadowed farm leaders' reception of the speech. It completely satisfied no one but perhaps a few who had had a hand in the writing. Even one of those, Wallace, left Topeka for Iowa far less enthusiastic about Roosevelt than he had been about Smith four years earlier. But it completely alienated not a one of them, representing as it did the consensus of all Roosevelt's correspondence and discussion with them throughout the summer.* At the same time, Roosevelt's financial and industrial friends thought it a masterpiece.[32]

Much of the speech was unexceptionable: his description of himself as a farmer, and of his farm program in New York State; his emphasis upon the economic necessity for farm prosperity; and his attacks upon the Hoover farm policies. Pungently he declared:

"When the futility of maintaining prices of wheat and cotton, through so-called stabilization, became apparent, the President's Farm Board . . . invented the cruel joke of advising farmers to allow twenty percent of their wheat lands to lie idle, to plow up every third row of cotton and to shoot every tenth dairy cow. Surely they knew that this advice would not – indeed, could not – be taken." [33]

Roosevelt was quite correct that this advice could not be taken, not without a guarantee of some financial return to the farmer. With all this, and with his positive demands for a reorganization of the Department of Agriculture, for land-use planning, tax reduction, and easier farm credit, few farmers would disagree. Some of them might take exception to his call for tariff reform. But they were all waiting for him to come to the crux of his program.

What this was, Roosevelt made clear only to those who knew the language of farm leaders of the West. He said he would compose the conflicting elements of their plans to arrive at the goal of economic

* Earl C. Smith, President of the Illinois Agricultural Association, unconsciously analyzed the political brilliance of the speech when he complained to Peek: "To those of us who have been very closely associated with previous efforts to solve the farm problem, a number of things could be read into his speech. Within the last two days I have been told by men in position to know that John Simpson . . . says 'The Governor was referring specially to the Farmers Union solution to the question. . . .' To many others, they are equally sure he was referring to the voluntary allotment plan of Mr. Wilson. Still others of us believe, as you well know, that his speech could refer to the principles of the Rainey bill." [31]

equality for agriculture with other industries within the United States. "I seek to give to that portion of the crop consumed in the United States," he asserted, "a benefit equivalent to a tariff sufficient to give you farmers an adequate price."

These were his specifications: First, it must provide a benefit of this size to the producers of staple surplus commodities such as wheat, cotton, hogs, and tobacco. Second, it must finance itself. Third, it must not involve dumping outside the United States. Fourth, it must use existing agencies and be decentralized outside of Washington. Fifth, it must operate as nearly as possible on a cooperative basis. Sixth, it must, so far as possible, be voluntary. It should not go into operation unless it had the support of a reasonable majority of the producers.[34]

At several points Roosevelt had departed from Wilson's draft and domestic-allotment proposals. He failed to mention production control or reduced acreage, or a processing tax, all of which were to form integral parts of the Agricultural Adjustment Administration. What he had said represented the ultimate point to which he was willing to go in outlining his agricultural program during the campaign. General Johnson assured Peek, "Of course the Governor will have to make another speech after Hoover shoots his blast. We will then tie up the loose ends." But Roosevelt saw only danger in the prospect of making himself any more explicit during the remaining weeks of the campaign. In further addresses on the farm problem at Sioux City, Iowa, Springfield, Illinois, and Atlanta, Georgia, he talked about tax relief and easier credit, but on the basic program simply referred his listeners to the six points he had set forth at Topeka.[35]

There was controversy about the reception of that key speech. Newspapers declared that the crowd numbered only ten to eighteen thousand people, and that it was relatively unenthusiastic. On the other hand, Murphy exuberantly estimated it at twenty-five thousand, and emphasized that it was strongly on Roosevelt's side. Wallace reported after his return to Des Moines that the speech had made a splendid impression upon the radio audience of Iowa. "They gained the idea from the air that your speech was more enthusiastically received than was actually the case," Wallace candidly asserted. "It seemed to me that the Kansas farmers listened to you very attentively and that they were so interested most of them did not care to applaud." [36]

The fact was that agricultural conditions were becoming so alarmingly desperate that an explosion threatened. Picketing in the Sioux

City area had gone on for five weeks, and several days after Roosevelt's speech, Reno ordered a general selling holiday to begin in all the Middle Western states. Arthur Capper's *Kansas Farmer* in July had editorially warned readers against violence, the use of guns, and mob rule. In Iowa, six hundred banks had failed, and the price of corn was so low that it took more than a ton to purchase a ton of the cheapest coal. Simpson reported to Roosevelt, "In North Dakota last week, wheat averaged thirty cents a bushel, oats and barley seven cents." [37]

The conclusion was clear to Simpson, who was holding meetings at which Roosevelt was lustily cheered and Hoover ridiculed and derided. "The Republicans are going to have to do some fast work to convince farmers they are bringing prosperity," he commented. Roosevelt need worry little about the Republicans, but they worried seriously about him. Senator Dickinson of Iowa sneered, "Glittering generalities will not bring farm relief," and the White House announced the day after the Topeka speech that President Hoover, contrary to his earlier plans, would take to the road to expound his principles. Roosevelt urged Baruch to "take a good crack in a formal statement at whoever among the Republican musketeers answers my Topeka agricultural speech." [38]

President Hoover hit repeatedly upon a more sensitive subject as he tried to force Roosevelt to commit himself upon his proposed monetary policies. If Roosevelt were to commit himself to inflation, it would do him irreparable damage in the East. And even the degree of inflation would be a matter of serious debate among the opposing farm groups. As a result of the farm strike, two clearly opposing organizations were consolidating their strength in the West, the Farmers' National Relief Conference, made up of those groups which had supported the holiday, and the National Agricultural Conference, made up of the Farm Bureau, the Grange, and the farm cooperative organizations. The more radical farmers wanted far more inflation, yet even the more conservative ones wanted some manipulation of the dollar. If Roosevelt came out as a sound-money man, it would hurt him with almost all farmers.[39]

Early in the campaign, a young economist working with the Brain Trust came to President Hoover to warn him that Roosevelt intended to tinker with currency if he were elected. This led Hoover to press Roosevelt on money again and again. But Roosevelt said nothing until the very end of the campaign, when he ambivalently declared at Brooklyn, "The President is seeing visions of rubber dollars." He went on to reiterate his belief in a sound currency not only for the United States but for the whole world, but this did not mean a deflated currency. His one firm commitment was to the gold clause in government bonds. He declared that Senator Carter Glass had made a devastating challenge to President Hoover "that no responsible government would have sold its securities payable in gold if it knew that the promise — yes, the covenant — embodied in these securities was as dubious as the President of the United States claims it was." [40]

Certainly Roosevelt followed a policy of wisdom in staying away from the money question during the campaign. Wallace granted this, but warned Roosevelt that many farm people were afraid that he was no better than Hoover on it. Privately, Wallace was pointing out to them exactly the things that Hoover feared, that Roosevelt was closely associated with Professor G. F. Warren of Cornell University, who favored modifying the gold content of the dollar. Further, Roosevelt at Columbus had assured one of Wallace's reporters that he favored the inflationary Goldsborough proposal which President Hoover was referring to as the "rubber dollar" bill.[41]

Thus through well-worded generalizations on the domestic-allotment plan and complete silence on inflation, Roosevelt campaigned past the perils and secured a decisive majority of the farm vote. Even before Roosevelt spoke at Topeka, Senator Thomas P. Gore of Oklahoma wired him, "If every Democrat in Iowa should be put in jail on election day you would carry President Hoover's native state anyway." [42]

Roosevelt was over the most difficult ideological hurdle in his campaign. When he appeared in the Mormon Tabernacle in Salt Lake City, he sat in the Mormon Apostle's chair, normally occupied by Republican Senator Reed Smoot of tariff fame. Senator Smoot was not there, but might just as well have been, for nothing in Roosevelt's speech would have offended his ears. Roosevelt promised increased government aid to railroads and Interstate Commerce Commission regulation of competing motor carriers.* What he said had come out of his conferences with heads of railroads; he declared that it differed from President Hoover's program in that he proposed rehabilitation, while the President would only loan more money and thus in the end increase the financial burden of the railroads. The differences, how-

* This speech was largely the work of Berle and of Donald Richberg, counsel of the Railroad Labor Executive Association. They drew upon William Woodin, Ralph Budd, and Joseph B. Eastman of the I.C.C. for suggestions.[43]

ever, were so slight that Republicans accused Roosevelt of stealing President Hoover's program.[44]

By the time Roosevelt reached Seattle on September 20, he was in full stride as a campaigner. The weather was so crisp that he wore a light overcoat and had to trade his Panama hat for a felt one. Between seventy-five and a hundred thousand people stood at the curbs, shouting "Hurrah for Franklin" as Roosevelt rode from the station to his hotel. The reception was so unexpectedly large and warm that he elaborated his planned remarks of a thousand words into a lengthier speech. The theme was his well-known position on reciprocal trade. The peroration was equally familiar, but it set the pattern of Roosevelt's campaigning in the West. "All my life I have been a doer, not a phrasemaker," he asserted, "and I ask your help in support of liberal views and liberal measures. I ask in the name of a stricken America and a stricken world." [45]

As a liberal, Roosevelt appeared in Portland the next day to set forth his power policies.* Up to this point, progressives had taken his position somewhat on faith. Judson King, Director of the National Popular Government League, had supported Roosevelt on the basis of what others had told him until he had a personal interview late in the summer. This sold King completely. "Outside of yourself," he wrote Norris, "I have never met an official in public life that has a firmer grip upon the technical requirements of the electrical fight." Norris himself was so convinced Roosevelt would follow his policies that he agreed to campaign actively, distasteful though the hustings were to him.[47]

What Norris felt he needed in order to win over Republican progressives was for Roosevelt to make a strong statement. He wrote Basil Manly, who was assisting Roosevelt on power matters, that Progressives would rally behind Roosevelt more on that issue than on any other. "Many of the Progressives have been somewhat disappointed with Roosevelt since his nomination because he has remained practically silent on that subject," Norris pointed out. "They ask me the concrete question as to what Roosevelt would have done with the Muscle Shoals bill which Hoover vetoed. Of course, I can give them only my opinion, which sometimes does not satisfy them." [48]

At Portland, Roosevelt said everything that Norris and King could

* It was well for FDR to display himself there in his full vigor, for Mayor Curley, speaking in Portland a few days earlier, had slipped by describing Roosevelt as nominating Al Smith, in 1928, seated in a wheel chair and against doctors' advice. This was untrue, and exactly what Republicans were whispering.[46]

wish. He set forth the same firm views on public-utility regulation that he had expressed so often as Governor of New York: regulatory commissions should be tribunes of the people, and they should set rates on a prudent-investment basis. Further he proposed full regulation of all utility securities, intercompany contracts, and holding companies. He did not advocate public ownership and operation of all utilities, but set forth his belief that where communities were not satisfied with private service or rates, they should have the right to establish their own government-owned and -operated service. This could create a yardstick to measure private rates. The Federal Government similarly should have the right to operate its own power business wherever essential to protect the public against inefficient service or exorbitant charges — and by implication this meant operation, as Norris wished, of the Federal facilities at Muscle Shoals on the Tennessee River.* And Roosevelt's peroration was a telling one:

"Judge me by the enemies I have made. Judge me by the selfish purposes of these utility leaders who have talked of radicalism while they were selling watered stock to the people and using our schools to deceive the coming generation." [50]

Indeed, Roosevelt had succeeded brilliantly in aligning himself with the Republican progressives on this issue. From Washington, Senator Norris proclaimed that Roosevelt's policy would "put the power trust out of business." [51]

It was as a progressive that Roosevelt traveled down into California, which before the First World War had been the greatest stronghold of the Progressive party, and where Republican Senator Hiram Johnson, who had run for Vice President on Theodore Roosevelt's Bull Moose ticket, was still powerful politically. General Johnson and Howe had wanted Roosevelt to speak at San Francisco in a conservative vein, on government economy. Instead, Roosevelt courted Senator Johnson and his following by delivering before the Commonwealth Club the most notable affirmation of his political liberalism of the entire campaign.† His Portland speech on power may have done much

* Leland Olds contributed substantially to the speech; Pittman helped some on it, and Owen D. Young contributed the suggestion that municipalities be allowed to build their own plants if they could not obtain satisfactory rates. Moley assembled the suggestions and wrote the draft.[49]

† Berle, who along with Tugwell and Frankfurter formed the left wing of FDR's advisers, wrote the memorandum which formed the basis for the Commonwealth Club speech. Moley later wished he had deleted some of Berle's contributions that appeared in the speech as FDR delivered it.[52]

to win over old Progressives; his San Francisco speech did much to fill them with enthusiasm.[53]

At the outset, Roosevelt sketched the history and political philosophies of the American people, aligning himself, as always, with the Jeffersonians. He pointed out how those who had built the railroads and industrial empires out of the great unused natural resources of the United States had done so at a high price to the public, and with government assistance during Republican administrations. Nevertheless, the return to the American people had outweighed the cost, until the frontier disappeared at about the turn of the century. Progressives at that point had tried to restore economic equality and curb the great uncontrolled and irresponsible power of the industrial combinations. President Wilson had tried to solve the problem, but had been diverted by war. Consequently, it remained unsolved into the 1930's. As Roosevelt saw it in 1932:

"Equality of opportunity as we have known it no longer exists. Our industrial plant is built; the problem just now is whether under existing conditions it is not overbuilt. Our last frontier has long since been reached, and there is practically no more free land. More than half of our people do not live on the farms or on lands and cannot derive a living by cultivating their own property. There is no safety valve in the form of a Western prairie to which those thrown out of work by the Eastern economic machines can go for a new start. We are not able to invite the immigration from Europe to share our endless plenty. We are now providing a drab living for our own people."

What did Roosevelt propose as solutions? The day of the great promoter or financial titan was over; Americans could not turn to them. "Our task now is not discovery or exploitation of natural resources, or necessarily producing more goods," he asserted. "It is the soberer, less dramatic business of administering resources and plants already in hand, of seeking to reestablish foreign markets for our surplus production, of meeting the problem of underconsumption, of adjusting production to consumption, of distributing wealth and products more equitably, of adapting existing economic organizations to the service of the people. The day of the enlightened administration has come."

There was no hint of the National Recovery Administration in what Roosevelt suggested, but he did declare that the government must assist business in developing an economic constitutional order. He broadened what he had applied to utilities at Portland to include all business when he declared, "Private economic power is, to enlarge an old phrase, a public trust as well." This meant a social contract as old as the Republic and as new as the modern economy:

> Every man has a right to life; and this means that he has also a right to make a comfortable living. He may by sloth or crime decline to exercise that right; but it may not be denied him. We have no actual famine or dearth; our industrial and agricultural mechanism can produce enough and to spare. Our Government formal and informal, political and economic, owes to everyone an avenue to possess himself of a portion of that plenty sufficient for his needs, through his own work.
>
> Every man has a right to his own property; which means a right to be assured, to the fullest extent attainable, in the safety of his savings. By no other means can men carry the burdens of those parts of his life which, in the nature of things, afford no chance of labor; childhood, sickness, old age. In all thought of property, this right is paramount; all other property rights must yield to it. If, in accord with this principle, we must restrict the operations of the speculator, the manipulator, even the financier, I believe we must accept the restrictions as needful, not to hamper individualism but to protect it.

The role of the government, Roosevelt affirmed, was to police irresponsible economic power in order to achieve these ends. It should assume economic regulation only as a last resort, when private initiative failed. "As yet," Roosevelt pointed out, "there has been no final failure, because there has been no attempt, and I decline to assume that this Nation is unable to meet the situation." [54]

There, in essence, was no detailed plan for a New Deal, but its fundamental philosophy: government should act as a regulator for the common good within the existing economic system. It was, as Roosevelt envisaged it, a philosophy in keeping with the objectives of Jefferson and Wilson, modified to meet a new and complex economic order. The means might change but the ends were the same.

The speech well met the immediate political end in California. Roosevelt had prefaced it at Sacramento with some felicitous remarks on Hiram Johnson which Moley had dashed off on the train. Johnson replied in kind the next day. The exchange was relatively spontaneous;

Johnson scoffed at reports of "the bright correspondents of the east" that it "was a deep laid conspiracy, carefully planned." He commented to his Republican colleague, Senator Charles L. McNary, "Apparently there isn't much doubt about my attitude in the State or any other place." Nor was there any doubt that Roosevelt was the beneficiary. Johnson candidly reported to McNary a few days later:

"Roosevelt has come and gone. He was cordially received by enormous crowds. He didn't evoke the enthusiasm that old T. R. could always arouse, nor even the hysterical approval that a portion of our population gave to Al Smith in 1928. His trip, however, I think was a success. . . . If the election were tomorrow, Roosevelt would carry this State very handily. I haven't the slightest idea what four and a half weeks may develop. I realize what the electric power people and big business can do, and realizing it, would not be surprised at anything that might transpire." [55]

As Roosevelt headed eastward again, he worried little about what the opposition might do. He was careful to engage only in fast footwork on the tariff. Moley had assigned Charles W. Taussig, a molasses manufacturer, to confer with Hull and write a draft speech; it called for a flat ten-per-cent cut.* Next Hugh Johnson prepared a draft which instead called for gradual bilateral negotiation of trade agreements. When Moley presented them to Roosevelt, he suggested Moley should weave the two together. In California, Roosevelt began seriously to think about the tariff, and was greatly impressed over M. L. Wilson's objection † that many farmers would not accept a low-tariff policy.[58]

This led Roosevelt to abandon one of the issues upon which he had longest been critical of Hoover and the Republicans. He instructed Moley to get to work on a speech draft along with Senators Walsh and Pittman, both of whom were high-tariff men. "No speech in the campaign was such a headache as this," Moley has written. Weave these things together indeed! One might as well weave glass fibers with cobwebs. Moley had to fight off both high-tariff men and low-

* Because Taussig was head of the American Molasses Company, Moley had hoped he would bring some campaign sugar with him, but he contributed only free-trade ideas during the campaign.[56]

† A few days later, October 7, Wilson wired Moley, "Great mass of Republican farmers north and west who are switching Roosevelt have had tariff instilled in them since Civil War stop will vote for Roosevelt not because of different tariff philosophy but because they are sore at Hoover farm prices economic conditions lack of action on surplus problems." [57]

tariff men to arrive at what Roosevelt wanted. The finished speech was in Roosevelt's eyes a compromise; in the eyes of Moley and anyone subsequently analyzing it, it was an abandonment of Hull's low-tariff position. Roosevelt himself did quite a lot of the final weaving upon it. As with other speeches, Moley had him dictate and write changes as much as time permitted between train stops. As Roosevelt delivered it in Sioux City on his way east, the only sop to Hull and his followers was the attack upon some of the outrageously high rates in the Hawley-Smoot Tariff.[59]

President Hoover, Eastern manufacturers, and farm leaders all pounded Roosevelt over even these indefinite remarks. He backtracked still further, and emphasized both in speeches and in telegrams to the farm leaders that of course it was absurd to talk of lowering tariff duties on farm products. Before the end of the campaign, he added that he favored continued protection for American industry. Hoover, feeling that he had Roosevelt at a disadvantage, continued to hammer upon this theme. He charged that Roosevelt on the tariff was like a chameleon on plaid. In his final speech at Madison Square Garden, he declared that as a result of Roosevelt's tariff policies, "the grass will grow in the streets of a hundred cities, a thousand towns; the weeds will overrun the fields of millions of farms." [60]

Whatever grass might grow in the future according to Hoover's prophecies, none was growing under Roosevelt's nimble feet. Both Republican opponents and low-tariff Democratic friends might gnash their teeth over Roosevelt's inconsistencies on the tariff, but he was correct in following Wilson's advice and relegating it to a minor place in his campaign. He likewise did nothing with foreign policy, although he had the Brain Trust gather materials so that if need be he could give a foreign-policy speech. There was some possibility of a Republican attack, for President Hoover had rejected an overture Colonel House had made to Secretary Stimson to take the question of war debts and reparations out of the campaign. When Moley asked Roosevelt if he should prepare a foreign-policy speech, Roosevelt replied that there was no need to do so, since Hoover was all right on the subject. More to the point, Republicans had avoided it except for one address by Secretary Stimson, and the public demonstrated little interest in the question. Had Roosevelt delivered a foreign-policy speech, Moley has written, his views would have been very popular in the Middle West and West, where he was already sure of winning, and would have cost him undecided votes in the East.[61]

Nor was there much of a labor issue in the campaign. In the eyes of most union leaders, Roosevelt was correct on labor matters and they gave him their wholehearted support. He did not have to say much. One of the officials of the United Mine Workers called Frank Walker's attention to the fact that there was no collective-bargaining plank in the Democratic platform although there was one in the Republican. Roosevelt himself wrote directly to the official that he regretted the oversight, and that of course the party was in favor of collective bargaining and unionism. He said he would be glad to refer to the subject as the campaign went on, but apparently did not bother to do so. His only reference to a labor subject in a major speech was his advocacy of a shorter working week.[62]

As he toured the West and stopped briefly in town after town, Roosevelt's policy was one of not saying anything much on much of anything. He saved what he had to say for his major addresses; the rest of the time he acted pleasant. At each whistle stop it was much the same, Clinton L. Mosher of the Brooklyn *Eagle* reported. The engineer would pull in the train usually for only about a minute. As the six cars slowly crawled in, the crowd would stare curiously at the reporters, politicians, and staff members, but concentrated their attention upon the last car.

As soon as the train came to a dead stop, Governor Roosevelt would step out, his hand tightly grasping the arm of his tall, prematurely bald, eldest son, James. Roosevelt would grin and remark, "It's nice to be back in so-and-so. I am just out here to look, learn, and listen." Then he would introduce the two attractive blonde women with him, his daughter-in-law Betsy Cushing Roosevelt and his daughter Anna, and finally turn to James. "And this is my little boy, James," he would laughingly conclude. "I have more hair than he has." The crowd would roar, but Moley observed that James Roosevelt grew rather depressed after about a score of these performances.[63]

By this time the train should be pulling out; if by some mischance it was not, Roosevelt would repeat a few sentences of his speech of the night or so before. And as the train left, he would wave warmly to the cheering throng. It was a splendid and effective performance, even to hard-boiled reporters who saw it ten times a day. "Roosevelt smiles and smiles and smiles and it doesn't get tiresome," Mosher wrote. "He can smile more than any man in American politics without being insipid."

Evenings, after his speeches, Roosevelt held open house to all comers in his rooms. He would shake hands and exchange pleasantries until after midnight, yet the next day be fresh and vigorous, making his appearances, conferring with local politicians, and polishing speeches.[64]

At times he varied the routine, as in Douglas County, Nebraska, where he ate fried chicken at Gus Sumnick's farm. While he was watching a threshing machine, the wind suddenly shifted and blew chaff over him. "That's all right," said Roosevelt, "but I won't wave my hat any more. I don't want chaff in my hair." He asked one of the Sumnick sons how heavy the yield of corn was. Better than forty bushels, was the reply. "That's pretty good," commented Roosevelt. "We can't get more than thirty back in New York State."

The President of the Nebraska Farmer's Holiday Association, Harry Parmenter of Yutan, gave Roosevelt a statement of harsh economic facts concerning Sumnick's productive but unprofitable farm. Roosevelt glanced at it, and assured Parmenter, "That will certainly get my attention." On the way back to Omaha, a woman asked Roosevelt for a shirt. He told her if she would come to the train, he would be glad to give her a clean one.[65]

And so it went as Roosevelt progressed across the land, doing all the things that are expected of a candidate for President, and doing them with unsurpassed showmanship. It was all very simple and effective, as Mosher of the Brooklyn *Eagle* pointed out, for the audiences were less interested in hearing Roosevelt's panaceas than in telling him what was wrong with President Hoover. On this subject, Roosevelt was a very good listener.[66]

CHAPTER XXIV

The Triumph

"This is the greatest night of my life –"
— FDR, *election evening, 1932.*

BY the time Roosevelt returned to Hyde Park from the West, every public-opinion poll showed him far in front of President Hoover.* As early as the beginning of August, one of the secret polls had indicated that Roosevelt would carry forty-four of the forty-eight states. "Of course, we won't do anything like that," he confided to Governor Dern of Utah, "but on that basis we could afford to lose several more!" At the beginning of October, Roosevelt's lead was so broad that Farley commented to O'Connor, "I am not going to worry very much about tabulations now, Doc. This is all over if someone doesn't rock the boat." [2]

Consequently, in October, which should have been the heavy campaign month, while President Hoover grimly took to the hustings to spread his record before the American voters, Roosevelt blithely planned a campaign trip into the again solidly safe South. It was undeniably a vacation junket rather than a fight for votes. Again all the experienced Democratic politicos voiced their vehement protests. Senator Pittman summarized them into five cogent points, of which the most important was that it would entail unnecessary expense. In a humble vein, Pittman concluded, "As I wrongfully advised against your western trip, I would not be disappointed if you turned down all of this advice. I would probably be encouraged because it would indicate that you were right and I was wrong." Pittman might well have been encouraged, for Roosevelt did ignore his advice, along with that of Farley and everyone else. Farley did not worry very much. The success of the Western trip convinced him that the Southern

* One of the most expert analysts of these polls, Emil Edward Hurja, had offered his services to Roosevelt, and from time to time prepared tabulations of the *Literary Digest* and Hearst polls, weighing them according to the methods used in collecting data, and projecting the trends that they indicated.[1]

junket would turn out all right. It did. Roosevelt might well have used the time and money to swing one or two critical Northern states from the Republican to the Democratic column, but he did not need the electoral votes and he simply wanted to campaign in the South.[3]

During October, Roosevelt did also swing through the Middle West and through New England, and he paid some attention to his own state of New York, but for the most part, as Farley later remembered, he coasted.[4]

There were a few critical problems upon which he had not yet spoken out. One was unemployment and social welfare. On October 13, he spoke over the radio from Albany, to answer a set of questions put to him by ten leading social-welfare workers. On every point he was correct in their eyes.* He outlined what he had advocated and had achieved as Governor of New York, and recommended Federal aid where local and state resources were inadequate. He favored not only self-sustaining public works, but also those essential to the community, such as playgrounds and public housing, as a means of alleviating unemployment. In addition, he endorsed a system of compulsory state unemployment insurance, and of federally coordinated state employment offices.[5]

A comprehensive program of social welfare and unemployment relief would cost money, and, as Roosevelt had said in outlining it, while he favored governmental economy, he was utterly unwilling that it should be practiced at the expense of starving people. Obviously he had not faced up to the magnitude of expenditure that his program would involve. Obviously too, he had not in the slightest accepted the views of those who felt that the way out of the depression was large-scale public spending and deficit financing.

On the eve of his nomination, Roosevelt wired Colonel McCormick of the Chicago *Tribune*, "Preliminary survey leads me to believe federal expenditures can be cut twenty percent by eliminating many functions not absolutely essential and by complete reorganization of many departments." On July 24, at the prodding of his friend Richard E. Byrd, the explorer, he sent his Harvard classmate Grenville Clark a telegram endorsing the work of the National Economy League.[6]

Roosevelt was well disposed, therefore, when Hugh Johnson drafted a strong economy speech for him. Johnson had Farley, who was travel-

* Interestingly, at no point did FDR draw directly upon the page of speech draft Harry Hopkins, his T.E.R.A. administrator, had submitted, nor upon the suggestions of his Industrial Commissioner, Frances Perkins.

ing West, take it to Roosevelt at Ogden, Utah. He was anxious for Roosevelt to deliver it at San Francisco. "It is a terrific indictment," Johnson wrote, "and I believe will do much to solidify the Governor in the East and do him no harm in the West." * When Roosevelt failed to use it in California, Howe, who had been converted by Johnson and Baruch, called Roosevelt to argue with him at every stop on his way back from the West Coast, and even wired him the speech (an eight-thousand-word telegram) at Williams, Arizona. Next Johnson with Baruch's endorsement tried to press Roosevelt into making the speech at Chicago, to "shoot first" before President Hoover could pledge heavy cuts in government spending at Des Moines.[7]

While Roosevelt refused to be stampeded into making the speech in the West, he did decide to deliver it at Pittsburgh on October 19. He was well aware of its implications and its alternatives, according to Moley.† Although Moley and the other Brain Trusters were not members of the public-spending school, they had outlined its tenets to him. He rejected them. The Pittsburgh speech was a strong avowal of financial conservatism. It is notorious that the speech plagued Roosevelt for a good many years;‡ it is less well understood that what he said represented his basic belief not only during the campaign but well into the New Deal. This is the significance of the Pittsburgh speech.

In hindsight what Roosevelt said seems rather ludicrous. He granted that a nation could borrow for a year or two without much danger, but warned that if like a spendthrift it threw discretion to the winds, it was on the road to bankruptcy. This, he charged, the Hoover Administration had done. The cost of national, state, and local government had risen to $125 a year per person. "Can we stand that?" Roosevelt inquired. "I do not believe it." The Federal budget had gone up

* Johnson had turned out his draft in twenty-four hours, and did not want to consider it final until he had gone over it with Baruch.

† Moley asked FDR to go over the speech very carefully since it committed him to such a conservative financial policy. FDR handed it to O'Connor, but apparently FDR and O'Connor did not revise it at all, because in Pittsburgh on the day of the speech it was still as Johnson had drafted it. That day, Moley revised it as best he could with the assistance of a conservative of conservatives, Swagar Sherley of Kentucky, whom Roosevelt liked. FDR made only stylistic changes in Moley's final revision.[8]

‡ In 1936, FDR, rankled by criticisms of the speech, ordered Rosenman to draft a speech giving good and convincing explanations of the 1932 statement which he could deliver on the same spot in Pittsburgh. When Rosenman reread it, he told FDR there was only one kind of explanation he could give — to deny categorically that he ever had made the speech.[9]

approximately a billion dollars, or roughly fifty per cent, between 1927 and 1931. This, charged Roosevelt, "is the most reckless and extravagant past that I have been able to discover in the statistical record of any peacetime Government anywhere, any time." He went on, "Now, I am going to give you good people a real shock. Instead of the Government running into the red for those two years to the tune of $150,000,000, the deficit on June 30, 1932, was, for the two fiscal years, three and three-quarters billion dollars."

The blame for this unbalanced budget and economic distress, Roosevelt asserted, was not some sequence of events originating abroad, as President Hoover was saying. "No, we need not look abroad for scapegoats," Roosevelt declared. "We had ventured into the economic stratosphere – which is a long way up – on the wings of President Hoover's novel, radical and unorthodox economic theories of 1928, the complete collapse of which brought the real crash in 1931. . . . As hard reality rushed up to meet our fall, this Administration did not see fit to adapt its fiscal policies to this inevitable consequence." Further, the Hoover Administration had unavoidably increased costs by centering "control of everything in Washington as rapidly as possible – Federal control."

As a remedy, Roosevelt pledged, "I shall approach the problem of carrying out the plain precept of our Party, which is to reduce the cost of current Federal Government operations by 25 percent." * No man would enter his cabinet, Roosevelt promised, until he had taken a pledge to cooperate in bringing about economy and reorganization in his department.

There was only one loophole. Roosevelt repeated, "If starvation and dire need on the part of any of our citizens make necessary the appropriation of additional funds which would keep the budget out of balance, I shall not hesitate to tell the American people the full truth and ask them to authorize the expenditure of that additional amount." [11]

* On the highly controversial question of the immediate payment of the veterans' bonus, Roosevelt took a conservative position, similar to that which had been suggested to him by his old acquaintance Admiral R. E. Coontz, who was Commander in Chief of the Veterans of Foreign Wars. He repeated a statement he had made the previous April, "I do not see how, as a matter of practical sense, a Government running behind two billion dollars annually can consider the anticipation of bonus payment until it has a balanced budget, not only on paper, but with a surplus of cash in the treasury." Admiral Coontz granted that this statement was all that could be expected during the campaign, since it was not a flat-footed acceptance or rejection. Father Coughlin, who had favored payment, assured FDR in advance that he would accept his stand whatever it might be.[10]

Even in the starvation year 1932, Roosevelt had no idea how large a loophole that would prove to be.

This sharp swing back toward the right stimulated much enthusiasm at the time among Roosevelt's supporters, liberal as well as conservative. As was to be expected, Roosevelt's 1920 running mate, Cox, wired it was the best effort of the campaign, and Colonel House hailed it as a knockout blow, but surprisingly Governor Dern of Utah also thought it "crackerjack," and Frankfurter regarded it as an extraordinarily effective and devastating presentation of national finance under Hoover's regime.[12]

Further to counter any Republican charge of radicalism, Roosevelt persuaded the conservative Senator Carter Glass of Virginia to deliver a vehement radio attack upon President Hoover's financial policies, and the highly respected Owen D. Young to speak reassuring the public that further economic disaster would not result from the election of Roosevelt. Within New York, Roosevelt himself delivered a strong speech at Buffalo, defending his administration from the onslaught of the Republican candidate for governor, William J. Donovan. He gave "Wild Bill" Donovan, who had been a classmate of his in Columbia Law School, a pleasant lambasting, and strongly emphasized the merits of the Democratic candidate for governor, Lehman. By this time, Al Smith was campaigning vigorously, and on the night of October 28, at Roosevelt's invitation, Smith called at the Executive Mansion for what headline writers happily called "an old fashioned love feast."[13]

All these tactics of Roosevelt were upsetting if not infuriating to President Hoover. Early in the campaign, he tried the technique of requesting one or another cabinet member to answer each of what he considered to be Roosevelt's untruths. Roosevelt declared at Columbus on August 20 that Hoover had favored development of backward or crippled countries by means of loans, and that the result had been a crop of worthless foreign bonds. Immediately the President called upon Secretary of State Stimson to refute this. Before Stimson could do so, Hoover persuaded Under Secretary William R. Castle to issue a denial. Stimson complained in his diary that this was getting to be a bit undignified. "Every time Roosevelt makes a speech," Stimson wrote, "Mr. Hoover has Mills or Hurley answer it, and the result is that it is rather wearing out the popularity of the two men."[14]

For weeks Hoover pressured Stimson to go into New York State and attack Roosevelt's record as governor. Stimson was thoroughly loyal to Hoover and, on the basis of some of his interchanges over Saint

Lawrence power, distrustful of Roosevelt. But he had regretted the attack he had been dragged into making in the campaign of 1930, and frankly told the President he would not repeat it. Instead, Stimson wanted to make a constructive speech about the Hoover Administration. This proposal drew no spark of interest from the embittered President, who was by now in the mood for attack. Stimson tried to placate him by making a speech on foreign policy, but this was not enough. Although eventually he agreed with reluctance to Hoover's request for an anti-Roosevelt diatribe, he never delivered it.* Hoover seems never to have forgiven him this, for in his *Memoirs,* he makes the remarkable statement that Stimson felt as Secretary of State he must be neutral in the campaign, and that he was the first cabinet leader in history to take that position. Distasteful though Stimson's stand was to President Hoover, it had great significance for the future, since it left Stimson in a relatively unembarrassed position after the election, from which he could take up foreign-policy matters with Roosevelt.[16]

As for President Hoover, he could rely upon few Republican leaders outside of his cabinet to speak up for him. In the end the campaign seemed to fall largely upon his own shoulders. He had few illusions about the outcome. The cabinet meeting on the day after the Maine election was a blue occasion for even that characteristically sober group. A few days later, on September 19, the President summoned Stimson to the White House to tell him something important. Stimson recorded:

"First, he summed up the situation in the campaign and said that it indicated that although he was gaining in the East, he would lose everything west of the Alleghenies and would lose the election. He then analyzed Roosevelt's campaign and the insincerity of it. With respect to the farm situation he said that he really had announced a campaign for a direct federal subsidy and yet had tied it up with conditions which prevented the East from getting the facts on it. Then he went through the steps of insincerity which marked his campaign in respect to railroads, where he was taking the plan made by the railroad companies and yet claiming that he was against them. He was

* As Stimson made clear in his diary when he finally acceded to Hoover's request, his objections were tactical rather than disloyal to Hoover. He wrote: "I think that to attack a presidential candidate who is a cripple and who has a pleasant appearance, particularly when the attack comes from a close adviser of the President, is about the most dangerous and probably unfortunate thing that the President and his foolish advisers can settle on, and I hate to be the goat."[15]

taking Hoover's plan in certain respects and yet denouncing Hoover." [17]

All President Hoover could seem to do was to go into the Middle West and make long earnest defenses of his administration. These could set the record straight, and perhaps force Roosevelt to commit himself on matters like the tariff and the gold standard. Unlike Roosevelt with his Brain Trust, Hoover wrote his speeches in entirety himself in time he snatched from his heavy duties as President. All nine of them, unlike Roosevelt's, which usually touched upon only one theme, were omnibus speeches which ranged widely over the campaign issues. Most of them he delivered when tired, or even on the point of exhaustion, in a dreary voice which all too often reflected his main theme: the depression could be worse, and if Roosevelt were elected, it would be.*

It was impossible for the President, even with the aid of Secretaries Mills and Hurley, to make Republican refutations catch up with Roosevelt's accusations. Roosevelt was always one step ahead of them and managed to keep them off balance throughout the campaign. Besides he was too far in front in the campaign for them to be able to press him very far. After Hoover had delivered his powerful jeremiad at Des Moines, William Allen White wrote enthusiastically, "It is hardly necessary to say what a tremendous impression the Iowa speech made on this Missouri Valley." Then he added with the realism of a good reporter, "I am not sure that it was enough of an impression." [19]

Even though he could not win the election, President Hoover was able to make his position clear. In subsequent years, feeling as bitter as ever, he fought the last battle of the campaign in his *Memoirs*, in which he devoted over a hundred pages to an analysis and comparison of his campaign speeches and Roosevelt's.[20]

As for Roosevelt, he delivered one last blast at President Hoover when he spoke at Baltimore on October 25. He declared he was waging a war against "the 'Four Horsemen' of the present Republican leadership: the Horsemen of Destruction, Delay, Deceit, Despair." It was in many respects the most belligerent speech of his campaign, and it contained an interesting portent for the future. Roosevelt ad libbed

* In his address at Des Moines, October 4, 1932, President Hoover asserted: "Thousands of our people in their bitter distress and losses today are saying that 'things could not be worse.' No person who has any remote understanding of the forces which confronted this country during these last eighteen months ever utters that remark. Had it not been for the immediate and unprecedented actions of our government things would be infinitely worse today." [18]

into it an implied criticism of the Supreme Court.* The Republicans, he said, controlled the Congress, the presidency — and the Supreme Court.[21]

This goaded Hoover into a waspish finale. Roosevelt, listening to it on the radio before making an address at Boston, was indignant. "I simply will not let Hoover question my Americanism," he snapped, as he stuffed into his pocket notes for a retort that his son James and Frankfurter had written for him. Moley and Marvin McIntyre pleaded with him to maintain a high level and not descend to personalities, but he made no reply to them. To their relief, when he began talking, he inserted none of his furious comments into the speech, but confined himself to a further exposition of his views on unemployment relief and long-range planning. Again, in his own summing up at Madison Square Garden on November 5, Roosevelt gave a confident, statesmanlike speech.[22]

In his final broadcast on election eve, delivered from Poughkeepsie, Roosevelt recounted the many miles he had traveled, his impressions of many cities and of millions of people.† He told the people that while they had not universally agreed with him, they had been universally kind and tolerant. Out of the unity he had seen, he said he hoped to build the strongest strand to lift the nation out of the depression. As for his own role, if he were to be the beneficiary of the united confidence of the people, he declared:

> A man comes to wisdom in many years of public life. He knows well that when the light of favor shines upon him, it comes not, of necessity, that he himself is important. Favor comes because for a brief moment in the great space of human change and progress some general human purpose finds in him a satisfactory embodiment.
>
> To be the means through which the ideal and hopes of the American people may find a greater realization calls for the best in any man; I seek to be only the humble element of this restoration.[23]

To Moley this speech best expressed the mood and spirit of the

* President Hoover immediately defended the Supreme Court from the charge, which he considered an atrocious slur.

† Altogether, FDR had traveled about thirteen thousand miles and had delivered sixteen important speeches, sixty-seven less significant ones, and had made countless back-platform appearances.

Roosevelt with whom he was so intimately and arduously associated during the 1932 campaign. Thus in the final week, as some newspapermen noted, Roosevelt was talking more like a President, Hoover like a desperate contender. On this ironic note the campaign ended.[24]

What had all the speechmaking accomplished? Villard's *Nation* complained that "neither of the two great parties, in the midst of the worst depression in our history, has had the intelligence or courage to propose a single fundamental measure that might conceivably put us on the road to recovery." Indeed, in many respects, for all the clash and clamor, Roosevelt and President Hoover had not differed greatly from each other. But the *Nation* was too harsh; it overlooked the political truth, not always appealing to intellectuals, that the purpose of campaigns is not to blueprint the future but to win elections.[25]

Surprisingly few voters were willing to turn that fall to the Socialist Norman Thomas or to other third-party candidates. Few were ready to stand as aloof as Senator William E. Borah, who gave a broadcast explaining why he could not support Hoover, yet did not come out for Roosevelt. It was indicative of the times that that cautious, detached intellectual, Walter Lippmann, who had been so critical of Roosevelt, in the end turned to him. Lippmann, in congratulating Borah upon his stand, confessed to him, "It'll be a great relief to have the election over, and to me at least, though I have the deepest reservations about Franklin Roosevelt, a relief to be rid of the present administration. It's so utterly discredited that it no longer has any usefulness as an instrument of government. And even assuming that Roosevelt isn't any better than Hoover, a new man for a little while will be better than a man who's worn out and used up." [26]

Certain basic differences other than this between the two candidates had emerged. President Hoover had seen the depression as being worldwide in origin and development; Roosevelt chose to view it as a domestic calamity, and capitalizing upon the popular tendency to make the President the scapegoat, blamed it upon the Republican party. This was not only shrewd politicking; it represented Roosevelt's sincere view, and marked the direction in which he was ready to take the New Deal. Since he had scuttled the tariff issue, and since he had beaten the League of Nations dead horse in February, he was free to move in the direction of economic nationalism. Through his speeches, too, there had run the theme of social and economic planning for the general welfare. Although this ran counter to the reiterated pledges of economy and a balanced budget, it was clearly the stronger of the two themes, and Roosevelt never winced at difficulties when two of his policies were contradictory. It is not surprising that Moley was able to see in the handiwork of Roosevelt and the Brain Trust an outline of everything the early New Deal was to bring, with the exception of the abandonment of gold, the borrow-and-spend policy, and the National Recovery Administration. And Moley thought there was even a hint of the N.R.A. in Roosevelt's October 6 remarks on cooperation with industry to bring about "regularization and planning for balance." [27]

This outline was clear only to the insiders, not to the voters who went to the polls on November 8 to record their protest against President Hoover and the depression. The outline is important mainly because it represents the great strides Roosevelt himself had taken in his self-education before and during the campaign, and because it set the direction in which he was to take the New Deal during its first two years.

On election eve, Roosevelt must have been thinking about these things. Moley remembers that Roosevelt sat quietly in front of an open fire in the old home at Hyde Park, talking "of the campaign, of the gathering economic storm clouds – the tumbling prices, the mounting unemployment." He would be assuming a gargantuan task and a terrible responsibility.[28]

The Roosevelts went to the polls at the Hyde Park town hall on election day, and posed almost interminably for the newspapers and motion-picture photographers. That evening they had the Rosenmans and a few other intimates to dinner at the house on Sixty-fifth Street in New York City. There was as yet no especial excitement or tension, since the result was a foregone conclusion. The final odds offered by those astute men who made book was five to one. But Rosenman noticed an unusual incident which was a symbol of the way in which Roosevelt's life was to change utterly in the future. Two strange men came into the room early in the evening and stood near Roosevelt. Rosenman inquired who they were, and found they were Secret Service men who had come to guard the man who that night would become President-elect. During the remainder of his life, Roosevelt was never to be free of them.[29]

After dinner, Roosevelt went to the Biltmore Hotel and established himself in a long room just inside the door of the Democratic headquarters. He sat at the head of the table with Farley and Flynn beside him; Howe sat pessimistically in his own little office. Twenty telephone girls along the table picked up the returns from all over the United States. As calls came in, they sent them up to Roosevelt and Farley, who spoke directly to O'Mahoney in Wyoming, Guffey in Pennsylvania, and scores of others. Almost all the returns were favorable as every sign pointed to a wide Roosevelt sweep.[30]

When the final vote was in, Roosevelt had carried forty-two states, and Hoover only six. Roosevelt won in the electoral college by a vote of 472 to 59. He received 22,800,000 popular votes, or 57.4 per cent, compared with 15,750,000, or 39.7 per cent, for Hoover.* Minor parties polled only 1,160,000, or 2.9 per cent of the vote.[31]

In Palo Alto, President Hoover, watching returns which were no surprise to him, wired his congratulations to the victor. At the Biltmore, Roosevelt made his way into the Grand Ballroom to make an appearance before the photographers and to speak into the microphone. "I want to say just a word," he remarked, gesturing to the two men beside him. "There are two people in the United States more than anybody else who are responsible for this great victory. One is my old friend and associate, Colonel Louis McHenry Howe, and the other is that splendid American, Jim Farley." [32]

Moley wrote Howe a few days later that he realized, as the votes came in from the farthest parts of the country, "the harvest was coming in from the seeds that you had sown there." To Moley, the significance of the victory was clear. "You and Jim have done more than elect a President," he declared. "You have created a new party that ought to hold power for twenty-five years." Moley himself could have the satisfaction of having played a key part in the campaign and in the formation of this "new party" that was to hold power almost as long as his enthusiasm prophesied it would.[33]

Amid the excitement, Eleanor Roosevelt was in a contemplative mood that night. John Boettiger, sensing this, told her he wished he knew what she was really thinking and feeling. She recalls:

> I was happy for my husband, of course, because I knew that in many ways it would make up for the blow that fate had dealt him when he was stricken with infantile paralysis; and I had

* FDR was weakest in New England, where he had 49.1 per cent of the vote compared to Hoover's 48.4 per cent, and in the Middle Atlantic states, which he carried 50.5 to 45.4 per cent. In other areas the percentages were: East North Central, 54.2 to 42.7; West North Central, 60.6 to 37.2; South Atlantic, 67.0 to 31.9; East South Central, 67.3 to 31.9; West South Central, 83.4 to 16.2; Mountain, 58.4 to 38.4; and Pacific, 58.2 to 36.7.

> implicit confidence in his ability to help the country in a crisis. . . .
> But for myself, I was probably more deeply troubled than even John Boettiger realized. As I saw it, this meant the end of any personal life of my own. I knew what traditionally should lie before me; I had watched Mrs. Theodore Roosevelt and had seen what it meant to be the wife of the president, and I cannot say that I was pleased at the prospect. By earning my own money, I had recently enjoyed a certain amount of financial independence, and had been able to do things in which I was personally interested. The turmoil in my heart and mind was rather great that night, and the next few months were not to make any clearer what the road ahead would be.[34]

If Roosevelt had any such misgivings, he never voiced them. At 1:40 in the morning he arrived back at his home on Sixty-fifth Street. His mother was there to embrace him as he stepped in the door. Reporters overheard him as he exclaimed to her, "This is the greatest night of my life." [35]

It was a great triumph for the man who had gone into politics with the minority party in 1910, who had never been taken entirely seriously because of his remarkable bounce, who had been considered politically through when he lost the use of his legs in 1921. It was also a great challenge, and one for which Roosevelt had well prepared in all his years of careful training in practical politics, his first-hand observation of diplomacy in Wilsonian Washington and his study of foreign affairs in years that followed, and especially in his superb administration of the State of New York during the trying early years of the depression. He had demonstrated a brilliant mastery of politics, a humble willingness to learn and grow, and a phenomenal capacity for hard work. His weaknesses – his tendencies to compromise and to accept things on the surface – were readily apparent to everyone. Most of his friends expected no more of him than that he would be a good President. Everything in Roosevelt's background, his sense of destiny in the many years he had worked toward the White House, the way in which he had gone about governing New York and winning the presidency, all of it together indicated that he would try for more than this. Assuredly he would dedicate everything in him to the objective of being a great President to the American people in a time of acute crisis.

Bibliographical Note

Three massive collections of manuscripts in the Franklin D. Roosevelt Library, Hyde Park, New York, are indispensable for a study of Roosevelt's career from 1928 through 1932. These are his official files as governor, on "permanent loan" from the State of New York; his personal files as governor; and the Democratic National Committee files on the campaign of 1932. In addition, there is a small but significant collection of letters loaned by the Roosevelt family, and some material in White House papers. The official Governorship files and the Democratic National Committee files are completely open for research. Only a few papers in the personal file are closed; there seems little likelihood that they would materially alter an account of Roosevelt's private life or career during these years.

Other useful manuscript collections at the Roosevelt Library covering the years 1928–1932 are the files of the Franklin D. Roosevelt Memorial Foundation, the official papers of Lieutenant Governor Herbert H. Lehman, on permanent loan from the State of New York, and the papers of Louis McHenry Howe, Mary W. Dewson, and the Roosevelt Business and Professional League. At the Library of Congress are the papers of William E. Borah, Josephus Daniels, Breckinridge Long, Charles L. McNary, George Norris, Henry T. Rainey, Thomas J. Walsh, William Allen White, and Robert Woolley. At the University of Missouri are the papers of George N. Peek, William Hirth, and other farm leaders. At Yale University are the papers of Henry L. Stimson and E. M. House. Finally, one of the richest and most indispensable sources of information upon the campaign of 1932 are the papers of Raymond Moley, which are in his possession. They amply corroborate his account of the campaign in *After Seven Years* (New York, 1939).

Interviews and manuscripts gathered by the Oral History Project at Columbia University, under the direction of Allan Nevins, contain much useful information.

Numerous people have been of invaluable help through talking or corresponding with me. Among them are: Joseph A. Broderick, James A. Farley, Nannine Joseph, Herbert H. Lehman, Raymond

Moley, Frances Perkins, Eleanor Roosevelt, Samuel I. Rosenman, Bernard Ryan, Lela Stiles, Rexford G. Tugwell, Henry A. Wallace, Louis B. Wehle, and Burton K. Wheeler.

Many of Roosevelt's letters of this period appear in print in *F.D.R.: His Personal Letters*, Elliott Roosevelt, editor (vol. 2 and vol. 3, pt. 1, New York, 1947–1950). Many of his speeches, and a wide variety of public papers, appear in *Public Papers of Franklin D. Roosevelt, Forty-eighth Governor of the State of New York* (4 vols., Albany, 1930–1939). A selection of his speeches is in the first volume of *The Public Papers and Addresses of Franklin D. Roosevelt*, Samuel I. Rosenman, editor (13 vols., New York, 1938–1950).

In addition to the general works and memoirs described in the previous two volumes, a few books are especially valuable. Bernard Bellush, *Franklin D. Roosevelt as Governor of New York* (New York, 1955) is an admirable analysis of his administration. Ernest K. Lindley, *Franklin D. Roosevelt, A Career in Progressive Democracy* (Indianapolis, 1931) is a vivid contemporary account, far above the level of the ordinary campaign biography. Another of the large crop, Earle Looker, *This Man Roosevelt* (New York, 1932), paints an intimate portrait. The two memoirs most valuable on Roosevelt as governor are Frances Perkins, *The Roosevelt I Knew* (New York, 1946), and Samuel I. Rosenman, *Working with Roosevelt* (New York, 1952). Eleanor Roosevelt's two memoirs, *This Is My Story* (New York, 1937), and *This I Remember* (New York, 1949), are illuminating upon her life and her husband's. Edgar Eugene Robinson, *The Roosevelt Leadership, 1933–1945* (Philadelphia, 1955) contains a critical estimate of Roosevelt as governor and a comprehensive bibliographical essay.

On the campaign of 1932, Roy V. Peel and Thomas C. Donnelly, *The 1932 Campaign, An Analysis* (New York, 1935) is succinct and useful; Herbert Hoover, *Memoirs* (3 vols., New York, 1951–1952), vol. 3, includes an indispensable analysis from Hoover's viewpoint; Harold F. Gosnell, *Champion Campaigner, Franklin D. Roosevelt* (New York, 1952) contains a clear general account; Edgar Eugene Robinson, *They Voted for Roosevelt* (Stanford University, California, 1947) presents the election statistics. James A. Farley, *Behind the Ballots* (New York, 1938) is a graphic and accurate narrative, especially valuable on the complicated maneuvering at the convention. A brilliantly hostile contemporary account of it is Henry L. Mencken, *Making a President* (New York, 1932). When Alfred A. Knopf sent a copy to Roosevelt, he promptly replied that Mencken was a dear old friend. Five minutes' skimming of the book would have disabused him. Raymond Moley, *After Seven Years* (New York, 1939) is a valuable analysis of the work of the Brain Trust. Lela Stiles, *The Man Behind Roosevelt; The Story of Louis McHenry Howe* (Cleveland, 1954) is most valuable as the memoir of a Democratic worker. Other useful memoirs are Edward J. Flynn, *You're the Boss* (New York, 1947); Charles Michelson, *The Ghost Talks* (New York, 1944); and Cordell Hull, *Memoirs* (2 vols., New York, 1948). See also Bascom N. Timmons, *Garner of Texas, A Personal History* (New York, 1948), and Russell Lord, *The Wallaces of Iowa* (Boston, 1947).

Other books and articles are cited in notes in the back of the book.

I have drawn especially heavily upon two unpublished theses at the University of Illinois: Earland I. Carlson, "Franklin D. Roosevelt's Fight for the Presidential Nomination, 1928–1932," and Gertrude Almy Slichter, "Political Backgrounds of New Deal Agricultural Policy: 1928–1932."

Acknowledgments

Without the unstinting generosity of many people, I could not have written this volume. I owe an especially large debt to those persons I have cited in the Bibliographical Note, who have made available their memories or manuscripts to me — often accompanied by warm personal hospitality. I am especially grateful to Raymond Moley, Eleanor Roosevelt, Frances Perkins, Samuel I. Rosenman, and Louis B. Wehle. Others have read sections of the manuscript or proofs and have made valuable critical suggestions concerning style and contents. These people, who are by no means responsible for my point of view, include: Thomas A. Bailey, Spencer Brodney, Earland I. Carlson, Richard N. Current, Don E. Fehrenbacher, Richard Hofstadter, Elisabeth Margo, Edgar E. Robinson, Arthur M. Schlesinger, Jr., and Gertrude Almy Slichter.

I am, as before, under heavy obligation to the staffs of numerous libraries, especially that of the Roosevelt Library, including the Director, Herman Kahn, and Edgar Nixon, George Roach, Margaret Suckley, William J. Nichols, and Raymond Corry. I wish also to thank George A. Palmer of the National Park Service, Katharine Brand of the Library of Congress, Jeannette M. Hitchcock and J. Terry Bender of Stanford University Library, and Lisette Fast of the Institute of American History, Stanford University.

I am indebted to the Roosevelt Library for permission to quote from manuscripts and to reproduce the photographs in this volume, and to the Roosevelt family for permission to quote from family letters, to McGeorge Bundy for permission to quote from Stimson papers, and to Charles Seymour for permission to quote from House papers.

The Institute of American History, Stanford University, provided me with several generous grants which aided materially in preparation of this volume.

Notes

Abbreviations

FDR: Franklin D. Roosevelt
ER: Eleanor Roosevelt
DNC: Democratic National Committee manuscripts, Roosevelt Library, Hyde Park, New York
FL: Family Letters, on loan to the Roosevelt Library
GO: Governor's Official file, on loan to the Roosevelt Library
GP: Governor's Personal file, Roosevelt Library
OHP: Oral History Project, Columbia University
PL: Elliott Roosevelt, editor, *F.D.R., His Personal Letters* (3 vols., New York, 1947–1950)
POF: President's Official File, Roosevelt Library
PPA: Samuel I. Rosenman, editor, *The Public Papers and Addresses of Franklin D. Roosevelt* (13 vols., New York, 1938–1950). These are cited by year covered by volume; i.e., PPA, 1936, etc.
PPF: President's Personal File, Roosevelt Library.
PPG: *Public Papers of Franklin D. Roosevelt, Forty-Eighth Governor of the State of New York* (4 vols., Albany, 1930–1939)
PSF: President's Secretary's File, Roosevelt Library
10. New York *Times*, November 13, 1928.

CHAPTER I

Roosevelt Takes Command

1. New York *Tribune*, January 2, 1929; New York *Times*, January 2, 1929.
2. Atlanta *Constitution*, June 26, 1947.
3. New York *Times*, November 10, 1928.
4. New York *Times*, November 12, 29, 30, 1928.
5. Frances Perkins, *The Roosevelt I Knew* (New York, 1946), 52.
6. PPA, 1928–1932: xii.
7. Samuel I. Rosenman, *Working with Roosevelt* (New York, 1952), 28, 29.
8. Warren Moscow, *Politics in the Empire State* (New York, 1948), 5.
9. New York *Times*, November 8, December 4, 1928; see editorials of November 13, December 10, 1928.
10. New York *Times*, November 13, 1928.

11. PL, 3:7
12. Samuel Lubell, *The Future of American Politics* (New York, 1952), 34; Edgar Eugene Robinson, *They Voted for Roosevelt, The Presidential Vote 1932–1944* (Stanford, California), 4.
13. New York *Times*, November 12, 1928.
14. New York *Times*, December 5, 10, 1928.
15. New York *Times*, November 12, 1928.
16. PL, 3:5–7; New York *Times*, November 12, 1928. Copies of all these form letters and an analysis of the replies are in a bound volume labeled "National Political Digest" in the FDR mss.
17. Fred M. Vinson to FDR, December 18, 1928, DNC '32, Ky.
18. Claude Pepper to FDR, December 22, 1928, DNC '32, Fla.
19. Henry T. Rainey to FDR, December 15, 1928, DNC '32, Ill.
20. Henry Pringle, *Alfred E. Smith, A Critical Study* (New York, 1927), 261, 282–287; Alfred E. Smith, *Up to Now, An Autobiography* (New York, 1929); Finla G. Crawford, "New York State Reorganization," *American Political Science Review* (February, 1926), 20:76–79; Richard S. Childs, "New York State Reorganizes," *National Municipal Review* (May, 1926), 15:265–269.
21. State of New York, *Public Papers of Alfred E. Smith . . . 1928* (Albany, 1928), 636–639.
22. PL, 3:11; New York *Times*, December 15, 30, 1928.
23. New York *Times*, December 30, 1928.
24. Rosenman, *Working with Roosevelt*, 28.
25. *Ibid*., 29.
26. New York *Times*, November 10, 17, December 16, 30, 1928.
27. PPA, 1938: xii.
28. New York *Times*, November 10, 15, 18, 22, 25, December 30, 1928.
29. New York *Times*, December 22, 23, 30, 1928.
30. New York *Times*, December 13, 1928.
31. New York *Times*, December 26, 30, 1928.
32. New York *Times*, December 17, 25, 1928; Perkins, *Roosevelt I Knew*, 54, 55.
33. New York *Times*, December 25, 1928.
34. Perkins, *Roosevelt I Knew*, 55–57.
35. Perkins, *Roosevelt I Knew*, 49–50; Edward J. Flynn, *You're the Boss* (New York, 1947), 73–77.
36. Perkins, *Roosevelt I Knew*, 51–52; PL, 3:772.
37. Interview with Frances Perkins, May, 1953.
38. Perkins, *Roosevelt I Knew*, 52–53.
39. New York *Times*, December 29, 1928.
40. PL, 3:10; New York *Times*, December 15, 23, 1928; FDR to Mary L. Hunn, January 7, 1929, GP.
41. PL, 3:772–773. The letter had been intended for Adolphus Ragan.
42. PL, 3:773.
43. New York *Times*, January 1, 1929; New York *Herald Tribune*, January 1, 1929.

44. New York *Times*, January 2, 1929; New York *Herald Tribune*, January 2, 1929; New York *World*, January 2, 1929.

45. *Loc. cit.*

46. *Loc. cit.;* Ernest K. Lindley, *Franklin D. Roosevelt, A Career in Progressive Democracy* (Indianapolis, 1931), 237.

47. PPG, 1929: 11–15; New York *Times*, January 2, 1929.

48. PL, 3:773. FDR's stenographer slipped and wrote "somebody's else."

49. New York *Times*, January 2, 1929; New York *World*, January 2, 1929.

CHAPTER II

A New Regime in Albany

1. PPG, 1929: 13.

2. PPG, 1929: 13, 39–47; New York *World*, January 3, 1929.

3. New York *Times*, January 3, 1929.

4. New York *Times*, January 3, 1929; New York *World*, January 3, 1929.

5. New York *World*, January 3, 1929.

6. Perkins, *Roosevelt I Knew*, 90–91.

7. New York *Times*, January 11, 1929.

8. Robert L. Duffus in New York *Times*, March 24, 1929.

9. New York *Times*, January 2, 1929.

10. Duffus, *op. cit.*

11. New York *Times*, January 3, 1929.

12. PPG, 1929: 681–683; see also FDR to Harry Kehoe, January 15, 1929, GP.

13. New York *Times*, January 3, 1929.

14. Lindley, *Roosevelt*, 237; New York *Times*, January 21, 25, February 3, 1929.

15. New York *Times*, January 21, 1929.

16. New York *Times*, January 18, 1929.

17. New York *Post*, January 2, 1929; New York *Times*, January 14, 15, 21, March 12, 1929.

18. Casper T. Gee to FDR, February 19, 1929, GP.

19. FDR (written by Howe) to Gee, March 12, 1929, GP.

20. New York *Times*, January 14, 1929.

21. PL, 3:26–31; New York *Times*, January 16, 1929; New York *World*, January 15, 1929.

22. FDR to Joseph W. Byrns, January 24, 1929; Byrns to FDR, January 14, 1929, DNC '32, Tenn.

23. New York *World*, January 15, 1929.

CHAPTER III

A "Sanely Radical" Program

1. PL, 3:25.
2. New York *Times*, February 15, 1929; FDR to Frank O. Lowden, January 7, 1929, GP.
3. New York *Times*, January 16, April 18, 1929.
4. PPA, 1928–1932: 127.
5. PPG, 1929: 40, 685.
6. PPG, 1929: 40, 686, 731.
7. Henry Morgenthau, Jr., to FDR, November, 1928; FDR to Robert M. Barker, May 7, 1929, GO.
8. New York *Times*, January 7, 8, 1929.
9. New York *Times*, January 16, 17, 1929.
10. New York *Times*, April 9, 1929.
11. FDR to Frederic A. Delano, February 1, 1927, FL; New York *Times*, November 9, 10, 1928; Berne A. Pyrke to FDR, November 15, 1928, GO.
12. New York *Times*, November 15, 1928.
13. New York *Times*, January 17, 1929; PPG, 1929: 683–685.
14. New York *Times*, January 21, 1929.
15. New York *Times*, January 31, 1929.
16. New York *Times*, January 21, 1929.
17. New York *Times*, February 2, 1929.
18. New York *Times*, February 3, 1929.
19. New York *Times*, February 16, 1929.
20. FDR to Robert M. Barker, May 7, 1929, GO.
21. PL, 3:39; FDR, radio address March 7, 1929, PPG, 1929: 688–692.
22. New York *Times*, January 21, 1929.
23. PPG, 1929: 120, 148–149; New York *Times*, March 6, 1929.
24. New York *Times*, March 6, 1929; Stephen S. Wise to FDR, March 6, 1929; FDR to Wise, March 19, 1929, GO.
25. PPG, 1929: 693–694; see also New York *Times* editorial, March 1, 1929.
26. Article by R. L. Duffus in New York *Times*, January 13, 1929.
27. Lindley, *Roosevelt*, 238–241; Duffus, *op. cit.*; see, for example, Stephen Raushenbush and Harry Laidler, *Power Control* (New York, 1928).
28. PPG, 1929: 153–157; New York *Times*, March 13, 1929.
29. PPG, 1929: 157.
30. New York *Times*, March 15, 1929.
31. *Loc. cit.*

CHAPTER IV

The Battle of the Budget

1. Richard S. Childs, "New York State Reorganizes," *National Municipal Review* (May, 1926), 15:268; New York *Times*, January 28, February 12, 1929.

2. PPG, 1929: 103–137; New York *Times,* January 30, 1929; New York *World,* January 30, 1929.

3. New York *Times,* January 28, 29, 30, 1929; New York *World,* January 29, 30, 1929.

4. PPG, 1929: 268; New York *Times,* February 6, 1929.

5. FDR to Corinne Alsop, February 6, 1929, GP.

6. New York *World,* February 25, 1929.

7. New York *Times,* February 18, 1929.

8. New York *Times,* February 18, 20, 27, 1929; PPG, 1929: 138–142.

9. New York *Times,* February 27, 1929; New York *World,* February 27, 1929.

10. PPG, 1929: 143.

11. PPG, 1929: 144. For the entire message, see *ibid.,* 142–147.

12. Lindley, *Roosevelt,* 246; New York *Times,* February 28, 1929; New York *World,* February 28, 1929.

13. PL, 3:42. The cartoon is reproduced in PL, 3, between pp. 140 and 141.

14. PPG, 1929: 148–171.

15. New York *Times,* March 29, 1929.

16. New York *Times,* February 27, 1929.

17. New York *World,* March 8, 1929.

18. New York *World,* March 9, 11, 1929.

19. PPG, 1929: 693.

20. New York *Times,* March 24, 1929.

21. New York *Times,* March 7, 1929.

22. New York *Times,* March 10, 24, 1929; New York *World,* March 11, 1929.

23. New York *Times,* March 14, 1929.

24. PPG, 1929: 196. See *ibid.,* 178–196.

25. PPG, 1929: 508–509, 510.

26. See also [FDR] to Editor, New York *Post,* March 16, 1929, GP.

27. New York *Times,* March 14, 18, 19, 21, 22, 26, 27, 1929; PPG, 1929: 510–514.

28. New York *World,* March 28, 1929.

29. New York *Times,* March 31, 1929.

30. New York *Herald Tribune,* March 29, 1929; New York *World,* March 30, 1929.

31. New York *Post,* March 29, 1929; New York *Herald Tribune,* March 29, 1929.

32. PPG, 1929: 518–519.

CHAPTER V

Appeal to the People — and the Courts

1. PL, 3:57.

2. See, for example, New York *Times,* April 19, 1929.

3. PPG, 1929: 698–703.

4. New York *Times*, April 6, 8, 1929.
5. PPG, 1929: 703–708.
6. New York *Times*, April 5, 1929.
7. PPG, 1929: 209–264.
8. FDR to George Wickersham, April 4, 1929; Wickersham to FDR, April 6, 1929, GP; PPG, 1929: 227–231.
9. FDR to John Crosby Brown, April 25, 1929, GP.
10. PPG, 1929: 528–531; New York *Times*, April 11, 12, 13, 1929; New York *Herald Tribune*, April 13, 1929.
11. New York *Post*, April 11, 1929; New York *Times*, April 27, 1929.
12. PL, 3:43.
13. Guernsey Cross to Jason Parker Thompson, September 4, 1929, GP.
14. FDR to Mrs. Thomas J. Preston, Jr., April 10, 1930, GP; see, for example, Charles Evans Hughes to FDR, April 12, 1930, GO; interview with ER.
15. New York *Times*, April 9, 1929.
16. FDR to Bernard Levy, April 9, 1929, GP; New York *Times*, April 8, 9, 1929.
17. FDR to Frances Perkins, July 24, 1930; Perkins to FDR, July 28, 1930, GO; New York *Times*, April 11, 1929; New York *Herald Tribune*, April 11, 1929.
18. PL, 3:81–82.
19. PL, 3:60.
20. New York *Times*, June 29, 1929.
21. PL, 3:51; New York *Times*, April 23, 24, May 14, 29, 1929.
22. FDR to Editor, Elmira *Advertiser*, June 10, 1929, GP. This letter contains quotations from the newspaper. Russell Lord, *The Wallaces of Iowa* (Boston, 1947), 321.
23. FDR to George W. Marble, editor, Fort Scott (Kans.) *Tribune*, May 15, 1929, GP.
24. Marble to FDR, May 19, 1929, GP.
25. Lehman to FDR, April 30, 1929, GP; New York *Times*, April 23, 24, 26, June 22, 24, 1929.

CHAPTER VI

A Quiet Summer Campaign

1. New York *Times*, April 14, 1929.
2. PL, 3:68.
3. PL, 3:56.
4. PPG, 1929: 710–713.
5. New York *Times*, June 13, 1929.
6. Copy in FDR mss.
7. New York *Times*, June 11, 13, 17, 18, 19, 21, 1929; FDR to William G. Howard, June 21, 1929, FL.
8. FDR to A. Lawrence Lowell, February 5, 1929, GP.
9. PL, 3:24, 64; FDR to Parmely L. Herrick, June 21, 1929, GP.

10. PL, 3:119–120. See also William I. Sirovich to FDR, May 11, 1930, GP.
11. New York *Times*, July 5, 1929.
12. New York *Times*, July 8, 1929.
13. PPA, 1928–1932: 367–376. See also PPG, 1929: 721–725; PL, 3:61; New York *Times*, July 17, 1929.
14. Wickersham to FDR, July 6, 1929, GO.
15. New York *Times*, July 18, 19, 1929.
16. Form letter in FDR GO file; correspondence with individual governors in DNC '32 file under various states.
17. FDR draft statement, July 20, 1929; Howe mss.; New York *Times*, July 22, 1929; PL, 3:67–69.
18. PL, 3:43.
19. PPG, 1929: 745.
20. PL, 3:69; New York *Times*, August 15, 1929.
21. Melvil Dewey to FDR, September 14, 1929, GP.
22. New York *Times*, July 14, 1929.
23. PPG, 1929: 728.
24. PPG, 1929: 729; New York *Times*, August 16, 1929.
25. PPG, 1929: 587–589; New York *Times*, July 12, September 5, 1929; FDR to Crawford, September 18, 1929, GP.
26. PL, 3:56–57.
27. PPG, 1929: 739, 745–747; Rosenman to FDR, undated, enclosing draft proposed constitutional amendment to transfer canals to Federal Government; John J. Boylan to FDR, April 16, 1930; Merchants Association of New York to FDR, April 15, 1930; Jere D. Tamblyn to FDR, May 2, 1930; FDR to Howard S. Cullman, November 4, 1931; FDR to Albert M. Garrison, January 21, 1930, GO; T. J. Walsh to Roy E. Ayers, May 13, 1930, Walsh mss.
28. New York *Times*, April 14, 1929.
29. PPG, 1929: 583; New York *Times*, May 30, June 27, 1929.
30. Interview with Eleanor Roosevelt, July 13, 1954; ER, *This I Remember*, 56–57.
31. New York *Times*, July 9, 13, 14, 15, August 9, 1929.
32. New York *Times*, July 6, 23, 29, 1929.
33. New York *Times*, July 30, 31, 1929.
34. FDR to Frank J. Donahue, June 26, 1929, GP.
35. New York *Times*, June 21, 1929.
36. PPG, 1929: 560–562.
37. New York *Times*, September 5, 1929.
38. New York *Times*, June 8, 9, 11, 16, 27, 1929. See also Moscow, *Politics in the Empire State*, 70–73.
39. PPG, 1929: 562–581.
40. New York *Times*, July 26, August 30, September 4, 16, 23, 1929.
41. PPG, 1929: 739.

CHAPTER VII

Crash and Ascent

1. New York *Times*, October 20, 1929.
2. John J. Raskob (interviewed by Samuel Crowther), "Everybody Ought to Be Rich," *Ladies' Home Journal*, August, 1929, 46:9.
3. New York *Times*, October 2, 13, 16, 19, 22, 23, 24, 25, 30, 1929.
4. New York *Times*, October 26, 1929; Herbert Hoover, *Memoirs*, 3:19, 29–37.
5. New York *Times*, October 26, 1929.
6. New York *Times*, October 30, 1929.
7. New York *Times*, November 25, 1929.
8. PL, 3:92.
9. PPG, 1929: 751.
10. PPG, 1929: 751; New York *Times*, October 31, 1929.
11. FDR to George Gordon Battle, October 12, 1929, GP.
12. Howe to FDR, October 3, 1929; FDR to Howe, October 5, 1929.
13. New York *Times*, September 25, 27, 1929; Howe to FDR, September 26, 1929, GP.
14. Howe to FDR, October 7, 11, 1929; FDR to Howe, October 12, 1929; FDR to Joseph Mahoney, October 8, 1929, GP.
15. PL, 3:96.
16. Frank Freidel, *Roosevelt: The Ordeal* (Boston, 1954), 219.
17. On the Republican machine, see Moscow, *Politics in the Empire State*, 129.
18. Lindley, *Roosevelt*, 263–264.
19. FDR to Isabel Hall, October 8, 1929, GO.
20. PL, 3:83–84.
21. PPG, 1929: 367–398.
22. PPG, 1929: 367–398; Lehman to FDR, April 30, 1929, GP.
23. New York *Times*, May 27, June 3, 9, 26, 1929.
24. Robert Moses, report, July 10, 1929, PPG, 1929: 385–386, 394, 395.
25. New York *Times*, November 6, 23, 1929. On November 7, 1929, most newspapers carried a somewhat misleading general story on a nationwide "Democratic trend."
26. New York *Times*, November 23, 1929.
27. New York *Times*, November 20, 1929; PPG, 1929: 638–654.
28. FDR to William D. Guthrie, October 3, 1929, GO.
29. FDR, address before City Club, November 23, 1929, PPG, 1929: 756.
30. See clipping under a Washington dateline from the Sioux City (Iowa) *Tribune*, in Box 163, GP; Howe to FDR, December 9, 1929, GP.
31. New York *Times*, December 11, 1929.
32. FDR, transcript of speech, December 10, 1929, enclosed in E. R. White to FDR, December 29, 1929, GP.
33. FDR to Bortius Sullivan, December 31, 1929, GP.
34. FDR to Howe, December 16, 1929; John N. Garner to FDR, December 18, 1929; C. C. Dill to FDR, December 18, 1929; see also Alben Barkley

to FDR, December 30, 1929; Henry T. Rainey to FDR, December 16, 1929, GP.

35. FDR to P. H. Callahan, December 5, 1929, GP.

36. Wright Patman to FDR, December 30, 1929; Marvin Jones to FDR, December 16, 1929; John E. Rankin to FDR, December 16, 1929, Box 33, Howe mss.

37. FDR to Bortius Sullivan, December 31, 1929, GP.

38. New York *Times*, December 11, 1929.

CHAPTER VIII

Victory over the Power Magnates

1. PPG, 1930: 29.

2. PPG, 1930: 29–36.

3. FDR to Frank Walsh, November 30, 1929, GO.

4. Morris Ernst to FDR, November 20, 1928; FDR to Ernst, November 28, 1928; Julius Henry Cohen to FDR, February 7, 1929, GO; see also Stephen Raushenbush and Harry Laidler, *Power Control.*

5. FDR to George Norris, December 22, 1928, Norris mss.; Norris to FDR, December 24, 1928; Thomas J. Walsh to FDR, December 26, 1928; Cordell Hull to FDR, January 4, 1929, GO.

6. Owen D. Young to Herbert Hoover, March 2, 1926, enclosed in Young to FDR, November 26, 1928; see also, for example, C. M. Palmer, Adirondack Civic League, to FDR, December 13, 1928, GO.

7. FDR to Frankfurter, July 5, 1929, GO.

8. Frankfurter to FDR, January 5, 1929, GO.

9. Frankfurter to FDR, June 27, 1929; see also Frankfurter to FDR, March 13, 1929, GO.

10. FDR to Frankfurter, July 5, 1929, GO.

11. Cohen to FDR, July 23, 1929, GO; New York *Times*, July 20, 1929. For Cohen's views, see Julius Henry Cohen, "Confiscatory Rates and Modern Finance," *Yale Law Journal*, December, 1929, 29:151–192.

12. FDR to Lionberger Davis, October 5, 1929, GO. FDR sent copies of the book to Davis, W. T. Anderson of the Macon (Georgia) *Telegraph*, and Frank P. Morgan of the Alabama Public Service Commission. FDR to Grace Tully, October 12, 1929, GP; William E. Mosher and Finla G. Crawford, *The Electric Utilities: A Crisis in Public Control* (New York, 1929).

13. William E. Mosher to FDR, November 19, 1929; FDR to Mosher, November 23, 1929, GO.

14. Morgenthau to FDR, November 27, 1929, GO. On rural electrification, see Agricultural Advisory Commission report, November 16, 1929, PPG, 1929: 637–638; FDR to Frank P. Walsh, November 30, 1929, GO.

15. James C. Bonbright to Guernsey Cross, September 14, 1929; FDR to Bonbright, October 12, 1929, GO.

16. FDR to Cohen, November 29, 1929.

17. Cohen to FDR, July 12, 1929, GO; Cohen, *op. cit.*, 151–152.

18. FDR, "The Real Meaning of the Power Problem," *Forum*, December, 1929, 82:327–332.

19. Martin J. Insull, "The Real Power Problem," *Forum*, February, 1930, 83:88–94.

20. New York *Times*, January 6, 1930.

21. PPG, 1930: 32–33.

22. FDR to Samuel Untermeyer, January 6, 1930; see also Untermeyer to FDR, January 2, 1930, GO.

23. New York *Times*, January 2, 3, 1930.

24. New York *Times*, January 6, 8, 1930.

25. New York *Times*, January 14, 1930; Thomas J. Walsh to FDR, February 4, 1930, Walsh mss.; Floyd L. Carlisle to FDR, January 10, 1930; FDR to Carlisle, January 14, 1930, GO.

26. New York *Times*, January 14, 1930.

27. Clinton L. Mosher in Brooklyn *Eagle*, March 16, 1930; New York *Times*, January 15, 1930.

28. FDR to Alfred E. Smith, January 14, 1930, GO.

29. PPG, 1929: 432, 433; 1930: 695.

30. Walter Lippmann to FDR, January 14, 1930; Frankfurter to FDR, January 17, 1930, GO; Walsh to FDR, February 4, 1930, Walsh mss.

31. FDR to Frankfurter, January 24, 1930, GO.

32. PPG, 1930: 439.

33. FDR to C. C. Dill, May 24, 1930, GO.

34. FDR to Frankfurter, January 28, 1931, GO.

35. Bernard Bellush, *Franklin D. Roosevelt as Governor of New York* (New York, 1955), 221–239.

36. New York *Times*, January 21, 1930.

37. FDR to Walsh, January 30, 1930, Walsh mss.; PPG, 1930: 75–76; New York *Times*, January 21, 25, 28, 1930.

38. New York *Times*, January 28, 29, 1930.

39. FDR to William A. Prendergast, January 27, 1930, PPG, 1930: 487–488.

40. New York *Times*, February 1, 1930.

41. Bonbright to FDR, December 21, 1930, GO.

42. New York *Times*, January 9, 10, 11, February 5, 1930.

43. New York *Times*, February 5, 1930.

44. New York *Times*, February 6, 1930. For an example of FDR's speeches, see PPG, 1930: 735.

45. New York *Times*, March 1, 1930; Brooklyn *Eagle*, March 16, 1930; Mosher to FDR, April 15, 1930, GO.

46. Milo R. Maltbie to FDR, May 2, 1930; FDR to Maltbie, May 9, 1930, GO; New York *Times*, May 2, 1930.

47. New York *Times*, February 25, March 2, 4, 1930.

48. New York *Times*, February 25, March 4, 1930.

49. FDR to Harry W. Laidler, March 4, 1930, GO; PPA, 1928–1932: 242.

50. Frankfurter to FDR, February 28, 1930, GO. For a summary of the minority report, see PPA, 1928–1932: 230–232.

51. Bonbright to FDR, December 21, 1929; Frankfurter to FDR, February 28, 1930, GO.

52. Frankfurter to FDR, February 28, 1930, GO.

53. Frankfurter to FDR, March 18, 1930, GO.

54. PPA, 1928–1932: 238–250.

55. PPA, 1928–1932: 236–259.

56. FDR to John R. Haynes, April 19, 1930, GP.

57. PPG, 1930: 738.

58. J. E. Roberts to FDR, April 26, 1930; Maltbie to FDR, June 16, 1930; FDR to Roberts, June 19, 1930, GO.

59. FDR to Mrs. LaRue Brown, February 17, 1930; Marguerite Owen to FDR, April 17, 1930; FDR to Frank Walsh, April 23, 1930, GO; PL, 3:107. Concerning national interest in FDR's program in New York, see W. M. Kiplinger in New York *Times*, March 9, 1930.

60. Chicago *Journal of Commerce*, May 10, 1930; Philadelphia *Public Ledger*, March 31, 1930; Archibald McNeil to FDR, May 12, 1930.

CHAPTER IX

Taming the Legislature

1. FDR to John H. Finley, January 22, 1930, GP.

2. PPG, 1930: 730.

3. Interview with Herbert H. Lehman, July, 1954; interview with Samuel I. Rosenman, August, 1954. See also Saul Streit to FDR, April 12, 1932, GP.

4. Lindley, *Roosevelt*, 315.

5. Clinton L. Mosher in Brooklyn *Eagle*, March 16, 1930; Lindley, *op. cit.*, 315.

6. Lindley, *op. cit.*, 317; New York *Times*, February 12, 13, 1930.

7. Lindley, *op. cit.*, 317–318; New York *Times*, February 22, 23, 26, 1930.

8. PPG, 1930: 528; Hastings H. Hart to FDR, November 18, 1929, GO.

9. PPG, 1930: 37–38.

10. New York *Times*, January 3, 6, 7, 1930.

11. FDR to Leonard Miscall, January 13, 1930; FDR to Clark D. Stearns, January 13, 1930, GO.

12. Rochester *Democrat and Chronicle*, February 1, 1930; see also Ellwood Williams to FDR, December 6, 1929, GO.

13. FDR to Lehman, November 22, 1929, GO.

14. Lehman to FDR, December 18, 1929; Attica Prison file, GO.

15. Greene to Lehman, November 28, 1929; Greene, statement to Prison Investigation Commission, February 18, 1930; Greene to Editor, Rochester *Democrat and Chronicle*, February 19, 1930, GO; New York *Times*, January 3, 6, 29, 1930.

16. PPG, 1930: 530.

17. FDR to Sam A. Lewisohn, February 4, 1930, GP.

18. FDR to Lewisohn, January 6, 1930, GO.

19. New York *Times*, January 22, 1930; Raymond Moley, *After Seven Years* (New York, 1939), 2.

20. FDR to Caleb H. Baumes, February 4, 1930, PPG, 1930: 490. For the report of the committee, see PPG, 1930: 491–504.

21. FDR to Gerard Swope, March 14, 1930, GO.

22. New York *Times*, March 14, 1930.

23. Brooklyn *Eagle*, March 16, 1930.

24. New York *Times*, August 23, 1931; Albany *Knickerbocker Press*, January 10, 1932.

25. For corroboration of FDR's statement, see Jane M. Hoey to FDR, March 14, 1930, GP; PPG, 1930: 294, 295, 528: Brooklyn *Eagle*, March 16, 1930; New York *Times*, August 15, 1930; George Gordon Battle to FDR, March 4, 1931; FDR to Battle, March 6, 1931, GO.

26. Brooklyn *Eagle*, March 16, 1930.

27. PPG, 1930: 171–172.

28. PPG, 1930: 728; FDR to Lehman, April 23, 1930, PL, 3:116.

29. PPG, 1930: 729.

CHAPTER X

Bread and Booze

1. Howe to FDR, January 30, 1930, GP.

2. Perkins, *Roosevelt I Knew*, 94–96; New York *Times*, January 22, 23, 1930.

3. Perkins, *op. cit.*, 93.

4. FDR statement, March 29, 1930, PPG, 1930: 506.

5. PPG, 1930: 505–507.

6. Perkins, *op. cit.*, 94.

7. Preliminary Report of Committee on Stabilization of Industry for the Prevention of Unemployment, April 21, 1930, PPG, 1930: 508–517. See also FDR to County and Municipal Officials, May 5, 1930, PPG, 1930: 537–538.

8. Felix Frankfurter to FDR, April 18, 1930; FDR to Frankfurter, April 22, 1930; FDR to Frances Perkins, April 22, May 15, 1930; Perkins to FDR, May 7, 1930, GO.

9. New York *Times*, April 27, 1930; interview with Burton K. Wheeler, July 8, 1954; interview with James A. Farley, July, 1954.

10. Interview with Wheeler, July 8, 1954; interview with Farley, August 7, 1954.

11. FDR to Wheeler, June 30, 1930, PL, 3:129; Wheeler to FDR, June 10, 1930; Wheeler to Byron Newton, May 15, 1930, GP.

12. New York *Times*, April 28, 29, 1930; interview with Wheeler, July 8, 1954; FDR to Nicholas Roosevelt, May 19, 1930, GP.

13. New York *Times*, June 30, July 1, 5, 1930.

14. New York *Times*, July 1, 6, 1930; for a complete stenographic transcript of FDR's remarks, see "Official Proceedings of the Twenty-second Annual Conference of Governors . . . Supplement to the *United States Daily*," July 14, 1930, 23.

15. Hollins N. Randolph to FDR, July 9, 1930; FDR to Randolph, July 16, 1930, GP.

16. New York *Times,* July 5, 1930; also see, for example, New York *Times,* April 28, 1930.
17. Rosenman, *Working with Roosevelt,* 40.
18. New York *Times,* May 6, 1930.
19. Arnold T. Koch to FDR, January 3, 1929; FDR to Martin T. Manton, January 28, 1929; FDR to Rev. G. T. Lemmon, March 20, 1929, GO.
20. Grover Whalen to Maurice Campbell, Prohibition Administrator, Treasury Department, undated, enclosed in Whalen to FDR, September 6, 1929, GO.
21. Resolution from Genesee Annual Conference of the Methodist Episcopal Church, October 1, 1929; Guernsey Cross to Daniel W. Howell, Secretary, Genesee Conference, October 18, 1929, GO.
22. Rosenman to FDR, May 23, 1930, GP.
23. New York *Times,* June 19, 21, July 26, 1930.
24. New York *Post,* June 19, 1930; FDR to Julian S. Mason, June 20, 1930, GP.
25. New York *Times,* July 15, August 5, 10, 13, 22, 1930.
26. Frank Gannett to FDR, August 12, 1930, GP.
27. FDR to Gannett, August 14, 1930, GP.
28. FDR to Henry S. Hooker, September 19, 1930, GO; FDR to William Adams Delano, December 8, 1930, GP.
29. FDR to Robert F. Wagner, September 9, 1930, PPG, 1930: 577–578.
30. New York *Times,* July 5, 1930.
31. Rosenman to FDR, September 17, 1930; W. J. Carpenter to FDR, September 15, 1930, GO.
32. John J. Raskob to FDR, September 11, 1930; Albert C. Ritchie to FDR, September 13, 1930; FDR to Ritchie, September 16, 1930, GO; New York *Times,* September 14, 1930. For further opinions, see New York *Times,* September 11, 1930.
33. FDR to Hugh C. Laughlin, September 23, 1930, GO.
34. FDR to George F. Carpenter, September, 1930, GO.

CHAPTER XI

The First Roosevelt Landslide

1. New York *Times,* September 26, 27, 1930.
2. Walter Millis in New York *Herald Tribune,* October 12, 1930.
3. New York *Times,* January 29, 1930; Lindley, *Roosevelt,* 266–267.
4. John Knight and J. J. McGinnies to FDR, July 3, 1930, GO; FDR to Knight and McGinnies, July 19, 1930, GP; New York *World,* July 24, 1930; FDR to Joseph Johnson, July 29, 1930, GO.
5. Lindley, *op. cit.,* 268–270.
6. Lindley, *op. cit.,* 270.
7. New York *Times,* August 22, 25, September 7, 21, 1930.
8. New York *Times,* September 26, 27, 1930.
9. FDR to James Walker, September 27, 1930, GO; New York *Times,* September 29, October 2, 4, 1930.

10. New York *World*, September 30, 1930; Lindley, *Roosevelt*, 277; Arthur Krock in New York *Times*, October 26, 1930.

11. John W. Davis to FDR, *c.* October 4, 1930, GO.

12. Regarding Max Steuer, see, for example, Charles C. Burlingham to FDR, October 17, 1930, GO.

13. W. Russell Bowie to FDR, October 4, 1930, GP.

14. Henry L. Stimson diary, October 28, 1930, Stimson mss.

15. Arthur Krock in New York *Times*, October 19, 1930.

16. T. A. Hendricks to Farley, October 13, 1930; L. J. Donohoe to Farley, October 10, 1930, copy, GP.

17. New York *Herald Tribune*, November 4, 1930.

18. Kingston *Leader* to FDR, undated [*c.* October, 1930].

19. FDR, informal acceptance address, September 30, 1930, PPG, 1930: 755; FDR, acceptance address, October 3, 1930, PPG, 1930: 761; Lindley, *Roosevelt*, 278–279.

20. FDR, Movietone talk, September 25, 1930, PPG, 1930: 758–759; Rosenman, *Working with Roosevelt*, 45; see also county survey of radio reception and theaters available in Howe mss.

21. Kansas City *Star*, October 8, 1930; Roy Roberts to FDR, September 16, 1930; FDR to Roberts, October 7, 1930, GP.

22. Circular with comment, enclosed in W. M. Odell to [James J. Mahoney], October 1, 1930, DNC '32.

23. Dr. Edgar W. Beckwith to FDR, October 21 [1930], Howe mss.

24. FDR to Editor, Elmira *Advertiser*, June 10, 1929, GP; Lindley, *Roosevelt*, 35, 36; New York *Times*, October 18, 19, 1930.

25. Survey by William Farquhar Payson, undated, GP.

26. James A. Farley, *Behind the Ballots* (New York, 1938), 54–55; also interview with Farley, August 7, 1954.

27. Howard Cullman to FDR, June 4, 1930; FDR to Cullman, June 16, 1930, GP; Frank Polk, Fred Osborn, and Cullman to Howe, September 24, 1930, Howe mss.

28. New York *Times*, November 22, 25, 26, 1930; Cullman to Howe, December 1, 1930, Howe mss.; on individual contributors, see FDR mss.

29. Rosenman, *Working with Roosevelt*, 42–43; Farley, *Behind the Ballots*, 54–55; Mary Dewson scrapbook, "Politics, 1932–1933," containing copy of flier and comments, Dewson mss.

30. New York State Federation of Labor, *Annual Report* (Rochester, 1929), 17–18; New York *Times*, August 27, 1930. See also a second endorsement, October 20, 1930, in PPG, 1930: 799.

31. FDR to Felix Frankfurter, May 14, 1930, GP; Rosenman, *Working with Roosevelt*, 41.

32. Rosenman, *Working with Roosevelt*, 42. Most of these speeches appear in the New York *Times*, and in PPG, 1930: 758–837.

33. Clinton W. Howard to FDR, October 10, 11, 1930; FDR to Howard, October 14, 1930, GP; New York *Times*, September 17, 27, 30, October 13, 1930.

34. Doggerel in Howe mss.; Louis Wiley to FDR, September 29, October 3, 1930, GP; New York *Times*, October 4, 1930.

35. PPG, 1930: 755, 761.

36. New York *Times*, September 30, October 1, 13, 15, 1930.

37. PPG, 1930: 762; Rosenman, *Working with Roosevelt*, 42.

38. Stimson diary, October 27, 1930, Stimson mss.

39. Stimson diary, October 23, 24, 1930, Stimson mss.; New York *Times*, October 26, 28, 29, November 2, 1930; New York *World*, November 3, 1930.

40. Rosenman, *Working with Roosevelt*, 43–44; New York *Times*, October 21, 26, 28, 29, November 2, 1930.

41. FDR address, November 1, 1930, PPG, 1930: 836–837.

42. PPG, 1930: 835.

43. Farley, *Behind the Ballots*, 63; Chicago *Tribune*, November 6, 1930; FDR to Owen Winston, November 15, 1930; FDR to Thomas H. Grace, December 6, 1930, GP.

44. Stimson diary, November 1, 1930, Stimson mss.

45. This analysis is based upon statistics in James Malcolm, ed., *New York Red Book 1931* (Albany, 1931), 393, 404, 406. In the *Red Book* and almost all other statistical tables, FDR is incorrectly credited with carrying 49 rather than 48 counties.

46. Howe mss.

CHAPTER XII

A Fast Start

1. New York *Times*, November 6, 1930.

2. Charleston (S.C.) *News and Courier*, November 7, 1930.

3. Calcutta *Statesman*, November 6, 1930, enclosed in Kermit Roosevelt to FDR, December 12, 1930, GP.

4. FDR to Jouett Shouse, September 13, 1930, PL, 3:143–144.

5. FDR to Howe, November 26, 1930, PL, 3:154.

6. Rosenman, *Working with Roosevelt*, 48.

7. Farley, *Behind the Ballots*, 62; New York *Times*, November 7, 1930.

8. Farley, *Behind the Ballots*, 62; Farley, *Jim Farley's Story* (New York, 1948), 6.

9. New York *World*, November 6, 1930; New York *Times*, November 8, 1930.

10. New York *Times*, November 8, 1932.

11. FDR to Harry Byrd, October 15, 1930, PL, 3:150; Ike B. Dunlap to FDR, November 12, 1930; FDR to Dunlap, December 3, 1930; Dunlap to FDR, February 15, 1932, DNC '32, Mo.; see also FDR mss.

12. Lela Stiles, *The Man Behind Roosevelt* (Cleveland, 1954), 127–137, 148, 160–161; Farley, *Behind the Ballots*, 66, 67.

13. Flynn, *You're the Boss*, 83, 84.

14. Flynn, *op. cit.*, 84–85; Farley, *Farley's Story*, 10.

15. Flynn, *op. cit.*, 84–85.

16. Advertisement in New York *Times*, October 30, 1930.

17. On Farley's background, see Farley, *Behind the Ballots*, 3–57.

18. FDR to Farley, November 21, 1930, in Farley, *Farley's Story*, 7–8; Farley to FDR, November 29, 1930, GP.

19. FDR to Scott Bullitt, April 3, 1931, DNC '32, Wash.

20. New York *Times,* November 6, 7, December 10, 1930; Mrs. John Greenway to FDR, undated; FDR to Mrs. Greenway, December 8, 1930, GP.

21. FDR to Editor, San Jose (Calif.) *Mercury-Herald,* January 20, 1931, GP.

22. New York *Times,* November 5, 1930; *Time,* January 19, 1931; Cross to Henry Luce, February 17, March 18, 1931 (the second of which was dictated by FDR); Luce to Cross, February 27, March 26, 1931, GP.

23. FDR to George F. Milton, February 17, 1931, GP.

24. Farley, *Behind the Ballots,* 69–70. Copies of these are in the Library and Research Bureau files, DNC '32.

25. New York *Times,* October 17, November 2, 1930; New York *Herald Tribune,* October 28, 1930.

26. See, for example, FDR to Shouse, March 29, September 13, 1930, PL, 3:113, 143–144.

27. Howe to FDR, December 6, 1928, Howe mss.; PL, 3:155. On the tariff, see Broadus Mitchell, *Depression Decade,* 72–74.

28. FDR to Charles H. McCarthy, November 20, 1930, GP.

29. Charles Michelson, *The Ghost Talks* (New York, 1944), 135; New York *Times,* February 11, 12, 22, 26, 1931; Hull to FDR, February 22, 1931; Byrd to FDR, February 23, 1931, GP.

30. Michelson, *op. cit.,* 137.

31. William Gibbs McAdoo to S. R. Bertron, March 31, 1931, copy in DNC '32, Calif.

32. FDR to Joseph P. Tumulty, February 16, 1931, GP.

33. Michelson, *op. cit.,* 34; U.S. 71st Congress, 3rd sess., *Congressional Record* (Washington, 1931), 6616; Cordell Hull, *Memoirs . . .* (2 vols., New York, 1948), 1:141–142; Hull to FDR, February 22, 1931, GP.

34. Hull to FDR, February 22, 1931, GP; New York *Times,* February 26, 1931.

35. S. R. Bertron to FDR, February 24, 1931, DNC '32, N.Y.C.; Harry Byrd to FDR, February 27, 1931, GP; New York *Times,* March 3, 1931.

36. FDR to Royal S. Copeland, February 23, 1931; Copeland to FDR, February 26, 1931, GP.

37. Farley, *Behind the Ballots,* 74; FDR to Al Smith, February 28, 1931; FDR to Jouett Shouse, February 28, 1931, PL, 3:179.

38. New York *Times,* March 3, 1931.

39. FDR to Norman Mack, Harry Byrd, John Garland Pollard, telegrams, March 2, 1931, GP; Hull, *Memoirs,* 1:143.

40. New York *Times,* March 3, 1931; see, for example, FDR to Mrs. Greenway, March 4, 1931, PL, 3:180–181.

41. Farley, *Behind the Ballots,* 75; Hull, *Memoirs,* 1:143.

42. New York *Times,* March 5, 6, 1931; Raleigh (N.C.) *News and Observer,* March 6, 1931, cited in New York *Times,* March 7, 1931.

43. Hull, *Memoirs,* 1:145; see also Sumner Welles to FDR, March 7, 1931, DNC '32, D.C.

44. FDR to Norman E. Mack, March 9, 1931, GP.

CHAPTER XIII

Depression Governor

1. New York *Times,* October 13, 27, November 2, 1930.

2. Memorandum for the press, December 4, 1930; FDR to Franklin Ward, November 29, 1930, GP.

3. Freidel, *Roosevelt: The Ordeal,* 141; New York *Times,* June 20, 1930, February 18, 1931; George S. Van Schaick interview, January-February, 1950, OHP.

4. Van Schaick interview, January-February, 1950, OHP.

5. *Loc. cit.*

6. FDR, message to legislature, March 23, 1931, transmitting Joseph A. Broderick to FDR [March 23, 1931], PPG, 1931: 124–127; Broderick to the present writer, December 23, 1954.

7. Broderick to FDR, March 21, 1931, GO.

8. Pedro de los Santos to FDR, April 19, 1932, GO.

9. For the most complete account, from which I have drawn extensively in the next few paragraphs, see M. R. Werner, *Little Napoleons and Dummy Directors, Being the Narrative of the Bank of United States* (New York, 1933).

10. The sharpest contemporary criticism is Norman Thomas, "The Banks of New York," *Nation* (February 11, 1931), 132:147–149; the ablest recent criticism is in Hofstadter, *American Political Tradition,* 322–323.

11. Robert Moses, press release, February 3, 1930, GO.

12. Joseph A. Broderick to FDR, May 21, 1930, GO.

13. John T. Flynn, "The Bank of United States," *New Republic* (January 28, 1931), 65:288–291.

14. Norman Thomas, "Bank of United States," 147–149.

15. Norman Thomas to FDR, December 20, 1930; January 3, 1931, GO; FDR to Thomas, January 5, 1931.

16. Frank Altschul to FDR, January 15, 1931, GO.

17. FDR to Altschul, January 16, 1931, GO.

18. FDR to Frederick A. Delano, April 10, 1931, PL, 3:189; FDR to Edmund Platt, March 24, 1931, GP.

19. FDR, message to legislature, March 24, 1931, PPG, 1931: 127–129.

20. PL, 3:188–189; Howard Cullman to FDR, March 27, 1931, GO; FDR, radio address, April 24, 1931, PPG, 1931: 725; PPG, 1931: 351; PPG, 1932: 31, 203.

21. Interview with Herbert Lehman, July 9, 1954; Broderick to the present writer, December 23, 1954.

22. *Loc. cit.;* FDR, statement for the press, October 19, 1931, GO. On bank-deposit insurance schemes, see FDR to Charles A. Burke, April 6, 1931 [written by Broderick]; FDR to Broderick, March 11, 1932; James J. Mahoney to FDR, March 15, 1932, GO.

23. Maxwell S. Stewart, *Social Security* (New York, 1937), 114.

24. Perkins, *Roosevelt I Knew,* 103–104; FDR to John B. Andrews, September 13, 1930; FDR to Jackson P. Olcott, October 1, 1930; Harold B.

Butler to FDR, November 18, 1930; FDR to Butler, November 21, 1930, GO.

25. FDR to G. Hall Roosevelt, February 24, 1931, GO.

26. FDR to S. N. Eben, November 15, 1930; see also FDR to Jackson P. Olcott, October 1, 1930, GO.

27. FDR, message to legislature, March 25, 1931, PPG, 1931: 130.

28. PPG, 1931: 723; Paul H. Douglas, *Social Security in the United States* (New York, 1936), 15.

29. FDR to Arthur H. Howland, October 8, 1930, GO.

30. Perkins, *op. cit.*, 104–105; FDR to governors, December 5, 1930, PPG, 1931: 530.

31. FDR, penciled memorandum, January 23, 1931, GO; Miss Perkins is incorrect in stating that John G. Winant was at the conference. For the papers presented there and some of the comments, see PPG, 1931: 531–582.

32. Perkins, *op. cit.*, 106.

33. FDR to G. Hall Roosevelt, February 24, 1931, GO.

34. Harry L. Hopkins, *Spending to Save* (New York, 1936), 42.

35. FDR, address to governors, June 2, 1931, PPG, 1931: 733–788.

CHAPTER XIV

Magic in the Name

1. K. Ford to FDR, November 20, 1944, OFP, 359.

2. Henry Fairfield Osborn to FDR, December 11, 1928; Mrs. Douglas Robinson (Corinne Roosevelt) to FDR, December 29, 1928; FDR to Mrs. Douglas Robinson, January 21, 1929; FDR to Osborn, December 30, 1930, GO; New York *Times*, October 28, 1931; Walter T. McCaleb to FDR, April 20, 1930; FDR to McCaleb, April 21, 1931, GP; McCaleb, *Theodore Roosevelt* (New York, 1931).

3. FDR to McCaleb, April 21, 1931, GP.

4. Isaiah Bowman to FDR, May 14, 1931, DNC, N.Y.

5. PPA, 1928–1932: 627–631.

6. E. M. House to Robert Woolley, November 5, 1930; House to Roper, May 9, 1931, House mss.

7. FDR, draft letter, Mary Dewson scrapbooks, letters, 1932–1934; FDR to Hamilton V. Miles, June 18, 1931, GP; New York *Times*, April 5, 1931.

8. House to FDR, March 23, 1931, PL, 3:201; see, for example, FDR to Miles, June 18, 1931, GP.

9. Earland Carlson interview with James A. Farley, July 25, 1953, in Carlson, "Franklin D. Roosevelt's Fight for the Presidential Nomination, 1928–1932," University of Illinois doctoral thesis; House to Howe, May 9, 1931, House mss.

10. House to Howe, May 5, 1931, Howe mss.

11. New York *Herald Tribune*, June 4, 1931; House to Robert Woolley, June 14, 1931, Woolley mss.

12. New York *Times*, June 17, 1931.

13. House to Roper, March 24, 1933, House mss.

14. New York *Times,* June 12, 1931; Dorothy G. Wayman, *David I. Walsh, Citizen-Patriot* (Milwaukee, 1952), 191.

15. New York *Times,* March 30, 31, 1931.

16. New York *Times,* April 18, 1931.

17. New York *Times,* June 1, 6, 1931.

18. Farley, *Behind the Ballots,* 81; Farley, *Farley's Story,* 11–12.

19. Farley, *Behind the Ballots,* 81; Howe to House, June 23, 1931, House mss.

20. The lists of names and itineraries are in the Howe mss.

21. Farley, *Behind the Ballots,* 83.

22. William V. Howes to Farley, July 4, 1931, Howe mss.; Howe to House, August 17, 1931, House mss.

23. Farley, *Behind the Ballots,* 83.

24. Farley to FDR, July 11, 1931, Howe mss.; Farley, *Behind the Ballots,* 85–86.

25. Farley to Howe, undated [July, 1931]; Howe to House, August 17, 1931, Howe mss.

26. Farley to Howe [July 14, 1931], Howe mss.; Arthur Mullen, *Western Democrat,* 260.

27. Howe to Daniel Roper, August 18, 1931, DNC, D.C.; Scott Bullitt to Farley, July 10, 1931, Howe mss.; New York *Times,* July 19, 1931.

28. FDR to [Adolphus Ragan], April 6, 1938 (not sent), PL, 3:771–772.

29. *Time,* April 27, 1931, 18.

30. FDR to Hamilton Miles, May 4, 1931, GP.

31. John Gunther, *Roosevelt in Retrospect* (New York, 1950), 267.

32. FDR to Dr. Linsly Williams, April 10, 1931; Dr. Foster Kennedy to FDR, April 29, 1931, with enclosed Kennedy and others to Looker, April 29, 1931, GP.

33. Earle Looker, "Is Franklin D. Roosevelt Physically Fit to Be President?" *Liberty,* July 25, 1931, 7–8; Looker, *This Man Roosevelt* (New York, 1932), 155–156.

34. Farley to FDR, July 17, 1931, Howe mss.; Joseph Davies to Howe, September 30, 1931, DNC, Wisc.; Howe to William C. Fitts, October 20, 1931, DNC, Ala.; John T. Gibbs to —— [form letter], August 12, 1931, Walsh mss.

35. FDR to Editor, Butte (Montana) *Standard,* December 29, 1931, GP.

36. George Marvin in New York *Times,* January 31, 1932.

37. Interview with Nannine Joseph.

38. Nicholas Roosevelt, *A Front Row Seat* (Norman, Okla., 1952), 224.

39. Clifford Ashley to FDR, April 28, 1930; FDR to Ashley, June 15, July 29, 1930; Francis D. Brinton to FDR, July 10, 1930; FDR to Brinton, July 29, 1930, GP.

40. FDR to Richard E. Byrd, July 7, 1930; Byrd to FDR, July 17, 1930, GP.

41. New York *Telegram,* October 1, 1930; FDR to James J. Carroll, October 7, 1930, GP.

42. FDR to Dr. Harvey Cushing, March 12, 1930, FL.

43. For a description of ER's routine, see Janet Scott in Albany *Knickerbocker Press,* November 8, 1931.

44. Interviews with ER; Sara Delano Roosevelt to FDR, May 8 [1932], FL.

45. ER to FDR, May 9 [1931].

CHAPTER XV

Pioneering Relief

1. FDR to Gifford Pinchot, June 11, 1931, GO.

2. Pinchot to FDR, June 11, 1931; FDR to Pinchot, June 15, 1931, GO.

3. FDR notes on back of Pinchot to FDR, June 18, 1931, GO.

4. FDR, form letter to mayors, August 8, 1931, GO.

5. PPG, 1931: 167–181.

6. PPG, 1931: 173, 174–180.

7. FDR to John H. McCrahon, September 15, 1931, GO.

8. Herbert Hoover, *Memoirs* . . . (3 vols., New York, 1951–1952), 3: 55–56.

9. New York *Times,* August 29, 1931.

10. FDR to Lewis A. Lincoln, September 2, 1931, GO.

11. Washington *Post,* August 31, 1931; Bainbridge Colby to FDR, August 31, 1931, GP.

12. Albany *Knickerbocker Press,* September 17, 1931.

13. New York *Journal,* September 18, 1931; Albany *Times Union,* September 18, 1931; New York *Times,* September 19, 20, 30, 1931.

14. FDR to Robert J. Caldwell, September 23, 1931, GP.

15. Frank Z. Glick, *The Illinois Emergency Relief Commission* (Chicago, 1940), 2, 5; Basil O'Connor to FDR, September 9, 1931, GO.

16. Jesse Isador Straus to FDR, September 8, 1931; Morris S. Tremaine to FDR, October 6, 1931, GP; New York *Times,* September 30, 1931.

17. Straus to Lehman, October 7, 1931, and attached memorandum, GO; New York *Times,* September 30, 1931; Robert E. Sherwood, *Roosevelt and Hopkins, An Intimate History* (New York, 1948), 17, 32.

18. Harry L. Hopkins to Raymond Moley [September, 1932], Moley mss.; Perkins, *Roosevelt I Knew,* 184.

19. Temporary Emergency Relief Administration, *Report . . . October 15, 1932* (Albany, 1932), 3; T.E.R.A., report, January 11, 1932, PPG, 1932: 448–458; FDR to Straus, January 26, 1932; Straus to FDR, March 4, 1932, enclosing report of February 23, 1932, GO.

20. T.E.R.A., *Report, October 15, 1932;* T.E.R.A., *Five Million People, One Billion Dollars; Final Report* . . . (Albany, 1937); Harry Hopkins, *Spending to Save,* 66.

21. Harry L. Hopkins to Raymond Moley [September, 1932], Moley mss.

22. FDR, "Block Aid," text enclosed in Milton Cross to NBC News Desk, March 16, 1932, GP.

23. J. M. O'Hanlon to FDR, June 7, 1932; FDR to Guernsey Cross, June 9, 1932, and attached memorandum, GO.

24. *American Agriculturalist*, June 25, 1932, 129:427; PPG, 1931: 752–759; see also *ibid.*, 780–782.

25. PPG, 1930: 568–569; Berne A. Pyrke to FDR, July 15, 1930, GO; PPG, 1931: 758–759.

26. See, for example, Guernsey Cross to Charles Cohen, May 4, 1932, GO; PPG, 1931: 780–782; 1932: 32–34, 508–509, 591–592.

27. FDR to William Church Osborn, May 31, 1932, GP; Clarence Roberts to FDR, August 23, 1932, DNC, Okla.

28. Rosenman to FDR, November 12, 1931; FDR to Rosenman, November 13, 1931; note in FDR's hand in 1932 Message file, GO.

29. PPG, 1932: 100–102; FDR to Robert F. Wagner, February 10, 1932, PPG, 1932: 463.

30. FDR to Cross, April 13, 1932; FDR to Perkins, April 7, 1932.

31. Henry Bruere to FDR, May 24, 1932; List of Acceptances to Dinner, Cosmopolitan Club, May 9, 1932, GO.

CHAPTER XVI

Break with the "Happy Warrior"

1. FDR [Howe?] to James J. Hoey, September 11, 1931, PL, 3:216.

2. Howe to Buell Brake, September 12, 1931, DNC, Ill.

3. FDR to House, July 21, 1931, DNC, N.Y.

4. FDR to William E. Dodd, August 26, 1931, DNC, Va.

5. PL, 3:216.

6. J. R. W. Lewis to FDR, October 9, 1931; FDR [Howe] to Lewis, November 9, 1931, DNC, S.C.

7. Howe to Farley, October 21, 1931; Fred B. Humphrey to FDR, September 10, 1931, Howe mss.; PL, 3:225.

8. J. Glenn Richards to FDR, November 26, 1931; Howe to FDR, undated; FDR to Richards, December 21, 1931, DNC, S.D.

9. FDR to Gerald Forbes, October 21, 1931, DNC, Texas.

10. FDR to Josephus Daniels, August 1, 1931, PL, 3:208; Howe to Hull, August 24, September 5, 1931, DNC, Tenn.

11. W. W. McDowell to Walsh, September 29, 1931; Hull to Walsh, October 8, 1931, enclosing memorandum, Walsh mss.

12. McDowell to Walsh, September 29, 1931; Walsh to McDowell, September 30, 1931, Walsh mss.

13. For a full discussion of the amendment, see Bellush, *Roosevelt as Governor*, 94–98.

14. New York *Times*, October 17, 1931.

15. New York *Times*, October 15, 16, 17, 18, 23, 25, 1931; PPA, 1928–1932: 526–530; Morgenthau to Howe, October 21, 1931, DNC, N.Y.C.

16. New York *Times*, December 4, 1931; George H. Dern to FDR, November 10, 1931, GP.

17. FDR to John Godfrey Saxe [November 3, 1931], PL, 3:228.

18. New York *Times*, November 16, 17, 18, 1931; FDR to Smith, November 10, 1931, PL, 3:229.

19. Edward J. Flynn, *You're the Boss,* 85–86.
20. Newton D. Baker to Edwin B. Smith, June 20, 1931, DNC, Ohio.
21. Farley, circular letter, September 17, 1931, DNC, N.Y.C.
22. Roy V. Peel and Thomas C. Donnelly, *The 1932 Campaign, An Analysis* (New York, 1935), 42–43; W. H. McIntyre to Howe, November 1, 1931, DNC, D.C.
23. E. G. Pinkham in Kansas City *Star,* November 6, 1931; New York *Times,* November 12, 13, 1931.
24. PL, 3:245.
25. FDR to Baruch, December 19, 1931, PL, 3:244.
26. Interview with Frederic Harris, April 7, 1948; Morris L. Cooke to Norris, June 23, 1932, Norris mss.
27. George S. Van Schaick interview, January-February, 1950, OHP.
28. PL, 3:229–232; Van Schaick interview, January-February, 1950, OHP.
29. *Collier's Weekly,* January 16, 1932, 34; Thomas H. Beck to FDR, January 15, 1932; FDR to Beck, January 22, 1932, Howe mss.
30. New York *Times,* February 9, 1932; Peel and Donnelly, *op. cit.,* 62–63.
31. Howe to Shouse, November 19, 1931, Howe mss.; FDR to Shouse, December 9, 1931, GP; Howe to W. C. Fitts, November 6, 1931, DNC, Ala.
32. PL, 3:231.
33. New York *Times,* November 22, 23, 24, 25, 1931.
34. New York *Times,* December 15, January 7, 1932; Harry F. Byrd to FDR, December 22, 1931, DNC, Va.; Robert Woolley to FDR, December 21, 1931, DNC, D.C.
35. New York *Times,* January 10, 1932.
36. *Loc. cit.;* Walsh to Mrs. J. C. Lenihan, January 9, 1932, Walsh mss.
37. New York *Times,* January 10, 1932.
38. Smith to FDR, January 30, 1932; FDR to Smith, February 8, 1932, GP.

CHAPTER XVII

Hat in the Ring

1. FDR to Fred W. McLean, January 22, 1932, GP; PPA, 1928–1932: 623–624.
2. FDR to Homer Cummings, January 25, 1932, DNC, D.C.
3. Farley, *Behind the Ballots,* 94; confidential source cited in Earland I. Carlson, "Franklin D. Roosevelt's Fight for the Presidential Nomination, 1928–1932," University of Illinois doctoral thesis.
4. Farley, *op. cit.,* 94; Peel and Donnelly, *The 1932 Campaign,* 72.
5. House to Robert Woolley, February 17, 1932, House mss.
6. Roper to FDR, February 15, 1932; Hull to House, January 2, 1933, DNC, special files; Walsh to Herbert J. Friedman, February 15, 1932, Walsh mss.; Carlson interview with Homer Cummings, August 28, 1953, Carlson, *op. cit.*
7. Peel and Donnelly, *op. cit.,* 60–61.
8. New York *Times,* January 24, 1932; Carlson, *op. cit.*

9. Breckinridge Long to William Gibbs McAdoo, January 25, 1932, Long mss.

10. Peel and Donnelly, *op. cit.*, 66.

11. Peel and Donnelly, *op. cit.*, 34–43.

12. Bascom N. Timmons, *Garner of Texas, A Personal History* (New York, 1948).

13. Chicago *Herald and American*, January 3, 1932, cited in Carlson, *op. cit.* For a definitive account of Hearst's support of Garner, see Carlson, *op. cit.*

14. Howe to T. W. Gregory, November 23, 1931, DNC, Texas; Timmons, *op. cit.*, 152–157.

15. Chicago *Herald and American*, January 6, 1932, cited in Carlson, *op. cit.*; Timmons, *op. cit.*, 152–157; Adolphus Ragan to FDR, February 16, 1932, DNC, N.Y.; Stephen Bonsal to Howe, January 31, 1932, DNC, D.C.

16. Ernest Foley to Howe, April 30, 1932, Howe mss.

17. FDR to Arthur Krock, July 3, 1931, PL, 3:204–205, 207.

18. Editor, London *Graphic*, to FDR, January 29, 1932; FDR to Editor, *Graphic*, January 29, 1932, GP.

19. Walter Lippmann, *Interpretations, 1931–1932* (Allan Nevins, editor, New York, 1932), 257–259.

20. On Lippmann's pro-Baker sympathies, see Lippmann, *op. cit.*, 300, 303–305; Friends of Al Smith pamphlets in FDR mss.

21. PL, 3:236, 254.

22. Bonsal to Howe, January 31, 1932, DNC, D.C.; New York *Times*, January 27, 1932.

23. Chicago *Herald and American*, January 17, 1932, cited in Carlson, *op. cit.*; Howell to Farley, January 23, 1932, DNC, Ga.; Howe to FDR, January 30, 1932, DNC, N.Y.

24. Howe to FDR, January 30, 1932, DNC, N.Y.; PL, 3:186; Chicago *Herald and American*, January 31, 1932, cited in Carlson, *op. cit.*

25. PPG, 1932: 551.

26. FDR, address before the New York State Grange, February 2, 1932, PPG, 1932: 550–552. Excerpts of this speech in PPA, 1928–1932: 155–157, omit sections on the League and war debts. For FDR's earlier views on war debts, see Freidel, *Roosevelt: The Ordeal*, 130–131, 235.

27. Freidel, *Roosevelt: The Ordeal*, 127–129, 239–240; New York *Times*, February 4, 1932.

28. PL, 3:213.

29. House to FDR, February 10, 1932, DNC, N.Y.C.

30. FDR to Robert Woolley, February 25, 1932, Woolley mss.; see also FDR to Florence E. Stryker, February 16, 1932, GP.

31. House to Farley, February 10, 1932, House mss.; Josephus Daniels to Hull, February 26, 1932; Mrs. Charles Hamlin to Daniels, March 1, 1932, Daniels mss.; Hull, *Memoirs*, 1:150.

32. New York *Times*, February 4, 1932.

33. New York *Times*, February 21, 1932; Norman Mack to FDR, February 23, 1932, GP.

34. Daniels to Hull, March 7, 1932, Daniels mss.

35. Hull to Daniels, February 29, 1932, Daniels mss.

36. PL, 3:186–187.

37. For a summary of the investigation during these months, see Bellush, *Roosevelt as Governor*, 270–273.

38. House to FDR, February 10, 1932, DNC, N.Y.

39. PPG, 1932: 248.

40. For a full account of the charges, defense, and proceedings, see PPG, 1932: 247–287.

41. J. Russell Bowie to FDR, February 11, 1932; FDR to Bowie, February 15, 1932, GO; see also FDR to James Byrnes, March 9, 1932, GO; FDR [Howe?] to Harold Bennett, February 25, 1932, Howe mss.

42. PPG, 1932: 296.

43. "Farley ouster" file, Moley mss.

44. John Haynes Holmes and Stephen S. Wise to FDR, March 17, 25, 1932, in PPG, 1932: 287–290.

45. FDR to Holmes and Wise, March 30, 1932, PPG, 1932: 290–293.

46. Lippmann, *op. cit.*, 250.

CHAPTER XVIII

A Champion for the Forgotten Man

1. Rosenman, *Working with Roosevelt*, 56; Moley, *After Seven Years*, 7–8.

2. Rosenman, *op. cit.*, 57–58.

3. Moley, *op. cit.*, 6.

4. Moley, *op. cit.*, 14–15; Rosenman, *op. cit.*, 59.

5. Moley, *op. cit.*, 18; interview with Moley, June 2, 1955.

6. Moley, *op. cit.*, 15.

7. Moley, *op. cit.*, 20–21.

8. Interview with Rexford G. Tugwell.

9. Moley, *op. cit.*, 10, 11.

10. New York *Times*, May 21, 1932; Rosenman, *op. cit.*, 58; Moley, *op. cit.*, 22.

11. Rosenman, *op. cit.*, 61; Moley, *op. cit.*, 11.

12. PPA, 1928–1932: 624–627.

13. J. C. Lenihan to FDR, April 8, 1932, DNC, Minn.; New York *Times*, April 9, 25, 1932; Lippmann, *Interpretations*, 275–278; Baruch to FDR, April 1, 1932, FL.

14. PL, 3:272–273; Howe to Kirke Simpson, March 28, 1932, DNC, D.C.; Homer Cummings to FDR, April 7, 1932, DNC, Conn.; New York *Times*, March 10, April 8, 10, 13, 17, 1932.

15. New York *Times*, April 14, 1932.

16. New York *Times*, April 15, 1932; Earle Looker, *The American Way: Franklin Roosevelt in Action* (New York, 1933), 31–33.

17. New York *Times*, April 15, 1932.

18. Albany *Knickerbocker Press*, April 14, 1932.

19. Arthur Mullen to FDR, April 16, 1932, DNC, Nebr.

20. Albany *News*, May 31, 1932.

21. Moley, *op. cit.*, 15–18.

22. PPA, 1928–1932: 627–639; New York *Times*, April 19, 1932.

23. Lippmann, *op. cit.*, 275–278; FDR to Walsh, April 20, 1932, Walsh mss.; House to FDR, April 14, 1932, House mss.

24. FDR to Walsh, April 20, 1932, Walsh mss.

25. Rosenman, *op. cit.*, 65; Moley, *op. cit.*, 24.

26. PPG, 1928–1932: 639–647.

27. Moley to FDR, May 19, 1932, Moley mss.

28. *The Prairie Farmer*, January 23, 1932, 104:1; *Wallace's Farmer*, April 2, 1932, 57:1.

29. George N. Peek to FDR, April 8, 1932, GP; Gilbert C. Fite, "John A. Simpson: The Southwest's Militant Farm Leader," *Mississippi Valley Historical Review*, March, 1949, 35:575–576.

30. Lord, *The Wallaces of Iowa*, 308–310, 318; Joseph S. Davis, *Wheat and the AAA* (Washington, 1935), 31, 32. For a succinct analysis of the program of this conference and a comparison with Roosevelt's ideas up to this point, see Gertrude Almy Slichter, "Political Backgrounds of New Deal Agricultural Policy, 1928–1932," University of Illinois master's thesis.

31. For example, Rexford G. Tugwell, "Farm Relief and a Permanent Agriculture," *American Academy of Political and Social Sciences, Annals*, March, 1929, 142:271 ff; Lord, *op. cit.*, 310–311; Tugwell, Diary, OHP; Moley, *op. cit.*, 41; interview with Moley, June 2, 1955.

32. FDR to Mr. Colbaugh, May 24, 1932, FL; PPA, 1928–1932: 655.

CHAPTER XIX

The Fight for Delegates

1. PL, 3:176–177.

2. For a detailed account, see Carlson, "Roosevelt's Fight for the Nomination." J. G. Baker to FDR, July 29, 1931; William C. Fitts to Baker, August 29, 1931, DNC, Ala.; F. B. Summers to FDR, April 21, 1931; FDR to C. W. Jones, April 16, 1931; Claude N. Sapp to F. B. Summers, August 10, 1931, DNC, Ga.; Arthur Rhorer to FDR, August 20, 1931, GO; PL, 3:214–215; Farley to Jones, January 17, 1932, DNC, Ga.

3. FDR to Pat Harrison, January 25, 1932, DNC, Miss.

4. Farley to Thomas A. Edwards, February 1, 1932, DNC, La.; F. B. Summers to FDR, February 18, 1932, DNC, Ga.; New York *Times*, May 23, 1932. Copies of the exposé are in the DNC mss.

5. New York *Times*, February 13, 1932; Peel and Donnelly, *The 1932 Campaign*, 73; "Georgia pre-convention file," DNC. Throughout this chapter, the analyses are largely based on the voluminous preconvention files for each state in the DNC mss. For detailed analyses of most of the state contests, see Carlson, *op. cit.* For a table summary, see Peel and Donnelly, *op. cit.*, 72–79.

6. William Crawford to Howe, January 29, 1932; Harry B. Hawes to FDR, March 29, 1932, DNC, Mo.

7. New York *Times*, April 1, 1932; Harvey Parnell to Farley, June 8, 1932;

Parnell to FDR, June 8, 1932; list of "Arkansas delegates from whom either Governor Roosevelt or Mr. Farley has heard" [June, 1932], DNC, Ark.

8. Confidential source cited in Carlson, *op. cit.;* Homer Cummings to House, March 18, 1932, House mss.; Cummings to Howe, March 21, 1932, DNC, Conn.; FDR to Robert Woolley, March 31, 1932, DNC, D.C.; New York *Times*, March 20, 23, April 7, 1932.

9. L. J. Bugg to Howe, December 18, 1931; FDR to Harlee Branch, April 4, 1932; Branch to Howe, April 11, 1932, DNC, Ala.; New York *Times*, May 4, 1932.

10. Byrnes to FDR, November 12, 1928, October 15, 1931, DNC, S.C.; Byrnes to FDR, May 26, 1932, FL; New York *Times*, May 11, 25, 1932.

11. Howe memorandum, January 22, 1932, DNC, La.; Howe to Burton K. Wheeler, January 29, 1932; Wheeler to Howe, February 2, 1932, DNC, Mont.; Elisabeth Marbury to Howe, February 5, 1932; Thomas A. Edwards to F. B. Summers, February 18, 1932, DNC, La.; Huey P. Long, *Every Man a King* (New Orleans, 1933), 301.

12. Harrison to FDR, June 9, 1932; FDR to Harrison, June 2, 7, 1932, DNC, Miss.; New York *Times*, June 8, 1932.

13. George B. Hills to Howe, December 19, 1931, January 15, 1932; R. H. Gore to FDR, February 23, 1932; Gore to Howe, June 6, 1932; Howe to Gore, June 7, 1932, DNC, Fla.; Cummings to FDR, April 2, 1932, DNC, Conn.; FDR to Josephus Daniels, June 16, 1932, Daniels mss.

14. New York *Times*, May 26, 1932.

15. Peel and Donnelly, *op. cit.*, 78, 79.

16. Michelson, *The Ghost Talks*, 4.

17. Robert Jackson to Farley, January 28, February 6, 1932; Jackson to Howe, March 15, 1932; Howe to Jackson, March 28, 1932, DNC, N.H.; New York *Times*, February 19, March 10, 1932; Arthur Krock in New York *Times*, February 15, 1952.

18. Howe to Marvin McIntyre, March 11, 1932, DNC, N.Y.C.; New York *Times*, March 8, 10, 11, 1932.

19. Farley, *Behind the Ballots*, 98; Jackson to Howe [April, 1932], DNC, N.H.

20. New York *Times*, April 6, 15, 16, 1932; Albany *Knickerbocker Press*, April 16, 1932.

21. New York *Times*, April 29, 1932.

22. James H. Guilfoyle, *On the Trail of the Forgotten Man* (Boston, 1933); New York *Times*, March 9, 10, 11, 12, 15, 17, 22, 24, April 21, 22, 24, 1932.

23. PL, 3:274; Homer Cummings to Howe, March 21, 1932, DNC, Conn.; New York *Times*, December 12, 1931, March 10, 11, 17, 22, 30, April 3, 9, 23, 26, May 3, 24, 25, 1932.

24. Howe to Stephen Bonsal, May 2, 1932, DNC, D.C.; New York *Times*, April 27, 1932.

25. PL, 3:252–253; Roy Howard to FDR, January 19, 1932; FDR to Howard, January 25, 1932, GP; Farley, *op. cit.*, 130.

26. Farley, *op. cit.*, 111, 130; Howe to Earl Peters, March 11, 1932, DNC, Ind.

27. "Illinois pre-convention file," DNC.

28. Howe to G. Hall Roosevelt, November 16, 1931, DNC, Mich.; New York *Times*, April 15, 1932.

29. G. Hall Roosevelt to FDR, March 7, 1932; Charles E. Coughlin to FDR, August 12, 1932, FL; September 16, 1932, DNC, Mich.

30. FDR to Fred W. McLean, March 7, 1932; McLean to FDR, March 2, 1932, GP; E. M. Mattingly to FDR, March 11, 1932; William Lemke to FDR, February 27, 1932; Melvin Hildreth to Howe, March 22, 1932, DNC, N.D.; New York *Times*, March 16, 17, 1932.

31. William F. Donahue to FDR, March 28, 1932, DNC, Minn. For a detailed account of the Minnesota dispute, see *Official Report of the Proceedings of the 1932 Democratic National Convention* (Washington, 1932), 524–549, also "Minnesota pre-convention file," DNC.

32. DNC, Iowa file; Farley, *op. cit.*, 111.

33. New York *Times*, March 27, April 6, 1932; circular enclosed in Robert Hayes to Farley, March 21, 1932, DNC, Wisc.

34. Charles W. Bryan to FDR, February 22, 1932; FDR [Farley?] to Bryan, February 26, 1932, FL; PL, 3:260; Arthur Mullen, *Western Democrat* (New York, 1940), 137–145.

35. William Crawford to Howe, January 30, 31, 1932, DNC, Kans.; New York *Times*, May 13, 1932.

36. E. J. Westerhouse to Farley, May 6, 1932, DNC, Calif.

37. Isidore Dockweiler to FDR, May 16, 1932; Justus Wardell to FDR, November 16, 1931, May 11, 1932; Will R. King to FDR, April 30, 1932, DNC, Calif.; Farley to Howe, July 11, 1931, Howe mss.; New York *Times*, May 5, 1932.

38. PL, 3:277.

39. Sara Delano Roosevelt to FDR [May 9, 1932], FL.

40. A. T. Kilcrease to Farley, May 18, 1932, DNC, Ariz.; New York *Times*, May 10, 1932.

41. See state preconvention files in DNC mss.

42. *Loc. cit.;* Peel and Donnelly, *op. cit.*, 78–79.

43. FDR to Josephus Daniels, May 5, 1932, Daniels mss.

CHAPTER XX

Roosevelt or Deadlock?

1. PL, 3:268–269.

2. Farley, *Behind the Ballots*, 104; Flynn, *You're the Boss*, 97–99; Michelson, *The Ghost Talks*, 4–8; Robert Jackson to FDR, April 7, 1932, DNC, N.H. Jackson's report to FDR, written immediately after the meeting, is the most useful account.

3. *Proceedings of the Democratic National Convention*, 125–126.

4. New York *Times*, April 5, 7, 1932; *Time*, April 11, 1932, 19:21.

5. New York *Times*, April 30, 1932.

6. Farley, *op. cit.*, 106–109; Claude G. Bowers to FDR, June 8, 1932, DNC,

N.Y.C.; Walsh to W. W. McDowell, June 6, 1932, Walsh mss.; interview with Burton K. Wheeler, July 8, 1954.

7. New York *Times*, June 7, 1932; New York *Sun*, June 6, 1932.

8. For the contents of the record, see *Time*, June 27, 1932, 19:13; there is apparently no copy of the record in the Roosevelt Library. Farley to Walsh, form letter, Walsh mss.; Howe to delegates, form letter, June 11, 1932; [Howe?] to A.T.&T., June 21, 1932, Howe mss.

9. Stiles, *The Man Behind Roosevelt*, 166–170.

10. Farley, *op. cit.*, 110–112; interview with Farley, August 7, 1954.

11. Bellush, *Roosevelt as Governor*, 274–276.

12. FDR to House, June 4, 1932, GP, partly in PL, 3:281; New York *Times*, June 4, 1932.

13. Lippmann, *Interpretations*, 251.

14. New York *Times*, June 22, 1932; Gene Fowler, *Beau James* . . . (New York, 1949), 314–315.

15. FDR to Harvey Parnell, June 14, 1932, DNC, Ark.

16. On the Republicans, see Peel and Donnelly, *The 1932 Campaign*, 19–25, 46–59, 82–91; Henry L. Mencken, *Making a President, A Footnote to the Saga of Democracy* (New York, 1932), 35–93.

17. Farley, *op. cit.*, 110; Flynn, *op. cit.*, 89.

18. Stiles, *op. cit.*, 172–173; Rosenman, *op. cit.*, 68; Farley, *op. cit.*, 121–122.

19. New York *Times*, June 23, 24, 1932; Farley, *op. cit.*, 114–115.

20. Farley, *op. cit.*, 115.

21. Farley, *op. cit.*, 139.

22. New York *Times*, June 23, 1932; Farley, *op. cit.*, 115–116; Flynn, *op. cit.*, 91; Mencken, *op. cit.*, 105, 106.

23. Stiles, *op. cit.*, 176–177.

24. New York *Times*, June 25, 1932; Flynn, *op. cit.*, 90; Farley, *op. cit.*, 116–117.

25. In Democratic National Committee folder, PSF.

26. Farley, *op. cit.*, 118; interview with Wheeler, July 8, 1954; New York *Times*, June 25, 26, 1932.

27. Farley, *op. cit.*, 119; New York *Times*, June 27, 28, 1932.

28. Farley, *op. cit.*, 120–121.

29. Hull, *Memoirs*, 1: 150–151.

30. Peel and Donnelly, *op. cit.*, 94, 95; Farley, *op. cit.*, 123; Alben W. Barkley, *That Reminds Me* (New York, 1954), 141.

31. Farley, *op. cit.*, 123–126; interview with Wheeler, July 8, 1954.

32. Farley, *op. cit.*, 126–127; Michelson, *op. cit*, 7–8; *Proceedings*, 133–134.

33. Mencken, *op. cit.*, 158–159, 167.

34. Farley, *op. cit.*, 127–128; *Proceedings*, 146–192.

35. Farley, *op. cit.*, 129, 137.

36. Farley, *op. cit.*, 129; Mencken, *op. cit.*, 105.

37. Farley, *op. cit.*, 129.

38. FDR to Stanley Prenosil, July 7, 1932, DNC, N.Y.C.; Stiles, *op. cit.*, 177.

39. Stiles, *op. cit.*, 183; *Proceedings*, 207–211.

40. Farley, *op. cit.*, 137; *Proceedings*, 211–287.
41. Rosenman, *op. cit.*, 70.
42. Farley, *op. cit.*, 139–141.
43. Farley, *op. cit.*, 141–142.
44. Rosenman, *op. cit.*, 70–71; Farley, *op. cit.*, 142–143.
45. *Proceedings*, 288–289, 302, 315.
46. Farley, *op. cit.*, 143, credits Harrison, but Flynn, *op. cit.*, 100–101, credits Long. Wheeler also credits Long. Interview with Wheeler, July 8, 1954.
47. New York *Herald Tribune*, July 1, 1932.
48. Mullen, *Western Democrat*, 274; Farley, *op. cit.*, 142; interview with Farley, August 7, 1954.
49. Farley, *op. cit.*, 144.
50. Farley, *op. cit.*, 145; George E. Allen, *Presidents Who Have Known Me* (New York, 1950), 55.
51. Farley, *op. cit.*, 131; interview with Wheeler, July 8, 1954.
52. Farley, *op. cit.*, 131, 148; Farley, *Farley's Story*, 24.
53. Mullen, *op. cit.*, 275; Farley, *Behind the Ballots*, 133–135.
54. Timmons, *Garner*, 159–161.
55. Farley, *op. cit.*, 132–133; Timmons, *op. cit.*, 165; E. D. Coblentz, editor, *William Randolph Hearst, A Portrait in His Own Words* (New York, 1952), 132–134.
56. Timmons, *op. cit.*, 165–166; Farley, *op. cit.*, 147.
57. Basil O'Connor to FDR, July 7, 1932, DNC, N.Y.C.; Farley, *op. cit.*, 149. For an analysis of the various claims, see Carlson, "Roosevelt's Fight for the Nomination."
58. Timmons, *op. cit.*, 166–167.
59. Daniel Roper and Frank Lovette, *Fifty Years of Public Life* (Durham, 1948), 258–260.
60. Farley, *op. cit.*, 150–151; *Proceedings*, 325.
61. *Proceedings*, 325–327.
62. Grace Tully, *F.D.R., My Boss* (New York, 1949), 51; Carlson interview with Miss Tully, August 27, 1953, cited in Carlson, *op. cit.*
63. *Proceedings*, 329.
64. Mencken, *op. cit.*, 166–167.

CHAPTER XXI

Toward a New Deal

1. Rosenman, *Working with Roosevelt*, 74.
2. *Proceedings of the Democratic National Convention*, 332; Rosenman, *op. cit.*, 73–74.
3. Farley, *Behind the Ballots*, 152–153.
4. *Proceedings*, 357–358.
5. Rosenman, *op. cit.*, 71, 75; Moley, *After Seven Years*, 23, 26–27, and illustration opposite p. 146.

6. Rosenman, *op. cit.*, 76–77; Moley, *op. cit.*, 33; Farley, *op. cit.*, 154; Stiles, *Man Behind Roosevelt*, 192–194; *Proceedings*, 365–366.

7. FDR to Walsh, July 26, 1932, DNC, Mont.; *Proceedings*, 290–292.

8. FDR, memorandum, March 25, 1933, speech files, FDR mss., and in Rosenman, *op. cit.*, 77.

9. *Proceedings*, 374; Rosenman, *op. cit.*, 77; Moley, *op. cit.*, 33–34.

10. PPA, 1928–1932: 647–659.

11. Rosenman, *op. cit.*, 78.

12. Farley, *op. cit.*, 155.

13. Dern to FDR, July 26, 1932, DNC, Utah; *Proceedings*, 596–597.

14. Rosenman, *op. cit.*, 75; Belle Moscowitz to FDR, July 7, 1932, DNC, N.Y.C.

15. Farley, *op. cit.*, 154–155.

16. Moley, *op. cit.*, 35; Stiles, *op. cit.*, 166.

17. Moley, *op. cit.*, 36.

18. Baruch to FDR, July 6, 1932, DNC, N.Y.C.; New York *Times*, July 6, 1932.

19. Hugh S. Johnson to Peek, May 11, 1932, Peek mss.; interview with Moley, June 2, 1955; Moley, *op. cit.*, 39, 43.

20. Moley, *op. cit.*, 45–46.

21. Moley, *op. cit.*, 41.

22. Moley, *op. cit.*, 19, 41, 45.

23. Farley, *op. cit.*, 178; Farley to M. M. Neely, July 27, 1932; see also Neely to Farley, July 21, 1932, DNC, D.C.; Howe to O'Connor, September 22, 1932, DNC, N.Y.C.

24. Michelson, *The Ghost Talks*, 141.

25. Michelson, *op. cit.*, 10.

26. Confidential source.

27. ER to Mary W. Dewson, July 16, 1932, Dewson mss.; Perkins, *Roosevelt I Knew*, 120–121; Farley, *op. cit.*, 160; see also Dewson mss.

28. Hull to Farley, July 14, 18, 1932; Farley to Hull, July 15, 1932, DNC, D.C.

29. Bernard Ryan to FDR, August 7, 1932; FDR to Ryan, August 11, 1932, DNC, Ala.

30. Democratic National Campaign Committee, 1932, Report of Literature and Circular Mail Department, Howe mss.; Farley, *op. cit.*, 159–160.

31. Howe notation on Francis H. Kinnicutt to FDR, October 20, 1932, DNC, N.Y.C.

32. FDR [CB] to Mrs. C. M. Begg, November 1, 1932, DNC, Ill.; FDR [GEF] to Adelaide M. Delany, October 6, 1932, DNC.

33. Moley, *op. cit.*, 40.

34. Peel and Donnelly, *The 1932 Campaign*, 115, citing Louis Howe, NANA article, December, 1932.

35. Arthur P. Homer to Howe, July 13, 1932; Frank C. Walker to FDR, September 6, 1932; FDR to Homer, September 15, 1932; Homer to FDR, November 1, 1932, DNC, N.Y.C.

36. Louise Overacker, "Campaign Funds in a Depression Year," *Ameri-*

can Political Science Review, October, 1933, 27:769–783; interview with Herbert Hoover, December 28, 1951.

37. Peel and Donnelly, *op. cit.,* 146.

CHAPTER XXII

To Starboard or Port?

1. Confidential source.
2. ER, *This I Remember* (New York, 1949), 60–61; interview with ER.
3. Garner to FDR, July 23, 1932; FDR to Garner, August 1, 1932, DNC. Texas.
4. Stimson diary, July 4, 1932.
5. *Ibid.,* July 5, 1932.
6. Lippmann, *Interpretations,* 298.
7. William Allen White to Jonathan Bourne, July 20, 1932, White mss.
8. Theodore Joslin, *Hoover Off the Record* (Garden City, N.Y., 1934), 330.
9. Claude Bowers to FDR, July 29, 1932; FDR to Bowers, August 1, 1932, DNC, N.Y.C.; see also William Jennings Bryan, Jr., to FDR [September, 1932], DNC, Calif.
10. Arthur F. Mullen to Bryan, September 27, 1932, DNC, Calif.; Berle to FDR, August 2, 1932, DNC, N.Y.C.
11. Miss Klenam to FDR [March], 1932, GO; H. G. Gue to FDR, September 9, 1932, DNC, Iowa.
12. New York *Times,* June 11, 1932.
13. Hoover, *Memoirs,* 3:225–232; New York *Times,* July 28, 29, 30, 1932.
14. Hoover, *Memoirs,* 3:195.
15. Timmons, *Garner,* 150–151; Hoover, *Memoirs,* 3:135, 136, 138, 146–147, 159–160.
16. Ike B. Dunlap to FDR, July 16, 1932, enclosing Kansas City *Star* editorial; Harry B. Hawes to Sam Rayburn, September 27, 1932, DNC, Mo.; Charles E. Marsh to House, July 20, 1932, DNC, Texas; Washington *Post,* July 20, 1932.
17. Mrs. John Nance (E.R.) Garner to FDR, July 26, 1932; FDR to Garner, August 1, 1932, DNC, Texas.
18. Garner to Farley, August 1, 1932; FDR to Mrs. Garner, August 7, 1932, DNC, Texas.
19. New York *Times,* August 15, 16, 1932; Garner to Howe, August 19, 1932, DNC, Texas.
20. Garner to Farley, September 2, 1932, DNC, Texas.
21. FDR to Garner, September 12, 1932, DNC, Texas; Stiles, *Man Behind Roosevelt,* 211–213; Timmons, *op. cit.,* 170.
22. Garner to Farley, September 2, 1932; see also Garner to Howe, September 2, 1932, DNC, Texas.
23. New York *Times,* section VI, July 17, 1932, July 8, 10, 12, 13, 14, 15, 16, 17, 1932.
24. New York *Times,* July 13, 16, 17, 24, 1932.

25. James T. Hague to FDR, July 7, 1932; Daniel A. Ambrose to M. A. Durand [summer, 1932], DNC, N.J.; Farley, *Behind the Ballots*, 158.

26. New York *Times*, July 24, 1932.

27. Owen D. Young to FDR, July 5, 1932, DNC, N.Y.C.; New York *Times*, July 24, 1932.

28. Millard Tydings to FDR [July, 1932], DNC, D.C.; O. Max Gardner to Josephus Daniels, July 28, 1932, Daniels mss.

29. Farley, *op. cit.*, 170–171.

30. New York *Times*, August 20, 1933; confidential source.

31. Lippmann to Morris Llewellyn Cooke, January 26, 1932, cc. encl. in Cooke to FDR, January 27, 1932, GO.

32. *Proceedings of the Democratic National Convention*, 362; Norris to R. Lowenthal, June 8, 1932, Norris mss.

33. PPA, 1928–1932: 203–205; New York *Times*, July 10, 1932.

34. Hoover to FDR, July 10, 1932, GO; PPA, 1928–1932: 205–206.

35. New York *Times*, July 10, 1932; Welles to FDR, July 13, 1932, DNC, Md.

36. Leland Olds to Frank Walsh, July 11, 1932, GO; Hoover, *op. cit.*, 3:234. For a detailed analysis, see Bellush, *Roosevelt as Governor*, 230–238.

37. Harold L. Ickes to William E. Borah, form letter, March 14, 1932, Borah mss.

38. Ickes to FDR, July 8, 1932, GO; William E. Dodd to FDR, July 30, 1932, DNC, Ill.; Herbert J. Friedman to Walsh, August 4, 1932, Walsh mss.

39. New York *Times*, July 26, 1932; PPG, 1932: 310–388; FDR to House, August 7, 1932, DNC, N.Y.C.

40. FDR to Felix Frankfurter, August 7, 1932, DNC, Mass.

41. New York *Times*, August 12, 1932; Rosenman, *Working with Roosevelt*, 83.

42. New York *Times*, August 24, 1932; FDR to Frankfurter, August 24, 1932, DNC, Mass.

43. Berle to FDR, August 17, 1932, GO.

44. FDR to Frankfurter, August 24, 1932, DNC, Mass.; Rosenman, *op. cit.*, 83; interview with Raymond Moley, September, 1954.

45. Walker to Michael J. Cruise, September 1, 1932, PPG, 1932: 393; Rosenman, *op. cit.*, 83; Moley to present writer, April 4, 1956.

46. Robert W. Bingham to FDR, September 5, 1932, DNC, Ky.

47. Joseph Tumulty to Jesse Isidor Straus, September 3, 1932, DNC, D.C.

48. Rosenman, *op. cit.*, 83–84; Farley, *op. cit.*, 172–176; Flynn, *You're the Boss*, 106–109.

49. Farley, *op. cit.*, 176, 177, 178.

CHAPTER XXIII

The Big Trip to the Coast

1. Clarence C. Dill to Farley, July 7, 1932. See also Dill to FDR, August 2, 1932; Key Pittman to Howe, August 19, 1932, DNC, D.C.

2. Michelson, *The Ghost Talks*, 11–12; Farley, *Behind the Ballots*, 163–167.

3. Farley to Dill, July 8, 1932, DNC, D.C.; FDR to Walsh, July 26, 1932; Walsh to FDR, August 3, 1932, DNC, Mont.; FDR to Daniels, September 12, 1932, Daniels mss.

4. Moley, *After Seven Years*, 52; FDR to Daniels, September 12, 1932, Daniels mss.

5. FDR to Walsh, July 26, 1932, DNC, Mont.

6. PPA, 1928–1932: 659–669.

7. *Ibid.*, 674–675.

8. Welles to Howe, August 26, 1932, DNC, D.C.; Bowers to FDR, August 24, 1932; House to FDR, August 26, 1932; Oswald Garrison Villard to FDR, August 22, 1932; Woolley to FDR, August 23, 1932, DNC, N.Y.C.

9. New York *Times*, August 28, 1932; Farley, *op. cit.*, 158.

10. PPA, 1928–1932: 684–692; Joseph C. O'Mahoney to FDR, undated, reporting suggestions of Mitchell Palmer and Frank Garvin, DNC mss.; Frankfurter to FDR, August 12, 1932, in "Prohibition file," Moley mss.; Clarence Roberts to FDR, August 23, 1932, DNC, Okla.

11. Robert R. McCormick to FDR, July 19, August 6, 1932, DNC, Ill.; New York *Herald Tribune*, August 1, 1932.

12. Richard Crane to FDR, July 20, 1932, DNC, Va.

13. Arthur Brisbane to FDR, September 6, 1932, DNC, N.Y.C.; William Randolph Hearst to FDR, July 8, September 6, 1932; FDR to Hearst, September 5, 1932, DNC, Calif.

14. New York *Times*, July 25, 1932; interview with Moley, June 2, 1955; FDR, *Government, Not Politics* (New York, 1932); FDR [Herbert E. Gaston?] to W. R. Ronald, August 15, 1932, DNC, S.D.; [Gaston], "Partial List of Men Interested in Farm Problems . . ." [September 12, 1932], GP.

15. Johnson to Peek, July 2, 15, 1932; Peek to Johnson, July 3, 15, 1932, Peek mss.

16. John D. Black, *Parity, Parity, Parity* (Cambridge, Mass., 1942), 53; Henry T. Rainey to Edwin S. Carr, August 22, 1932; Earl C. Smith to Rainey, September 23, 1932, Rainey mss.; Peek to [Johnson], July 15, 1932, Peek mss.

17. Peek to Louis S. Clarke, July 15, 1932, Peek mss.; New York *Times*, August 12, 1932.

18. FDR to Hatton W. Sumners, July 19, 1932, DNC, D.C.; New York *Times*, August 8, 10, 1932; Lord, *Wallaces of Iowa*, 323.

19. Dunlap to FDR, July 10, 1932; FDR to Dunlap, July 28, 1932, DNC, Mo.; FDR to Harry H. Woodring, July 29, 1932, GO; FDR to Milo Reno, August 29, 1932, DNC, Iowa.

20. [Gaston], "Partial List . . ." [September 12, 1932], GP; Edward A. O'Neal to FDR, July 21, 1932, DNC, Ill.; Chester H. Gray to FDR, August 3, 1932, DNC, D.C.

21. FDR to Frank O. Lowden, July 22, 1932, GO.

22. *Wallace's Farmer*, September 3, 1932, 57:1, 18; Lord, *op. cit.*, 319–322; Wallace to FDR, August 26, 1932, DNC, Iowa.

23. John A. Simpson to FDR, July 5, 1932, DNC, Okla.; Fite, "Simpson," *Mississippi Valley Historical Review*, March, 1949, 35:576.

24. On silver, see Pittman to Howe, August 19, 1932, DNC, D.C.

25. Simpson to FDR, August 27, 1932, DNC, D.C.; Fite, *op. cit.*, 35:575–576.

26. Dunlap to FDR, July 10, 1932, DNC, Mo.; FDR to Woodring, July 29, 1932, GO; Moley, *op. cit.*, 41–45; Wilson's outline is in Box 5, "Library and Research bureau file," DNC mss.; Tugwell diary, December 31, 1932, OHP.

27. Interview with Moley, June 2, 1955; FDR to Woolley, September 12, 1932, DNC, D.C.

28. Moley, *op. cit.*, 55.

29. John S. Cohen to FDR, September 13, 1932; FDR to Cohen, September 13, 1932, DNC, Ga.

30. Moley, *op. cit.*, 55–56; Frank W. Murphy to Peek, September 18, 1932; Peek to Murphy, September 23, 1932, Peek mss.

31. Earl C. Smith to Peek, September 23, 1932, Peek mss.

32. Johnson to Moley, September 15, 1932, Moley mss.; interview with Henry A. Wallace, August 24, 1952.

33. PPA, 1928–1932: 709.

34. *Ibid.*, 704–705.

35. *Ibid.*, 756–770, 812–819; New York *Times*, October 25, 1932; Democratic National Committee, *The Forgotten Farmer* (New York? 1932).

36. Murphy to Peek, September 18, 1932, Peek mss.; Wallace to FDR, September 16, 1932, Moley mss.

37. *Kansas Farmer*, July 10, 1932, 4; Theodore Saloutos and John D. Hicks, *Agricultural Discontent in the Midwest, 1900–1939* (Madison, 1951), 435–451; Earle D. Ross, *Iowa Agriculture: An Historical Survey* (Iowa City, 1951), 161; New York *Times*, October 5, 1932; Simpson to FDR, October 10, 1932, DNC, D.C.

38. FDR to Baruch, September, 1932, DNC, N.Y.C.; New York *Times*, September 19, 23, 1932.

39. Mary Heaton Vorde, "Farmers' National Relief Conference," *New Republic*, December 28, 1932, 73:183–185; Donald C. Blaisdell, *Government and Agriculture* (New York, 1940), 42.

40. Hoover, *Memoirs*, 3: 285–286; New York *Times*, November 5, 1932.

41. Hoover, *op. cit.*, 3:119; Wallace to FDR, October 25, 1932, DNC, Iowa.

42. Thomas P. Gore to FDR, September 14, 1932, DNC, Okla.

43. Moley mss.; Moley, *op. cit.*, 45; interview with Moley, June 2, 1955.

44. PPA, 1928–1932: 711–723; New York *Times*, September 18, 20, 1932.

45. New York *Times*, September 21, 1933.

46. Carl C. Donaugh to Howe, September 12, 1932; Howe to Robert Jackson, September 16, 1932, DNC, Ore.

47. Judson King to Norris, September 13, 1932; Norris to Frank P. Walsh, September 15, 1932, Norris mss.

48. Norris to Basil Manly, September 1, 1932, Norris mss.; see also Kenneth McKellar to FDR, July 23, 1932, DNC, Tenn., urging FDR to come out for Muscle Shoals.

49. Moley mss.; interview with Moley, June 2, 1955. See also Berle to FDR, September 20, 1932, Moley mss.

50. PPA, 1928–1932: 727–742.
51. New York *Times*, September 24, 1932.
52. Interview with Moley, June 2, 1955.
53. Interview with Farley, August 7, 1954.
54. PPA, 1928–1932: 742–756.
55. Hiram Johnson to Charles L. McNary, October 7, 1932, McNary mss.
56. Interview with Moley, June 2, 1955.
57. M. L. Wilson to Moley, October 7, 1932, Moley mss.
58. Moley to Hull, August 27, 1933; also Taussig to Moley, September 14, 1932, and drafts of Walsh, Johnson, Berle, and Taussig proposals in "Tariff file," Moley mss.
59. PPA, 1928–1932: 756–770.
60. *Ibid.*, 835–836; FDR to Ralph Snyder, October 28, 1932, DNC, Kans., and similar wires in DNC mss.; New York *Times*, November 1, 5, 1932; Moley, *op. cit.*, 48–52. For Hoover's analysis of his attack upon FDR's tariff statements (but not Hoover's grass-growing remark), see Hoover, *op. cit.*, 3:287–301.
61. Stimson diary, July 12, 1932; Moley, *op. cit.*, 62; Hoover, *op. cit.*, 3:236; see "foreign policy file" in Moley mss., especially James T. Shotwell to Berle, September 2, 1932, Raymond Leslie Buell to Moley, September 30, 1932, Welles to Le Hand, October 6, 1932, and enclosures.
62. Patrick T. Fagan to Frank C. Walker, July 6, 1932; FDR to Fagan, July 29, 1932, DNC, Pa.
63. Moley, *op. cit.*, 53.
64. Brooklyn *Eagle*, September 25, 1932.
65. Omaha *News Bee*, September 29, 1932.
66. Brooklyn *Eagle*, September 25, 1932.

CHAPTER XXIV

The Triumph

1. E. Edward Hurja to FDR, July 15, 1932; Hurja to Howe, August 31, 1932, and attached memo, DNC, N.Y.; Hurja, memo on New Jersey, September 16, 1932, DNC, N.J.; Hurja to Howe, October 25, 1932, DNC, Kans.
2. FDR to George H. Dern, August 1, 1932, DNC, Utah; Farley to Basil O'Connor, October 1, 1932, DNC, N.Y.C.
3. Pittman to FDR, October 4, 1932; Farley to Roper, October 12, 1932, DNC, D.C.
4. Farley, *Behind the Ballots*, 184.
5. PPA, 1928–1932: 786–795; see Hopkins draft and Perkins to FDR, July 15, 1932, copy, Moley mss.
6. FDR to McCormick, June 24, 1932, DNC, Ill.; Richard E. Byrd to FDR, July 22, 1932; FDR to Grenville Clark, July 24, 1932, DNC, N.Y.C.
7. Johnson to Moley, September 15, 27, 1932; Howe to FDR, September 26, 1932, Moley mss.; Moley, *After Seven Years*, 59–60.
8. Interview with Moley, June 2, 1955; drafts of speech, Moley mss.

9. Rosenman, *Working with Roosevelt*, 86–87.

10. PPA, 1928–1932: 809; R. E. Coontz to Howe, September 30, 1932; Howe to Coontz, October 7, 1932; Coontz to FDR, October 17, November 2, 1932, DNC, D.C.; Charles E. Coughlin to FDR, September 16, 1932, DNC, Mich.

11. PPA, 1928–1932: 795–811.

12. Cox to FDR, October 20, 1932, DNC, Ohio; House to FDR, October 20, 1932, DNC, N.Y.C.; Dern to FDR, October 21, 1932, DNC, Utah; Frankfurter to FDR, October 20, 1932, DNC, Mass.

13. Farley to Cary T. Grayson, October 13, November 2, 1932; Robert Woolley to FDR, November 2, 1932, DNC, D.C.; FDR to Owen D. Young, October 13, 1932, GP; Farley to Young, November 4, 1932, and copy of Young speech with Howe note attached, DNC, N.Y.C.; FDR, address at Buffalo, October 18, 1932, GO; Albany *Knickerbocker Press*, October 29, 1932.

14. Stimson diary, September 6, 1932.

15. Stimson diary, September 22, 1932.

16. Stimson diary, September 6, 21, 1932; Hoover, *Memoirs*, 3:233.

17. Stimson diary, September 19, 1932.

18. New York *Times*, October 5, 1932.

19. White to Walter Newton, October 14, 1932, White mss.

20. Hoover, *op. cit.*, 3:218–347.

21. PPA, 1928–1932: 832; New York *Times*, October 26, 1932; Hoover, *op. cit.*, 333.

22. Moley, *op. cit.*, 52, 63–64; PPA, 1928–1932: 842–855, 860–865; New York *Times*, November 1, 6, 1932.

23. Moley, *op. cit.*, Appendix A, 401–402.

24. Moley, *op. cit.*, 65; New York *Times*, November 6, 1932.

25. *Nation*, November 9, 1932, 135:442.

26. Lippmann to Borah, November 3, 1932; Borah to Lippmann, November 9, 1932; Borah to C. W. Brown, November 12, 1932, Borah mss.

27. Moley, *op. cit.*, 62, 63.

28. Moley, *op. cit.*, 65.

29. Mimeographed "Special Bulletin" on letterhead of C. Woodruff Valentine & Co., vertical file, campaign literature 1932, DNC; Rosenman, *op. cit.*, 87; New York *Times*, November 9, 1932.

30. New York *Times*, November 9, 1932; Stiles, *Man Behind Roosevelt*. 215–216.

31. Robinson, *They Voted for Roosevelt*, 41.

32. Stiles, *op. cit.*, 218.

33. Moley to Howe, November 12, 1932, Moley mss.

34. ER, *This I Remember*, 74–75.

35. New York *Times*, November 9, 1932.

INDEX

Index